Spectator Politics

Spectator Politics

*Metatheatre and Performance
in Aristophanes*

NIALL W. SLATER

PENN

University of Pennsylvania Press
Philadelphia

10 9 8 7 6 5 4 3 2 1

Published by
University of Pennsylvania Press
Philadelphia, Pennsylvania 19104-4011

Library of Congress Cataloging-in-Publication Data

Slater, Niall W., 1954–
    Spectator politics : metatheatre and performance in
Aristophanes / Niall W. Slater.
        p. cm.
    Includes bibliographical references (p.) and indexes.
    ISBN 0-8122-3652-1 (acid-free paper)
    1. Aristophanes—Technique.   2. Political plays, Greek—
History and criticism.   3. Greek drama (Comedy)—History
and criticism.   4. Aristophanes—Political and social views.
5. Athens (Greece)—Politics and government.   6. Aristophanes—
Dramatic production.   7. Politics and literature—Greece.
8. Theater audiences—Greece.   9. Drama—Technique.
10. Rhetoric, Ancient.   11. Theater—Greece.   I. Title.
PA3879 .S58   2002
882'.01—dc21   2001050752

D.M.

Isabell B. Steiner

Contents

Preface

THE ORIGINS OF THIS BOOK lie in my previous work on Plautus's comedies and his use of metatheatre (a term coined by Lionel Abel in his book of
the same title; I have followed his spelling of the term). Even as I sought to
explain the metatheatricality of Plautus's plays as a reaction against the illusionism of the earlier Greek New Comedy he employed as raw material, I
was well aware that Aristophanes' comedies often displayed a theatrical self-
consciousness exceeding anything in Plautus — and yet there was no illusionistic tradition within the earliest Greek comedy for Aristophanes himself to
be reacting against. Nor did parody seem to account for all the phenomena:
I found the notion of treating metatheatre in Aristophanes simply as paratragedy wholly inadequate to the range and power of his theatrical strategies.
At the same time, the polarized debate over Aristophanes' politics (conservative or democrat, satirist or clown, even subversive or agent of repression)
seemed trapped in a rather dreary hermeneutic shuttle between a complete
identification of comedy and politics (where no one who laughed at Cleon
in the theater was allowed to vote for him in the elections) and a complete
divorce (where festival laughter never reechoed for a moment after holiday
time ceased). This book seeks, through attention to performance not just as
stage practice but also as cultural practice, to help get Aristophanes off this
particular MTA.

This book has had a long gestation, and many audiences have listened
to, and bracingly challenged, parts of it. I am grateful for the opportunity to
present parts to audiences at the Centre Louis Gernet in Paris (thanks to Pierre
Vidal-Naquet and Pauline Schmitt); a colloquium at the University of Konstanz (thanks to Bernhard Zimmermann and H-J. Newiger); the Institute for
Classical Studies in London (thanks to J. Barron); the Universities of Edin-
burgh, Cambridge, Glasgow, Oxford, Birmingham, and Dunedin (thanks to
Dory Scaltsas, Richard Hunter, Douglas MacDowell, Ewen Bowie, Stephen
Halliwell, and John Barsby); "Tragedy, Comedy, and the Polis" at Notting-
ham (thanks to Alan Sommerstein and to the American Council of Learned
Societies for a travel grant which partially funded that trip); the Notting-
ham Classical Literature Symposium IV; and as an invited speaker at a gradu-

ate student conference on performance at the University of Texas (thanks to Bryan James and Sarah Dougher). My warm thanks go also to those who have read and criticized portions of this book in manuscript or shared their own work in advance of publication with me: Elizabeth Bobrick, Jeffrey Henderson, Alan Sommerstein, and Mark Toher. None of these scholars necessarily shares my views, however.

I am most grateful for a number of opportunities that have helped me to develop my thinking about performance. I thank the Faculty Research and Innovation Fund of the University of Southern California and the NEH for travel grants that allowed me to work on representations of performances in the splendid Institute for Classical Studies archive in London; and the Folger Institute at the Folger Shakespeare Library in Washington, D.C., for grants to attend a conference by Keir Elam on semiotics and Shakespeare, a workshop by Harry Berger on "Fictions of the Pose," and a memorable seminar led by Anthony Grafton on popular culture in the Renaissance. Special thanks are owed to the Greek Archaeological Service and the Ephoreia of the Acropolis for permission to work in the orchestra of the Theater of Dionysus and try out various movements there, as well as to the American School of Classical Studies at Athens for their assistance in arranging the permit.

This book has also benefited from very generous support of research leave. It was begun during a memorable year as a junior fellow at the Center for Hellenic Studies in Washington, D.C. It continued during a year as an Alexander von Humboldt fellow at the University of Konstanz, where my sponsors, Bernhard Zimmermann and H-J. Newiger, offered great help and enormous personal kindness. The Humboldt Foundation also funded my work in Greece in the winter of that year. Generous visiting fellowships at the Humanities Research Centre of the Australian National University in Canberra in the (northern) summer of 1994 and at Clare Hall, Cambridge, in the following academic year allowed me to prepare most of a manuscript. Finally, a visiting fellowship for a term at Magdalen College, Oxford, allowed me to complete it in the most congenial circumstances and company imaginable.

I

The Naming of Parts

To-day we have naming of parts. Yesterday,
We had daily cleaning. And to-morrow morning,
We shall have what to do after firing. But to-day,
To-day we have naming of parts.

—Henry Reed, *Lessons of the War*

ARISTOPHANIC COMEDY KNOWS AND NAMES ITSELF. No tragedy tells us
it is a tragedy, but Old Comedy from its beginning proclaims itself comedy
and soon proceeds to discuss its various parts with its audience—which itself
is one of the parts. It is this awareness of itself as theater that we now generally
term metatheatre.

Yet precise definitions of metatheatre vary widely. The term itself was
coined almost forty years ago by Lionel Abel in his book *Metatheatre: A New
View of Dramatic Form*. He saw it as a third genre, distinct from both comedy
and tragedy, one that emerged only in the Renaissance. He defined it epigra-
matically as "the world is a stage, life is a dream" and functionally by the presence of the play-within-the-play.[1] Representatives of this new genre he termed
metaplays. Abel's book sparked a lively discussion, especially in the fields of
his best examples, Shakespearean drama and that of the Spanish Golden Age.
While Abel's claim of separate generic status for metatheatre was largely rejected, the work of James Calderwood and Richard Hornby, among others,
built upon his insights into theatrical self-consciousness to demonstrate playwrights' fascination with metatheatrical effects from the Renaissance on.[2]
Hornby in particular sought to identify particular elements of metatheatre, including the play-within-the-play, ceremonies within in the play, role-playing
within the role, literary or real-life references, and self-reference.[3] One effect,
however, of Abel's original generic claim persisted: his insistence that metatheatre was different from comedy (as well as tragedy), his use of *Hamlet* as the
archetypal metaplay, and the traditional dominance of tragedy over comedy in

the canon combined to focus most discussion of metatheatre on its presence in, and relation to, "serious" forms of drama.[4]

Much has changed in recent years, primarily through the increasing influence of performance studies. Metatheatre is fundamentally an experience of performance. Abel's work, and the insights of those who followed him, would not have been possible without the transformations in theater practice, especially in performance of Shakespeare, which have been pursued throughout the twentieth century.[5] While classicists have always acknowledged that most ancient literature was performed, systematic investigations of performance are a more recent phenomenon. Moreover, that interest seemed to follow the hierarchy of established canons, with discussion of epic dominating for decades. Only with the publication of Oliver Taplin's landmark work, *The Stagecraft of Aeschylus*,[6] did performance criticism of ancient drama come into its own, and here too books on Sophoclean and Euripidean stagecraft followed in their canonical order before much performance-oriented criticism of comedy appeared.[7] When I wrote on Plautus in 1985, the press that published that book strenuously resisted my desire to use the word "metatheatre" in its title on the grounds that few of its likely readers would recognize or sympathize with this neologism.

The rise of performance studies has not been uncontested in the field of classics. Where insights from contemporary performance experiments have influenced criticism of Renaissance and later drama from the 1920s on, significant stagings of ancient drama and discourse between stage practitioners and publishing scholars are very hard to find before the late 1960s. Performance studies thus arrived in classics after the first and even second waves of structuralist and poststructuralist criticism and were not always welcomed by practitioners of the latter,[8] although Charles Segal was one of the first scholars in classics to investigate what he termed metatragedy.[9] Given Abel's insistence on its generic distinction from true tragedy, it is not surprising that metatheatre was first explored in the late works of Euripides.[10] Gradually, however, metatheatrical criticism has gained more and more currency in studies of tragedy. Many would now accept a definition such as Mark Ringer gives in his recent book on Sophoclean metatheatre:

Metatheater . . . encompasses all forms of theatrical self-referentiality. These may include role playing, various forms of self-conscious reference to dramatic convention and other plays, and the many ways in which a playwright may toy with the perceived boundaries of his or her craft. Other elements of metatheatrical phenomena include ritual or ceremonial enactments within the play. . . . Metatheater calls attention to the semiotic systems of dramatic performance.[11]

Earlier discussions of metatheatre in ancient comedy have been heavily influenced by peculiarly nineteenth-century notions of illusion. Thus some acknowledge the presence of metatheatre only when the audience is addressed directly (ὦνδρες and the like) or when a character on stage refers explicitly to a piece of stage machinery such as the *ekkyklema*, thereby "breaking the illusion" of the stage world. Such a view implies that this "illusion" is somehow prior, the natural state of affairs on stage, into which metatheatre is a later and artificial intrusion. This view suppresses the fact that illusion itself is an artifice. A sustained, illusionistic representation of character and situation is a creation of a particular, historical moment. It is a convention, an agreement or contract (usually implicit but sometimes explicitly negotiated) between performers and audience on certain expectations about character and action. When we speak of "breaking the illusion," we imply that this contract is somehow violated, the audience cheated of some legitimate expectation. It would be better to speak of a renegotiation of the contract, for most of the time even sudden changes in the nature of the performers' contract with the audience are designed to delight rather than cheat the audience. In a theater that rewards novelty (as the Greek theater certainly did), the poet must constantly search for those variations on what has gone before that will delight and amuse rather than baffle and alienate the audience.

Old Comedy, certainly as we see it instantiated in Aristophanes, constantly renegotiates its relationship with its audience. Within Aristophanes' career we can observe a number of changes in the formal structure of a comedy, among them a relative diminution in the importance of the chorus and a related curtailment in the parabasis. Such changes are sometimes categorized with organic metaphors of decline or decay, as though there were a Platonic Form of Old Comedy, a standard from which an aging Aristophanes increasingly falls away, or alternatively as a slow but inevitable evolution toward a more fully developed plot and the consistently maintained illusion of Menandrean comedy.[12] Both views falsify by abstracting the plays and their changing strategies from the immediate concerns of their original audiences. In particular, the evolutionary view inclines its adherents to view metatheatre as primitive or crude, easily jettisoned in the great historical march forward, and therefore not all that important even in earlier comedy.

Metatheatre, even once it had been recognized as a phenomenon present both at the beginnings of Western comedy and in some of the most interesting plays of more recent centuries, has still often been treated as one more variation on comic formulae, amusing solely through momentary unexpectedness or at most as something to be subsumed into the category of parody, especially parody of tragedy.[13] Indeed, many of the metatheatrical devices and moments in Aristophanes arise from parody of tragedy and more particularly Euripides, but there has been little inclination, beyond claiming that Aristophanes is a "conservative" in both taste and politics, to look for a deeper or broader explanation for the comic poet's fascination with the theatrical process itself and his delight in exposing its working and its deceptions to an apparently fascinated audience (at least to judge from his success in winning a slot at the festivals and his share of prizes).

My aim in this book is to explore the possibility that there is more to Aristophanic metatheatre than a series of one-line gags, a dislike of Euripidean tragedy, or even the characteristic feature of the parabasis with its direct address to the audience in the theater. To make such a case, it will be helpful to examine first the range of metatheatre in Old Comedy. This chapter attempts a rapid, synchronic survey of various metatheatrical techniques and devices in Aristophanes, with occasional forays into the fragments of the other writers of Old Comedy. Its aim is to cast the net widely, to be suggestive in scope rather than exhaustive in detail.

Having outlined a number of techniques, we turn then to the nexus of most of them: the actor, the performer whose words and actions make us conscious of performance as performance. It will be my contention that the actor and acting are more problematic categories for the late fifth century than most have acknowledged. With this background we will then be able to examine not just the varieties but the patterns and purposes of metatheatre in eight of Aristophanes' plays, for which such issues are central.

Comedy is notoriously difficult to study and analyze. The creation of taxonomies of jokes or comic techniques risks destroying the very subject it studies, eliminating any sense of what is really funny or creative through the atomization of the dramatic experience into a series of lifeless specimens, pinned onto the collector's display board. Yet some preliminary survey does seem necessary, if only to orient ourselves. If linguistic analogies were not so worn out by overuse in literary criticism, I would defend the surveys of this chapter as a grammar of metatheatrical techniques whose syntax will be explored subsequently in the context of the whole plays. Perhaps we should rather consider these preliminary inventories of the repertoire of metatheatrical techniques to be analogous to a rummage through the costumes and stage properties of Old Comedy,[14] some of which turn up only occasionally, others with considerable regularity.

In the subsequent individual play readings, we will see more clearly the changes in the uses of metatheatre over Aristophanes' career. My goal, however, is not merely an increasingly refined categorization of literary technique or even literary evolution. A central contention of this book is that Aristophanes believes that teaching his audience to be aware of, and to think critically about, performance, both in the theater and elsewhere in the life of the city, is a matter of vital importance for the Athenians. His ambition for comedy to rival tragedy as a teacher of the people is intimately related to precisely this self-consciousness about acting and stage technique in which his comedy is so rich.

In focusing attention thus, I hope to move discussion beyond what now seems an entrenched impasse between a "political" and an "aesthetic" approach to Aristophanes. The presence of characters who express themselves forcefully on issues of politics and war and even direct caricatures of contemporary politicians lends an obvious plausibility to the notion that Aristophanes wrote to represent and advocate his own views about politics. The Aristophanes of this view, now especially associated with G. M. de Ste. Croix,[15] is a simple conservative, nostalgic for the good old days before the riffraff became involved in Athenian politics, impatient with democracy, and rather fond of Sparta. The problem with this view is a certain circularity: since we "know" that Aristophanes is a conservative, we can recognize various statements and passages apparently approving of the democracy and its practices as "cover," designed to sugarcoat for the masses an advocacy of policies that would ultimately disenfranchise them. The aesthetic view on the other hand, represented in perhaps its purest form by Malcolm Heath,[16] sees Aristophanes purely as an entertainer, willing to write and portray anything that will raise a laugh successfully from the audience and thereby conduce to his winning the prize.[17] Argument has oscillated between these poles, with certain variations, for more than a century: is Aristophanes "just" a comedian, or is he "serious" about something—which we will be able to find if we only peel away all the layers of comic camouflage?

Simon Goldhill, drawing especially on Bakhtin's discussions of carnival and the carnivalesque but including a masterful survey of other, more anthropologically grounded work,[18] has argued forcefully that neither model suffices. In the face-to-face society of Athens, comedy's attacks on individuals cannot simply be written off as "licensed transgression," mere fun that does not count after holiday time is over. If Old Comedy offered just a temporary release from and reversal of existing power structures, serving ultimately to cement them ever more firmly in place, Cleon and other politicians would have paid no attention to its gibes: comedy's "negative *kleos*" is real and matters.[19] At the same time Goldhill is unwilling to see comedy as an unambiguous or straightforward challenge to existing social and political order. He propounds a dyadic model for poetry and performance in the classical democratic city, in which the Homeric poems, especially as performed at the Panathenaea, function as the "normative" voice of poetry, which the poetry of the Dionysiac festivals, both tragic and comic, challenges and transgresses.[20] Such a model of struggle over the interpretation and therefore control of the mythic past works well for the uniformly mythic corpus of surviving tragedy. It also enriches our picture of tragic parody within Old Comedy. Yet it verges on turning comedy into tragedy pursued by other means: while the multiple layers of parody and fantasy in Aristophanes' appropriations of Euripides, for example, may make for shifting and manifold ambiguities in the audience's reception of such scenes, it is not obvious that all the other parts of comedy are similarly ambiguous or contested in meaning.[21] In particular, while comedy is to some degree reactive to and dependent on tragedy, it need not follow that comedy's self-conscious discussion of poetic performance and its reception is also dependent on and subordinate to tragedy. Aristophanes is not just worried about tragedy's state of artistic health; he offers his own comedy as an alternative way of thinking and talking directly, not mythically, about Athens and its problems.

It is my belief that we can recuperate a much more specific political dimension of Aristophanic comedy through attention to its metatheatricality, a proposition that may well sound counterintuitive. If metatheatre is defined as Lionel Abel does, as "the world is a stage, life is a dream,"[22] then its aesthetic can seem fundamentally disengaged and apolitical or antipolitical. I want to argue, however, that Aristophanes uses metatheatre as a means to critique certain kinds of politics, not the whole notion of politics. His challenge is procedural, an objection to certain ways of conducting politics, not to the right of ordinary citizens to participate in politics at all.

Some groundwork is necessary before making the case for such a proposition. Metatheatre in Aristophanes is usually comic in its effect, although the degree of comedy may vary: Trygaeus in the *Peace* calling to the crane operator to save him when the beetle sways alarmingly beneath him appeals more obviously for audience laughter than a chorus's simple reference to "our comic poet," although both bespeak the fictive and created status of the play in which the speaker is engaged. Trygaeus might be able to be subsumed into the category of comedy as surprise: actors on stage do not normally address the stagehands behind the scene, and when they do, the surprise may be "funny." The notion that metatheatre works solely through the violation of illusionistic expectations to make the audience laugh renders it simply one technique or tool among many, indistinguishable in kind or purpose from padded costuming or insults directed at contemporary public figures. Such a notion is inadequate to account for other metatheatrical moments which are not immediately funny, or which are sustained too long to count any longer as "surprise." Moreover, if we think that the plays actually engage with ideas, then the idea of meta-theatre can have implications beyond its immediate comic effect. Metatheatre is by nature metacritical: by opening up the theatrical process to our gaze, it invites our contemplation not only of the *quality* but the *goals* of the theatrical performance.

The presence of metatheatre in Aristophanic comedy calls for some ac-counting, even if we cannot immediate give a full explanation of its emer-gence. While it has become obvious in the last forty years that Lionel Abel was wrong to claim that metatheatre was a third genre that emerged only in the Renaissance, quite separate from tragedy and comedy, it is equally obvi-ous that jokes calling attention to the play as play and an awareness of itself as a theatrical performance are not features of all comedy. Greek New Com-edy developed a style in which awareness of its own status as performance played very little role—necessarily so, I would argue, as the story patterns that predominate there (sentimental fictions of young lovers separated by chance or social barriers but ultimately reunited by the benevolent workings of fate) would have engaged their audience's emotions far less successfully if the fic-tive status of these stories were too obvious. Indeed, when Plautus takes over the stories of Greek New Comedy but begins to play with them in ways that make obvious their fictive status, the result is a diminution of interest in the love stories per se and the figures central to them and a corresponding increase of interest in, and audience engagement with, the scheming and plotting slave characters who so obviously control the fictional process within the plays.

From Greek New Comedy descends a long and rich tradition in western comedy, whose variations still play themselves out on stage and screen; only the details of the blocking forces seem to change. Most of these plays rely on a sentimental identification of audience with the play's participants and avoid any disruption of that identification with a stage illusion. When familiarity becomes formula and sentiment stifling rather than satisfying, however, the form may be ripe for metatheatrical self-criticism. Any authority or structure, including the conventions of the stage itself, becomes fair game for mockery.[23] If the dominant theatrical tradition (comic or otherwise) begins to seem hack-neyed or oppressive, metatheatre offers an avenue for renewal. I have argued elsewhere that such a creative reaction against a rigid inherited formula for comedy helps to account for Plautine metatheatre.[24]

Such a reactive explanation for the appearance of metatheatre will not suffice in the case of Old Comedy. Attic comedy becomes representational in the sense of a plotted narrative fiction only with Crates—at least according to Aristotle.[25] Whatever the facts behind the claim that plot in comedy originated in Sicily and only came late to Attica, the history of comedy within the Athenian festivals (with the first comedies being added to the program only fifty years after the organization of tragic competition[26]) suggests that comedy lagged behind its tragic counterpart in organization and development. Aristophanes and his contemporaries were part of only the second generation to write plays with a semblance of a continuous narrative. There was therefore no already hackneyed plot formula against which Aristophanes was necessarily reacting.

One could seek a reactive explanation in sibling rivalry. Tragedy was already well established on the Athenian stage when *komoi* or comedies in honor of Dionysus were added to the program at his festivals. As we have already noted, much of Old Comedy criticizes contemporary tragedy's practices and practitioners (not just Euripides, but a host of justly forgotten minor figures as well). In the *Acharnians* the poet uses the broadest of strokes to mock Euripides, suggesting that he must be crippled himself if he produces so many crippled heroes, while a few years later in the *Clouds* the focus turns to audience reception and the possibility that the young will imitate the actions of the scandalous women (and men) of Euripidean tragedy (a claim also found in the *Thesmophoriazusae*). Comedy's relentless examination of both the production and reception of tragedy must partially explain its own theatrical self-consciousness. Yet not all that is metatheatrical in Old Comedy can be reduced to paratragedy. When a play discusses itself in relation to other comedies (even if only in boasting its own superiority to the competition), it rubs the audience's nose in the fact of its own constructedness. It is the very status of theatrical representation that Old Comedy's play with its own form calls in question.

Plays and Playwrights

Let us turn then to comedy's self-awareness and its own naming of parts. My examples are of necessity drawn primarily from Aristophanes, but where useful fragments of other writers of Old Comedy survive, I have included these in our survey as well. Aristophanes' plays do refer to themselves as comedies: the revised version of the *Clouds* laments the audience's reception of the premiere of what he considers "the cleverest of my comedies" (σοφώτατ᾽ . . . τῶν ἐμῶν κωμῳδιῶν, 522) and compares "her" to Electra (534–535).[27] The poet had already alluded more circumspectly to this fate of his "comic verses" (ἔπη . . . κωμῳδικά, 1047) in his *Wasps*. More often, he refers to the low-brow comedy of both named and unnamed rivals (*Wasps* 66, *Peace* 751, *Frogs* 15).

While comedy possesses an independent language of self-description, to a significant degree it also comes to know itself through describing its other, that is, tragedy. By self-differentiation, by naming tragedy as the other which it is *not*, comedy both articulates its own sense of self and yet acknowledges a certain dependence on tragedy. On one level tragedy is simply an important part of contemporary culture, calling forth either praise or (more often) blame from the comic poet: Dicaeopolis is hoping to see Aeschylus when he goes to the theater (*Acharnians* 10), but tragedians such as Morsimus (*Knights* 401, *Peace* 802–807), Agathon (*Thesmophoriazusae* passim and Aristophanes fr. 592 K-A., lines 33–35), and above all Euripides regularly arouse Aristophanes' scorn.

Beyond simple aesthetic appreciation of tragedy as art, however, comedy ventures to evaluate tragedy's believability, its claims to accurate representation of reality. Lysistrata sees the weakness and unreliability of women as justification for writing tragedies about them (*Lysistrata* 138). Other references suggest that tragedy is a world inhabited by strange figures not otherwise to be encountered: Trygaeus's daughter first suggests he acquire Pegasus as a steed in order to appear "more tragic" (τραγικώτερος, *Peace* 136) but then warns him to take care not to fall and become crippled, lest he become a (Euripidean) tragedy (τραγῳδία γένῃ, *Peace* 148). Tragedy is also where one might encounter a Priam (*Birds* 512) or a fury (*Wealth* 423–424).

Beneath this ambiguous love-hate relationship of Old Comedy with tragedy lies an unmistakable envy: Aristophanes (and doubtless other comedians) wanted some of the public admiration and respect accorded the rival genre. In his attempt to put comedy on a par with tragedy Aristophanes may have invented a term that, while punning on the name of tragedy, attempts to construct comedy as an alternate (and equally important) source of poetic authority in the city. This term is "trugedy" (τρυγῳδία), punning on τρύξ, meaning "wine lees" or "new wine."[28] The word and its derivatives seem to be a feature only of early Aristophanic comedy.[29] By using it, Aristophanes stakes his claim to the authority and public voice of tragedy, while differentiating his own comic art from the corruption and sophistic influence predominant in contemporary tragedy.

Key to this claim of authority is the poet's traditional role as teacher.

Advocates of tragedy were presumably asserting (as Aristotle later would) that it was the proper successor of Homeric verse as an instructor of the citizenry. Already in the *Acharnians* (658) Aristophanes claims for his own poetry this power of teaching the city,[30] and the claim regularly reappears in his plays. Moreover, Aristophanes is adept at exploiting the semantic slippage between this kind of teaching and the dramatic poet's role in constructing the performance. As the term κωμῳδοδιδάσκαλος (*Knights* 507, *Peace* 737) shows, the poet (though occasionally he delegated it to someone else) "taught" the play to the performers, a process for the choristers at least that was surely oral. Though a late source, Plutarch gives us a picture of this in an anecdote where Euripides is singing one of his odes to teach it to his chorus—and one of the choristers laughs at the old poet.[31] Both comic and tragic poets had to teach their performers; it is an easy step (which Aristophanes eagerly takes) to claim that *both* kinds of performance then teach the audience in turn. Given the haphazard survival of substantial passages from other writers of Old Comedy, it is impossible to be certain, but it seems likely that this claim of a teaching function for comedy within the city was peculiar, if not unique, to Aristophanes. The nature and ramifications of this "teaching" will be one of the most important themes in what follows.

In pursuit of his claims for the status of comedy, Aristophanes thus pursues a typically double-edged strategy: on the one hand he emphasizes that comedy is poetry and therefore that the comic poet, like any other, is entitled to respect as a teacher of the people, while on the other hand he criticizes tragedy, explicitly or implicitly, for neglecting that crucial duty. For example, when Hermes in the *Peace* describes Euripides as a "poet of little lawcourt phrases" (ποιητῇ ῥηματίων δικανικῶν, 534), the yawning gap, both aesthetic and moral, between poetry and legal sophistry is intended to be painfully clear.

Aristophanic comedy's discussion of poets, both its own and others, carries with it recognition of its own "made" status: it is itself poetry, composed by a poet. Many types of poet appear or are referred to in Old Comedy under the term ποιητής.[32] While these poets may be dithyrambic, epinician, or quite often tragic, Aristophanes is already using the term of himself without further qualification in the *Acharnians*: he is the poet (lines 644, 649, 654) who gives such good advice to the city that the Spartans try to claim him in the proposed peace treaty.[33] He refers to his comic predecessors simply as poets (τοὺς προτέρους τῶν ποιητῶν, *Knights* 519), although he also can specify a practitioner of comic poetry (κωμῳδοδιδάσκαλος, *Knights* 507, *Peace* 737; κωμῳδοποιητής, *Peace* 734). In an unknown lost play he discusses the demos' general taste in poetry (fr. 688 K-A.): it rejects those who are dry (σκληρός) and hard (ἀστεμφής).[34] Aristophanes even shows us the poet at work: the brilliant opening scene of the *Thesmophoriazusae* shows us Agathon, composing his poetry (τῆς ποιήσεως, 38).[35] Among Aristophanes' lost plays are included *Poetry* (Ποίησις) and *Dramas* (Δράματα), whose titles suggest plots perhaps even more metatheatrical than anything that has survived. All of this explicit discussion separates the world of Old Comedy from that of tragedy.

Poetic Form

Poets compose Old Comedy within the parameters of a known set of both verse forms and larger structures. The full technical vocabulary for describing these forms and structures is not present in the plays, but significant elements are. Plays possess prologues (προλόγους, *Frogs* 1119 and passim), episodes (Metagenes fr. 15 K-A.), and a final exodos (ἔξοδον, *Wasps* 582; cf. τοὺς ἐξοδίους . . . νόμους, Cratinus fr. 308 K-A.). Much of this language is of course used to describe tragedy, which also displays these formal features, but the existence of a language to describe and analyze plays is a key step to self-consciousness about its own form, and in fact some of this language is explicitly applied to comedy. In Cratinus's lost play, *The Wineflask*, he may have shown himself onstage writing a comedy; at any rate, someone advises putting Cleisthenes in an episode (ἐπεισοδίῳ, fr. 208 K-A.) of a play and suggests how to write about Hyperbolus as well (fr. 209 K-A.).[36] The plays also have some language to describe features unique to them as comedies. The chorus regularly acknowledges when it is about to begin the parabasis, which it often refers to as "the anapaests" from the verse form predominant in its opening (ἀναπαίστοις, *Acharnians* 627; cf. *Knights* 504, *Peace* 735, *Birds* 684) and which it frames as "stepping aside" from the play's action (πρὸς τὸ θέατρον παραβάς, *Peace* 735).[37]

The *agon* or formal contest is often considered a standard part of an Old Comedy, even though its form can vary considerably, from Dicaeopolis's attempts to persuade the chorus of his play not to lynch him to the debate between the two Logoi in *Clouds* down to the contest of tragic poets in *Frogs*.[38] The Greek term is generic in application; Aristophanes uses it for the Olympic games (τὸν Ὀλυμπικὸν . . . ἀγῶνα, *Wealth* 583) as well as musical and other gymnastic contests (ἀγῶνας μουσικοὺς καὶ γυμνικούς, *Wealth* 1163). At times, though, Aristophanes seems to use the word in a more tech-

nical sense, as when the chorus in the *Clouds* proclaims a "great contest" between the two Logoi (ἀγὼν μέγιστος, 958; so too the chorus of *Wasps* on
Bdelycleon and Philocleon's dispute: μέγας . . . ἀγών, 534), and both Aeacus
and Dionysus refer to the upcoming struggle between Aeschylus and Euripides in the *Frogs* as an *agon* (785, 873). It is context, however, rather than the
word itself that determines how self-conscious any given instance is. We would
dearly love to know, for example, if the confrontation between the two sons
of Œdipus in Aristophanes' *Phoenissae*, described as an ἀγῶνα in fr. 570 K-A.,
was the formal *agon* in that play, but we cannot be sure.[39]

Not all the technical poetic and rhetorical vocabulary for describing the
plays and their features is fully developed or consistently employed, but those
terms that do occur underline the self-consciousness of the descriptions and
discussions. Iambs (ἐν τοῖς ἰαμβείοισι, *Frogs* 1204) are the only meter apart
from anapests to be mentioned specifically, but the metrical parodies of the
Frogs and elsewhere are highly sophisticated and precise. Aristophanes employs no single word for "verse" or "line." In *Thesmophoriazusae* 412, τοὖπος
τοδί clearly means "the following (iambic) line," as does τοὖπος in *Frogs* 1381
at the beginning of the verse-weighing contest, but at 1395 ἔπος equally clearly
means only a single word within the line (i.e., pointing out the word "persuasion").[40] At *Frogs* 1379 (and probably 1155 and 1199 as well), ῥῆμα seems to
mean "line," yet at 924 and 929, the ῥήματα are more likely "words," while
elsewhere the plural is more likely to mean "speech" (e.g., Aristophanes fr.
719, *Peace* 604,[41] *Birds* 1257, *Frogs* 97, 821, 824, 828). At least "speeches" somehow differ from "shavings of words" at *Frogs* 881 (ῥήματα καὶ παραπρίσματ᾽
ἐπῶν). A ῥῆσις is certainly a "speech": we hear of a defendant reciting one
in court in *Wasps* 580, and of the "crime" of writing out one by Morsimus
in *Frogs* 151, while at *Clouds* 1371 Pheidippides scandalizes his father by reciting a speech of Euripides, after he has specifically refused to sing.[42] Yet
when Dionysus tells both contestants to pray before the poetry contest (πρὶν
τἄπη λέγειν, *Frogs* 885), ἔπη here seems best translated "speeches" also, not
just "lines" or "words." In short, while ἔπος, ῥῆμα, and ῥῆσις are neither
completely synonymous nor perfectly differentiated, Aristophanes' vocabulary does allow him to discuss recognizable features of plays in a relatively
precise and technically self-conscious manner.

Musical Form

The situation with musical vocabulary is quite similar. The plays refer to
songs, odes, hymns, and melodies, both their own and those belonging to

tragedy. This terminology is used to critique both the performances of others and the performers' own efforts. Perhaps the commonest term for song in the plays is μέλος. After the discussion of their prologues, Aeschylus and Euripides in the *Frogs* turn to a competition over their respective μέλη (1248ff.).⁴³ The Old Relative is captivated by the μέλος Agathon sings (*Thesmophoriazusae* 130, 144), clearly a parody of the poet's tragic style, but when the old men in the chorus of the *Lysistrata* invite the old women to join them (τοῦ μέλους ἀρξώμεθα, 1040), the μέλος in question is clearly the comic choral song they proceed to sing. Animals sing such songs too: Charon tells Dionysus to listen to the beautiful songs of the frog chorus (μέλη, *Frogs* 205), and Carion refers to the songs of goats (αἰγῶν . . . μέλη, *Wealth* 294). The frog chorus refers to its own singing as "the oft-diving melodies of the ode" (χαίροντες ᾠδῆς / πολυκολύμβοισι μέλεσιν, *Frogs* 245–246).⁴⁴ The later chorus of initiates in the same play call the god to their ode (*Frogs* 396), the same term used by the chorus of the *Thesmophoriazusae* (ᾠδήν, 986). The bird chorus at the end of their play sings wedding songs (νυμφιδίοισι . . . ᾠδαῖς, 1729) for Peisetaerus. The chorus refers to its own activity in choosing to sing a hymn (ὑμνίωμες, *Lysistrata* 1304) or changing the focus of a hymn (*Frogs* 383).⁴⁵ Specific to the theater, and therefore all the more pointedly metatheatrical, is the notion of singing a monody. It occurs as early as *Peace*, where Trygaeus uses the term to mock the tragic poet Melanthius, imagined as singing in the character of his own *Medea* (μονῳδεῖν ἐκ Μηδείας, 1012),⁴⁶ but the Old Relative in *Thesmophoriazusae* (1077) wants to perform one in full.⁴⁷

Now the mere mention of the word "melody" or "ode" is not necessarily in and of itself metatheatrical. Even tragedy can portray its performers referring to their own performances, as when Aeschylus's chorus of Furies refer to the melody and hymn that they sing (*Eumenides* 329–331), but such references are not inconsistent with the maintenance of a continuous characterization or illusion.⁴⁸ When Carion in *Wealth* 290ff. imitates the sound of the cithara⁴⁹ and dances as first the Cyclops and then Circe, these songs do foreground the adoption of role along with the musical form.

At the same time, another very important element of musical criticism, aimed neither at tragedy nor at comedy itself, nonetheless functions metatheatrically in that it calls attention to both comedy and its competitors for public attention as parts of the larger Dionysiac festival. Old Comedy's criticism of both contemporary comedy and tragedy demonstrates an important truth: the comic poet strives not just for the prize within his particular *agon* but for status within the festival as a whole and therefore before the public in general. This helps explain both comedy's hostility to dithyramb and its scathing personal attacks on its practitioners. In some ways the most intrigu-

ing attack is in the famous fragment 155 K-A. of Pherecrates' *Cheiron*, where
Music herself laments (in startling double entendre) the outrages she has suf-
fered at the hands of contemporary dithyrambists, but Aristophanes too gives
us memorable portraits of these woolly and incomprehensible hucksters such
as Cinesias in *Birds* 1372ff. As Bernhard Zimmermann has shown, Aristophanes with cheerful inconsistency both criticizes the New Music, as exemplified
by dithyramb, and steals from it as well, all in the continuing competition for
public attention and status.[50]

Dance

The element of dance, as (if not more) essential to comedy as to tragedy, is
also the subject of explicit comment on its own performance. In Greek culture
dance was a natural way to express joy: the entering chorus of the *Peace* break
into spontaneous dance and cannot restrain themselves, despite Trygaeus's
pleas for them to be quiet (*Peace* 326, 329, 330[51]). Dance was even more appropriate to the choral finale.[52] Some specific types of dances are mentioned, such
as the pyrrhic (*Frogs* 153) and a comic dance (ἀπόκινον, *Knights* 20; Aristophanes *Dramata* fr. 287 K-A.; Cratinus *Nemesis* fr. 127 K-A.). There are also instructions on how to dance: in circular formation (*Thesmophoriazusae* 954), in
Cretan style (*Ecclesiazusae* 1165–1166), or simply with good rhythm (εὐρύθμῳ
ποδί, *Thesmophoriazusae* 985). The *Wasps* ends with a dance contest in which
Philocleon undertakes to demonstrate the superiority of the old dances of
Thespis and Phrynichus over the tragic dancers of the present (1474ff.), and
Plato Comicus similarly complains about the degeneracy of modern dance.[53]
    Perhaps not surprisingly, the technical language of dance in Aristophanes
is less developed than that for music and poetic meters, but the word σχῆμα
seems to mean an individual dance figure in *Wasps* 1485 and *Peace* 323 (cf. the
discussion of Aeschylus's dance figures in Aristophanes fr. 696 K-A.).[54] At the
same time, this word can be used of the posture or pose of a performer (*Ecclesiazusae* 150) and even of a costume or disguise (*Ecclesiazusae* 482, 503).

Chorus

Reference to the chorus, by itself and by others, is very common, though
not all such mentions are actively metatheatrical. The choruses regularly invoke the gods to help them in their singing (*Knights* 559, 586; *Clouds* 564;

Peace 775; *Frogs* 326–327, 674–675; etc.) or refer to the delight the gods take in their performances (*Peace* 976, *Thesmophoriazusae* 975, 992). Such language is traditional, both in the theater and in other choral performance venues, and presumably calls no special attention to itself. At the other end of the spectrum, however, is the use of the term as a metonym for the play as a whole or for the opportunity to perform represented by the grant of a chorus. The chorus at *Knights* 513 discusses why Aristophanes had not applied for a chorus in his own name before and speaks (521) of Magnes' victories over his rivals' choruses, while Dionysus at *Frogs* 94–95 disparages those poets who receive only one chorus, then disappear from the cultural landscape.

At other times the chorus's separate identity or role within the whole performance is singled out. Dicaeopolis plans a speech to win over the chorus (*Acharnians* 416), while the chorus leader demands that Strepsiades tell the chorus what happened offstage (*Clouds* 1352). In both these instances Aristophanes dispenses with any specific identity for the chorus (as Acharnians or Clouds) and shows us the fundamental mechanism of the play at work, the hero's struggle against the chorus. One-word fragments appear to refer to individual choral performers (frr. 503, 894 K-A.), but without a context it is hard to say more.

Plays even refer to the behavior of past choruses. The chorus in *Knights* insists (507ff.) that they would not have obliged past poets by performing a parabasis, although they are willing to do so for Aristophanes. *Frogs* contains discussion of both Aeschylean and Euripidean choruses, including details of gesture and sound effects (e.g., 914–915, 1029).

Costumes, Props, and Stage Machinery

Paradoxically, costumes, stage properties, and effects, the most concrete parts of a comic performance, provide us with examples of both the subtlest and the most blatant kinds of metatheatre. Ancient comedies, like modern ones, are much more prop-laden than their tragic counterparts, a testament to the inherent comic potential of the things that surround and limit us.[55] The *Agamemnon* can be done with a carpet, a chariot, and a net (and can dispense with the chariot in a pinch), but the *Acharnians* requires a wealth of props and costumes, from feathered helmet crests to Copaic eels.

No single term or set of terms exhaustively indicates when props are being used metatheatrically. For the most part, they are simply there, in abundance, successfully representing what they simply are: a chair, a bed, a chopping block. A lamp (like a cigar) is just a lamp—unless it becomes the occasion for Euripidean parody, as in the remarkable opening of the *Ecclesiazusae*. At other times, as when Dicaeopolis begs for Telephus's basket or Trygaeus moves a sacrifice indoors without completing it, to "save the choregus a sheep" (*Peace* 1022), the prop is fully foregrounded as a counter in the theatrical game.

Costumes and stage properties are not such differentiable categories for the ancient Greek theater as they are for us today. A number of related terms can be used to designate costumes and props: σκευή (often costume), σκεῦος, σκευάριον, and the verb σκευάζω). At *Frogs* 108 Dionysus refers to his Heracles costume as σκευήν. Both the desperate Megarian and the desperate Euripides costume others in order to forward schemes of deception (*Acharnians* 739, σκευάσας; *Thesmophoriazusae* 591, ἐσκεύασεν).[56] Plato Comicus wrote an entire play called *Skeuai*, whose fragments mostly deal with theatrical (especially tragic) performers and performances.[57] A mask seems to fall in the category of σκεῦος, for it is the prop-makers (τῶν σκευοποιῶν, *Knights* 232) who refuse to make a portrait mask of Cleon in that play. Neither σκεῦος nor its diminutive σκευάριον is as specialized as the word "props" in English: both can simply mean "equipment, furnishings" and are used to refer to equipment or luggage in the *Frogs* (12, 172). Yet when Xanthias as *Wasps* 1313 refers to Sthenelos, a known theatrical figure, as having lost his σκευάρια, this is surely stage equipment.

As with props, most costumes simply represent, conveying information the audience is asked to accept about the wearer. Usually the details of costume in the plays must be inferred from various references in the texts that do not forcibly call the audience's attention to its status as costume.[58] Only occasionally, as in Peisetaerus's reference to the piper's mouthstrap (*Birds* 861), is a single costume detail in and of itself metatheatrical, although a clash between costumes (for example, Dionysus's yellow gown slipping out from under the lion skin in *Frogs* 45–46) functions in the same way.

Much more important, yet signaled by no single word or gesture, is the device of putting on and taking off costumes in the sight of the audience, which recurs regularly from Dicaeopolis's borrowing of the Telephus costume from Euripides in the *Acharnians* to the women disguising themselves as men in *Ecclesiazusae*. Hamlet never changes into tennis clothes: to do so would be to imply a dangerous instability of identity and purpose. Yet Aristophanes' characters, particularly his comic heroes, can change their clothes and with them their roles with surprisingly freedom. There can also be forced changes of identity. Lysistrata and her followers drive the Proboulos from the stage by first costuming him as a woman with veil and wool basket (*Lysistrata* 531–535), while Carion in the *Wealth* forcibly strips the Informer and makes him change clothes with the Just Man (lines 926ff.), clearly demonstrating the results of the new regime in which Wealth can see the difference between the deserving and undeserving. In a delightful variation, Dicaeopolis transforms the informer Nicarchus in *Acharnians* into a piece of pottery by packing him up and selling him off to the Boeotian (926–953). We shall consider the metatheatrical strategy of costume change in detail in the individual play readings below.

There is, however, surprisingly little metatheatrical play with masks in the surviving plays of Aristophanes. Apart from the discussion of the portrait mask of Cleon that was *not* made for the *Knights*, there is nothing in the early plays that makes masks an issue for the audience. In the *Birds* Aristophanes makes a joke of the fact that Procne is both a bird and a piper, but her mask is far from standard.[59] At *Frogs* 912, when Euripides criticizes Aeschylus's use of a silent character who does not show his or her πρόσωπον to the audience, the word might mean mask rather than face, but the latter is probably more likely. I have argued elsewhere that some of the references to lekythoi in the young man's encounter with the old women in the *Ecclesiazusae* play on the resemblance of their painted white masks to white ground lekythoi,[60] but the allusions are subtle, and the broad comedy of the scene could be appreciated without this dimension. So too I suspect that the reference to "the rags of her face" (τοῦ προσώπου τὰ ῥάκη, *Wealth* 1065) subtly plays on the fact that masks were made of painted linen, but it could simply be a bold metaphor for the ravages of age in the old woman's face. In short, there is nothing in surviving comedy quite so bold as the scene in Aeschylus's satyr play, the *Theoroi*, where the satyrs appear carrying masks of themselves.[61]

The most unambiguous markers of metatheatricality in Old Comedy are the references to those props and stage effects that simply do not exist outside the world of the theater. A fragment of the *Banqueters* (fr. 234 K-A.) preserves a reference to the ἀχυρόν, a means of creating a fire effect on stage, while a fragment of the *Danaids* (fr. 259 K-A.) mentions the σώρακος, a box in which actors kept stage props (τὰ σκεύη), as Pollux 10. 129, which preserves the fragment, tells us. Given their fragmentary state, we cannot fully gauge what effect these references had in context, although the *Banqueters* fragment almost certainly is making a point or joke about tragedy, since it cites a *Hekabe*.

The references to the *mechane* and the *ekkyklema*, resources developed for the tragic stage but gleefully pirated by comedy, give us a better notion. The use of the *ekkyklema* seems always to be indicated by verbs: Dicaeopolis calls on Euripides to have himself wheeled out (*Acharnians* 408), and his fellow tragic poet Agathon makes a similar appearance (*Thesmophoriazusae* 96, 265). The defeated Paphlagon is rolled back into the *skene* on the *ekkyklema* like a fallen tragic hero at *Knights* 1249, but most untragically requests this conveyance: κυλίνδετ᾽ εἴσω τόνδε τὸν δυσδαίμονα.[62]

The crane or *mechane* was an even more spectacular stage effect and therefore all the more ripe for comic exploitation. Trygaeus's terrified appeal to the crane operator or μηχανοποιός at *Peace* 174, when his beetle begins to sway alarmingly, is the most obvious instance but apparently had its parallels in lost plays as well.[63] More startlingly innovative than this tragic parody of Bellerophon, however, is the use of the crane to suspend Socrates in his basket at *Clouds* 218 in a typical Aristophanic literalization of metaphor. In both cases, Aristophanes simultaneously exposes the effect for the stage device that it is and incorporates it into the narrative of his play.

Theater Space, Audience, and Festival

More generally, Aristophanic comedy displays a full awareness of its setting in the theater, performed before an audience, competing against the work of other poets before a chosen body of judges, as part of a festival in honor of Dionysus. One of the women in the *Thesmophoriazusae* gives the formula for (tragic) theater thus: θεαταὶ καὶ τραγῳδοὶ καὶ χοροί, (391), "spectators and actors and choruses," but with the substitution of κωμῳδοί it defines the comic theater equally well. Performers and audience are alike essential parts of the theatrical experience. The spectators are addressed directly, whether as "gentlemen" (ὦνδρες ἥλικες, Strepsiades to the audience in *Clouds* 1437; ὦνδρες, Peisetaerus[64] to the audience in *Birds* 30) or as "spectators" (e.g., ὦ θεαταί at *Wasps* 1071; ὦ σοφώτατοι θεαταί, *Clouds* 575; ὑμῶν τῶν θεατῶν at *Birds* 786) or simply as "you" (ὑμεῖς δ᾽ ἡμῖν προσέχετε τὸν νοῦν, the chorus to the audience at *Knights* 503). The performers even give each other stage directions (*Knights* 36, *Clouds* 890) for the explicit benefit of the spectators and instruct the spectators how to behave (*Knights* 228, *Wasps* 1013).[65]

Explicit mention of the theater itself (the θέατρον) in which the performance takes place functions as a metonym for the audience (*Acharnians* 629, *Knights* 233, 508, 1318, *Peace* 735),[66] but there are also very specific references to parts of the theater: the stage (περὶ τὰς σκηνάς, *Peace* 731), the orchestra (Aristophanes fr. 968 K-A.; also κύκλον, *Frogs* 441[67]), the side entrances for the chorus (εἴσοδον, *Clouds* 326, *Birds* 296, *Islands* fr. 403 K-A.), the rows of audience members (τὰς στίχας, *Knights* 163), and the benches they sit on (ἀπὸ τῶν ἰκρίων, *Thesmophoriazusae* 395). Sometimes the audience is treated just as an undifferentiated crowd (ὄχλον, *Frogs* 676; τὸ πλῆθος, *Ecclesiazusae* 440), but there are also references to privileged seating up front for members of the boule (ἐν βουλευτικῷ, *Birds* 794) and others (προεδρίαν, *Knights* 575, 703, 704).

The fact that the plays are produced in a competition is never far from the poet's mind. In most cases it is in his best interest to assume that there is no difference of opinion possible between the audience as a whole and the judges whose votes actually determine the prizes at the competitions (thus the servant in the finale of the *Ecclesiazusae* invites both to dinner, but the audience first: τῶν θεατῶν . . . τις / καὶ τῶν κριτῶν . . . τις, 1141–1142), but there are explicit appeals to the judges as well: the chorus of birds in its play both attempts to bribe the judges with "owls of Laureion" and threatens them with a rain of bird droppings from above if they fail to give the victory to their play.[68] On one occasion, Aristophanes is even bold enough to remind the judges of their oath and their duty to "judge the choruses fairly" (κρίνειν τοὺς χοροὺς ὀρθῶς ἀεί, *Ecclesiazusae* 1160).[69] While a tragic poet (Aeschylus or Phrynichus, say) may be praised, other comic poets, unless dead or no longer competing, are usually only mentioned when they can be criticized.[70]

The plays also acknowledge the festival of which they are a part, and with that the festival's place in the life of the city. Dicaeopolis, speaking for Aristophanes in response to the attacks of Cleon, notes that the *Acharnians* is being performed "at the Lenaean competition" (οὑπὶ Ληναίῳ τ' ἀγών, *Acharnians* 504), and the chorus of Knights asks its audience for "a Lenaean clamor [of approval]" (θόρυβον . . . Ληναΐτην, *Knights* 547). The chorus even refers to the structure of the day's program in the theater: the Birds entice their audience with the prospect of wings which would allow them to escape from the boring performances of tragedy for lunch and then return, presumably for the satyr play and comedy that rounded out the day (*Birds* 786–789).[71] For Dionysus in the *Frogs*, his desire to save the city is grounded in the desire to keep the choruses at these dramatic festivals singing in his honor (lines 1418–19).

Evidence from Aristophanes supports the proposition that there were separate performance venues for the play performances of the Greater or City Dionysia and the Lenaea. Early dramatic performances took place in the old Agora, probably located east of the Acropolis, although this remains controversial.[72] At some point in the early fifth century, the ἴκρια on which the spectators sat collapsed during a performance, after which "the theater" (certainly the Theater of Dionysus on the south slope of the Acropolis) was built. It seems likely that this collapse took place in the old Agora and resulted in moving the performances of the City Dionysia from temporary stands to the natural slope of the present theater site.[73] Though not firmly dateable (it could be anywhere between 499 and 467 B.C.), this disaster took place well before the institution of dramatic performances at the Lenaea. It seems unlikely that, when a new contest of performances at the Lenaea was inaugurated, these would have returned to the site of the former disaster. At the same time, performances at the Lenaean festival are always designated as taking place ἐπὶ Ληναίῳ, that is, not at the *time* of the Lenaean festival but in a physical *space* called the Lenaion. No such shrine has ever been located archaeologically at the present Theater of Dionysus on the south slope of the Acropolis or in the present Agora. Although the provision of a second new performance space may seem uneconomic, once the first on the south slope of the Acropolis existed, the Athenians may well have valued the separate identity of the two festivals and their contests and have chosen to reinforce this spatially. I have argued elsewhere at length for the existence of two theaters, relying especially on evidence from the *Frogs*.[74] In the case of tragedy at least there was a clear status differentiation between the two festivals.[75] Poets competed with tragic tetralogies at the City Dionysia but with pairs of plays only at the Lenaea.[76] No surviving play of Greek tragedy is known to have been performed at the Lenaea. In comedy the status distinction is much less sharp, and Aristophanes produced plays for both festivals.

Such a rapid survey of terms as that undertaken in this chapter so far has the potential to bog down in details. We have looked at a number of ways in which the plays call attention to themselves as plays, ranging from passing jokes about minor tragedians to straightforward comparisons of one comedy to another (always to Aristophanes' advantage!). Yet such a synoptic preliminary view is essential to prevent limiting our view of metatheatre in Old Comedy to the most obvious and isolated examples. Moreover, it has become clear that no one explanation accounts for every instance in the plays. Much that is metatheatrical occurs in the parabases, but it is also clear that the phenomenon is not confined to this particular structural element of an Aristophanic comedy. While some metatheatrical comments are just jokes for a moment, other passages display a frequency and density of metatheatrical play that suggests that the phenomenon is of more than passing interest to Aristophanes. Not all of his plays evince an equal interest in, or emphasis on, the metatheatrical, although I will in due course argue that it is a key element in all eight plays to be analyzed in detail here.

The survey has also clarified and I hope refined the point made by Gregory Sifakis a number of years ago: Old Comedy is nonillusory drama.[77] It is not a theater of illusion occasionally disrupted by primitive choral interventions (i.e., the parabasis) or occasional asides by the actors; illusion is not "broken" and then seamlessly glued back together. Instead, Old Comedy exhibits a spectrum of performance modes and methods of relating to its audience, moving freely from the illusory to the nonillusory and capable of foregrounding its status as performance in varying degrees of prominence.

Before turning to the individual play analyses, it is necessary to examine one element of the original performance in greater detail and more precise historical context. In our survey up until this point, we have touched on all the means of representation, save the most essential: the human being, the actor on the stage. Though we are not yet (and may never be) in a position to determine whether play with the forms of staging or with the notion of acting came first, it seems essential to explore, insofar as the fragmentary sources allow, the growth of a self-consciousness of—and about—actors and acting. It is my contention that there is a relation between the self-consciousness of the individual actor as actor, his awareness of the nature and techniques of his own representations, and the manifestations of self-consciousness within the comedies themselves. If we can trace the steps whereby actors developed a sense of themselves and their craft, if we can follow the development of audience awareness of actors and acting, we will be better able to contextualize, historically and socially, the rise of metatheatre within Old Comedy. We will also be better able to understand what made acting and the transparency of representation (or lack thereof) in the late fifth century such debatable commodities.

2

The Emergence of the Actor

A WELL-KNOWN ANECDOTE IN PLUTARCH'S *Life of Solon* tells of the encounter of the lawgiver with Thespis, the traditional originator of dramatic performances in Athens. The story is no doubt apocryphal, but that does not mean it need be a very late invention, for it bespeaks an anxiety about performance and the idea of acting that is by no means out of place in the late fifth century. Solon has gone to see Thespis act one of his own plays:

μετὰ δὲ τὴν θέαν προσαγορεύσας αὐτὸν ἠρώτησεν εἰ τοσούτων ἐναντίον οὐκ αἰσχύνεται τηλικαῦτα ψευδόμενος. φήσαντος δὲ τοῦ Θέσπιδος μὴ δεινὸν εἶναι τὸ μετὰ παιδιᾶς λέγειν τὰ τοιαῦτα καὶ πράσσειν, σφόδρα τῇ βακτηρίᾳ τὴν γῆν ὁ Σόλων πατάξας· "Ταχὺ μέντοι τὴν παιδιάν," ἔφη, "ταύτην ἐπαινοῦντες οὕτω καὶ τιμῶντες εὑρήσομεν ἐν τοῖς συμβολαίοις." (Plutarch, *Solon* 29.5)

After the performance [Solon] called to him and asked if he was not ashamed to tell such lies in front of so many people. When Thespis replied that there was no harm in speaking and acting as he did in play, Solon struck the earth with his walking stick, saying, "if we so praise and admire play of this sort, we will soon find it in our solemn contracts." [1]

Extracted from its context, this may seem simply an anecdote about Solon's lack of imagination or sense of play. In fact, Plutarch goes on to show just what ἐν τοῖς συμβολαίοις entails. No translation quite captures this phrase, but I have opted for Perrin's "solemn contracts" to catch the echo of the social contract, for Plutarch follows this directly with the story of how Peisistratus intentionally wounded himself, then rushed to the agora to ask for a bodyguard to protect him against the assaults of his "enemies." [2] Solon accuses him of "playing the part of Homer's Odysseus" (ὑποκρίνῃ τὸν Ὁμηρικὸν Ὀδυσσέα, 30.1), who used deception to trick his enemies (*Odyssey* 4.244ff.). Solon fails, however, to induce the rest of his fellow citizens to see through Peisistratus's playacting, and the foundations of the tyranny are laid through this bodyguard.

The encounter between Solon and Thespis is too apt to its context to be true, even apart from the unlikehood of such a datum being successfully transmitted from the middle of the sixth century. It nonetheless functions as a useful reminder that "acting" and the "actor" are not timeless categories always present to us, but have a historical origin at some point in a given culture—and that point may also be a point of resistance.

Nor are acting and drama coterminous in the historical consciousness. The emergence of drama from ritual has occasioned much speculation and debate, which we cannot (and need not) revisit here. Suffice it to say that the institution of poetic performances with mythic subject matter was not enough to create the notions of actor and acting. The actor as a conceptual category is posterior to the playing of drama before an audience. At first, performing in comedy or tragedy must have seemed just one more form of participating in the public festivals in honor of Dionysus. Mimesis alone does not create the actor, for other forms of poetry before had spoken in character voices. Plutarch's story is an anachronism in the sixth century: when Thespis first separated himself from his chorus (or whoever it was who first took that formal step), he was not yet an actor, a practioner of the art called acting, in the sense we use these terms today. The creation of acting was a gradual process, whose full development in fact destroyed the original notions of festival performance from which it grew. Only through the creation of concepts of actor and acting is a single poetic enactment at a festival (the status of drama in the early fifth century) transformed into a portable and repeatable play in our modern sense.

Acting begins on the margins of choral performance. According to traditional early accounts of the theater, drama arises from a leader responding to a chorus and thereby creating dialogic performance. Acting of course did not remain on the margins. It is a commonplace that over time the balance between acting and choral performance reverses, and the chorus in its turn becomes marginal, the actor central. Less common is any attempt to explain this change other than in terms of the "degeneracy" of poets and audience alike, the latter often seen to derive from a growing cult of personality around the actors. Such a view, part Aristotle, part Aristophanes, may conceal more than it reveals—in particular, the changing nature of the relation between the actor and the performance as a whole. I suggest that we can detect at least three rather loosely delimited stages in this transformation. At first, the actor's relation to the form of drama is essentially unselfconscious: acting is judged in relation to the myth it enacts. As drama becomes a more familiar form and the audience builds up its repertoire of experience in seeing performances, there is a growing self-consciousness of acting; actors are compared and judged in similar but not identical performances. Finally (and this development lies essentially beyond the limits of the fifth century), reperformance becomes possible,[3] and comparisons can be made of actors playing precisely the same roles. At this point, the subject matter of theater has become classical; acting is the primary source of innovation and renewal within the form.[4]

An exploration of the emergence of actors and acting as conceptual categories in the course of the fifth century is a necessary background to understanding performance and self-consciousness about that performance in the plays of Aristophanes. It is not just that actors (mostly tragic) are known and named in comedy, just as other elements of the stage performance are in various places foregrounded. Even more important is the role of the actor as the visible agent and intelligence assembling and guiding the performance. When Dicaeopolis performs in the guise of Telephus for the chorus of the *Acharnians*, he is an actor putting together a performance from costumes and props that he rifles through in front of the audience, before putting them together in that performance. He is an actor enacting the process of acting, and an audience cannot understand what he is doing without some awareness of actors and acting.

Our sources for the emergence of actors and acting are both meager and scattered over a significant period of time. In this material, tragic actors and acting are much better documented than their comic counterparts. While tragic acting and comic acting were in the fifth century quite separate professions, just as the writing of the plays was,[5] this should not be a serious impediment to us: it is the portrayal of the mythic characters of tragedy that most obviously evokes anxieties (at least in Aristophanes) as to whether the portrayals are "proper." Nor should we forget that virtually every actor in a Greek performance played multiple roles: while we hear of some actors excelling in their portrayals of certain roles (mostly from the next century), none could confine themselves to such roles, since three (or perhaps four) actors played *all* the roles in a Greek drama.[6] This very multiplicity, if the audience is aware of it,[7] can help highlight the performer apart from his role. We shall begin by looking at the evidence for tragic actors, not just because they are much better documented than their comic counterparts, but also because comedy's metatheatrical critiques of performance so often focus on tragedy. Whether they are Euripides' ragged and pathetic heroes, which so offended Aristophanes, or the portentous and baffling heroes that he portrays Euripides as criticizing in Aeschylus (*Frogs* 907–926), the tragic actors are seen as powerfully manipulating audience response.

Tragic Actors: The Literary Sources

The evidence for the history of actors in the early fifth century is very sketchy, and a significant portion of it comes from the lives of the poets. M. R. Lefkowitz has contended that "virtually all the material in all the lives is fictional."[8] Many of her criticisms of the lives as a whole are well founded. With regard to actors and acting, however, her general thesis (i.e., that the lives draw simply on the texts of the poets' own plays or from the comic poets' attacks and comments on other plays and playwrights) is much more questionable, especially as regards tragic actors and acting. As we shall see, the information on actors preserved in the texts we have of comedy (and in the scholia) in general would not suffice to give us the general picture of the development of acting presented in the lives (a picture that is further supported by Aristotle).

Tradition tells us that originally poets acted in their own plays, and we have no particular reason to doubt this. Aristotle *Rhetoric* 3.1 (1403b) makes this claim for the earliest poets of tragedy, and the tradition for Thespis as both poet and performer of his pieces is quite clear. Now it is obvious that a poet was not granted a chorus on the basis of his acting ability but for his skill in composition, and it equally obvious that poets will have differed in their personal histrionic skills. The question of when poets ceased to act in their own plays is an important one for an understanding of the emergence of the concepts of actor and acting.

It is interesting that the *Life of Aeschylus* 15 is not terribly clear on this point:

ἐχρήσατο δὲ ὑποκριτῇ πρώτῳ μὲν Κλεάνδρῳ, ἔπειτα καὶ τὸν δεύτερον αὐτῷ προσῆψε Μυννίσκον τὸν Χαλκιδέα. τὸν δὲ τρίτον ὑποκριτὴν αὐτὸς ἐξεῦρεν, ὡς δὲ Δικαίαρχος ὁ Μεσσήνιος, Σοφοκλῆς.

He employed as first actor Cleandrus, and then he added to him as second actor Mynniscus of Chalcis, and he invented the third actor (though Dicaearchus of Messene says it was Sophocles).

Does this mean that Aeschylus at first employed Cleandrus as his other actor and then added Mynniscus as the third actor? This is the usual interpretation,[9] but the use of the term "first actor" for Cleandrus seems puzzling. Would Aeschylus have taken any other than the protagonist's roles?[10] The *Life* is our only source for Cleandrus, whose acting career may have been over by the time contests for tragic actors began, but Mynniscus appears in the victory lists in 447,[11] and his appearance in those lists means that he too is now the protagonist in his performances.[12]

The *Life of Sophocles* tells us some important things about his use of actors but associates no names with him particularly. The most important passage for our purposes is sections 4–6:

Παρ' Αἰσχύλῳ δὲ τὴν τραγῳδίαν ἔμαθε. καὶ πολλὰ ἐκαινούργησεν ἐν τοῖς ἀγῶσι, πρῶτον μὲν καταλύσας τὴν ὑπόκρισιν τοῦ ποιητοῦ διὰ τὴν ἰδίαν μικρο-φωνίαν (πάλαι γὰρ καὶ ὁ ποιητὴς ὑπεκρίνετο αὐτός), τοὺς δὲ χορευτὰς ποιήσας ἀντὶ ιβ' ιε' καὶ τὸν τρίτον ὑποκριτὴν ἐξεῦρε.

Φασὶ δὲ ὅτι καὶ κιθάραν ἀναλαβὼν ἐν μόνῳ τῷ Θαμύριδί ποτε ἐκιθάρισεν, ὅθεν καὶ ἐν τῇ ποικίλῃ στοᾷ μετὰ κιθάρας αὐτὸν γεγράφθαι.

Σάτυρος δέ φησιν ὅτι καὶ τὴν καμπύλην βακτηρίαν αὐτὸς ἐπενόησε. φησὶ δὲ καὶ Ἴστρος τὰς λευκὰς κρηπῖδας αὐτὸν ἐξευρηκέναι, αἷς ὑποδεσμεύονται οἵ τε ὑποκριταὶ καὶ οἱ χορευταί· καὶ πρὸς τὰς φύσεις αὐτῶν γράψαι τὰ δράματα· ταῖς δὲ Μούσαις θίασον ἐκ τῶν πεπαιδευμένων συναγαγεῖν.

He learned tragedy from Aeschylus. And he introduced many innovations in the contests, being the first to abandon the tradition of the poet's acting through the weakness of his own voice (for of old the poet himself acted) and making the chorus fifteen in place of twelve. He also invented the third actor.

They say also that only in the *Thamyras* did he once take up the cithara and play it, for which reason he is painted in the Stoa Poikile with a cithara.

Satyrus says that he thought up the bent walking stick. And Ister also says that he invented the white boots that both the actors and the choristers wear, and he wrote his plays according to their natures, and he gathered together a thiasos of the educated in honor of the Muses.

Let us consider first the statement that Sophocles gave up acting in his own plays because of his weak voice. If true, this would be an important milestone: not merely the quality of the poetry but the quality of the acting now makes a difference to the success of a drama.[13] Lefkowitz attempts to discredit this statement by claiming that it is introduced solely in order to explain Sophocles' traditional invention of the third actor. Now Aristotle's neat, teleological scheme whereby Aeschylus invents the second actor and Sophocles the third *is* suspicious. But the *Life* makes no causal link between Sophocles' ceasing to act and the invention of the third actor; indeed the author's statement about Sophocles' changes in the size of the chorus intervenes between the two. I can see no reason to believe that the author of the *Life* or anyone else thought Sophocles' abandonment of acting *explained* his invention of the third actor. The specificity of the anecdotes about his performances as Nausicaa and Thamyras suggests strongly that Sophocles did begin by acting in his own plays, but it is not essential to argue that he was the first poet to abandon acting. At some point the poets gave up acting in their own plays because the actors' contributions made a difference to the success of the whole piece. Dating this change to Sophocles' early career may be wrong, but it is not likely to be far out of the actual historical sequence.

Cleandrus is our only name from the period when actors were presumably just friends of the poet. By the time of Sophocles' "innovations" in the competitions, actors seem to have worked with several poets. What would the capacities and characteristics of actors of this stage of development be? Let us look again at the last part of the *Life* cited, where three statements are attributed to Ister, particularly the claim that Sophocles wrote his plays according to φύσεις αὐτῶν. Does this mean that Sophocles had in mind the peculiar capabilities of his performers in the composition process? Like so much of the lives of the poets, this is a laundry list, and the relation of one item to another is far from clear. Though the grammatical antecedent of αὐτῶν seems to be both ὑποκριταὶ and χορευταί, these two statements may not have been connected in Ister—what have white boots to do with typecasting? Interpreting this way also presents us with an extreme improbability, especially if we accept John Winkler's contention that tragic choristers were young men drawn from a pool that probably changed every year.[14] What on earth can it then mean to write a chorus according to the φύσις of its performers? Did Sophocles walk into rehearsal, look over the pimply throng, and say, "You lads look much more like Lemnian maidens than Argive elders"? But the notion that he wrote *actors'* parts according to their performance capacities is far from improbable.

The principal objection to accepting this as a historical datum is the possibility that actors were allotted to the poets in the later fifth century, not chosen by them, but there is no proof that allotment of actors was introduced this early; indeed, it seems inherently improbable. A poet who writes according to the capacities of his actors is another important milestone, whoever that poet was. Fifty years ago, A. S. Owen argued that Sophocles was just such a poet, to the extent that he changed the distribution of singing parts based on the capacities of his actors.[15]

Thus in the early fifth century actors existed primarily in relation to the piece they enacted. Their performance was not separable from the overall performance of the drama. Gradually, as actors' capacities and talents began to differ, so poets began to see advantages in using different actors for differently conceived roles. The process that led eventually to specialization of actors in roles by gender, age, and class such as we know from the fourth century begins here. The separation of poets from actors is a natural result as the latter's part in the drama increased in both size and complexity.

The narrowing in the choice of tragic subjects that seems to begin in the course of the fifth century may be related to the developing skills of the actors. In *Poetics* 13 (1453a) Aristotle argues that some myths are better suited to tragedy than others. One can only speculate that acting plays a part here. One representation of Orestes can build on another, both histrionically as well as poetically. The urn supposedly containing the ashes of Orestes is as much a creation of performance as of poetry, if not more so. How an actor realizes a scene on stage creates just as much an "anxiety of influence" for future performers as the words of the text. Mrs. Siddons's "tender" Lady Macbeth still exerts an influence over performers today. Thus as the storehouse of myths for tragedy begins to contract ever so slightly, the actors begin to portray characters whom other actors have portrayed before. As this process accelerates, it creates standards by which quality of acting can be judged and actors typed by their skills in representing certain kinds of characters.

Our only direct glimpse of this process is the reference to Sophocles writing according to his actors' φύσεις. Nonetheless, some such process must have taken place, for we see its result in the institution of contests for actors of tragedy at the City Dionysia almost certainly in 449, at the Lenaea perhaps in 442. The situation for comedy is somewhat more complicated. There was definitely a comic actors' contest at the Lenaea, starting perhaps in 442, but the traditional view has been that there was no corresponding contest for comic actors at the City Dionysia until the latter half of the fourth century.[16] The evidence for these dates is inscriptional and fragmentary. The date of 449 for the tragic actors' contest at the City Dionysia rests on a seemingly secure calculation of when an additional line began to be added to each year's records in the so-called "Fasti," I.G. ii² 2318. It seems equally certain that no line was added to this inscription to record a comic actor's contest in the fifth century. There *was* such a contest, however, when a different series of inscriptions, the so-called "Didascalia" (I.G. ii² 2319–2323), gives us records for the next century. It seems very curious that three acting contests should be begun within ten years of each other (tragic actors' at both City Dionysia and Lenaea, comic actors' at Lenaea), and yet the fourth, the logical complement, would not be introduced until a century later. I have argued at length elsewhere that there is evidence for a comic actors' contest at the City Dionysia already in the fifth century in the unfortunately corrupt text of one of the hypotheses to Aristophanes' *Peace*.[17] Whether my argument is accepted or not, the author of the hypothesis certainly knew that an actor named Apollodorus was the lead actor in Aristophanes' play. That such knowledge was still available to the hypothesis writer over a century later is a signficant fact in itself and quite consistent with the absolutely certain foundation of three actors' contests in the 440s.

The importance of the institution of the contests cannot be overemphasized. Their existence means that acting is now conceptually separate from the drama. Actors have an ontology in and for themselves. Standards exist by which one actor's performance can be judged superior to another's. If actors do not yet have the same status as the poets, they nonetheless are seen to be doing something very different—for it is now possible for a victorious actor to play in a losing play. No doubt at the beginning the prize for acting tended to go to the protagonist of the victorious play, just as today there is some association in the Academy Awards for films, for example, between those for best actor or actress and best picture. The possibility nonetheless exists that a great play can be inadequately acted or that extraordinary acting can be done in inadequate plays. We are first sure of this occurring in 418, when we have inscriptional evidence for a victorious protagonist in a losing play.[18]

It would be a great help to know when the system of allotment for protagonists began. What we know of it comes from the Suda, where we also learn that the victor of one year's contest was entitled to be one of the protagonists for the following year:

νεμήσεις ὑποκριτῶν· οἱ ποιηταὶ ἐλάμβανον τρεῖς ὑποκριτὰς κλήρῳ νεμηθέντας ὑποκρινουμένους τὰ δράματα, ὧν ὁ νικήσας εἰς τοὐπιὸν ἀκρίτως παρελαμβάνετο.

allotment of actors: the poets received three actors allotted to them to act their dramas; the victorious actor [of the three] was entered into the next year's pool without preliminary selection.

We know nothing else of how the group of actors to be allotted was drawn up. Though Haigh argued that allotment is contemporary with the initiation of the contests, that presupposes an extraordinarily swift change in the status of actors in the middle of the fifth century, from nonentities to a controlled and rationed commodity. The provision that a victor had an automatic right to compete the next year also seems very suspicious this early, and the Suda clearly links this with allotment. Such a formal provision sounds much more at home in the fourth century, when the number of available actors was large and even the chance to appear had to be fought for.

The contests therefore made it possible to earn recognition and fame as an actor. Acting in the fifth century, however, was not yet a way of making a living: there simply were not enough performance opportunities. It is therefore no surprise to learn that it was often a family pursuit, although actors may well have begun to train nonfamily members as well.[19]

Whether actors' self-recognition and identity involved banding together in groups larger than master and apprentice in the fifth century is another question. Sophocles' *thiasos* in honor of the Muses (cited above, section six of his *Life*) has been long and unfruitfully discussed. There is no way to determine whether this was a "professional" group in any sense. For many, including Pickard-Cambridge,[20] the history of actors only begins with the formation of the great Hellenistic guilds, the Artists of Dionysus; our first proofs of their existence are third-century inscriptions recording contracts for productions between the guilds and festival producers. Pickard-Cambridge discounts Aristotle's references in the fourth century to *Dionysokolakes* and *technitai* (*Rhetoric* 3.2 [1405a]), because there is no evidence that those so designated formed groups which functioned as the later guilds did.[21] For our question, though, when actors acquired a self-consciousness of themselves and their art, such evidence is most welcome.

Pickard-Cambridge dismisses as an anachronism the earliest reference to the *technitai* of Dionysus.[22] Athenaeus 9, 406e–407c, relates a story about the comic poet Hegemon, who dates to the end of the fifth century, citing as his source book six of Chamaeleon *On Comedy*.[23] Hegemon, summoned in a lawsuit, goes to seek the help of Alcibiades, who obligingly goes down to the Metroon and wipes out the indictment with his thumb. The fascinating—and inorganic—detail Chamaeleon adds is that Hegemon, on his visit to Alcibiades, was accompanied by τοὺς περὶ τὸν Διόνυσον τεχνίτας. Many simply discount this reference as a Hellenistic embellishment, but it is hard to see why Chamaeleon would choose to invent this detail, which serves no obvious narrative purpose.[24] It suggests rather that Hegemon, in appealing for help, could now summon professional, not just personal, friends to his aid.

A further intriguing question arises: are these comic *technitai* in particular (since Hegemon is a comic poet), or despite the sharp division between tragic and comic performers noted above, did both kinds of performers identify themselves as *technitai* of Dionysus? While we will come to no clear answer about Hegemon's companions, it is time to turn to the much more shadowy evidence for comic performers.

Comic Performers

We have virtually no names of comic actors from the period before inscriptional records begin. Athenaeus 14, 659ab, tells us of Maison, an actor from Megara who originated a comic cook role and had a mask named after him. He may be a sixth-century figure. Recent work on the mid-fifth century comic poet Magnes suggests that he acted in his own plays and was famous for his animal imitations.[25] It is hard to tell with certainty, however, whether the references to Magnes in *Knights* (520–525), where Aristophanes claims the older poet used to "buzz like a fly and dye himself frog-green" refer to the choruses he staged or to his own individual performances. Crates, whom Aristotle credits with changing the nature of Old Comedy by moving from simple iambic abuse to a more plotted entertainment, may still have been an actor when Magnes was performing, for we have a tradition that Crates began by acting for Cratinus.[26] In comedy, the poet was then still hard to separate from the whole performance. It has even been suggested that a poet as late as Aristophanes played in his own comedies.[27]

This dearth of evidence for comic actors seems at first glance no different from the relative lack of evidence for early comedy as a whole (as compared to tragedy). Axel Seeberg, however, has recently suggested a radical reconsideration of our picture of comedy before the mid-fifth century, particularly with regard to actors:

In iconography the typical comic *actor* is altogether a late-comer . . . debut[ing] . . . around 430; it is legitimate to wonder how long Athenian artists had kept this rather spectacular apparition up their sleeve[s]. . . . Plots need actors, of course. On the other hand actors need plots. Would they have loitered for many years without them? There could be a case, on negative evidence only, for thinking that the classic comic actor came in relatively late and by degrees, and the Comedy went on much as before in the first decades after its official establishment, any individual parts that it offered being tackled in ways not yet standardized.[28]

As Seeberg shows, the history of the *komos* or comic chorus is much more visible in the iconographic record, beginning with the Corinthian padded dancers, who also appear in Attica, but then are replaced in the latter part of the sixth century by theriomorphic or other characterized choruses, accompanied by a flute-player. The flute-player implies an organized chorus and a shared song, presumably composed by a poet for such a characterized chorus, but there is no clear necessity for an actor to respond to or interact with the choristers.[29] No doubt there could be individual comic performers who differentiated themselves from their fellows, whether performing animal imitations (perhaps Magnes[30]) or even playing human types (Maison as cook), but these need not imply plots or sustained representations of characters, which, as Aristotle again tells us, come in only with Crates, probably around mid-century.

Aristophanes is not just in the second generation of Athenian comic poets to write *komoi* with plots. He may be in the second generation writing *komoi* with actors as well—actors defined as performers sustaining an individualized character involved in a narrative plot. Nor are all comic performers equally engaged in what we from our modern point of view might consider acting: so-called "bomolochic" characters such as Euelpides in the *Birds* are defined more by their comedic interactions with the lead player than by any notion of through-characterization. Even the lead performer need not be tightly bound by consistency of either psychology or action.[31]

The question of why comedy adopts plots at all lies beyond the scope of our argument here. The influence of tragedy is obvious, but the specific aetiology and mechanisms of change are less so. We must emphasize, however, that acting and sustained plots are not "natural" elements of the *komoi* in honor of Dionysus; even if Aristophanes grew up watching comedies with actors and plots, there was ample living memory of comic performances organized in quite different ways. It may well be that the introduction of an actor (as opposed to a *komast*) and therefore a notion of acting into comedy was a key step in general recognition of their existence. That which was seamlessly sutured into the whole in tragic performance became identifiable when borrowed (whether in parody or simply imitation) by comedy. Not only that—as comedy exposed the constructedness of acting in tragedy through parody of both tragic style and individual performers, it created an observational point outside the tragic system of representation from which to recognize and observe analogues to tragic acting in the construction of other kinds of cultural performances.

Our picture thus far of the evolution of acting in the century preceding Aristophanes shows quite disparate stories for tragedy and comedy. In tragedy, the earliest actors were the poets themselves with the assistance of others more or less regularly attached to one poet. As the balance between the contributions of chorus and actors to the drama shifted steadily toward the actors, the importance of histrionic skill increased. Many poets ceased to act, and they took care to suit the actors they chose to the part and vice versa. At some point in Sophocles' career then, we pass from the first of our hypothetical stages in the evolution of Greek acting to the second, from actors who existed primarily in relation to the poetry to actors with a craft of their own who competed with each other. Tragic actors began to have a public presence. It is a change embodied in the transition from Cleandrus, whom we know only as Aeschylus' actor, to Callippides, who doubtless acted for Sophocles but also for many other poets as well. It is difficult to say how far this process had advanced when the first contest was held at the City Dionysia, but enough certainly for the public to take an interest. When the contest for tragic actors was instituted, Magnes was probably still performing in his own comedies and Crates just beginning his career. By the time of Alcibiades, there had been actors' contests for a generation, long enough to establish actors as a presence in the public mind and certainly long enough for the actors themselves to have developed a consciousness of themselves and their art. Whether or not that self-consciousness had been translated into professional organization, by the last quarter of the fifth century the actor certainly has arrived.

Actors in the Visual Arts

Recent work on the scanty but growing body of visual evidence for the fifth-century theater has greatly enriched our understanding not just of the individual images but of the systems of representation that underlie them. In particular the work of Richard Green has shown us that the metatheatricality of comedy and the general illusionism of tragedy find their parallels in systems of representation that tend to expose comic performers as performers but efface any evidence of the stage (masks, actors' footwear, the details of stage props) from representations of tragic myth, even when there are strong grounds to suspect the influence of a particular tragedian's play. The problems of using vase paintings and other representational art as evidence for the fifth-century theater are well known.[32] Vase painters are not cameras; they record what they *wish* to see. But their wishes are generically conditioned.

It would be vain in brief compass here (or indeed in wider compass) to attempt to improve on Green's illuminating studies, and I must refer the reader to his work for a full account and for excellent reproductions of the key vases and other material on which they are based.[33] His conclusions are succinct: "the figures seen in the theatre recreated myth-history and they were to that degree 'real.' When the vase-painter showed them, he therefore showed them as real."[34] Even a growing trend toward representing performers (almost all choristers) putting on or taking off their masks and costumes or rehearsing dance steps or movements for their portrayals still respects this boundary of the actual performance itself. Once the vase painter chooses to portray part of the play's action, however, it becomes indistinguishable from a painting of the myth itself. Masks are exposed as masks when carried in the performers' hands or pushed up on their foreheads as they rehearse,[35] but once in place as part of the play itself, they melt into the performer's own face. The result, as Green succinctly puts it, is that "we have no representations of tragic actors acting in the fifth century."[36]

The vase painter's eye sees comedy quite differently. As Green shows, "the depictions of comedy . . . are literal in their approach."[37] From a well-known black-figure amphora in Berlin, depicting a chorus of men in bird masks but otherwise simply muffled in heavy mantles, and an oinochoe in London with a dancing chorus of men in bird suits,[38] on down through the fifth century and into the fourth, the vase painters enjoy and even emphasize the grotesquery and ridiculousness of the comic masks and costumes. The contrast in ways of viewing the two genres is superbly summarized in the so-called "Choregus Vase" of the fourth century, well studied by Oliver Taplin and others.[39] Here a character labeled "Aegisthus" has stepped onto a stage already inhabited by padded comic performers with typically exaggerated masks. "Aegisthus" is portrayed just as he would be in myth, with no indication of a mask: only the contrasting figures already on stage make him a performer as well.

The vases do not supply us with significant evidence for individual actors with a public following.[40] For that we must turn to the jokes about some of them employed in Old Comedy. There may be one piece of visual evidence, however, for the existence of associations and self-identity of actors at the very end of the century, such as the story about Alcibiades, Hegemon, and his fellow Dionysiac artists implies. It is the well-known sculptured actors' relief from the Peiraeus, which I have argued elsewhere must represent a dedication by actors (not their choregus) and may even imply an ongoing partnership or even association among these actors.[41]

Evidence from the Plays

Thus at the end of the fifth century, actors had a public presence, though still far from equal to that of the poets. Once again we must remind ourselves that fifth-century plays were written for a single performance. While a poet might subsequently take his play to Syracuse or the court of Macedon, Athens would not see it performed at a festival again. The sole exception is Aeschylus, but we know nothing about the mechanics and organization of these revivals. While Dicaeopolis at *Acharnians* 10 looks forward to seeing a revival of Aeschylus (but is disappointed by the arrival of a new play instead), we do not know if a revived Aeschylus play competed for the prize with the works of the living or not.[42] In any case he is the great exception. Thus in the fifth century an actor could not make a reputation in a particular performance. There were no legendary interpretations such as again Mrs. Siddons's Lady Macbeth or Irving's Hamlet.

Nonetheless a growing self-consciousness of acting is reflected in comedy's comments on tragic actors toward the end of the century. Note that comedy does not much concern itself with comments on other comic actors.[43] This might seem an odd omission—until we consider the possibility that comic poets may still have been performing their own plays at this period; in this case, the obvious target is the poet as creator rather than performer of the play.[44] Thus, while comments on rival poets as poets are common in Old Comedy, so far only Aristophanes' comments on Magnes at *Knights* 520–525 seem particularly to address performance style, suggesting that Magnes' animal imitations finally lost their appeal for the audience.

We may take references to four tragic actors mentioned in Aristophanes as representative for how consciousness of actors and acting shapes dramatic meaning. These four are Oiagrus, Callippides, Hegelochus, and Sthenelus. We know the first, Oiagrus, only from one passage in *Wasps*. Philocleon, in enumerating the pleasures of being on a jury, counts among them:

κἂν Οἴαγρος εἰσέλθῃ φεύγων, οὐκ ἀποφεύγει πρὶν ἂν ἡμῖν
ἐκ τῆς Νιόβης εἴπῃ ῥῆσιν τὴν καλλίστην ἀπολέξας.   (579–580)

And if Oeagrus comes into court as a defendant, he doesn't get off until
he's picked out the finest speech in *Niobe* and recited it to us.

Many things could be noted about this passage, particularly its equation of the courts to the theater (discussed more fully below), where the jurymen function as an audience to be pleased by the contending parties just as they are by actors, an equation reinforced by the reference in the next two lines to the flute-player, who when acquitted rewards the jurymen by playing an ἔξοδος for them. More to our purpose, however, is the fact that this actor, of whom we unfortunately know nothing more, is somehow associated with performance of the *Niobe*, and the jurymen make use of their power in order to receive a command performance. Neither do we know if this is the *Niobe* of Aeschylus or of Sophocles. If the latter, it would likely have been performed at a recent festival and would not be evidence for an actor having a certain part permanently in his repertoire. If the Aeschylean version is meant, that would be a little more surprising, implying a recent revival or a sense that this particular play is now a classic which an actor might be expected to have in his repertoire. Circular argument is a danger here. We cannot use this passage as evidence for or against an assumption of multiple performances of a play at this period. The most we can say, and this is quite a bit in itself, is that this particular actor enjoyed at least passing fame for his portrayal of Niobe, and his performance was so good that a repetition of it constitutes an acceptable bribe to the jury.

One of the most famous actors of the end of the century was Callippides. He is the unwitting agent in the version of Sophocles' death, which the *Life* 14 attributes to Ister and Neanthes. They say:

Καλλιππίδην ὑποκριτὴν ἀπὸ ἐργασίας ἐξ Ὁποῦντος ἥκοντα περὶ τοὺς Χόας πέμψαι αὐτῷ σταφυλήν, τόν δὲ Σοφοκλέα λαβόντα ῥᾶγα εἰς τὸ στόμα ἔτι ὀμφακίζουσαν ὑπὸ τοῦ ἄγαν γήρως ἀποπνιγέντα τελευτῆσαι.

Callippides the actor coming from an engagement in Opous around the festival of Choes sent him a bunch of grapes, and Sophocles taking an unripe grape into his mouth on account of his great age choked on it and died.[45]

This actor's fame was such that Strattis even wrote a play about him, certainly another milestone in the growing importance of actors. By this point the influence of a single leading actor on the art has become so important that he merits attack in comedy. The case of the New Music is similar. It had really "arrived" when Connus was attacked in an eponymous play. The date of Strattis's *Callippides* is not certainly known but is likely before 390.[46] On the other hand Strattis was somewhat younger than Aristophanes and was active well into the fourth century. How early can the *Callippides* be? The question makes a difference in how we interpret a fragment of Aristophanes' play Σκηνὰς καταλαμβάνουσαι. Kassel and Austin in the new *Poetae Comici Graeci* have chosen to follow the reading of the manuscripts of Pollux, the fragment's source, while Kock and Edmonds prefer an emendation proposed by Brunck:

fr. 490 K-A.:

> ὥσπερ ἐν Καλλιππίδῃ
> ἐπὶ τοῦ κορήματος καθέζομαι χαμαί.

Just as in the *Callippides*, I sit on the ground in the refuse.

Edmonds (474 Kock):

> ὡσπερεὶ Καλλιππίδης
> ἐπὶ τοῦ κορήματος καθέζομαι χαμαί.

Just like Callippides, I sit on the ground in the refuse.

Naturally the date of Aristophanes' play from which the fragment stems is not known either.[47] No other playwright is recorded as having written a play entitled *Callippides*, nor would we expect one. It is possible that the Σκηνὰς καταλαμβάνουσαι is later than Strattis' play, but it seems unlikely (*pace* Kassel-Austin), nor are references to other comedians' plays by title all that common in Old Comedy; the one good parallel is Aristophanes' reference to Eupolis' *Maricas* in the *Knights*.[48] In any case, the reference points to a considerable public awareness of the actor. I prefer Brunck's emendation and see in this fragment of Aristophanes a reference to a famous scene Callippides played, rolling around in dirt on the ground.[49] This seems quite in keeping with what we know of Callippides' style; Aristotle (*Poetics* 1461b) records that the great actor of the previous generation, Aeschylus' second actor Mynniscus, called Callippides a "monkey" because his gestures were so extravagant.

Two other actors at least are ridiculed *qua* actor, Sthenelus and Hegelochus. Here I leave out of account those ridiculed for a personal characteristic such as gluttony. Sthenelus is a somewhat problematic figure: was he an actor, a poet, or both? We first encounter him in the *Wasps*. Philocleon is recounting some of the conversation at the party he has attended. There someone compares Lysistratus, one of the guests, to a locust that has lost its wings and to "Sthenelus bereft of his stage equipment" (Σθενέλῳ τε τὰ σκευάρια διακεκαρμένῳ, 1312). A scholion on this line identifies Sthenelus as a tragic actor (τραγικὸς ὑποκριτής) who, through poverty, was forced to sell his equipment and thereby incurred ridicule. He also is mentioned in a fragment of Aristophanes' *Gerytades* preserved by Athenaeus:

fr. 158 K-A.:

καὶ πῶς ἐγὼ Σθενέλου φάγοιμ' ἂν ῥήματα;

And how could I eat the speeches of Sthenelus?

This is more ambiguous. Athanaeus identifies Sthenelus as a τραγικός, which can unfortunately mean either poet or actor. When Aristophanes ridicules a ῥῆσιν of Morsimus in *Frogs* 151, he is known to be a poet, but one could argue that the ῥήματα of Sthenelus are made "inedible" by his delivery of them rather than his authorship.[50]

The most infamous actor, as far as the comic poets were concerned, was the unfortunate Hegelochus, who so memorably mispronounced the word γαλήν' ("calm," with a final vowel elided) as γαλῆν ("weasel") in his performance of Euripides' *Orestes*. Aristophanes had his fun with this in the *Frogs* (lines 302–03), but Strattis fr. 1 K-A. (cf. his fr. 63 K-A., Plato fr. 235 K-A.) also notes it:

> καί τῶν μὲν ἄλλων οὐκ ἐμέλησέ μοι μελῶν,
> Εὐριπίδου δὲ δρᾶμα δεξιώτατον
> διέκναισ᾽ Ὀρέστην, Ἡγέλοχον τὸν Κιννάρου
> μισθωσάμενος τὰ πρῶτα τῶν ἐπῶν λέγειν.

> As for the rest, he's
> Left me quite cold, I grant you, but the Orestes,
> Euripides' clever play, he spoilt for us
> By giving the name part to Hegelochus. (trans. Edmonds)[51]

In Sannyrion's *Danae* (fr. 8 K-A.), Zeus imagines changing himself into a field mouse, then worries about Hegelochus seeing him:

> τί οὖν γενόμενος εἰς ὀπὴν ἐνδύσομαι;
> ζητητέον. φέρ᾽ εἰ γενοίμην ⟨-⟩ γαλῆ·
> ἀλλ᾽ Ἡγέλοχος ⟨εὐθὺς⟩ με μηνύσειεν ⟨ἂν⟩
> ὁ τραγικός, ἀνακράγοι τ᾽ ἂν εἰσιδὼν μέγα·
> 'ἐκ κυμάτων γὰρ αὖθις αὖ γαλῆν᾽ ὁρῶ.'

> What shall I change to to creep in, and where?
> Let's look; a shrew-mouse, say; but if I do,
> That player Hegelochus will take the cue,
> And peach by shouting till the benches shake
> "The storm is o'er; I see the kitty wake." (trans. Edmonds)[52]

Note the way in which Strattis designates Hegelochus's role as protagonist: he is hired to speak the first part.[53] One would very much like to know who it was (the choregus?) who is conceived of as employing Hegelochus. At any rate the effects on the audience of this mispronunciation were memorably unfortunate, and some have even speculated that the result may have influenced Euripides' departure from Athens for Macedon.

We have seen very clearly the harm that bad acting can do to the overall effect of a play in the theater. What constituted good acting is harder to say—perhaps not surprisingly, since it is not the function of comedy to praise. The prominence enjoyed by actors, particularly of tragedy, is obvious by the end of the century. They are not yet so frequently mocked in comedy as the tragic poets, but we are well on the road to the situation Aristotle would complain of in the next century, when the actors were more important than the poets.

To review briefly: at the beginning of the century, actors as a category of public attention simply did not exist. As performers they were not differentiated from the singers of dithyramb—volunteer amateurs participating in the city's festival. The principal actors were usually the poets and thus simply identified with the pieces they wrote. As the first half of the century progressed, however, acting skill began to be recognized as something apart from the poetry. Histrionic skill could make or mar. The poets gradually abandoned acting to men of more specifically performative skills. The recognition of this change came with the establishment of acting contests in the middle of the century. Now performances were judged in relation to each other as well as to the work. At the same time the storehouse of myths suitable for dramatic representation seems to have been shrinking; it is tempting to speculate that acting helped in this winnowing process as one performance built on, and of course competed with, another.

The development of acting skills in comedy may have contributed to a different winnowing process. As one poet famously complained,[54] comedy was much harder work than tragedy because the poet had to invent all the characters and action. While a tragic actor could expect to play Orestes several times, in several different plays, there were no such repeated characters in Old Comedy. A comic actor on the other hand could develop a skill as a certain "type" of character; thus improvements of comic acting skills may have contributed materially to the development of the character types that came to dominate New Comedy.

The art of the second half of the century shows us actors as such for the first time, both as their audiences saw them and as they saw themselves. Comic actors are recognizable as such, wherever they appear, while tragic actors and choristers come into focus only as the vase painter's eye dwells on the margins, on the transitions into and out of the illusion of the mythic enactment. Nonetheless, this interest in the events beyond the illusionistic frame shows how actors are the new and exciting focus of an increasing amount of public attention. We also see actors as they pay to have themselves represented. There is considerable pride in the craft and a sense of self-worth behind the Peiraeus actors' relief. Even so the final stage of our process, where actors begin to compete in representing precisely the same role, where a play has become a repeatable event in which acting is a principal source of its interest, still lies beyond the end of the fifth century. Only in the fourth century do we reach the point where an actor like Polos can become famous for his representation of a particular role.

The Integrity of Performance

These two introductory chapters have attempted to survey the vocabulary, both verbal and visual, by which performance and performers are made perceptible categories within the theatrical events we label Old Comedy. The following studies of individual plays pursue patterns and thematic significance in the deployment of this language of performance. I do not argue that metatheatre is a "masterplot," the study of which unlocks every one of Aristophanes' works. Rather, I have chosen to study eight of the plays where self-consciousness play with the notion of performance forms a key, indeed sometimes essential, theme. There are certainly metatheatrical elements in the three surviving plays not treated in detail in this book (*Clouds*, *Lysistrata*, and *Wealth*), but I have chosen to concentrate on those plays that seem best to illustrate the range and development, not just of Aristophanes' dramatic technique, but of his contribution to the debates of democratic Athens as well. The early, anti-Cleon plays all offer critiques of the demagogue's performative style of leadership in the various venues of the democracy. The political focus of the later plays is more varied. It is not just that the "demagogue comedy" has run its course as an artistic form; Aristophanes also begins to explore much more abstract issues such as the power of self-conscious dramaturgy to create an alternative political order (as in *Birds* and *Ecclesiazusae*) and the direct relations between political and artistic order (at play in both *Thesmophoriazusae* and *Frogs*).

Finally, metatheatre must be understood as one mode or performance practice among many others. The significance of metatheatrical self-consciousness within the plays of Aristophanes does not lie in itself but in the contribution it makes to the impact of the entire theatrical event. Therefore we must study it in context. That context is, first and foremost, the unique performance that competed with other performances in the presence of the Athenian demos at one of the Dionysiac festivals.

Plays exist in time. Critical analysis that abstracts the play from the stage and even more importantly from its original linear presentation risks distorting the play beyond recognition. I stress this point, because the reading (and frequent rereading) of a text is so overwhelmingly often the modern experience of Aristophanes, rather than a performance. Even for those fortunate enough to see a performance, the first experience has likely been one of reading a text. While Aeschylus's audience probably had a good idea of Agamemnon's fate before the first performance of the *Oresteia*, no one but the poet's friends in the audience will have known what Dicaeopolis would do in the

Acharnians. We must suspend, not our disbelief, but our anachronistic fore-knowledge of the action of these plays in order to recapture their original performative meaning. This is not the only possible critical approach to the plays—but it is the only approach that respects their integrity as performances in context. Experienced readers of the plays may therefore find in what follows a bit more detailing of stage action than they feel they need; its purpose, however, is to reanimate the whole of the performance within which the metatheatrical makes its contribution. But enough of prologue: let the plays begin.

3

Euripides' Rag and Bone Shop:
Acharnians

IN THE BEGINNING, as Peter Brook has taught us, there is only an empty space. No matter how many props we pile into that space, it is not a theater until an actor appears—and even then, until the actor engages the audience, it is still only a space. It is the speaking voice, the moving body of the actor that creates the theater around him and defines the space, even as he begins the action.

Within that space, once created, an extraordinary range of transactions take place. In its realm, representations or symbols from the world outside its magic circle can be played with and transvalued. In the case of Old Comedy, set within the institution of the fifth-century radical democracy, those transactions are especially complex, and analogies from the modern theater are far more likely to mislead than illuminate. We must consider in detail for all Aristophanes' comedies first, how theatrical space is created and transformed within the play and second, what equivalencies or areas of exchange Aristophanes sets up between the theatrical space and other public spaces in Athens. In the case of our earliest surviving play, we must also consider how Aristophanes uses the fluidity of both character and space in this play to meditate upon the dangers and the potentials of the process of representation. We begin with the creation of theatrical space.

Thus our first surviving Old Comedy, the *Acharnians*, begins with a voice speaking into an empty, open-air space on a riverbank or a hillside[1] in the city of Athens in the winter of 425 B.C. Where does that voice come from? We will subsequently learn that the mask from which it comes, the body which supports it, portray an old—or at least no longer young—farmer. When we ask how this character moves within the theatrical space even as he generates it, we may seem to grasp for ghosts. From texts without melodies, from a few battered stones and a highly dubious wall in the Theater of Dionysus, we must, as best we can, recover that space.

Where does the actor appear from? We can only say with certainty where he does *not* come from: that is, from an opening in the front of the stage building. That would anchor the space (by implying it was his house or some building closely associated with him) in a way that the following action makes impossible. Perhaps he comes from one of the side entrances, the *parodoi*, which led both to the sides of the stage and into the orchestra space. Perhaps he emerges from the audience.[2]

But where does he go, what does he do to define this space he has entered? Before the first word of this play is spoken, essential information has been conveyed to its audience—information that we, twenty-three hundred years later, simply do not have handed to us. With every step he takes, this character shapes the world around him—and we cannot see those steps. We must imagine them, but in doing so we must confront a choice between at least two opposing views of what was permitted to the actors of this period. Is this character on the stage or in the orchestra when he begins to speak?

A considerable body of opinion holds that the space of the fifth-century theater was already firmly divided, that actors acted on the stage and the chorus danced in the orchestra, with the only interaction between the two being verbal, never physical. This picture, in my view, is fundamentally mistaken, a projection of the practices of tragedy (and quite possibly fourth-century tragedy at that) back onto the comic stage of the fifth century.[3] Neither convention nor the physical conditions of production forbade the actor from appearing in the orchestra. The most natural use of the space available, and the staging that will most convincingly suggest the space that is about to be defined, is to have the actor on his entrance step forward into the orchestra and deliver his first speech from there.[4]

That choice, however, makes possible a rich ambiguity which the actor's first speech exploits to the full. The stage of Old Comedy is notoriously fluid; that fluidity, like that of the Elizabethan-Jacobean stage a couple millenia later, is made possible by use of the minimum of actual, physical markers to define the setting of the particular play. We have only the open orchestra, a low stage at its back, and probably three openings in stage building behind it, which will be used as the doors to three different interior spaces in the course of the play.[5] That stage was most probably empty—no particular props or background pieces are required for the functioning of the first scene.

If the actor indeed entered the orchestra and there began his first speech, how does that speech proceed to shape and define the space through which he moves? Let us look at the opening 16 lines:

ὅσα δὴ δέδηγμαι τὴν ἐμαυτοῦ καρδίαν,
ἥσθην δὲ βαιά, πάνυ δὲ βαιά, τέτταρα·
ἃ δ᾽ ὠδυνήθην, ψαμμακοσιογάργαρα.
φέρ᾽ ἴδω, τί δ᾽ ἥσθην ἄξιον χαιρηδόνος;
ἐγῷδ᾽ ἐφ᾽ ᾧ γε τὸ κέαρ εὐφράνθην ἰδών,   5
τοῖς πέντε ταλάντοις οἷς Κλέων ἐξήμεσεν.
ταῦθ᾽ ὡς ἐγανώθην, καὶ φιλῶ τοὺς ἱππέας
διὰ τοῦτο τοὔργον· ἄξιον γὰρ Ἑλλάδι.
ἀλλ᾽ ὠδυνήθην ἕτερον αὖ τραγῳδικόν,
ὅτε δὴ ᾽κεχήνη προσδοκῶν τὸν Αἰσχύλον,   10
ὁ δ᾽ ἀνεῖπεν· "εἴσαγ᾽, ὦ Θέογνι, τὸν χορόν".
πῶς τοῦτ᾽ ἔσεισέ μου δοκεῖς τὴν καρδίαν;
ἀλλ᾽ ἕτερον ἥσθην, ἡνίκ᾽ ἐπὶ Μόσχῳ ποτὲ
Δεξίθεος εἰσῆλθ᾽ ᾀσόμενος Βοιώτιον.
τῆτες δ᾽ ἀπέθανον καὶ διεστράφην ἰδών,   15
ὅτε δὴ παρέκυψε Χαῖρις ἐπὶ τὸν ὄρθιον.

How many times I've bitten my own heart with rage,
but my pleasures—few, very few—just four!
My pains have been sandheap-hundreds.
Come now, what did I find worthy of joy?
I know—what gave my heart joy to see:
those five talents Cleon barfed up.
That brightened my day, and I love the Knights
for that deed: it was worthy of Greece.
But another pain I felt—a tragic one—
with my mouth hanging open, waiting for Aeschylus,
the herald announced: "Bring in your chorus, Theognis!"
Can you imagine my heart attack at that?
Another pleasure: once when Dexitheus came on
after Mochus, playing a Boeotian tune.
But this year the sight nearly killed and tortured me,
when Chairis came slouching in to play the Orthian.

The actor claims to have had only four pleasures in a life of miseries—and then proceeds to name two pleasures and two miseries. Three of the four are certainly festival entertainments: being cheated of a revival of Aeschylus in favor of a tragedy by Theognis,[6] enjoying Dexitheus's performance on the lyre, and suffering through Chaeris's rendition of Terpander. Thus we have three different festival entertainments. What sort of pleasure was the first and obviously greatest, that of seeing Cleon humiliated?

No fifth-century source tells us of an event involving Cleon that lines 5–8 could be describing. The obvious conclusion is that this too is a pleasure of *theoria*, of watching a festival performance: the events described took place in a comedy, which, since the reference is made within another comedy, naturally enjoys pride of place in the list of four festivals pleasures and pains. It is tempting, but not completely certain, to see this as a reference to Aristophanes' own *Babylonians*, a play that got him into considerable trouble.[7]

This discussion of comedy, tragedy, and musical performance then exploits the ambiguity of the empty space into which the actor has stepped. Where are we, and what is he waiting for? We are physically in a theater, watching a comedy. Could it be that he too is in a theater, waiting for a performance to begin? Lines 17ff. will dispel this notion and show us that the empty space is in fact the Pnyx, and the actor is waiting for a session of the assembly to begin. Nonetheless, an equation made by the initial ambiguity of the space lingers in the minds of the audience. Theater and assembly are remarkably congruent spaces (and indeed the assembly could meet in the Theater of Dionysus on certain occasions).[8] In two forms only was the full body of citizens gathered together, seated, and called upon to judge (in competitive fashion) the words and deeds put before them: in the theater at the festivals of Dionysus and on the Pnyx in the sovereign democratic assembly.[9]

The staging itself continues to support the equation. At line 40 the actor informs us that the *prytaneis* are finally arriving to open the session. We have no idea how many figures actually appear now; only a herald actually speaks.[10] Certainly the Herald appears on the stage, and his presence transforms it into the speaker's bema on the Pnyx. If silent extras representing the prytaneis themselves followed him in, where did they appear?

We have until this point spoken only of "the actor." Since the play has by now established enough of the outline of this character (Athenian citizen from the country, trapped in the city by the war and resenting it) that he can no longer be considered "undefined," and since other actors will now be appearing, for the sake of clarity I shall begin using the character name Aristophanes has given him, Dicaeopolis. Note, though, that we do not learn the character's name until line 406, at which time some interesting things are already happening with the notion of character. It is worth keeping in mind that the very use of this name can be a distortion of our experience of the play at this point, for Aristophanes quite probably had a very good reason for not revealing this name until the play is already one-third over.[11]

The final line of Dicaeopolis' opening speech, then, may hold a clue to how the entry of the *prytaneis* was staged. He speaks of them all fighting for front-row seats (42, εἰς τὴν προεδρίαν πᾶς ἀνὴρ ὠστίζεται). It is very difficult to imagine a staging that would place these front-row seats on the stage itself. Such seats were certainly *not* on the speaker's bema on the Pnyx—placing them on the stage here would only confuse the picture. If we try to imagine the stage as the whole of the Pnyx, however, the problem only gets worse. Then the only possible staging would be to put the *prytaneis* on one end of the stage and the speakers (first the Herald, then the Ambassadors and others) at the other. The resulting stage picture is visually distorted and moreover quite bad acoustically, even when (as they must) the speakers turn full front in order to be heard by the audience. There are only two real possibilities: first, that the *prytaneis* are quite imaginary, or second, that they too move into the orchestra. The first view cannot be disproved and indeed has much to favor it; it gives the producer much less to worry about. Nonetheless the second view is appealing. It gives some point to Dicaeopolis's line, especially the reference to *proedria*—which in turn further reinforces the visual equation of theater and Pnyx, since priests (most notably the priest of Dionysus, as witnessed by the reference in the *Frogs*) and other officials enjoyed the right of *proedria* in the theater as well. The easiest and most effective way to stage the appearance of the *prytaneis* here is to add a couple of wooden benches at the tips of the horseshoe of seats of honor around the orchestra[12] and bring in a few extras (in perfectly normal Athenian street clothes, therefore involving no expense to the choregus) at this point to occupy them.

On either view, the audience in the theater must represent the assembly of citizens on the Pnyx.[13] No tiny group of extras on the stage could successfully portray this essential element. As the succeeding characters on the bema speak, they transform the body of citizens gathered to see a comedy into their political counterpart, the sovereign assembly on the Pnyx.

And where is Dicaeopolis while the Herald and any silent extras enter? Still in the orchestra, I submit, and his position frames and conditions our subsequent experience of the scene. In response to the Herald's call for all to enter the assembly area, Amphitheus comes bursting in, from a *parodos* onto the stage, announcing his divine mission to make peace with the Spartans (45ff.).[14] When the Herald orders the archers to drag him away, Dicaeopolis protests, and the Herald replies κάθησο, σῖγα (59).[15] This implies either that Dicaeopolis rose from his seat to protest or at least that he has the opportunity to sit—but where? He could be seated on the stage, but we have seen the objections above to this particular stage picture, with or without extras. It is also important to note that nowhere before he interrogates the "King's Eye" does Dicaeopolis express the intention of speaking to the assembly himself. Although in theory any citizen could speak in the assembly, in practice a fairly limited number of citizens spoke with any regularity. The vast majority came to the assembly to hear the others speak and vote on their performance. Dicaeopolis has in fact already told us what he has in mind: his plan is to shout, interrupt, and revile any speakers who discuss anything except peace (37, βοᾶν, ὑποκρούειν, λοιδορεῖν τοὺς ῥήτορας).[16] This is just what he proceeds to do, and the procedure works most effectively if his interruptions and abuse[17] come, not from the stage, but from the audience.

He presumably mounts the stage only at 109 in order to confront the King's Eye with threats of violence (111–112).[18] This effect transforms the theatrical space; it resembles the action of an audience member joining the play in progress. The result, though, is to strip away layers of illusion. Dicaeopolis forces the King's Eye to speak more clearly and discovers that the attendants are in fact Athenian pathics (one of them is Cleisthenes) hidden under beards and Persian costumes. This is the first use of a major theme in this play, that of putting on and stripping off costumes. Dicaeopolis can then remain on the bema for the remainder of the scene without seriously disturbing the stage picture. This facilitates the five-line exchange (129–133) in which he commissions Amphitheus to make a private peace with Sparta.

Theorus now appears, makes another joke about the tragedian Theognis (138–140), and introduces the mercenaries he brought back from Thrace. These appear in the orchestra, and one of them steals Dicaeopolis's lunch (163ff.), presumably left at the seat he abandoned (the lunch ought to be real; this sort of comedy works best with an actual object to focus the attention of the audience). Dicaeopolis probably at this point attempts to leave the stage to rescue his lunch but is restrained by Theorus, who warns him that the Thracians are too dangerous, once they have eaten garlic (165–166).

As this episode shows, Dicaeopolis is not yet able to control the play. The political illusions continue, and finally he must use a false omen to force adjournment of the assembly: he claims to have felt a drop of rain, an omen that means the assembly must be adjourned for the day, and the assembly around him dissolves both legally and theatrically as the other characters depart. When Amphitheus returns with the three vintages of peace treaties (175), the space is as empty and undefined as when the play began.[19]

The effect of the prologue up until this point is complex. Dicaeopolis begins as both theatrical and political spectator. He invades the political space presented to him but fails to seize control of it. His only resource then is to create a new space, for which his separate peace with Sparta is the means. There follows the famous scene in which the three possible peace treaties are presented as *spondai*, as vintages of wine. This interlude of typically brilliant Aristophanic fantasy has its own power to transform the theatrical space. It has often been noted how absolutely right the image of properly aged wine is for a peace treaty;[20] little noted is how the images associated with the successive vintages range further and further spatially from the city setting of the play up until this moment. The five-year treaty vintage smells of tar and naval preparations (190) and therefore sticks close to the isolated imperial city, now cut off from the land. The ten-year vintage smells of embassies to the allied cities (192), ranging out into the empire but no further. Only the thirty-year treaty smells of complete freedom of movement (198, "βαῖν' ὅπη 'θέλεις").[21] Only when he drains this vintage is Dicaeopolis ready, metaphorically as well as theatrically, to escape the city for the countryside, where he now announces that he will celebrate the Rural Dionysia (202)—and thus the spatial transformation of the undefined theater space into Dicaeopolis's country home is complete.

With Dicaeopolis's departure, the prologue is over. It is then a good time to assess what Aristophanes has accomplished through the prologue as he has structured it. He has used the flexibility of the theatrical space to the fullest—the playing space has moved from the undefined theater to the Pnyx, back to an undefined space and now, with the first entrance into the *skene*, into Dicaeopolis's country home. The entrance of the old Acharnians, heralded by Amphitheus's reference to their pursuit of him, will provide a certain spatial anchor hereafter, but we should not be surprised that Aristophanes will continue to use the flexibility of his theater space in novel ways.

He has also used this flexibility to establish some important and persisting equivalencies, or perhaps we should say areas of exchange, between the theatrical space and political space. Dicaeopolis begins the play as a spectator, an observer on the edge of a playing space looking in, enjoying Aeschylus and Aristophanic comedy but nauseated by the decadent modern entertainments offered by Theognis and his ilk. When the playing space turns into the Pnyx (and the audience thereby into the members of the assembly), he intends at first to remain a spectator, though an obnoxious and obstreperous one, shouting and heckling in order to direct the political players toward the scenario he wishes to see played out, a discussion of peace. Only when the political spectacle is too much to bear does he mount the stage and begin to expose the fraud for what it is. His exposure of the handlers of the King's Eye as two Athenian pathics is a promising start, but he fails to seize control of what goes on in the assembly; he can only halt its proceedings by a fraudulent omen (as others had doubtless done before him). His only real hope is to invent a space in which the peace he longs for can be achieved. With the help of Amphitheus he does just that: he concludes his private peace treaty with Sparta. This fantasy space is quickly distanced from the "real," historical space as depicted in the assembly, though it will continue to function as a distorting mirror of Athenian politics in miniature. We noted above how the five-, ten-, and thirty-year peace treaties range farther and farther geographically from Athens; as we follow this ever-widening circle away from Athens and out into the countryside, the fantasy space finally breaks free and becomes self-sufficient. Its first task, however, will be to defend itself against the chorus's attempt to collapse it back into Athenian political space, into the old world of resentments and enmity.

The chorus of Acharnians arrives, singing of their hunt for the traitor who has dared to make peace with Sparta.[22] Their physical presence, filling the orchestra, defines and divides the space. The unified space through which an undefined actor moved freely at the beginning of the play is now split (though not insurmountably) into stage and orchestra, whose occupants are sharply opposed to each other.[23] Once won over, the chorus will more more forcefully reunite the space, acting as a bridge between audience and stage.[24] For the moment, however, when Dicaeopolis emerges from the *skene*, leading his festival procession, the chorus forms an audience for his celebration of the Rural Dionysia.[25] More than that, as Lauren Taaffe has cogently observed,[26] Dicaeopolis functions as a director here, instructing his daughter in her proper performance[27] before the gaze of so many spectators, internal and external.

The ensuing scenes with their justly famous Euripidean parody now add exchanges between tragic and comic space to those between the theater and Athenian political space. I wish to argue here that Aristophanes' metatheatrical play with the boundaries between his own and the competing genre is no isolated literary game but has a political function. He defends both his past career and the future usefulness of his brand of comedy to the city.

Dicaeopolis's song celebrating the joys of peace is interrupted by a shower of stones from the chorus,[28] and the argument between Dicaeopolis and the chorus is played out.[29] Dicaeopolis saves himself from further attack only by his brilliant recycling of a plot sequence from Euripides' *Telephus* (325ff.): he seizes a basket of charcoal and threatens to kill it, just as the disguised Telephus threatens to kill the baby Orestes.[30] The threat to their "fellow demesman" (333, ὁ λάρκος δημότης ὅδ᾽ ἔστ᾽ ἐμός) is effective: the Acharnians agree at least to listen to Dicaeopolis, who further offers to speak with his head on a chopping block (355).[31]

While the chorus speaks a few lines to cover the action, Dicaeopolis brings out the block, places it, and specifies the chorus's function with a simple imperative: they are to be *spectators* of what follows ("hey, take a look!" ἰδοὺ θεᾶσθε, 366). The situation on stage is somewhat unusual, since monologues are not all that common in Old Comedy.³²

I think an intended irony becomes clear when he begins his defense speech, which once more draws political and theatrical space together. He notes how gullible the citizens in the assembly are and cites the dangers of speaking before the predominantly old men of Athenian juries (367–376). Yet he is speaking to an audience, a chorus of old men whom he has just tricked with a device from tragedy and before an outer audience of the play who a few minutes before represented the assembly. The unsettling effect is to demonstrate his point: assembly and juries can be tricked by theatrical devices. The result is to draw three supposedly distinct venues within the polis (assembly, juries, and theater audiences) together. When Dicaeopolis cites the problems and dangers of speaking in the first two situations as preparation for speaking in the third, he thereby prepares the way for testing the boundaries of the dramatic illusion here. All are simply places of performance.

This introduction paves the way for an astounding bit of metatheatre, whose surprise value we should in no way minimize. In this play alone does a character on stage (as opposed to the chorus, who are traditionally licensed to do so in the parabasis) speak directly in the first person as the poet. At line 377 Dicaeopolis first speaks in a way which identifies him as a specific, historical comic poet, that is, Aristophanes:³³

> αὐτός τ᾽ ἐμαυτὸν ὑπὸ Κλέωνος ἅπαθον
> ἐπίσταμαι διὰ τὴν πέρυσι κωμῳδίαν.
> εἰσελκύσας γάρ μ᾽ εἰς τὸ βουλευτήριον
> διέβαλλε καὶ ψευδῆ κατεγλώττιζέ μου
> κἀκυκλοβόρει κἄπλυνεν, ὥστ᾽ ὀλίγου πάνυ
> ἀπωλόμην μολυνοπραγμονούμενος.   (377–382)

> And I know myself what I suffered from Cleon
> because of last year's comedy.
> He dragged me to the bouleterion, attacked me,
> slobbered insults over me,
> stormed and flooded, so that I was almost
> drowned by his sewer-mouth.

He tells how as the result of the political satire he employed in a previous production he was dragged before the *boule* by Cleon.³⁴ The precise details of Cleon's action (i.e., what legal form his attempted prosecution took³⁵) remain unclear but are not material to our purpose for the moment. The *boule* too, of course, was a representative of the whole citizen body, though it was the smallest and therefore perhaps more easily bullied by a popular politician like Cleon. Halliwell suggests, I think rightly, that Aristophanes was probably forced to make some sort of concession or apology for whatever he had said in the *Babylonians* in order to settle the matter.[36] We must not allow the paucity of detail to divert us from the theatrical impact of these lines: the playwright has stepped out from behind the persona of one of his characters.

The nature or very existence of "illusion" in Old Comedy is a much-debated topic.[37] The phrase "breaking the illusion" is itself part of the problem, for it seems to imply that illusion is an on-off switch: either there is one or there is not. The strong version of Gregory Sifakis's claim that there was no attempt to create a dramatic illusion in Old Comedy has not won wide acceptance, precisely because there are places in which the plays seem to behave like scenes in tragedy or modern illusory drama. His position, however, is much closer to a correct description of what goes on in Aristophanic comedy at least than the general notion of some of his opponents that illusion or "pretense" was maintained on the stage, with other things being allowed (as traditional forms) from the orchestra. It is much better to classify the whole of Old Comedy under John Styan's term, nonillusory theater.[38] The term non-illusory theater covers a wide range of phenomena, including highly conventionalized theater forms. Episodes within such forms will often behave like illusory forms of theater—but the consistent maintenance of illusion is not an unbreakable requirement. Even if Old Comedy behaves like modern theater much of the time, that is no reason to classify it as an illusionistic form of theater and label all breaks in this "illusion" as exceptions. We must study the patterns and conventions as Aristophanes uses them. And by those standards, the moments in which Aristophanes speaks from the stage in first person, through the character of Dicaeopolis, are absolutely extraordinary.

The explanation for this exception to the usual conventions of his stage may well lie outside the play itself, in the historical context.[39] For the present interpretation of our linear experience of Aristophanes' play, we need only note how unusual this step is and try to gauge its effect within its context. An explanation must wait for a little more material.

Dicaeopolis's first speech as Aristophanes is surprisingly short: only lines 377–382 must be attributed to the persona of Aristophanes. It is as though he is testing the waters with these lines, but then steps back quickly to his narrative and character. The whole abortive beginning of his attempt to win over the chorus, that is, from when Dicaeopolis reenters with the chopping block until he goes to Euripides' door, proceeds very rapidly. The sequence is (1) I will speak in favor of the Lacedaemonians, but (2) I have reason to fear; (a) witness the gullibility of the assembly and (b) the ferocity of jurors. Then the persona shifts: I also have reason to fear, because of what I experienced from Cleon. Therefore I need to outfit myself as pitiably as possible; the verb in line 384, ἐνσκευάσασθαι, is clearly theatrical in its connotations, but it can as easily apply to props as well as costumes.

The only preparation for what Dicaeopolis/Aristophanes now does is in the chorus's suggestion that he can go get a "cap of invisibility" from Hieronymus—that is, a tragic prop from a tragic poet.[40] Even so, the goal of his movement from the chopping block to the door in the *skene*, which probably needs all the chorus's lines (385–392) to cover it, is not clear until he speaks Euripides' name at the end of line 394: the door in the *skene* thereafter represents Euripides' house. Aristophanes in effect doffs the mask of Dicaeopolis[41] when he speaks *in propria persona* as a comic poet but then short-circuits much of this astonishing effect by his sudden movement and commencement of the sequence with Euripides. It is also only at this point that we hear the character's name: in his banter with Euripides' servant, he finally gives his name,[42] Dicaeopolis (406), though the notion that this is meant to be any sort of triumphant revelation is undercut by Euripides' sudden and spectacular appearance on the *ekkyklema* (407ff.).

The scene between Dicaeopolis and Euripides is so familiar that I fear we may wrongly assume that just such a scene is what the audience expected here. Rather, much in this scene is meant to surprise. Dicaeopolis immediately makes two standard jokes about Euripides and his plays (they do not have their "feet on the ground," and all his heroes are ragged), but the form of the second joke deserves more attention than it has gotten heretofore:

> ἀναβάδην ποιεῖς,
> ἐξὸν καταβάδην; οὐκ ἐτὸς χωλοὺς ποιεῖς.
> ἀτὰρ τί τὰ ῥάκι᾽ ἐκ τραγῳδίας ἔχεις,
> ἐσθῆτ᾽ ἐλεινήν; οὐκ ἐτὸς πτωχοὺς ποιεῖς. (410–413)

So you write with your feet up, when you could
with your feet on the ground? No wonder you create cripples.
But why do you have the rags from tragedy,
pitiful tatters? No wonder you create beggars.

On one level the two jokes simply explicate what the audience sees. Euripides is lying down with his feet up, and tragic rags (ῥάκια) are lying around him. Just what form the ragged costumes take and where they are situated are subjects of considerable speculation.[43] Clearly there are props mixed in among the costumes as well. The notion that Euripides has at hand book rolls containing his plays as well has been suggested; perhaps better is the suggestion of Colin Macleod that the costumes, or at least some hanging on the wall (which must then be a back wall) of the *ekkyklema*, resemble book rolls.[44] We will speculate a bit further about the nature of these props in a moment.

At present, the form of Dicaeopolis's question is of particular interest: "but why do you have the rags from tragedy . . . ?"[45] Since Euripides does not answer the question, it is a little difficult to be sure how Dicaeopolis means it, but it surely has more function than simply drawing attention to the costumes. The ἀτάρ seems to suggest surprise as well as a marked change of subject or direction.[46] The question then becomes: why is it surprising that Euripides has the costumes from his tragedies? Is there something unusual in a poet having such "souvenirs" of past productions?

Our ignorance of the details of how theater at Athens was funded in this period are profound. Pickard-Cambridge's magisterial work on the dramatic festivals states that the choregus paid for the costumes of the chorus but had no responsibility for the actors' costumes.[47] He cites no evidence to support this statement, which seems on its face questionable. If the actors' costumes were not part of the liturgy of choregeia, who paid for them? We have no idea how the actors themselves in this period were remunerated; they can hardly have been expected to pay for costumes out of their own funds (costumes could be quite expensive) when the state funded the rest of the performance. The only item Pickard-Cambridge cites in support of his thesis in fact speaks against his interpretation. Plutarch's *Life of Phocion* (19.2–3) tells the story of an actor playing a queen who refused to go on unless the choregus provided a larger retinue of "maid servants dressed richly" (κεκοσμημένας πολλὰς ὀπαδοὺς πολυτελῶς). The choregus refused and pushed the actor onto the stage, saying he should be contented with one servant, just like the wife of Phocion. The implication of the story is clear; the choregus would have had to pay for costuming any additional players (we have no reason to believe that he paid wages to such silent extras for appearing). Now a queen's retinue were supernumeraries who appeared on stage, not part of the chorus. Thus there was no invisible dividing line between stage and orchestra in terms of funding; the choregus paid for costumes on the stage just as he did for those worn in the orchestra. It would be exceedingly strange if he were expected to pay for everything except what the protagonist wore; the simplest explanation is that he bore all the costs of outfitting the production and its players.

That in turn sheds a rather different light on the function of stage cos-

tumes in the democratic scheme of things at Athens. We know that an elaborate choregeia was a socially acceptable, indeed expected, form for the display
of wealth, because this display of wealth was in the service of the democracy.
A lavish choregeia enhanced a man's status; a miserly one could call down
ridicule on him.[48] Moreover, costumes were a part of the spectator's visual
pleasure in the performance. Euripides' "beggar" heroes therefore deprived
the spectators of an expected part of their enjoyment of theatrical experience.

The costumes of the actors were just as integral a part of a choregeia as
those of the choristers. A good choregus did not reuse old costumes but had
them made new for the production.[49] What happened to the costumes after
the production? Unfortunately, we have no evidence. We can say with certainty that they were not used for reperformance, because there were no reperformances in this period. They were not saved for the touring production,
because there were no tours.[50] It is an open question what happened to chorus
costumes, especially ones such the animal costumes of Old Comedy;[51] there is
no obvious secondary function for such things, although expensive materials
might be salvageable. Costumes suitable for civic elders or serving women
(which would not have been rags, save for special cases like *Trojan Women*),
though, would have been too useful simply to discard. There is no prima facie
reason to assume that such clothing would be given to those who had worn
it.[52] Either it remained the property of the choregus or became state property
after the performance. In either case, it had a value and was most probably
sold (by choregus or state), not given away. This would be particularly true of
elaborate costumes of kings or gods.[53] Euripides' peculiar ideas about tragedy,
then, may have deprived the choregus or the state of an expected source of
postproduction income as well.

In any case, it is hard to imagine why the author of the play should end
up with the costumes—unless those costumes were so worthless that no one
else wanted them. Dicaeopolis is surprised that Euripides has these costumes
(ἀτάρ), because a playwright normally would not possess leftover costumes—
and who would want such ragged things to begin with? Once he sees them,
however, he conceives that the obvious way to make himself "as pitiable as
possible" is to borrow one of the costumes.[54]

On one level, this may be somewhat of an "in" joke—how many people
in the city were really familiar enough with the financial and production ar-
rangements behind what they saw at festivals?—but on another, it helps us
recover some of the sense of outrage Euripides' ragged heroes evoked. Aristophanes' depiction of Euripides' rag and bone shop is not simply a highly
imaginative piece of aesthetic criticism. It is rather a telling depiction of how

Euripides has depreciated the value of certain accepted symbols. The Athenians were not fifth-century Victorians, outraged that a playwright should put "noble" characters in rags. They eventually learned to respond so well to such extreme contradictions that Euripides became for posterity "the most tragic" of poets. They were, however, upset when an important form of civic display of wealth was turned into its opposite. Imagine the feelings of that citizen who, having enjoyed the parades, the display of the tribute from the allies, the presentation of the war orphans and all those other parts of the Dionysia that showed his city to be great, rich, and powerful, suddenly discovers that during the tragedies he is looking, not at the noble and beautifully turned out kings and nobles of the plays of his youth, but beggars just as ragged as the ones he spurned in the Agora on his way to the theater.[55] Even the comparison of the shock in opera houses when the Valkyries arrive on motorcycles or in theaters when characters perform the whole play in trash cans is not completely apt, for these are experiences of a small segment of society who have preselected themselves as enthusiasts of "culture." A more apt comparison would be the First Lady turning up at a state funeral in a dress from Goodwill or a military band wearing tattered uniforms, for the dramatic festivals of Athens were not art in the modern sense but politics in the ancient sense, expressions of the political life of the city.

The discussion between the actor and Euripides is among the most richly metatheatrical comedy in Aristophanes. We should again speak of "the actor," for, having shed his role as Dicaeopolis, he now rummages through the Euripidean rag-and-bone shop, looking for a scrap of an old play to make him truly pitiable.[56] Euripides' plays are reduced to the physical remnants left behind after a production, costumes and a few props (which are also so worthless that, unlike kingly scepters and crowns, we might well imagine the author being allowed to keep them).[57] In the course of the scene the actor speaks only one line that could with any plausibility be ascribed to the character of Dicaeopolis. At the very beginning of the scene, the actor explains why he needs the costume:

δεῖ γάρ με λέξαι τῷ χορῷ ῥῆσιν μακράν·
αὕτη δὲ θάνατον, ἢν κακῶς λέξω, φέρει. (416–417)

I need to make a long speech to the chorus;
it means my death, if I speak badly.

The first line is clearly spoken as an actor, outside any illusionistic space. By naming the chorus he expresses his superiority to it; they remain within the space of the play and therefore can be manipulated by such theatrical means as a ῥῆσις. The second line seems to step back into the illusion, but the question is, which illusion? It envisions the penalty the character, not the actor, will suffer if his theatrical manipulations fail. This could as easily be Telephus as Dicaeopolis speaking, and we noted above that the process of assuming the character of Telephus really began with the threat against the basket of coal.

After four wrong guesses (Oineus, Phoenix, Philoctetes, and Bellerophon), each insufficiently wretched, Euripides finally hits upon the character that Dicaeopolis wants: Telephus. The servant digs his rags out, and the actor apparently puts them on. The actor's line, "O Zeus, who seest through and over all" (435, ὦ Ζεῦ διόπτα καὶ κατόπτα πανταχῇ—), makes clear that this costume is so ragged that the comic costume remains clearly visible underneath it. But a costume alone will not suffice. The actor needs props to flesh out this portrayal.[58] He asks for a Mysian cap,[59] quotes two lines on seeming and reality which may be from the *Telephus*,[60] and then makes a most interesting statement:

τοὺς μὲν θεατὰς εἰδέναι μ' ὅς εἰμ' ἐγώ,
τοὺς δ' αὖ χορευτὰς ἠλιθίους παρεστάναι,
ὅπως ἄν αὐτοὺς ῥηματίοις σκιμαλίσω.   (441–443)

The spectators must know me for who I am,
but the chorus must stand by like idiots,
while I give them the finger with my little speeches.

The general sense of this is perfectly clear: parody relies on the audience's superiority of knowledge. They must know what is really going on, while the chorus must be deceived. So the passage is usually taken—but I think it means rather more. Surely neither Aristophanes nor Dicaeopolis (if he comes into question here at all) thought the audience would truly be deceived into thinking that Telephus was really speaking in the story. The joke, for the purposes of the parody, lies simply in knowing that the performer is *not* the person the chorus take him for, that a successful theatrical deception is being pulled off. Line 442 makes a much more explicit demand, however, more explicit than is requisite for the dynamics of the parody: the audience must know who the actor *is*—and that, I submit, is not Dicaeopolis but Aristophanes himself.[61]

The suggestion that Aristophanes himself played Dicaeopolis is not a new one, having first been put forward in developed form by Cyril Bailey sixty years ago.[62] The great appeal of this suggestion is that it explains why, as happens in no other surviving play of Aristophanes', a player on stage and not the chorus speaks for the poet here.[63] The two passages, in which the actor playing Dicaeopolis presents himself rather as Aristophanes himself, form a ring around the scene with Euripides. Both passages in which Aristophanes slips out from behind the character mask do so by making explicit mention of his troubles with Cleon. It is as though he tests the waters in the first passage (377–384), then quickly diverts the audience's attention to the broad comedy of the scene with Euripides. Once literally and metaphorically garbed with the persona of Telephus, however, he returns to the attack.

The *Telephus* parody has been under way, of course, since the hostage scene (331ff.), though it is perhaps open to question how many of the audience will have recognized the parodied original at once. The original performance of the *Telephus* now lay some fourteen years in the past.[64] The dressing scene with Euripides has the function not only of allowing the actor to rehearse his way gradually into the part of Telephus but to recall the key points to the audience's mind. Though verbal parody has been underway for some time,[65] textual echoes naturally concentrate themselves in Dicaeopolis/Telephus' speech in favor of peace. The actor is still talking himself into this part as he returns from Euripides' door. It requires a final soliloquy, addressed to his θυμός and his καρδία, before the new role is firmly in place (480–490).

And then Aristophanes confounds the audience again, for, after just a few line of *Telephus* parody, the actor suddenly drops that character and again speaks as Aristophanes. He asserts that Cleon will not be able to charge him with slandering the city in front of foreigners again, since it is the festival of the Lenaea, and no foreigners are present in the audience (οὑπὶ Ληναίῳ τ' ἀγών / κοὔπω ξένοι πάρεισιν, 504–505).[66] He then proceeds to give the justly famous and hilariously distorted account of the Megarian decree and the origins of the Peloponnesian War. This account he then in effect signs "Telephus" with his mention of the name at the very end of his account:

> ταῦτ' οἶδ' ὅτι ἂν ἐδρᾶτε· τὸν δὲ Τήλεφον
> οὐκ οἰόμεσθα; νοῦς ἄρ' ἡμῖν οὐκ ἔνι.   (555–556)

> I know that you would have done this; do we think
> that Telephus wouldn't? Then we have no brains!

It is therefore by no means so clear as Sommerstein would have it that the actor ceases to speak as Aristophanes at line 509 and thereafter consistently speaks as Dicaeopolis.[67] No element of this speech is explicable only on the basis that we see it proceeding from the character of Dicaeopolis as we have come to know it. The account is of course comic and exaggerated, but that is hardly proof that it must be based in the persona of Dicaeopolis. I suspect that Aristophanes, by wrapping himself in the parody of the *Telephus* and yet at the same time deliberately signaling that he is speaking behind the mask (which is the whole point of 442–444, a clear yet unprosecutable signal of authorship), is in effect giving, not the chorus, but Cleon the finger.

Dicaeopolis's speech in favor of peace[68] persuades half the chorus, who then come to blows with the other half. The split that occurred during the prologue between Athenian political space and Dicaeopolis's theatrical space now reduplicates itself among the chorus. Half choose the vision that Dicaeopolis offers them, while the other half cling to the world and assumptions they arrived with. In an equal fight, the war-mongers are bested. In an attempt to save themselves, they call the Athenian general Lamachus (a real, historical personage) to their defense. This simply carries the fight back onto the stage.

The general appears, only to be mocked, flouted, and stripped of his dignity by Dicaeopolis. Having dressed himself up as a beggar, Dicaeopolis now proceeds to the undressing of Lamachus. Lamachus arrives, flourishing the Gorgon on his shield and trailing helmet feathers and troops behind him (575). Dicaeopolis first transforms the Gorgon ($\Gamma o \rho \gamma \acute{o} \nu$, 574) into a bogey ($\tau \grave{\eta} \nu \mu o \rho \mu \acute{o} \nu a$, 581), simply by renaming it but also succeeds in persuading Lamachus either to discard the shield or to turn it away so that the Gorgon no longer shows. He then requests a feather from Lamachus's plumes—but plans to use it to vomit with. He caps this sequence by making an outrageously insulting homosexual proposition to Lamachus, topped by a multivalent pun (592): $\tau \acute{\iota} \mu$ ' $o \mathring{v} \kappa$ $\mathring{a} \pi \epsilon \psi \acute{\omega} \lambda \eta \sigma a \varsigma ; \epsilon \mathring{v} o \pi \lambda o \varsigma \gamma \grave{a} \rho \epsilon \mathring{\iota}$. Just what sexual act Dicaeopolis suggests with $\mathring{a} \pi \epsilon \psi \acute{\omega} \lambda \eta \sigma a \varsigma$ is not entirely clear,[69] but the pun in $\epsilon \mathring{v} o \pi \lambda o \varsigma$ is. Having stripped Lamachus of shield and part of his helmet decoration (entirely by verbal persuasion, we should note), the general has lost the weapons (*hopla*) of his profession. At the same time, by putting down his shield, he reveals how well (or ill) equipped he is with the comic phallus.[70] By stripping him of the symbols of his military function, Dicaeopolis has revealed Lamachus as just one more poor bugger.

The stripping continues metaphorically as Dicaeopolis attacks Lamachus as a place-hunter who profits from his war-time position (595ff.). Lamachus's claim to popular election is simply brushed aside.[71] As a result, Dicaeopolis's jeers at young men who get cushy jobs and serve on embassies while old citizens bear the brunt of fighting persuade the recalcitrant half of the chorus. Lamachus withdraws with a ringing patriotic declaration (620–622), but the chorus announces that Dicaeopolis has won over not just them but the whole demos on the subject of the peace treaty (626–627).

The fantasy world of a separate peace has successfully defended itself and incorporated the chorus within it. Lamachus, the war, and the other ills of the city that Dicaeopolis has come to hate will hereafter have a place only on the stage, and then only as occasional intruders. The remainder of the play will demonstrate how differently these two worlds, Dicaeopolis's world of peace and Lamachus's world of war, function.

The chorus with a typically metatheatrical reference to this traditional element of the play ("Let's strip and get on with the anapaests," 627) now embark on the parabasis. The stripping metaphor has provoked concern in the past. The notion that the choristers remove their masks can certainly be rejected, since there is no obvious point for them to reassume them; most probably they remove their cloaks.[72] Yet the motivation seems not to be purely physical, since they engage in no vigorous dancing immediately thereafter. Ketterer has suggested a visual joke he himself admits is complicated: the old men strip as a preparation to oratory, which is meant to play off the normal image of young men stripping for athletics.[73] In light of the elaborate "divestment" of Lamachus just preceding, we would expect some more obvious meaning to the chorus's action. It is in fact the visual demonstration of their conversion to Dicaeopolis's point of view. The *tribones*, a type of garment associated with the poor and the ascetic, are cast aside along with their pro-war views.[74]

Their first theme in the parabasis is the third, most developed, and climactic reference to Aristophanes' troubles with Cleon:[75]

> ἐξ οὗ γε χοροῖσιν ἐφέστηκεν τρυγικοῖς ὁ διδάσκαλος ἡμῶν,
> οὔπω παρέβη πρὸς τὸ θέατρον λέξων ὡς δεξιός ἐστιν·
> διαβαλλόμενος δ᾽ ὑπὸ τῶν ἐχθρῶν ἐν Ἀθηναίοις ταχυβούλοις,
> ὡς κωμῳδεῖ τὴν πόλιν ἡμῶν καὶ τὸν δῆμον καθυβρίζει,
> ἀποκρίνασθαι δεῖται νυνὶ πρὸς Ἀθηναίους μεταβούλους.
> φησὶν δ᾽ εἶναι πολλῶν ἀγαθῶν αἴτιος ὑμῖν ὁ ποιητής,
> παύσας ὑμᾶς ξενικοῖσι λόγοις μὴ λίαν ἐξαπατᾶσθαι,
> μήθ᾽ ἥδεσθαι θωπευομένους, μήτ᾽ εἶναι χαυνοπολίτας.   (628–635)

Now ever since our producer has been in charge of comic choruses,
he's never yet turned to the audience to say how clever he is.
But he's been charged by his enemies in front of the swift-judging Athenians
with mocking our city and insulting the people;
now he must answer the swift-*changing* Athenians.
Our poet says you owe him for a lot of benefits:
stopping you from being deceived too easily by foreigners' speeches,
from enjoying flattery, from being mouth-breathing proles.

Attempts have been made to distinguish between the διδάσκαλος of line 628 and the ποιητής of 633, but none have been convincing: both must signify Aristophanes.[76] This is the traditional place for the poet to defend himself and his work, so it is not surprising that Aristophanes here strikes back at Cleon.

More interesting is the nature of his defense of his work: he claims to have taught the audience to be good literary critics, to have helped them achieve distance from, and therefore control over, the traditional emotional effects of poetic language.[77] The key word here is ἐξαπατᾶσθαι (634; cf. 636, ἐξαπατῶντες), to deceive. Ambassadors, says Aristophanes, come from other cities, intent on deceiving the Athenian assembly, and they do so through the use of traditional poetic language to flatter Athens, calling her "violet-crowned" (ἰοστεφάνους, 637) or "gleaming" (λιπαράς, 639), but he has taught the demos to see through such devices.

Discussion of deception in a theatrical context in the second half of the fifth century naturally brings to mind the famous comment of Gorgias, preserved for us (with a clarification) in Plutarch (de glor. Ath. 348c = Diels-Kranz 82 [76] B 23):

ὅ τ᾽ ἀπατήσας δικαιότερος τοῦ μὴ ἀπατήσαντος, καὶ ὁ ἀπατηθεὶς σοφώτερος τοῦ μὴ ἀπατηθέντος. ὁ μὲν γὰρ ἀπατήσας δικαιότερος, ὅτι τοῦθ᾽ ὑποσχόμενος πεποίηκεν· ὁ δ᾽ ἀπατηθεὶς σοφώτερος· εὐάλωτον γὰρ ὑφ᾽ ἡδονῆς λόγων τὸ μὴ ἀναίσθητον.

He who deceives is honester than he who does not deceive, and he who is deceived is wiser than he who is not deceived. He who deceives is honester because he has done what he undertook to do; he who is deceived is wiser, because what is not imperceptive is easily captivated by pleasure of speech. (trans. D. M. MacDowell)[78]

We need not delve into the whole discussion about the nature of illusion in the theater or suspension of disbelief in our experience of literature generally to realize that Aristophanes in his defense of his own comedy is playing with, or perhaps rather against, Gorgianic notions about the nature of deception (in the theater and elsewhere).[79] The spectator who is deceived in the theater is normally the wiser, for he enjoys and benefits from being deceived. But what applies in the theater or while listening to poetry emphatically does not apply in the assembly. There he who is deceived is certainly not wiser. If politics becomes a form of theater, the city will be the worse for it. Aristophanes claims his plays benefit the city by teaching the citizens to be critical "readers" of the texts that others present before the assembly.

The mediating term here is Euripidean tragedy. For Aristophanes, the value that deception usually has in the theater becomes a positive danger in the case of Euripides, for the power of poetry there can inure the audience to things they should instead be outraged by.[80] His defense against this danger is to view Euripidean tragedy in a way that distances us from the text. Aristophanes "deconstructs" the *Telephus* in more ways than one. By unmaking the dangerous new plays of Euripides into their constituent rags and shoddy props, the equation set up between theater and assembly at the beginning of the *Acharnians*, which seemed to imply a dangerous political cynicism, is suddenly inverted: the alert spectator who learns how to view theater as a process of role-playing and the creation of illusions out of burnt wicker baskets and broken crockery will be equipped to see through the literary deceptions of wily foreigners—or dangerous mountebanks such as Cleon. No wonder, then, that Aristophanes claims that the Spartans are trying to reclaim Aegina in order to get hold of himself, because a poet with that kind of power is Athens' best weapon in the fight.[81]

The chorus closes the first section of the parabasis with a ringing declaration of the value of comedy and specifically Aristophanic comedy to the city (655–658). His comedy offers the city "the right stuff" (τὰ δίκαια, 655) and teaches it best (656; διδάσκων, 658).[82] Equally interesting is the series of things his comedy will *not* do: "not flattering or bribing or deceiving you, nor cheating or drenching you with praise" (οὐ θωπεύων οὐδ' ὑποτείνων μισθοὺς οὐδ' ἐξαπατύλλων, / οὐδὲ πανουργῶν οὐδὲ κατάρδων, 657–658). Perhaps comedy might flatter the city (θωπεύων), but the rest of these activities are much more appropriate to the assembly; Aristophanes is promising (however hyperbolically) that his comedy will display political, not just artistic, honesty.

The invocation of the Acharnian muse of fire (665ff.) returns the chorus to their Acharnian character and functions as the prologue to more usual complaints about the abuses of the jury system in Athens. As representatives of the old, they complain of their ill treatment in the courts by the young. Once again, though, the deceptive power of language is the theme. The young prosecutor attacks his victim with well-rounded phrases (στρογγύλοις τοῖς ῥήμασιν, 686), using word-traps (σκανδάληθρ' ἱστὰς ἐπῶν, 687). Most interesting, however, is the reference to a specific case, the prosecution of Thucydides by Euathlus, son of Cephisodemus, who is marked with a deictic, indicating that he is present in the theater (705): τῷδε τῷ Κηφισοδήμου.[83] Such direct references to audience members are not unknown in Aristophanes; in this play, though, the presence of the prosecutor functions to draw the theater space closer to juridical space and once more threatens to collapse the theatrical and political modes into one. The threat to the court system (which Aristophanes develops at length in the *Wasps*) is that it too will become theatricalized, a realm of poetic *apate* where justice lies with the best rhetorician.

The remainder of the play is devoted to the illustration of the results of Dicaeopolis's peace settlement. The first two scenes contain relatively little in the way of metatheatrical reference; this is comedy celebrating the sensual joys of life. Dicaeopolis sets up his free market, and a Megarian, blocked from trading in Athens by the Megarian decree that Dicaeopolis ridiculed in his history of the war (512ff.), arrives, starving and willing to sell his daughters for food.[84] The Megarian, having nothing else worth trading, resorts to a theatrical trick (Μεγαρικά τις μαχανά, 738)[85] and outfits (σκευάσας, 739) his daughters as pigs, a joke based on an untranslatable, obscene pun. An informer threatens to abort the proceedings but is driven away by Dicaeopolis. After a choral interlude, a Theban arrives (860), bringing Copaic eels to trade, which Dicaeopolis greets in paratragic style as the "dear desire of the comic choruses" (ποθεινὴ μὲν τρυγῳδικοῖς χοροῖς, 886).[86] Once again an informer arrives, Nicarchus, to denounce the Theban's goods as contraband. He also charges the Theban with a wild scheme to set fire to the dockyards; most interestingly, he explains this extravagant charge τῶν περιεστώτων χάριν (915, literally, "for the sake of those standing about"). Sommerstein translates this "for the sake of the audience" and then notes (*ad loc*) that this is the usual phrase a speaker uses when addressing those in court. On either construction the metatheatrical effect is powerful. If we understand Nicarchus to mean the audience in the theater, he is making a direct appeal for their support against Dicaeopolis and his vision of peace, an appeal doomed to failure. I do not attach much weight to the literal point that the audience is seated about, not standing about. Nonetheless, the comic appeal seems more powerful if Nicarchus is such a creature of habit (mechanically encrusted, as Bergson would say) and so much a professional informer that he speaks in the language of the law courts even when out on the street. At the same time the latter interpretation once again temporarily moves the world of the theater closer to the world of the lawcourts, only to generate an audience reaction against such an elision. The audience is meant to see through both the stage informer and his real counterpart, employing just such shabby tricks in the law courts. Dicaeopolis solves two problems in one by packing up the informer as a piece of pottery and selling him to the Theban in exchange for his goods.

Just as the Theban is carting Nicarchus away, a slave from Lamachus' house runs up, bringing the general's request to buy thrushes and an eel for his celebration of the feast of Choes (961). Dicaeopolis refuses the request and goes inside, leaving the chorus to sing his praises on those of reconciliation. The exchange with the slave, however, not only heralds the scene with Lamachus which will follow but also makes clear the fluidity of time in this play. In the absence of any other indications, we should assume the temporal setting of the *Acharnians* at its opening to be "now," that is, around the feast of the Lenaea (which fell during the month of Gamelion, sometime in January according to our calendar),[87] and the opening flirtation with the notion that we are actually in the theater, waiting for the performance to begin, supports this belief. When Dicaeopolis then celebrates his own Rural Dionysia, the season has changed significantly, for the Rural Dionysia fell in Poseideon, roughly our December.[88] Now, by bringing us back to the feast of Choes (later we hear of Chutroi too: 1076), which were part of the Anthesteria,[89] Aristophanes has taken us through the full cycle of the seasons, to the beginning of a new year. Dicaeopolis's separate peace becomes, not the one-day diversion of the comic festival, but the image of the full agricultural year, with all its Dionysiac riches. Geographically, the play has moved through a cycle, too: away from the city at war at the beginning, out into the countryside, and now back to the city, where Choes and Chutroi would be celebrated.[90]

The herald proclaims the beginning of the drinking contest:

> ἀκούετε λεώ· κατὰ τὰ πάτρια τοὺς Χοᾶς
> πίνειν ὑπὸ τῆς σάλπιγγος   (1000–1001)

Hear ye, hear ye! According to ancestral custom
drink your tankards at the sound of the trumpet!

but the call finds Dicaeopolis still struggling to finish his cooking. He is probably rolled out on the *ekkyklema*, complete with cooking pot and roasting spits.[91] More intruders come, wanting a little share of Dicaeopolis's peace. The first, a farmer named Dercetes who has lost his oxen, is turned away empty-handed. Modern commentators are often bothered by this scene, since Dicaeopolis spurns a fellow Athenian, but some personal joke at Dercetes' expense seems quite likely.[92] It is worth noting that the chorus is unhappy, too: they complain of Dicaeopolis's selfishness (1037–1039) and suggest he is going to kill them by making them smell the cooking aromas, when they do not get to share (1044–1046), thus making it clear that, although supporters of Dicaeopolis's plan, the chorus do not yet share in its benefits. Next come representatives of a bride and groom, who want a share of the peace so that the groom will not have to go off to war. The groomsman's attempt to bribe Dicaeopolis fails, but the appeal transmitted from the bride tickles Dicaeopolis's sense of humor (1059–1060), and Dicaeopolis gives her a share of the peace. He grounds his generosity, though, very specifically: he will share with her because "she is a woman and not to blame for the war" (1062).

A messenger now comes running on, calling for Lamachus to come out and deal with an incursion of bandits from Boeotia. Immediately thereafter another messenger arrives to invite Dicaeopolis to dine with the priest of Dionysus. A splendidly funny "mirror" scene follows, in which Dicaeopolis equips himself with food and other comforts for the feast, while Lamachus must equip himself for war. Not only do these two mirror each other's actions (spears and sausage spits, rounded shields and rounded cakes are carefully matched to each other), but both look into mirrors and see through their own frame of reference: Lamachus sees Dicaeopolis reflected in the surface of his oiled bronze shield ("I see an old man on the shield, about to be prosecuted for cowardice," ἐν τῷ χαλκίῳ / ἐνορῶ γέροντα δειλίας φευξούμενον, 1128–1129), while Dicaeopolis sees himself reflected in a pool of honey on a cake, making a fool of Lamachus (1130–1131).[93] Lamachus does his best to ignore the visual parody of his every move but does burst out with the demand that Dicaeopolis stop making fun of his "weapons" (παῦσαι καταγελῶν μου τῶν ὅπλων, 1107). This makes clear verbally what is already clear visually: this scene is the counterpart to the earlier one in which Dicaeopolis stripped the general of his military equipment.[94]

Each finally goes his way with the chorus's blessing (1143ff.), an opening that often signals a parabasis.[95] What follows strongly resembles a parabasis in its metatheatricality, for the chorus complains of their mistreatment at the hands of the choregus Antimachus at last year's Lenaea.[96] Antimachus failed to provide the customary dinner thereafter and here gets his just reward. It has been suggested, with some probability, that the chorus is in fact speaking for Aristophanes, who competed with a play at the Lenaea of 426 with Antimachus as choregus.[97] In any case the chorus's speech once again calls our attention to the play as play, as competitor (just like Dicaeopolis in the drinking contest) in a Dionysiac agon.

Lamachus is the first to return, having twisted his ankle and incurred other minor injuries by falling into a ditch, but he is more troubled by the prospect of Dicaeopolis's scorn. And well he may be, for Dicaeopolis arrives supported by dancing girls and proclaiming his victory in the drinking contest (1202, 1227). The play comes to a swift end, though not before Dicaeopolis gets in a few last digs, as Lamachus is carried off to the doctor and Dicaeopolis demands to be carried off to the judges and the king archon.

The ending of the *Acharnians* with Dicaeopolis's triumph does more than simply ratify the sensual joys (food, wine, and sex) that will accompany peace. Aristophanes is once again playing with the boundaries of the comic stage. As many other of his plays show, he knew how to orchestrate a festive ending without invoking a real Athenian festival. Why does he choose to set Dicaeopolis's triumph at the drinking contest of Choes during the Anthesteria?[98] One answer has already been suggested: it completes both a temporal cycle of Dionysiac festivals in which the whole year is encompassed and a geographical cycle which carries the play out of the corrupt and war-oppressed city into a peaceful countryside and now back into a renewed and revitalized city, which Dicaeopolis' peace has now somehow come to include. The image of the drinking contest forms a good though not perfect counterbalance to Lamachus's wartime operations; Dicaeopolis matches Lamachus's breastplate with his *chous*, for example (1132–1135), though the two are not particularly visually similar.

The contest must have other advantages from Aristophanes' point of view. The obvious one is proleptic; Aristophanes uses the device as a very broad suggestion to the judges that his play deserves to be crowned with the same success as Dicaeopolis's drinking. At 1224 ("Take me to the judges! Where's the king?" ὡς τοὺς κριτάς με φέρετε. ποῦ 'στιν ὁ βασιλεύς;), Dicaeopolis is really speaking to the judges in the theater—and the appeal worked, for *Acharnians* placed first.

One problem with interpreting what is going on in the contest at the end of this play is that Aristophanes is not writing to provide the historians of religion with information, though the text is often read as if he did. Though it seems quite logical and nothing else contradicts it, the only positive evidence that the king archon presided over the drinking contest on Choes is line 1224. We do know (from Aristotle *Ath. Pol.* 57.1) that the king archon presided over the Lenaea. If Aristophanes, in eliding the two occasions together here for his dramatic purposes, thereby suppressed the existence of another priest or official who presided at the drinking contest, we would never know. I hasten to add that I do not argue for that as fact but simply point out the possibility. And if the king archon did preside, did he require the help of other judges (κριτάς) in making a decision, or do they come from the theater setting?

Though it is close to pure speculation, one wonders if there could be yet one more meaning. There is later and not perfectly clear evidence for another kind of contest at the Anthesteria on the day of Chutroi. Lycurgus among his various theatrical reforms in the later fourth century apparently revived the ἀγῶνες χύτρινοι after they had fallen into abeyance. Pseudo-Plutarch in the *Lives of the Ten Orators* 841f. records:

εἰσήνεγκεν δὲ καὶ νόμους, τὸν μὲν περὶ τῶν κωμῳδῶν, ἀγῶνα τοῖς Χύτροις ἐπιτε-
λεῖν ἐφάμιλλον ἐν τῷ θεάτρῳ καὶ τὸν νικήσαντα εἰς ἄστυ καταλέγεσθαι, πρότερον
οὐκ ἐξόν, ἀναλαμβάνων τὸν ἀγῶνα ἐκλελοιπότα.[99]

He also brought in laws, including one about the comedians, providing that they
should compete on the day of Chutroi in the theater and the victor should be selected
for the City, a thing previously not possible, reviving the contest which had been abandoned.

Pickard-Cambridge interprets this to be a contest of comic actors, in which
the victor gained the right to appear at the next City Dionysia. The unanswer-
able question is whether the practice Lycurgus revived goes back into the fifth
century. Much is unclear about actors and their relations to poets and producers in the fifth century. I have argued elsewhere against a system of allotment for tragic actors at the end of the fifth century but accepted the notion
that the right of the victorious protagonist in one year's acting contest to be
chosen to act at the next year's festival was in fact a separate issue and could
well go back into the fifth century.[100] Many developments in the comic theater
lag behind their counterparts in the tragic theater, including in the development of the acting profession. In itself the notion of a contest for a guaranteed
place as a comic protagonist at the City Dionysia (and Pickard-Cambridge is
surely right to assume that the contest must be for a protagonist's position)
seems to imply more actors, and more struggle for a place on the bill of the
festival, so to speak, than we have evidence for, certainly in the 420s.[101] In iso-
lation then, the actors' contest on Chutroi seems more likely to be a creation
of the fourth century.

The ending of *Acharnians*, however, hints at another possibility. We have
seen above that the unique moments in which Aristophanes steps out from
behind the character of Dicaeopolis suggests that Aristophanes himself played
the character. If the ἀγῶνες χύτρινοι existed in 425 B.C., Dicaeopolis's victory in the contest of the Choes may be meant to be proleptic not only of the
Acharnians' victory at the Lenaea but of Aristophanes' own hoped-for victory
in the contest at the coming Anthesteria, thus vindicating him as both poet
and actor. This must be ranked a tenuous possibility at best, but it does offer a
slightly better justification for Aristophanes' choice of the Anthesteria as the
climax of his play's cycle through the Dionysiac festivals.[102]

The *Acharnians* is a splendid celebration of the power and the range of
the Aristophanic theater. It is a deeply political play, not just in its supremely
funny and devious counterattack on Cleon, but in its suggestion that the audience can learn from its deconstruction of the dangerous pretensions of Eu-

ripidean tragedy how to see through the even more dangerous strategems of dishonest speakers in the assembly (including, but not limited to, Cleon) and the lawcourts. Its playful and rapid transitions from theater to assembly to lawcourt and back again, while temporarily raising the specter of a collapse of all forms of Athenian civic life into a form of *theoria*, a city populated only by Open-Mouthenians, as Alan Sommerstein so aptly translates χαυνοπολίτας (635),[103] in fact teaches the spectators to see the differences and restores distinctions and boundaries that Sophists such as Gorgias seemed to be undermining. These were lessons Aristophanes thought worth repeating, as he shows in his next play, which resumes the frontal assault on Cleon and his influence over the demos.

4

The Politics of Performance: *Knights*

> Conservative—n., a statesman who is enamored of existing
> evils, as distinguished from the Liberal, who wishes to re-
> place them with others.
>
> —Ambrose Bierce, *The Devil's Dictionary*

THE *KNIGHTS* IS TODAY one of the less studied and least produced of Aristophanes' plays. His most direct attack on the demagogue Cleon, the play therefore seems closely tied to its immediate historical context, the aftermath of Cleon's successful capture of the Spartan garrison on Pylos. Yet Cleon's specific actions are much less at issue than, once again, the transactional nature of his approach to politics. A performance analysis will show that role-playing is as central to the *Knights* as to the *Acharnians*, but a key part of its effect lies in not making this completely clear too early. Like Dicaeopolis in the *Acharnians*, the central character of this play, the Sausage-seller, is invited onto the stage and into the fiction; only at the end do we fully realize how much acting the assumption of this role has entailed.[1] That revelation has troubled many, particularly those of a more Aristotelian turn of mind,[2] but the plot of the play as a whole uses the same devices already employed in the prologue of the *Acharnians* to demonstrate the consequences of failure to learn the earlier play's lessons in reading political performance.

The play opens with two slaves on stage discussing their unhappy oppression by the new slave in the household, Paphlagon. These two slaves are never given personal names in the text, and nothing in the opening lines compels us to identify them as particular individuals. The mediaeval manuscripts of the play label them as the two well-known Athenian statesmen, Demosthenes and Nicias. The two most recent editors of the play disagree on whether or not this identification is reliable. Sommerstein accepts it and suggests the comedy may even be pointed up by having the two slaves wearing portrait masks.[3] Henderson reviews the statements of each character in great detail, noting some points that are consistent with an identification (notably Slave A's first-person reference to being robbed of the credit for the victory at Pylos) and others not, and argues that the two slaves are generic politicians rather than these two particular individuals, although he of course accepts that Paphlagon is a satire of Cleon.[4] Characterization in Aristophanes is always a rather fluid concept, and certainly some touches, particularly in the character of Slave B, are reminiscent of what other sources tell us about Nicias. I prefer to think that these touches are deliberate and part of the setup of the notion that there are individuals behind these slave roles (as Cleon certainly lies behind the role of Paphlagon). I have therefore followed Sommerstein in referring to the two characters by the names of Nicias and Demosthenes. It might well be charged that this procedure is both prejudicial and inconsistent, since I will refer to the hero of the play when he appears as the Sausage-seller until this character (like Dicaeopolis) later reveals he has a personal name as well. To the arguments already given for audience recognition of these figures, I would simply plead the greater intelligibility of using personal names: whereas the Sausage-seller is both correct and unambiguous as a designation, I find one is much more likely to confuse Slave A and Slave B so named than Nicias and Demosthenes.

The reference to Paphlagon is the only concrete bit of exposition we get in the play's opening moments, since the first thirty-five lines are otherwise devoted to a series of slave jokes and outrageous puns.[5] The feeling of the scene is highly improvisational: stock slave characterizations and language itself generate the comedy. This opening movement ends rather abruptly with this exchange:

> {Δε.} βούλει τὸ πρᾶγμα τοῖς θεαταῖσιν φράσω;
> {Νι.} οὐ χεῖρον· ἐν δ᾽ αὐτοὺς παραιτησώμεθα,
> ἐπίδηλον ἡμῖν τοῖς προσώποισιν ποιεῖν,
> ἢν τοῖς ἔπεσι χαίρωσι καὶ τοῖς πράγμασιν.   (36–39)

Demosthenes. You want me to explain the plot to the spectators?
Nicias. Not a bad idea. Let's ask them one thing, though:
to show us plainly in their faces,
if they enjoy our words and deeds.

They will explain the plot, but first they ask the audience directly for a sign of approval. This induction thus puts in lots of jokes to warm the audience up, builds to a peak, and then by asking for applause creates a caesura and readies the audience for exposition of the political allegory which will accustom the audience to think of the figures on stage as simultaneously slaves and statesmen.

The succeeding lines make it very clear that Paphlagon is Cleon, now riding high on his recent success at Pylos, and the two slaves of the opening are his envious and fearful displaced competitors. Demosthenes fleshes out this basic scenario by telling the audience of Demos,[6] the master they serve, and his acquisition of the new slave Paphlagon. The political allegory of the play comes into focus only at this point: the city as a single household, ruled by the as yet unseen Demos. The initial characterization of Demos is not flattering: "a little old guy, grouchy and deaf" ($\delta\dot{\upsilon}\sigma\kappa o\lambda o\nu$ $\gamma\epsilon\rho\acute{o}\nu\tau\iota o\nu$ / $\dot{\upsilon}\pi\acute{o}\kappa\omega\phi o\nu$, 41–42). The bulk of Demosthenes' description, however, focuses on Paphlagon as flatterer and toady in this household; the audience does not necessarily know whether Demos will in fact appear in this play at all.

While mixing in liberal amounts of further slave comedy, the play does move slowly from improvisation to scripted drama. Demosthenes establishes himself as the dominant partner of the two, ordering the reluctant Nicias into the house to steal some wine. With this obviously Dionysiac inspiration,[7] he now has the idea that sets the plot itself in motion: he sends Nicias in again, this time to steal from the sleeping Paphlagon the oracles on which his influence over Demos rests. Nicias returns with scroll in hand, and it becomes the script of the play: the traditional "great idea" of the Aristophanic hero is here *not* conceived by Demosthenes but provided in already written form. The oracle (129ff.) "foretells" a succession of leaders of the city, all tradesmen ("mongers") of various sorts. Like all effective prophecy, it is mostly already history: under the names of their trades the audience recognizes the first three as Eucrates, Lysicles, and Cleon (= Paphlagon). The oracle then foretells the fourth "monger" who will overthrow Paphlagon: a sausage-monger, who will out-Cleon Cleon. In typically Aristophanic fashion, the fulfillment of this prophecy immediately appears.

The staging of the Sausage-seller's entrance is key to our understanding of his role and the function of the play as a whole. He appears, miraculously as far as the two slaves are concerned, heading to the market.[8] While we cannot be absolutely certain, the subsequent verbs suggest that, like the chorus, he enters from a *parodos* and is then invited up onto the stage, for Demosthenes says: "Come here, o dearest one, mount up, savior to the city" ($\delta\epsilon\hat{\upsilon}\rho o$ $\delta\epsilon\hat{\upsilon}\rho$', ὦ φίλτατε, / ἀνάβαινε σωτὴρ τῇ πόλει, 149–150).⁹ Unlike Dicaeopolis, then, who watches and criticizes the spectacle on stage for some time before joining in, the Sausage-seller becomes part of the performance immediately: we have no opportunity to discover what he is "really" like before he joins in. He is immediately instructed in the role he is to play from the script of Paphlagon's oracle. Note the verb: "*teach* (him) the oracle" (τὸν χρησμὸν ἀναδίδαξον, 153). There is a substantial difference here from "telling" or even "explaining" the oracle. Demosthenes relates to him not merely the contents of the oracle but instructs him about the actions he must take, teaching him in the process the role he must play to defeat Paphlagon.

As if to drive the point home even further, Demosthenes not only divests the Sausage-seller of the butcher's table he carries but, after inviting him to survey the audience in the theater ("do you see the rows of people?" τὰς στίχας ὁρᾷς τὰς τῶνδε τῶν λαῶν; 163), causes him to climb up on that table (τοὐλεὸν τοδί, 169) for a view that will allow him to survey all the surrounding islands of Athens' empire (170).¹⁰ At the very least, like Dicaeopolis, he is "framed" by this action and our attention focused tightly on him. One wonders, however, if at least some in the audience would have recognized a further theatrical encoding in this movement. Before Thespis, according to Pollux 4. 123 (an admittedly late source), the actor who responded to the chorus stood on an ἐλεός.¹¹ One wonders what Pollux's source of information was. Could the use of such a table still have been seen in rustic performances in honor of Dionysus? If so, then the audience is being told even more unambiguously that the Sausage-seller has been invited into the play to perform a role.

The Sausage-seller has doubts about his ability to play this part, which sets up a number of jokes about his low origins as the perfect qualifications for political leadership.¹² He requires further instruction from the oracle script (ἀναδίδασκέ με, 202), which Demosthenes supplies.¹³ He is to be the opponent of "this Paphlagon" (ὁ Παφλαγών ἐσθ᾽ οὑτοσί, 203), and the deictic suggests that Demosthenes gestures to where the real Cleon is sitting in the front row of the audience.¹⁴ The Sausage-seller says that he is afraid of his opponent, just as both rich and poor already are (222–224), a statement that can apply only to the real Cleon, since he can have no knowledge of "Paphlagon" yet. Demosthenes reassures him of support in a cleverly constructed reply. First he notes that the Knights will support him, thereby pointing ahead to the chorus of the play and building audience anticipation for their arrival. Then he asserts that the καλοί τε κἀγαθοί will support the Sausage-seller, as well as all the spectators who are intelligent (τῶν θεατῶν ὅστις ἐστὶ δεξιός, 228). This metatheatrical reference prompts another such joke: we learn that Paphlagon's mask will not be a portrait because the prop-makers were too frightened to create one (231–232)! Demosthenes insists that the audience will have no trouble recognizing him, however, since they are all "intelligent" (τὸ γὰρ θέατρον δεξιόν, 233).[15] Aristophanes has neatly framed the joke at Cleon's expense with the premises of a syllogism: the intelligent (δεξιός, 228) in the audience will all support the Sausage-seller; the whole theater is intelligent (233); therefore. . . .

We are thus as prepared as we can be for the roaring entrance of Paphlagon, who is consistently portrayed throughout the play as an inhuman monster.[16] The Sausage-seller is terrified at Paphlagon's approach and may retreat from the stage temporarily (witness Demosthenes' worried question, "Aren't you staying?" οὐ μενεῖς; 240) but returns on the arrival of the chorus of Knights, who support him.

The choice of the Knights for a chorus is determined by their opposition to Cleon, signaled already in the *Acharnians*.[17] Unfortunately, we have no indication of their appearance, other than their own reference to their long hair (ἡμῖν κομῶσι, 580). A black-figure vase of the previous century shows a chorus of Knights mounted on the backs of other men, playing their horses, but we cannot assume that Aristophanes' chorus was so represented.[18] While their active role as a mobile defense force against Spartan raids should have benefitted them in public opinion,[19] their wealth and traditional arrogance means that Aristophanes must tread carefully in his presentation of them.

The ensuing argument, laying out the very important theme of Cleon's disturbance of the city,[20] occupies the stage until Paphlagon (at 481) and the Sausage-seller (at 495) leave to carry on their battle in front of a new audience, the *boule*. Very little in this first encounter emphasizes the theatrical nature of the combatants' performances, although R. A. Neil (*ad loc.*) calls our attention to some of the associations of lines 395–396:

{Πα.} οὐ δέδοιχ᾽ ὑμᾶς, ἕως ἂν ζῇ τὸ βουλευτήριον
καὶ τὸ τοῦ δήμου πρόσωπον μακκοᾷ καθήμενον . . .

Paphlagon. I'm not afraid of you, as long as council chamber lives
and the demos sits there looking blank.

πρόσωπον may or may not anticipate the expression on the mask of Demos, as Neil suggests, but his point is well taken that the use of τὸ βουλευτήριον for ἡ βουλή is rare and parallels the use of τὸ θέατρον for the theater audience at 233. Neil further suggests that καθήμενον may be underscored with a gesture toward the audience sitting in the theater. He proposes here an echo of Cleon during the Mytilene debate of 427, as recorded by Thucydides. In defending his harsh policy against the Mytilenians, Cleon charges the demos with behaving like spectators sitting at a sophists' debate (σοφιστῶν θεαταῖς ἐοικότες καθημένοις, Thucydides 3.38.7). One might go further and suggest that Paphlagon's mockery of the Sausage-seller for thinking that he can be a speaker (ᾤου δυνατὸς εἶναι λέγειν, 350) recalls Cleon's derisive comments on the demos, where he charges that all of them think they are qualified to speak in the assembly (καὶ μάλιστα μὲν αὐτὸς εἰπεῖν ἕκαστος βουλόμενος δύνασθαι, Thucydides 3.38.6).

The subsequent self-consciousness of the chorus reinforces these performative echoes in Paphlagon's speech. Immediately following his lines, the chorus expresses its hatred of him by offering two profoundly metatheatrical curses on themselves:

εἴ σε μὴ μισῶ, γενοίμην ἐν Κρατίνου κῴδιον
καὶ διδασκοίμην προσᾴδειν Μορσίμου τραγῳδίᾳ. (400–401)

If I don't hate you, may I become a blanket in Cratinus's house
and be learning to sing in Morsimus's tragedy.

To be a blanket in the house of Cratinus is to be urinated upon. We will hear more about Cratinus as a broken-down, incontinent, and drunken old poet very soon in the parabasis (526ff.), but the brief yet very specific joke here implies that jokes about his lack of bladder control are already standard, the equivalent of Dan Quayle / potato jokes, and therefore can be used quite elliptically. The insult to the tragedian Morsimus is more direct and also more explicitly metatheatrical. Rehearsing his songs is the worst fate the chorus can imagine. Note the specificity of διδασκοίμην (401), which emphasizes the repetition that only comes in a rehearsal situation. To sing in Morsimus's chorus is to suffer the horror over and over again.[21] While not direct comments on Paphlagon's performance, these reminders that a comedy is in progress do highlight the theatricality of both contenders for Demos's affections.

The function of Demosthenes in this contest also emphasizes the staged nature of the scene, for he at least attempts at crucial moments to direct the action and coach the Sausage-seller in his part. While his comments are not asides in that they do not explicitly address the audience,[22] at the same time he stands a little apart from the action. His comments help shape audience re-action to the conflict between Paphlagon and the Sausage-seller, consistently reinforcing sympathy for the latter. Paphlagon and the Sausage-seller both denounce each other in the third person (278–281), thereby apparently call-ing the audience to witness. Demosthenes' first interjection is to endorse and expand on the Sausage-seller's accusation against Paphlagon (282–283), who promptly rounds on them both. Only once does Demosthenes speak directly to Paphlagon (366); otherwise he abuses him in the third person (319–321, 375–381) or directs his comments to the Sausage-seller.

Given the structure of the scene, these comments might lead us to see Demosthenes as virtually a Plautine *poeta* figure, directing the performance of the Sausage-seller, but the power relationships at this point are more ambigu-ous than they first seem. Demosthenes gives both simple if powerful stage di-rections ("hit him good and hard!" παῖ' ἀνδρικῶς, 451; παῖ' αὐτὸν ἀνδρικώ-τατα, 453) and script advice ("if that doesn't work, tell him you're descended from scoundrels, too!" ἐὰν δὲ μὴ ταύτῃ γ' ὑπείκῃ, λέγ' ὅτι κἀκ πονηρῶν, 337). Toward the end of the scene, Demosthenes criticizes the Sausage-seller's first response to one of Paphlagon's attacks (464), then voices his approval when the Sausage-seller does pick up the proper line of attack (470). Other comments suggest that the Sausage-seller is *not* under Demosthenes' control, which worries the latter. The first is the most significant:

τὰ μὲν ἄλλα μ' ἤρεσας λέγων· ἓν δ' οὐ προσίεταί με,
τῶν πραγμάτων ὁτιὴ μόνος τὸν ζωμὸν ἐκροφήσεις. (359–360)

The rest of what you said pleased me—except this:
that you'd slurp up the public gravy all by yourself.

When the Sausage-seller states clearly that he intends to eliminate not only the competition of Paphlagon but that of all the other would-be leaders, thereby acquiring for himself all the benefits of public office (356–358), Demosthenes realizes that he does not control the other's performance. Two later comments move from ambiguous admiration to outright criticism of the Sausage-seller: one compliments his ability to steal through deception (421–422), the other labels him a typically lying and pathic politician (427–428).[23]

Demosthenes concludes the scene by giving the Sausage-seller a num-ber of instructions, preparing him for the *agon* in the *boule* (482–497); their form, however, is no longer strictly that between director and actor, but a con-versation between two theater professionals. Demosthenes concedes a crucial function to the Sausage-seller, when he says that the latter will now be the one to *teach* (διδάξεις, 483). While no object is specified, it clearly means that the Sausage-seller will teach both the *boule* and the theater audience in the process of defeating Paphlagon. With this word, Demosthenes surrenders his claim to be in control of the Sausage-seller's performance and becomes rather a consultant (though he will vainly try to claim some credit at 1254–1255). The Sausage-seller departs to continue the battle before another audience.

The dramatic time for this battle before the *boule* is filled onstage by the parabasis. Interest in the metatheatrical elements of this parabasis has traditionally focused on its opening and the philological and historical question of Aristophanes' early career, for the poet asserts that this is the first time he has "asked for a chorus" (χορὸν αἰτοίη καθ' ἑαυτόν, 513) in his own name, his previous productions having been put on by other *chorodidaskaloi*. Rather than revisit the technicalities of authorship and sponsorship at this point, however, I suggest we look a little more carefully at what has often been seen as a conventional, if not formulaic opening:

εἰ μέν τις ἀνὴρ τῶν ἀρχαίων κωμῳδοδιδάσκαλος ἡμᾶς
ἠνάγκαζεν λέξοντας ἔπη πρὸς τὸ θέατρον παραβῆναι,
οὐκ ἂν φαύλως ἔτυχεν τούτου· νῦν δ' ἄξιός ἐσθ' ὁ ποιητής,
ὅτι τοὺς αὐτοὺς ἡμῖν μισεῖ τολμᾷ τε λέγειν τὰ δίκαια,
καὶ γενναίως πρὸς τὸν Τυφῶ χωρεῖ καὶ τὴν ἐριώλην.   (507–511)

If some comic producer of old had pressured us
to turn and speak our piece to the audience,
he wouldn't have done it easily. But now our poet's worth it,
because he dares to hate the same guys we do and speak justly
and nobly braves the Typhoon and the whirlwind.

On the traditional view of the parabasis, which recognizes that the chorus here steps out of its character in the fictional world of the play, this statement is positively ludicrous. Many scholars still hold, following the view of the ritualist school, that the parabasis and its direct address to the audience are the oldest, most traditional, and most formulaic part of Old Comedy. Thomas Hubbard has recently offered some invigorating criticism of this view, suggesting in fact that the dramatic self-consciousness of the parabasis may be a relatively late development,[24] but does not address the specific audience reception of these lines. Why, if every poet of Old Comedy has his chorus turn to the audience and make direct comments on contemporary events, would Aristophanes pretend that doing this very thing was a large favor on the part of the chorus toward a young poet, indeed a mark of their especial favor? The laugh that would earn would not conduce to the poet's benefit in the current competition. One might deny the step out of character and attempt to filter these statements through the chorus's fictive identity as Knights. Choruses do employ their character for comedy (witness the Clouds in their play). The problems with that explanation here are twofold: one, there is no inherent comic appeal in Knights praising a poet, and two, the explicit comparison of old and new poets makes no sense in the mouths of Knights in the absence of evidence that Knights regularly appeared as the choruses of Old Comedies.

If we do not start with the assumption that Aristophanes is joking, what are the implications of this opening gambit? For one, it implies that the chorus is prior—as well as superior—to the poet: this chorus speaks as though it has ongoing existence, while poets come and go.[25] We might just consider taking this seriously. The *komoi* in honor of Dionysus existed long before the state took on the function of organizing those *komoi* through the official festivals (and funding them through public liturgies). We know even less about the organization of the comic choruses than we do about their tragic counterparts.[26] One wonders whether singing in a *komos* was in fact a traditional activity and whether the participants therein had some corporate existence over time, as the speakers of 507ff. seem to imply. Analogy can easily be pressed too far, but the parallel of comic mumming groups in later periods, such as the carnival Narren in Germany, is intriguing: comic choristers in Athens might well have repeated from year to year. If there were traditions of participation in the Dionysiac *komoi*, their members might well resist innovations—such as the innovation of speaking directly for the poet on matters of individual concern to him, rather than singing more general and less centrally organized comic or even mocking verses to the populace at large. Whether or not Aristophanes is strictly innovative at this moment is not the question—certainly he has already had the chorus speak directly on quite specific issues to the audience in *Acharnians*. The point is rather that this appeal for audience sympathy for the poet, framed by the chorus's claim that this poet deserves the indulgence of a hearing more than any of the poets of a previous generation, works best if it is meant to be taken at face value. The chorus speaks corporately from its past experience with poets and vouchsafes the remarkable quality and moreover political acumen of the young Aristophanes.

The chorus, continuing to praise and encourage Aristophanes (just as it encouraged the Sausage-seller moments before), justifies his career up till now in the light of the experience of other comic poets. A. M. Bowie makes the intriguing suggestion that this succession of comic poets is meant to parallel the prophesied political succession in Athens: just as the Sausage-seller is fated to succeed the previous salesmen/political leaders, so Aristophanes, we are to understand, is fated to succeed the comic poets of previous generations.[27] Aristophanes' account, however, which sandwiches the still-active though elderly Cratinus between the long-dead Magnes and the more recently departed Crates (514–540),[28] turned out to be too clever by half. It roused Cratinus to reply in the form of his play, the *Wineflask*, which was to triumph over Aristophanes' *Clouds* the next year. The chorus concludes the parabasis by reverting to its character as Knights in order to fuse patriotic appeals for victory in war to appeals for the victory of the chorus in the comic competition (581ff.).

The returning Sausage-seller gives an account of his victory over Paphlagon in the *boule*. He thus establishes himself ever more firmly in the estimation of chorus and audience alike before Paphlagon returns for another round of argument. The mutual threats resume as before. One point of particular interest for our purposes is when Paphlagon reinforces a threat with an oath by his προεδρία (702), literally his seat up front at public gatherings.[29] Cleon is presumably sitting in that seat of honor right up front in the theater even as these lines are spoken, drawing attention once more to the equation of Paphlagon and Cleon. The Sausage-seller's reply not merely derides this claim to honor but looks forward to its reversal:

ἰδοὺ προεδρίαν· οἷον ὄψομαί σ' ἐγὼ
ἐκ τῆς προεδρίας ἔσχατον θεώμενον. (703–704)

Up your front row seat! I want to see you
booted from front to last row, craning for a look.

He hopes to see Paphlagon/Cleon not just pushed out of his front row seat and shoved to the back, but emphatically cast as a *spectator* (θεώμενον), no longer a performer in the theater of politics.[30]

The squabbling here is brief and preparatory to the appearance of Demos himself to judge between the two contenders for his favor. The staging of this scene is peculiarly important but frustratingly difficult to reconstruct. Sommerstein believes that Demos appears from a door in the *skene* but at line 751 moves to sit on a rock located near the orchestra.[31] While this staging does not admit of definitive proof, it both focuses attention on the two contenders by moving Demos away from center stage and underlines his identification with the audience by moving him closer to them in the theater. As Henderson has pointed out, the theater and the Pnyx, where the action in the play now moves, were homologous spaces in which the citizen body judged competitive displays.[32] On the Pnyx as in the theater, the place for the judges is in the audience. The opening prayers (763ff.) offered by Paphlagon and the Sausage-seller seal the transformation of the theater space into the assembly.

We need not delve into every charge and countercharge of this debate. Skillfully employing little bribes (a cushion for Demos' hard stone seat, some ointment), straightforward attacks, and reinterpretations of what Paphlagon claims were his past services, the Sausage-seller successfully shakes Demos' confidence in his current steward. Demos takes his ring of office back from Paphlagon, but when he is about to appoint the Sausage-seller in his stead, Paphlagon appeals to his final weapon, his oracles. The Sausage-seller claims to have oracles too, and Demos agrees to hear them both.

While both contenders leave the stage in quest of their respective scripts, the chorus sings a short ode (973ff.) denouncing Cleon—by name. Despite the very broad hints elsewhere, this is the only moment in the whole play in which Cleon is directly named. B. B. Rogers calls attention to this fact and offers a very intriguing explanation: he suggests that Aristophanes may have hoped that this song would move into popular circulation, as other songs from comedy apparently had,[33] and thereby continue to undermine Cleon's political position. For the success of the song, Cleon must needs appear under his own name, not as Paphlagon.

The oracle contest allows ample scope for parody of the fulsome and obscure style of these prophecies, and most of the audience surely enjoyed this scene on the level of wordplay. It may or may not be legitimate to ask what is "really" going on in this scene, given the absence of any attempt in Old Comedy to maintain a consistent illusion or dramatic verisimilitude. When the Aristophanic hero needs something to carry out his plan, it is provided, and it can be a distraction to ask where the resource came from or how the hero might reasonably be expected to have acquired it. Still, if we are permitted to ask the question in this scene, where do the Sausage-seller's oracles come from, the answer surely is that the Sausage-seller is improvising them. His oracles respond to and top those of Paphlagon too neatly to be a preexisting script. There are no texts on his scrolls: he is composing poetry in oracular style on the spot.[34] If on the other hand (as is frankly more likely in this scene)

Aristophanes does not want his audience to worry about such details, I would suggest that the improvisatory character of this competition in insulting verse, perhaps related to the verses improvised by the predramatic *komoi*,[35] nonetheless remains detectable. Of course Paphlagon and the Sausage-seller have been insulting each other in verse from the very beginning: that is the fundamental form of Old Comedy. The oracle contest simply takes the competition to a new level.

The Sausage-seller's repeated successes drive Paphlagon briefly to a new weapon, dreams (1090ff.). Here too the Sausage-seller concocts a better dream, and Demos immediately declares himself ready to turn himself over to the Sausage-seller for "reeducation."[36] Once again Paphlagon shifts ground and decides to compete in feeding Demos. He and the Sausage-seller both dash from the stage to get their next set of props, leaving Demos to converse with the chorus.

In their absence comes a startling (and to some shocking) revelation.[37] The chorus begins by praising Demos for his power but then accuses him of being too easily led astray and indeed taking pleasure in being deceived (χαίρεις κἀξαπατώμενος, 1116–1117).[38] From his reply (1123–1124) we learn that Demos *himself* has been playing a role: he claims that he has been deliberately pretending to be a fool (ἐγὼ δ' ἑκὼν / ταῦτ' ἠλιθιάζω) to lull Paphlagon and other demagogues like him into a false sense of security. Yet Aristophanes is not too explicit about the theatricality of Demos' own performance but rather chooses his words carefully here. The verb ἠλιθιάζω indicates youthful folly more than conscious acting technique and thus fits into the sequence of images that presents Demos as in his second childhood.[39] If Aristophanes wanted to portray Demos clearly as an actor, as an equal theatrical competitor, he would need to use a verb such as the chorus's own term, ἐξαπατάω (cf. Paphlagon's deceptive performance in the *boule* at 633).

Nor is Demos' policy unequivocally folly: there is a rudimentary political theory behind his actions. He claims to be fattening up these various political leaders, who think they are deceiving *him*, like victims for sacrifice. The politicians temporarily steal for themselves but are forced to disgorge their ill-gotten gains when Demos needs the money and turns on them.[40] R. W. Brock has pointed out that sounds like a parody of the political theory of the Old Oligarch, whose pamphlet on the Athenian constitution may have been written around this time.[41] The problem with the theory, however, is that it is both unjust and inefficient: the politicians mistreat citizens, acquire their wealth, and presumably spend some of it on themselves before the remainder is squeezed out of them by Demos. On the other hand, most of the victims of the politicians will be the wealthy, for whom the populace at large had little sympathy. After all, the very institution of the Dionysiac festivals themselves relied on a similar procedure: the system of choregeia provided entertainment for the demos of Athens at the expense of a rotating group of rich individuals on whom the liturgy fell. The chorus praises Demos for his wisdom. The only repudiation of the theory of governance he propounds here will be a silent one at the end.

The final contest relies on props, as the Sausage-seller and Paphlagon strive to outdo each other in providing delicacies from their baskets for Demos. Aristophanes' theatrical instincts are surely sound here: there is ample scope for physical comedy and a steady buildup to the climactic moment. In the first several exchanges the Sausage-seller simply produces something bigger or better than Paphlagon's gift. Then Paphlagon brings out hare's meat, a delicacy for those shut up in the besieged city,[42] and the Sausage-seller has nothing to outdo it. He is stymied only for a moment: he uses the old "look! here come ambassadors with bribes" trick (the same trick for which Demosthenes complimented him back at 419–422) to steal the hare's meat from Paphlagon and offers it to Demos.[43] Demos, who has twice been ready to hand over rule to the Sausage-seller already, now is a bit coy. He expressly wants the approval of the theater audience for whatever decision he makes:

τῷ δῆτ᾽ ἂν ὑμᾶς χρησάμενος τεκμηρίῳ
δόξαιμι κρίνειν τοῖς θεαταῖσιν σοφῶς;   (1209–1210)

What evidence should I use to judge you
in order to seem wise to the spectators?

This coyness is not simply a delaying tactic on Aristophanes' part; it is the beginning of a key shift in the characterization of Demos. Heretofore, Demos has been primarily a figure of fun and therefore not someone with whom the audience identifies, despite his name. The audience cannot yet know it, but very soon it will see a quite different Demos, with whom it will be expected to identify; this appeal for audience endorsement of his reasoning and judgement is groundwork for that.

The Sausage-seller suggests a simple but decisive test: look and see what in their respective baskets each has *not* yet given to Demos. The Sausage-seller knows his basket is empty. Paphlagon's, of course, is still full of all the things he was keeping for himself. We will never know how this was staged, but surely one of the most effective means would be turning the baskets upside down and watching the ill-gotten gains pouring out of Paphlagon's basket, like silverware out of Harpo Marx's overcoat.

Even this moment of revelation does not cow Paphlagon. He puts his faith in the script he has mastered, the sacred oracle he thinks he has guarded so carefully. Like Macbeth about to have his little chat with MacDuff, Paphlagon feels secure in the knowledge that no one has yet appeared who matches the characteristics of the one the oracle foretells will triumph over him. This play is not tragedy, however, nor is the Sausage-seller's fate really written in the stars. There was a purpose to the theft of the oracle at the beginning of the play: instructed in its details, the Sausage-seller now knows how to answer Paphlagon's questions, and with each reply tears away at the foundations of the latter's previously unshakable confidence.

He who lives by the oracle dies by the oracle. The Sausage-seller's victory is the archetypal one of improvisational hero over scripted hero. Paphlagon might claim to be able to tell any lie in order to hold on to power—but he has made the mistake of believing in his own oracles. It is the Sausage-seller who possesses what Greenblatt terms the "mobile sensibility,"[44] the ability to stand outside and manipulate others' belief structures. When Paphlagon quizzes him, he can give whatever answer the oracle script requires,[45] while Paphlagon is trapped by his belief in what is written in his scrolls. There is a deep structural appropriateness then in Paphlagon's profoundly metatheatrical exit speech:

οἴμοι, πέπρακται τοῦ θεοῦ τὸ θέσφατον.
κυλίνδετ᾽ εἴσω τόνδε τὸν δυσδαίμονα.
ὦ στέφανε, χαίρων ἄπιθι, καί σ᾽ ἄκων ἐγὼ
λείπω· σὲ δ᾽ ἄλλος τις λαβὼν κεκτήσεται,
κλέπτης μὲν οὐκ ἂν μᾶλλον, εὐτυχὴς δ᾽ ἴσως. (1248–1252)

Alack, the god's prophecy is fulfilled.
Roll ill-fated me within.
Garland, fare thee well, for I unwillingly
leave you. Some other will take you up,
no greater thief indeed, yet mayhap more fortunate.

The lines are a pastiche of Euripides. The first part parodies his *Bellerophon* (fr. 310), with the substitution of the emphatically theatrical "roll" (κυλίνδετ᾽), a reference to the *ekkyklema*,[46] substituting for the original "accompany" (κομίζετ'). The physical staging therefore, with Paphlagon collapsing onto the *ekkyklema*, frames this as a theatrical event. The second part even more interestingly reworks Alcestis' famous farewell speech to her bed.[47] In a familiar move, comedy puts onstage what tragedy reported from offstage (Alcestis' speech in her play is quoted by a messenger). The point is certainly not just to mock Euripides, eager though Aristophanes was to take every opportunity to do so.[48] Rather, by using a memorably emotional scene from a previous drama (and twisting it toward bathos) he emphasizes that Paphlagon/Cleon has been a bombastic performer too—and it is Aristophanes' job to teach the Athenian public to see through such performances.

With Paphlagon finally vanquished, Demos can now hand himself over to the Sausage-seller—whose name we at last learn. It is Agoracritus, which he etymologizes as "raised to argue in the Agora" (1259–1260).[49] Demosthenes makes a final appearance, asking to be a henchman (ὑπογραφεύς, 1256) in the new regime. This, combined with the Sausage-seller/Agoracritus' exiting reference to the citizens as "Openmouthenians" (Κεχηναίων, 1263), a far from complimentary title, should signal to us that this is not a satisfactory ending.[50] Changing leaders, especially if they simply acquire new henchmen, is no real solution to the problems of the city.[51] Indeed, the very fact that Paphlagon can only imagine being succeeded by another thief (1252) shows the impasse his politics have reached.

One hint of the direction in which the play is now moving is Agoracritus's revelation of his real identity. In one sense it is even clearer here than in the case of Dicaeopolis that the character's name is more a function than an identity. The moment of revelation is not randomly chosen, however. Agoracritus chooses this moment to step out from behind his role as the Sausage-seller in order to prepare the audience for Demos' rejection of the role *he* has hitherto played.

The second parabasis fills the interval while Agoracritus and Demos are offstage. The first part of this choral interlude attacks various individuals, including Ariphrades, pilloried for his devotion to cunnilingus. These attacks link the oral sexual impurity of sophistic politicians to their impurity of political speech.[52] The concluding element offers the intriguing fantasy of a conversation between triremes of the city's fleet.[53] The ships declare their unwillingness to obey the orders of so unworthy a commander as the orator Hyperbolus (1300ff.), who would in reality become one of the contenders for leadership in the city after the death of Cleon. These verses too then reinforce the growing notion that what the city needs is not just a change of the current dominant politician—new rascals for old—but a change in the nature of politics.

That is precisely what Aristophanes provides. Agoracritus returns to the stage proclaiming good news and asking for a paean of joy from the theater audience (παιωνίζειν τὸ θέατρον, 1318). He announces that Demos has been magically restored, boiled down and rejuvenated as Medea did for Jason's father Aeson.[54] The *ekkyklema* which removed the failed performer Paphlagon from the stage now rolls forward again.[55] In his place stands Demos, now no longer a spectator but an active participant in the drama, revealed in old-fashioned and therefore dignified costume (ἀρχαίῳ σχήματι, 1331).

The transition from passive spectator to active performer is not simply an exchange of roles but a process of maturation. Demos will not become a deceptive performer himself, simply substituting for Paphlagon; rather, he ceases to play the deceptive role of gullible audience and becomes himself the entire embodiment of the democracy.

Demos undergoes a similar maturation in erotic self-image. He apparently has no recollection of how he has behaved recently and must be told by Agoracritus how he once played the submissive role to the politicians' claims to be his lovers (ἐραστής εἰμι σός, 1341)[56] and was regularly deceived by them (ἐξαπατήσας σ', 1345). When Demos hangs his head in shame,[57] however, Agoracritus reassures him that the blame belongs entirely to those who practiced these deceptions (ἐξηπάτων, 1357).

Aristophanes thus plays on the ambiguities inherent in Greek pederasty to underscore his points about political spectatorship and passivity. There are limits to both erotic and political passivity, and Demos may have been rather close to them. No blame attaches to the passive younger partner in Greek pederastic relationships—so long as he outgrows that role at the proper time. Nor does the maturation process cease when the young *eromenos* grows up enough to take on the role of *erastes* and pursue younger males in his turn; that is only a further transitional stage. Leaving both erotic and political passivity far behind, Demos will not simply become a demagogic deceiver in turn but will pass immediately beyond that stage to full self-control.

Demos' complete restoration to power is assured when Agoracritus asks him how he will act in the lawcourts and in public policy. Demos shows himself again capable of deciding for himself: he no longer needs Agoracritus or anyone else to rule over him. Agoracritus now leads out the female embodiments of the thirty-year peace treaty Demos will now enjoy, which Paphlagon had hidden away, and the play moves rapidly to a conclusion.

There are a few final insults for the fallen Paphlagon. His fittingly theatrical punishment will simply be to take on Agoracritus's original role as
Sausage-seller, plying his trade at the city gate and engaging in screaming
matches with prostitutes and other lowlife types.[58] From center stage in the
city's politics he will be led away to be a spectacle (ἴδωσιν, 1408) for foreigners
at the edge of the city.

The text we have ends without a choral exit song, although it is extremely
likely there once was one. Sommerstein and others have speculated that Aristophanes employed traditional songs at this point, which were therefore not
preserved.[59] We would give much to know the staging of this exit, but surely
its broad outlines are clear: Paphlagon is carted away, and a restored Demos
rules.

The connection between this ending, showing Demos restored to his
former glory, and the whole plot of the competition between the Sausage-
seller and Paphlagon, which ends with the latter's downfall, has become a traditional problem in scholarship on the play. Even Landfester, who set out to
defend the integrity of the play, seems to say that the clues that should prepare us for this ending are detectable only after we have experienced the play's
conclusion.[60]

The connection, however, lies in the theme of spectatorship. The *Knights*
enacts the cure of Demos, a cure that includes rejection of his role as spectator
in a theater of politics dominated by other actors and his assumption of center
stage in the drama of his own political existence. The play continues the message laid out by Aristophanes in the *Acharnians* the year before: the Athenians
must learn to see through the costumes, props, and role-playing of those who
claim to love the city. If they do so, Athens will regain her past glory.

The *Knights* is not numbered among Aristophanes' peace plays. While
Demos is rewarded in the end with the thirty-year peace treaties for his enjoyment and the opportunity to return to his country home,[61] the play as a whole
does not dwell so much on the hardships of the war as on the fact that the
lying, self-interested politicians have done nothing to relieve the people from
those hardships, despite their elaborate protestations of love for the people
(cf. 792–794). This suggests that those who have recently questioned the characterization of Aristophanes as first and foremost an advocate of peace[62] may
well be right. In the *Acharnians* Aristophanes attempted to use the yearning
for peace as a weapon against Cleon. The fact that he does not return heavily
to that theme in this year's play suggests either that it was not as effective
as he had hoped (indeed, after Cleon's victory at Pylos perhaps could not be

as effective) or just not his main concern. The theme that does persist is the fraudulence of the city's leaders and the necessity for teaching the people to see through their costumes and their lying speeches. When that happens, Aristophanes seems to say, the city will be restored to real democratic control and peace will come automatically.

5

Bringing Up Father: *Wasps*

Should a Happiness Machine, he wondered, be something
you can carry in your pocket?
Or, he went on, should it be something that carries you in
its pocket?

—Ray Bradbury, "The Happiness Machine"

IN COMPARISON TO ITS PREDECESSORS the *Wasps* has often seemed to possess a surfeit of plot. Where *Acharnians* displays the typical pattern of fairly steady plot development through the enactment of the great idea, followed by a series of *alazones* trying to share in it who illustrate its effect, and *Knights* gives us a succession of *agones* culminating in Paphlagon's defeat, followed by the revelation of the restored Demos, *Wasps* develops three ideas in succession (Philocleon's sickness, his "cure" through the private court, and finally his introduction into "good" society), followed by a much briefer illustration of the results. Many see the play as falling into a "diptych" form, with its satire of the law courts rather unrelated to the more farcical comedy of the attempts to introduction old Philocleon to "good society."[1] I shall suggest that the play is in fact more unified than many will grant and unified precisely by themes of spectatorship and performance.

The *Wasps* begins in a deceptively easy fashion: two slave comedians, Sosias and Xanthias, warm up the audience while bantering with each other about falling asleep on duty.[2] One drops a hint about the "monster" (4) they are guarding, but Aristophanes wants to introduce his theme gradually. The conversation turns quite naturally to dreams. Each wants to tell the other his dream and have it interpreted. Xanthias's dream turns out to be a standard joke about Cleonymus, who threw away his shield,[3] but Sosias's dream, he announces, is much more significant, dealing with the city's whole "ship of state" (29). It takes us once more, as *Acharnians* and *Knights* both do, to the assembly on the Pnyx, only here the citizen sheep are assembled to be harangued by a whale (clearly Cleon). The joke is obvious, but the purpose is not. After Xanthias "interprets" this dream, Sosias dismisses the whole subject by labeling dream interpretation as "two-obol work" (52).[4]

Then, as if he had just noticed their presence, Xanthias announces he will "explain the plot to the audience" (κατείπω τοῖς θεαταῖς τὸν λόγον, 54), but this metatheatrical explicitness is first the prelude to the disparagement of other kinds of comedy. Their play will be neither too grand nor too cheap[5]—no slaves throwing goodies to the audience, no mythological parody, and above all, no abuse of Euripides (55–60). This last promise is particularly interesting in light of the fact that one of the *Wasps*' competitors was a play entitled *Proagon*, in which mockery of Euripides was prominent, perhaps central—and the play seems to have been written by Aristophanes! (See Appendix I to this chapter.) Xanthias closes this section, though, with another reassurance that this is a story with a point (γνώμη) and neither too intellectual nor too slapstick:

> ἀλλ᾽ ἔστιν ἡμῖν λογίδιον γνώμην ἔχον,
> ὑμῶν μὲν αὐτῶν οὐχὶ δεξιώτερον,
> κωμῳδίας δὲ φορτικῆς σοφώτερον.   (64–66)

But our little story has wit:
it's not cleverer than you are,
but it is smarter than the average comedy.

He now embarks on the plot exposition, announcing that they are guarding the father of their master, who suffers from a dread disease—and then challenges the audience to guess what it is (ἐπεὶ τοπάζετε, 73). The ensuing sequence offers a marvelous imitation of improvisation in the theater. Sosias reports several guesses from the audience in response to this challenge, all of which prove to be wrong, of course.[6] MacDowell (*ad loc.*) has offered the splendid suggestion that Sosias walks along the front row of seats around the orchestra while doing so, pretending to catch the comments of those seated nearby.[7] The result is a lively sense of improvisation, which more than compensates for Xanthias's lengthy exposition (83–135), when he finally settles down to it.

This exposition lays out the basic conflict between father and son. The father's disease is a rabid desire to serve as a juror in the law courts. His physical symptoms include sleeplessness, a hand cramped up as if constantly holding a voting pebble (94–95), and even a serious misplacement of his erotic impulses. When he sees the typical graffito, "Demos is beautiful" (Δῆμον καλόν, 98), the old man scribbles up beside it, "The voting funnel is beautiful" (κημὸς καλός, 99).[8] There is probably more than one level to this rhyming pun. Certainly it is proof of comic dementia to prefer this part of the voting apparatus in the court to a beautiful young man.[9] Why does Aristophanes cite this particular young man? No doubt he was reasonably well known, but I would suggest he is chosen for his name rather than his outstanding attractions.[10] His name of course is the same as that of the master in *Knights*, the sovereign in the democracy, the people themselves. Moreover, Socrates employs the same pun on the name of this young man in Plato's *Gorgias* (481de), when he compares Callicles' behavior toward the people in the assembly to his behavior toward Demos, son of Pyrilampes. This suggests that the joke was already a familiar one. Philocleon, as the play will illustrate, has confused the instruments of the democracy with the democracy itself and therefore adores the process of serving in the law courts, not the rule by the people which the law courts are intended to embody.

The son's previous attempts to cure his father (persuasion, ritual bathing, Corybantic rites, even incubation at the shrine of Aesclepius on Aegina) are detailed. Nothing has worked, so now the household is relying simply on physical restraints, including nets. The setup for the physical comedy to ensue is now complete. Only at this point do we the audience learn the significant names of this father and son: they are Philocleon ("Lover of Cleon") and Bdelycleon ("Hater of Cleon"), the embodiments of the partisanship created by the divisive demagogue, Cleon.[11]

The scene that develops now is one of the finest examples of physical comedy in the ancient theater. Its underlying mechanism is purely Bergsonian: in his desperation to get to the law courts Philocleon tries anything to escape from the house. First he tries to climb out a chimney and, when detected, claims to be smoke.[12] Then in a superb visual parody of Odysseus's escape from the Cyclops he clings to the underbelly of a donkey being sent to market—but his son is sharper than Polyphemus and catches him.[13] Finally he tries to crawl out from under the roof tiles.

With his father temporarily checked, Bdelycleon's worries now turn to preparation for the entrance of the chorus of the old man's fellow jurors, whose appearance to collect old Philocleon and take him along to the day's cases is imminently expected. Though his slaves claim to be ready to drive them off with stones, Bdelycleon warns against that, describing them as a swarm of wasps only likely to be enraged, not dispersed, by such treatment.

The arrival of the chorus bears out this prediction, for though they move with the comically slow gait of the elderly,[14] their tempers are as fierce as Bdelycleon has said. In fact, egged on by Cleon, they are eagerly anticipating the conviction of Laches today (240ff.). Note the reason they are so eager to convict: Laches is said to have lots of money (241), which the state will take through either fines or outright confiscation on his conviction. Here is an echo of Demos' theory of governance in *Knights* (1126–1130), still being practiced under Cleon's guidance: fattening up the leaders of the democracy and then squeezing their ill-gotten wealth out of them to support the citizens through jury pay and other benefits.

The emphasis on physical comedy includes interplay between the old men of the chorus and young boys leading them. In the fiction of the play, it is still so early that the old men need lamps to see their way, which their young sons carry for them. Fussing over the lamps (reminiscent of Strepsiades' complaints in the opening of *Clouds*) and worries over how the meagre jury pay can put enough food on the table establish the theme of generational conflict for the chorus, paralleling what we have already seen between Philocleon and Bdelycleon.[15] These quarrels could be pathetic, for as MacDowell points out,[16] even in wartime inflation men who could not afford to buy figs for their children were very poor indeed, but the boys' extravagant laments quoting Euripides' *Theseus* (312, 314 = Eur. frr. 385–386) plus an irrelevant bit of Pindar (308 = Pind. fr. 189) shifts the tone to bathos.

Though he fails to respond to the chorus's first song, Philocleon now pops his head out of a window in the *skene* and sings that he is unable to sing under the circumstances (318–319)! The joke is of course a metatheatrical one, calling attention to the poetic form of comedy.[17] His fellow jurors encourage him in his attempts to escape, recalling at the same time their past military exploits together to encourage. Philocleon then gnaws through the net covering the window and begins to descend on rope.

Bdelycleon, sleeping with Xanthias in front of the doorway, is at last aroused by the noise that "encircles" him (395), and, while Xanthias climbs up the exterior of the house and flails at Philocleon with the harvest wreath from the door, Bdelycleon ascends inside the house and begins to pull up on the rope.[18] There is considerable scope for physical comedy here, demonstrating among other things that the actor playing Philocleon must have been something of an acrobat. As the old man is finally hauled back in, he appeals to his fellow jurors for their assistance.

The choristers now remove their cloaks and in the process reveal themselves to be equipped with wasp stings.[19] The boys who accompanied their entrance carry away the cloaks and are also ordered to report this outrage against the jurors to Cleon (409). One wonders if Aristophanes is toying with audience expectation here: those spectators who attended the proagon would know that Cleon does not appear *in propria persona* in the play, but the public at large might be tempted to hope for yet another caricature such as we have already seen in *Knights* (and probably in *Babylonians* as well). Aristophanes will eventually fulfill that hope with a surprising twist.

The chorus attempts to storm the stage,[20] but with the help of sticks and smoke pots Bdelycleon and his slaves fend off the attack. The disappointed Philocleon offers one very interesting observation: he claims that if the chorus had been "drinking the melodies of Philocles" (462), a tragedian known for the bitterness of his verse, they would have put up a much better fight. The joke is typically two-edged, making fun of a tragedian's style, but also anticipating the view (fully expounded in *Frogs*) that dramatic poetry is not just aesthetically pleasing but a direct instigator of action.

Bdelycleon now tries to reason with the chorus, but to no avail. They accuse him of scheming to set up a tyranny, a powerful charge in democratic Athens. Bdelycleon's mocking response is telling:

ὡς ἅπανθ᾽ ὑμῖν τυραννίς ἐστι καὶ ξυνωμόται,
ἤν τε μεῖζον ἤν τ᾽ ἔλαττον πρᾶγμά τις κατηγορῇ.
ἧς ἐγὼ οὐκ ἤκουσα τοὔνομ᾽ οὐδὲ πεντήκοντ᾽ ἐτῶν·
νῦν δὲ πολλῷ τοῦ ταρίχους ἐστὶν ἀξιωτέρα,
ὥστε καὶ δὴ τοὔνομ᾽ αὐτῆς ἐν ἀγορᾷ κυλίνδεται.   (488–492)

Everything with you is "tyranny" and "conspirators,"
whether somebody criticizes something big *or* small!
I haven't heard the word "tyranny" for fifty years,
but now it's commoner than salt fish,
so that in the marketplace this word is on a roll.

The last word here, κυλίνδεται, is particularly interesting: it is the root of the words used for the operations of the *ekkyklema*,[21] the tragic stage device Aristophanes loves to satirize. Could Aristophanes be suggesting here that all this talk of tyranny at Athens is, if not inspired directly by the discourse of the stage (comic or tragic), at least as insubstantial as theatrical plots? Bdelycleon goes on to make the point that all of this talk of tyranny must be gratifying some public desire (503), or it could not circulate so widely.

This theme of gratification forms an important transition in the argument. After Bdelycleon decries the public taste for accusations of tyranny, Philocleon insists the charges are deserved in his son's case because the latter is trying to deprive him of the pleasure (ἥδιον, 510) of judging lawsuits. Bdely-cleon replies that his father has gotten used to such gratifications (ἥδεσθαι, 512), but he now proposes to teach (ἀναδιδάξειν, 514) his father the errors of his ways, charging that his father has in fact been enslaved by the jury sys-tem he thinks is sustaining him. Bdelycleon accepts the challenge (as does the chorus), which sets up the *agon* of the comedy.

Though framed more subtly than in *Acharnians* or *Knights*, the charge here against the demos is very similar. They become titillated spectators of a drama orchestrated by the corrupt political leaders of Athens. They have allowed the pleasures of spectatorship (and its modest financial rewards) to delude them, chaining them to their miserable lives on the jury benches when they could be living as free men. The charge that jury service enslaves is a shocking one in a society where slavery existed, where in fact participation in such activities of the democracy as jury service was considered an essen-tial marker of the status of free man. Bdelycleon, like the Sausage-seller before him, undertakes the reeducation of the citizens away from their couch potato existence in law courts—but first he challenges his father to instruct him and the chorus (δίδαξον ἡμᾶς, 519)—and by extension the whole theater[22]—in the benefits of the present system.

By getting his father to agree to this challenge, Bdelycleon has in effect already won the argument, for he has enticed his father out of his role as spectatorial consumer and into the competition as a performer. Moreover, this is a performance that Bdelycleon will now critique—and on which he will take notes. A silent extra playing a slave has brought writing materials out of the house for Bdelycleon. From the verb forms used when notes are made on Philocleon's arguments, I think it slightly more probable that the slave remains and takes notes for Bdelycleon than that he takes notes for him-self.[23] MacDowell thinks that Bdelycleon sits on the steps leading up to the stage during Philocleon's speech; if so, the slave sits beside him. Now these notes have no later function in the play: nothing suggests that Bdelycleon reads from them while delivering his own speech. Apart from the function of marking divisions within Philocleon's speech, why is Bdelycleon taking notes? The stage picture bears an interesting resemblance to a well-known scene on a chous from Anavyssos (*ARV*[2] 1215.1), very close in time to *Wasps*,[24] portray-ing an older and a younger man watching a comic performer on a low stage. The scene on the vase has been variously interpreted, but one possibility is as poet and *chorodidaskalos* or *chorodidaskalos* and attendant, watching a rehearsal for a performance, since the temporary chairs on which the two spectators sit are unlike anything one would expect for audience accommodations at a regular performance. Bdelycleon and his note-taker then may well offer a strong visual association with dramatic rehearsals.[25]

Philocleon's encomium of the pleasures of the juror's life divides into five sections, structured somewhat chronologically. First he describes how defendants are already waiting at the court when he arrives and attempt to gain his sympathy even before the trial begins (548–558). Then he describes the general run of defendants' performances, ranging from tragic descriptions of poverty and misery (564–565) to attempts at comedy (note 567: "so that I'll laugh and let go of my anger," ἵν' ἐγὼ γελάσω καὶ τὸν θυμὸν καταθῶμαι); then, if this fails, back to appeals for pity when the accused brings out his sons and daughters to plead for him (568ff.).[26] He concludes with the triumphant rhetorical question: "isn't this a great power and mockery of wealth?" (ἆρ' οὐ μεγάλη τοῦτ' ἔστ' ἀρχὴ καὶ τοῦ πλούτου καταχήνη; 575).

The term καταχήνη (mockery) is of particular interest here. Philocleon sees the jury system not just as political power in the abstract (μεγάλη . . . ἀρχή) but as a source of emotional gratification, as Schadenfreude, in fact. This emotional gratification is what Bdelycleon finds worthy of noting down from this section of his father's speech (576), and it again reminds us of the Old Oligarch's notions of the function of comedy in a democratic society.[27] Comedy, like the courts, provide the populace with a satisfying sense of superiority over those otherwise more materially advantaged in the society. The comic poet Lysippus even produced a play called Καταχῆναι in 409 B.C.[28] Bdelycleon does not challenge his father on this point directly but simply asks him what specific benefits the jurors derive from their supposed rule over Greece.

Philocleon's answer (and the third section of his speech) is a curious mixture of theatrical and voyeuristic pleasures. He first mentions the pleasures of looking at boys' genitals at their *dokimasia* or deme registration (δοκιμαζομένων αἰδοῖα πάρεστι θεᾶσθαι, 578).[29] Then he turns to theater and music:

κἂν Οἴαγρος εἰσέλθῃ φεύγων, οὐκ ἀποφεύγει πρὶν ἂν ἡμῖν
ἐκ τῆς Νιόβης εἴπῃ ῥῆσιν τὴν καλλίστην ἀπολέξας.
κἂν αὐλητής γε δίκην νικᾷ, ταύτης ἡμῖν ἐπίχειρα
ἐν φορβειᾷ τοῖσι δικασταῖς ἔξοδον ηὔλησ' ἀπιοῦσιν.   (579–582)

And if Oeagrus comes in as a defendant, he doesn't get off
until he picks out and performs the best speech in the *Niobe* for us.
And if an aulos-player wins his case, as our reward
he straps on his aulos and plays an exit tune for the jury.

Oeagrus is known only from this passage and is presumably a tragic actor rather than a poet. The assumption that he was recently involved in a case is plausible but not necessary. Nor do I think that the actor chose to quote the *Niobe* in his own defense.[30] The most straightforward reading of the passage suggests that the jury demand a performance from him as the price of acquitting him on the charge. At this period, tragedies were still given only a single performance at the dramatic festivals.[31] An actor might well be asked to reprise a famous speech as a party piece—but jurors of Philocleon's sort were not invited to those parties. Here the court is turned into a form of symposium, with Oeagrus put on the spot by his "hosts."[32] Philocleon's next example returns us unambiguously to public performance: when a flute-player (the kind of musician accompanying the performance of *Wasps* even now in progress) wins his case, he plays an exit tune ($\emph{ἔξοδος}$) for the departing jurors. A symposium does not need an exit tune, and the flute-player there would be female in any case.[33] The term $\emph{ἔξοδος}$ is clearly theatrical,[34] underscoring the equation between the jury in the law courts and the chorus of jurors in this production (who have a surprising $\emph{ἔξοδος}$ yet to perform!). The final pleasure Philocleon enumerates in this section is their power over heiresses (583), where the jury can disregard the wishes of the deceased about her marriage and grant her to any claimant who persuades them—and, as Philocleon triumphantly concludes, juries are the only government officials whose acts are not subject to review.

After a brief comment from Bdelycleon, protesting this treatment of heiresses, Philocleon offers as proof of his importance the political matters referred to the courts by the *boule* and the assembly and the fact that Cleon terrorizes everyone else but protects the juries. He concludes by illustrating the independence from his son's authority that his meager juryman's income provides—an income nonetheless important enough to earn him the assiduous attentions of his wife and daughter, who want the money from him. Philocleon even claims an explicit likeness to Zeus, in that the jurymen can make such an uproar in court that it sounds like thunder to passers-by. The chorus congratulates their fellow juryman, fully convinced by his speech, which has delighted them ($\emph{ἡδόμενος}$, 641). Philocleon's first venture as a performer rather than a spectator seems to have succeeded.

Bdelycleon begins by protesting that the task of curing the city of its addiction to the law courts is far above the stuff of comedy ($\emph{μείζονος ἢ 'πὶ τρυγῳδοῖς}$, 650), certainly an ironic touch in the midst of a comic performance. He then calls upon "father Zeus" but is interrupted by Philocleon. The text does not and cannot on its own make clear whether Bdelycleon is sincerely offering a prayer (presumably for his own success in the contest) or addressing his father, since the old man just claimed to be a Zeus in his own realm. Presumably the actor playing Bdelycleon made clear his intention by stance and gesture. What is clear and ultimately more important is that Philocleon certainly takes it as addressed to himself—and shows at once that this tactic is not about to persuade him. Bdelycleon cuts to the chase at once. His argument is purely economic. Reckon up, he says, the revenues of the empire, then compare with the fees paid the jurymen. Their "profit" from the empire is a tiny fraction of the whole—and less than what goes into the pockets of their supposed defenders. In historical actuality, Bdelycleon's figures for empire revenues may be questionable[35] but the conclusion he draws is not: if the intention of jury pay was to share the wealth, it was a miserable failure.

Philocleon seems shaken but not yet convinced, for he demands to know wherein his "slavery" consists. Bdelycleon's response is to follow the money and pursue the politics of envy.[36] First he demonstrates that the prosecutors and others always get paid, while the jurors are treated as "wage slaves" (note τὸν μισθὸν ἔχοντι, 712) and turned away empty-handed if they arrive late. He suggests that if the tributary states supported the Athenian poor directly (cutting out the jury system altogether), the result would be a vast increase in their standard of living.

The men of the chorus proclaim themselves persuaded (725), but Philocleon, after one expression of weakness (713–714) remains silent as his fellow jurymen appeal to him to join them. Apparently he is frozen to the spot: his silence is paratragic and appropriately Aeschylean for an old man.[37] When he does break his silence, his speech of lament parodies Admetus in the *Alcestis*, expressing his wish to be with his dead wife: Philocleon wants to be back in the law courts, which are now dead to him.[38] When Bdelycleon begs him to calm down, Philocleon says he will do anything—except give up judging.

Bdelycleon's solution for his father's dilemma is at once so brilliant and so familiar to anyone who knows anything of Aristophanes that we risk missing some of its implications. Bdelycleon promises to create a law court at home, so that Philocleon can continue judging without having to leave the house—and it has been Bdelycleon's goal from the beginning of the play to keep his father at home, out of public view.[39] In the language of recent American political discourse, Philocleon will become the crazy aunt in the cellar. At this point the second stage of Bdelycleon's plan (to wean his father from this behavior) has not yet been revealed. Instead, we are left to imagine that Bdelycleon will be happy so long as his father does not go out in public and disgrace him by his desperate obsession with judging. In a bizarre anticipation of cocooning, the civic function of judging will be confined to the *oikos*.

We have known from the beginning that Philocleon is a man with an obsession. Transferring the obsession to the private realm immediately generates Bergsonian comedy, as we watch him pursue the servants and even household pets with the zeal he once reserved for the purported enemies of the state. We should not lose sight of the fact that the ease with which Philocleon makes the move from public to private realm demonstrates how completely the emotional gratification of judging is all that matters to him. There is not now and apparently has never been any belief on his part that his jury duty served any real social purpose.

In his book *Anarchy, State, and Utopia*, the philosopher Robert Nozick postulated a fascinating construct he dubbed "the experience machine."[40] In more recent years we have begun the pursuit of such a device under the name of "virtual reality," for Nozick's experience machine would be designed to feed directly into a human being's nerve endings and thereby produce the complete sensory impression of any experience that a human being desired to have. Nozick devised the experience machine as a thought experiment to test the difference between feeling and doing, between experience and action. The vigor with which virtual reality is now being pursued suggests Nozick was somewhat naive to assume that the natural conclusion, having conceived the very idea of the experience machine, is to realize one would not use it. On a less lofty plane, various science fiction writers had already imagined the experience machine, both as a means for allowing individuals to have experiences that are immoral or illegal in everyday life and as a punishment for those who need to be "reeducated."[41] The experience machine therefore raises both ethical and ontological questions.

I submit, however, that some twenty-four centuries earlier Aristophanes had already invented the experience machine: it is the law court Bdelycleon designs for his father to judge in. Moreover, I suggest that it was every bit as much a thought experiment in political philosophy for Aristophanes as Nozick's machine is for him. It allows Aristophanes to explore the consequences of detaching the profoundly emotional and theatrical experience of acting as a juror in the law courts from any practical consequence. Philocleon can have all the pleasures he associates with the experience of the actual law courts without either embarrassing his son or wreaking havoc in the state (although the latter theme is surprisingly muted by this point). What is striking in the Aristophanic experiment, in this paralleling Nozick's, is that Aristophanes is not content to leave Philocleon inside the experience machine. Instead his son reprograms the machine in order to cure his father of his mania for judging. The results, however, prove far from what the son expects them to be.

We anticipate, however. First Bdelycleon must build his private law court, in negotiation with his father. He first shows that judging at home will be superior in comfort to the public version: Philocleon can work in the sun when it is pleasant, by the fire if it snows, and inside if it rains (771ff.). He can begin at noon if he likes, eat while the speeches are going on, never miss his pay, and even relieve himself in a handy urinal—which will function as the water clock to regulate the length of speeches (cf. 856)! The comic by-play over the various furnishings of the private court keeps the audience well entertained as the stage setting is changed.

When everything is ready for the court session to begin, Bdelycleon offers a prayer that foreshadows the next theme, the transformation of Philo-cleon's disposition (874ff.). The chorus joins in this prayer for the new political order[42] and praises Bdelycleon for his love of the demos (888–889). This latter phrase should alert us to the ambiguities of Bdelycleon's role in this play. He has become one of the demagogues himself by creating and soon manipulat-ing this private court. Old Philocleon may be better cared for, but he will be just as deluded in his new court as he was in the old one.

The structure of the scene has all the hallmarks of a play-within-a-play,[43] and Bdelycleon is the obvious candidate for director. Before we simply iden-tify him with Aristophanes, however, we need to observe him in action. At the same time, the trial is also a dogfight. This element of the fantasy con-nects the scene to the traditions of animal comedy, but by employing domes-tic and familiar animals it also enacts the trivialization and domestication of justice that the demagogues have brought about in Athens' courts (similar to the effect of staging the agon of the Logoi in *Clouds* as a cockfight: see Ap-pendix II). Bdelycleon as presiding magistrate in this new court calls for trial of the dog Labes on the charge of stealing a cheese. The prosecutor is "Dog of Cydathenaeum" (Κύων Κυδαθηναιεύς, 895), a clear send-up of Cleon, while the unfortunate Labes ("Grabber") stands for the contemporary gen-eral Laches, accused of embezzlement.[44] The historical actualities behind this satire, however, are of less interest that its dramatic form. Aristophanes has previously travestied Cleon as a household slave and now puts him on stage as a greedy dog, both brilliant literalizations of metaphors Cleon himself had employed to express his devotion to the people of Athens.[45] The language used points the comparison between theater and law court: Bdelycleon calls on Dog to take the platform and begin his speech, using the same verb as for "take the stage" (ἀναβάς, 905).[46] No stage property for the speaker's platform has been mentioned in the process of constructing the private law court: apparently it simply means here "take center stage." As his prosecutorial speech shows, Dog's complaint against Labes is not so much the theft as the fact that Labes failed to share the illicit proceeds with him. Philocleon, however, ignores these details and is ready to convict before he has even heard the defense speech.

Bdelycleon pleads with his father at least to listen to the other side, but the unfortunate Labes is so stricken by the ferocity of Dog's assault that he cannot speak, and so Bdelycleon must himself undertake the defense. The silence of Labes (for which the precedent is cited of the breakdown at his trial of Thucydides, son of Melesias) may make a joke out of a stage necessity[47] and certainly allows Bdelycleon to play a larger role in his father's cure.

His defense speech is a rich parody of the genre, compounded of praise of Labes' past service, testimony from a kitchen cheese grater, attacks on Dog, and extravagant appeals for sympathy, including bringing Labes' puppies on stage to plead for their father (975–978).[48] Philocleon displays signs of weakening in the face of this onslaught (973–974) and cries out for Bdelycleon and the puppies to step down:[49]

> {Φι.} κατάβα, κατάβα, κατάβα, κατάβα.
> {Βδ.}   καταβήσομαι.
> καίτοι τὸ "κατάβα" τοῦτο πολλοὺς δὴ πάνυ
> ἐξηπάτηκεν. ἀτὰρ ὅμως καταβήσομαι.   (979–981)

> Phil. Step down, step down, step down, step down!
> Bdel.   I will—
> even though that "step down" has tricked so many
> before—but still, I'll step down.

This exchange is extremely interesting in terms of performance dynamics. It shows that the rowdy Athenian juries were quite capable of shouting to a speaker to sit down when they had had enough.[50] It suggests also, however, that the juries might well play with an unfortunate defendant. The cry is open to two interpretations: either "We are convinced: you need not say any more," or "Sit down: nothing you can say will persuade us." The use of the active ἐξηπάτηκεν suggests, however, that the confusion is not the result of the speaker's failure to read the mood of the jury correctly but a deliberate deception on the part of the jurors. If so, it shows a rare burst of resistance from the jury, who are normally the objects of the deceptions of the speakers.

Bdelycleon does step down and thereby out of his formal role as advocate for the defense. He nonetheless continues to attempt to persuade his father to acquit Labes. The old man has been crying, moved against his will by these pleas, although he blames his tears on the hot soup he has been drinking (982–984). I think the audience is meant to imagine that he continues to be blinded by his tears even while he declares his intention to vote for condemnation. Bdelycleon takes advantage of his father's state, leading him first not to the voting urn for condemnation (the usual position) but by a circuitous route to the voting urn for acquittal. He plays on the ambiguity of the word πρότερος and tells Philocleon that this is indeed the first urn—that he has come to. Bdelycleon then informs the audience in an aside what should already be clear from the stage business: Philocleon has been deceived (ἐξηπάτηται, 992) and thereby induced to vote for acquittal rather than condemnation.

When Bdelycleon declares the result of the voting and Labes' consequent acquittal, Philocleon faints from the shock. Even when he revives, he remains conscience-stricken.[51] Interestingly, he makes no accusations against his son: even as he begs the gods to forgive him, he accepts responsibility for his own actions. Bdelycleon holds out the vision of a new life of parties and entertainments (ἐπὶ θεωρίαν, 1005). He assures his father that now he will no longer be deceived by Hyperbolus (ἐξαπατῶν Ὑπέρβολος, 1007)—which rings rather false immediately after the old man has been deceived by his son. Philocleon now disconsolately follows his son off, leaving the chorus to deliver the parabasis.

It seems reasonable to pause here as well and consider the structure and development of the play up until this point. Bdelycleon has accomplished his goal of curing his father of a mania for judging. If it is not entirely clear why one vote for acquittal has destroyed forever Philocleon's pleasure in his old way of life, the audience is not likely to quibble over that point in the rush of comic events. Less certain is how clearly they are meant to see that Bdelycleon has behaved in ways no better than Cleon, Hyperbolus, and the other demagogues he affects to despise. He has stage-managed the whole trial. While he has indulged his father in recreating the atmosphere of the law court and even "improving" it with certain creature comforts, he has deprived his father of the fundamental pleasure of condemning the defendant—even when the defendant was just a dog.

It is tempting but I think quite unjustified to assume, based on Aristophanes' well-known antipathy for Cleon personally, that Bdelycleon in this play represents the poet's point of view: the enemy of my enemy may be my friend, but that does not make him *me*. Bdelycleon has indeed been fighting the good fight up until this point to detach his father from his old position as an open-mouthed consumer of the illusions that Cleon and his ilk create. Like the Sausage-seller in *Knights*, Bdelycleon has done this by becoming a better purveyor of deceptions than his (here offstage) rival Cleon. Unlike the Sausage-seller, however, Bdelycleon does not now renounce his position as a creator of illusions. Instead, as we shall see following the parabasis, he tries to script a new role for his father to perform—but with much less success than he has enjoyed heretofore.[52]

The parabasis represents Aristophanes' first opportunity to address the Athenians in this form since the (to him) shocking failure of the *Clouds* the year before. The first words are flattering (he exaggerates and calls the audience "countless myriads"[53]) but soon acquire an edge. He urges them not to leave his good advice unheeded (1011), as stupid spectators do (1013). This negative example forms the transition to his direct criticism of the audience ("Now our poet wants to blame the audience . . ." μέμψασθαι γὰρ τοῖσι θεαταῖς ὁ ποιητὴς νῦν ἐπιθυμεῖ, 1016) for their failure to appreciate his previous play. It is interesting that he criticizes the audience as a whole and not just the judges, for the ranking of plays was determined by five randomly selected ballots from ten judges, and so it would seem to be open to the poet to claim that their judgment was unrepresentative of the audience as a whole.[54] This implies, despite the various explicit appeals to the judges for victory, that the judges were seen to be influenced by popular opinion as expressed in the theater.[55]

The chorus then expatiates on Aristophanes' career and his selfless devotion to comedy. Elements of this account of his career remain controversial, but the details need not occupy us for long here.[56] He insists that he has not prostituted his muse in settling private scores (1025–1028) but resolutely attacked the snaggle-toothed monster of the age, Cleon. He again expresses disappointment over the failure of the *Clouds* but compares himself to a racing chariot driver who was wrecked trying to overtake his rivals. The chorus concludes with a *pnigos* urging the audience to accept poets (such as Aristophanes) who purvey new ideas.

In the epirrhematic syzygy the choristers return to their characters as wasps, but they do so with reminisces of their past exploits both as choristers and as soldiers (1060–1061).[57] The specific mention of their past service as choristers helps frame their direct address to the audience on the subject of their unusual, only partially theriomorphic costumes:

εἴ τις ὑμῶν, ὦ θεαταί, τὴν ἐμὴν ἰδὼν φύσιν
εἶτα θαυμάζει μ' ὁρῶν μέσον διεσφηκωμένον,

ἥτις ἡμῶν ἐστιν ἡ 'πίνοια τῆς ἐγκεντρίδος,
ῥᾳδίως ἐγὼ διδάξω, κἂν ἄμουσος ᾖ τὸ πρίν.   (1071–1074)

If any of you, spectators, is amazed to see
what I look like, with my wasp waist,
and wonders what the idea of our sting is,
I will easily clue him in, even if he was ignorant before.

The verb διδάξω here carries theatrical associations beyond the simple meaning of "instruct." The chorus rehearse the audience in their role as recipients
of the theatrical event and cement the association by the Euripidean tag at the
end of line 1074. The full quotation is: ποιητὴν δ' ἄρα *Ἔρως* διδάσκει, κἂν
ἄμουσος ᾖ τὸ πρίν ("Love indeed teaches the poet, even if he was ignorant
before," *Stheneboea* fr. 663). Love teaches the poet—who in turn teaches his
audience. The dramatic poet teaches his audience not only in the grand moral
sense (agreed upon by Euripides and Aeschylus alike in the *Frogs*) but in the
purely performative sense: he shows his audience how to respond.

The response that Aristophanes now teaches his audience is a more nuanced one than we have had heretofore. The ferocity of the wasp chorus has
been a negative quality until now, a force simply to be placated or turned aside
by Bdelycleon's manoeuverings. Now we see this fierceness in a new light,
as the authentic (and autochthonous, 1076) Athenian character. The chorus
makes clear that they had no interest in rhetorical performance or legal accusations when they were young (1095, 1096) but now pursue the juror's life as
a continuation of their previous military service. The message then is deeply
mixed: though they reject the kinds of performance they constantly witness
in the courts (speeches and accusations), they now seem less persuaded than
they were that Philocleon—or they themselves—should give up their wasp-
like spectatorial role in this interactive legal drama.

In an important article (now subsumed into his book),[58] A. M. Bowie
has addressed the problem of how the satire of the Athenian law courts before
the parabasis of the *Wasps* relates to the scenes following it, where Philocleon
undergoes a rejuvenation into a particularly rowdy young man. He analyzes
the first part of the play as a series of three *agones* (Philocleon's individual attempts to escape, the combined effort with his fellow jurymen, and the whole
trial sequence) in which Philocleon fails each time. In Bowie's scheme the
three contests also correspond to three stages of Philocleon's life: as ephebe,
as adult hoplite warrior, and as old juror. Like various elements of coming of
age rituals in Greece, Philocleon's failures strip him of the key elements of his

existing identity and ready him for a new one. That new identity is a return to the ephebic stage of life, one marked by theft, youthful exuberance, and disorder. Bowie seems somewhat doubtful, however, as to whether the finale of the play points to a successful reintegration of Philocleon into society or simply a comic return to the beginning.[59]

Bowie offers an important insight into one deep structure of the play. I believe the ephebic elements point to a new and remarkable interpretation of the ending of the play in particular. The ephebic resonances work, I suggest, in concert with the performative and metatheatrical elements we have already been considering. Ritual, like theater, is performative. Some, regarding ritual as somehow deeper, truer, or more significant than theater, may find the interpretation of the play as a "reversed ephebeia" fully satisfying. I believe, however, that we can say more. Bowie focuses on Philocleon as one who fails to act successfully, fails various tests of performance. This seems to neglect the very important element of Philocleon as spectator: the whole of the first part of the play is obsessed with extracting Philocleon from his role as spectator in the law courts in favor of action. Let us follow this reversal and its performative associations through the remainder of the play.

Philocleon and his son return to the stage arguing. Bdelycleon is attempting to persuade his father to give up his old, worn, homespun cloak (τρίβων', 1131) in favor of a warm and stylish new Persian mantle (καυνάκην, 1137). Now, while changing clothes may have ritual and even ephebic associations,[60] on stage it has even more obvious theatrical associations. Bdelycleon wants his father to adopt a new role: therefore he must costume the old man in a new way. Just as Dicaeopolis must put on Telephus's tragic rags in order to play his new part, so too must Philocleon. It is also profoundly comic: only comedy regularly shows us the kind of instability of identity associated with changing clothes on stage (compare the Old Relative in *Thesmophoriazusae* and all the women in *Ecclesiazusae*), and when it happens in tragedy, as in Euripides' *Bacchae*, it is profoundly unsettling.[61]

It certainly unsettles Philocleon, but after a number of puns and jokes about the cloak (including the idea that it will be so hot it will bake him like an oven), he finally puts it on. Then comes a struggle over whether to put on "Spartan" shoes. Despite the old man's protests that one of his toes is "very anti-Spartan" (1165),[62] Bdelycleon wins this argument too, and his new costume is complete.

Costume of course is not enough: Philocleon must now be taught how to behave in his new clothes. First comes a lesson in walking: Bdelycleon demonstrates (note the deictic ὡδί, 1169). Then Philocleon tries to imitate and asks his son to judge his σχῆμα (1170), meaning both his pose and movement.[63] In a "feed" line, he asks his son which rich man he resembles; Bdelycleon says he looks like a man with a boil.[64] Next come lessons in storytelling and polite conversation, but here too Philocleon's coarse myths about Lamia and animal fables are far below his son's standards.[65]

A fairly clear class distinction is being drawn in these performance lessons.[66] It may be pressing character probability in Aristophanes a bit far to say so, but either Bdelycleon is quite ignorant of his father's life (not improbable in the young) or he is deliberately trying to fabricate a higher class past life for Philocleon to talk about in his new surroundings. A key exchange is the following:

{Φι.} ποίους τινὰς δὲ χρὴ λέγειν;
{Βδ.}   μεγαλοπρεπεῖς·
ὡς ξυνεθεώρεις Ἀνδροκλεῖ καὶ Κλεισθένει.
{Φι.} ἐγὼ δὲ τεθεώρηκα πώποτ᾽ οὐδαμοῖ,
πλὴν ἐς Πάρον, καὶ ταῦτα δύ᾽ ὀβολὼ φέρων.   (1186–1189)

Phil. What sort of stories are the right ones to tell?
Bdel.   Grand ones:
how you went on an embassy with Androcles and Cleisthenes.
Phil. I *never* went on an embassy—
except once to Paros, and then I got two obols.

Bdelycleon wants his father to talk about past ambassadorial service, but on Philocleon's only voyages abroad he was a member of the crew: he earned two obols for rowing, instead of a more lordly ambassadorial per diem.[67]

Bdelycleon then tries to rehearse his father in proper behavior at a symposium. Once again some of the comedy is physical: the old man does not know how to recline "elegantly" (εὐσχημόνως, 1210; cf. 1170) and makes fun of his son miming eating and drinking (1218). Most curious, though, is the guest list for this imaginary banquet, which includes Cleon, Phanus, Theorus, and other political leaders;[68] in fact, Bdelycleon now takes on the part of Cleon himself: καὶ δὴ γάρ εἰμ᾽ ἐγὼ Κλέων (1224)! It seems very odd that Bdelycleon, who is defined by his hatred of Cleon, should now so calmly imagine his father and himself dining in his company. Again, character consistency is not a notable Aristophanic virtue, but this seems a fairly egregious violation. MacDowell (*ad* 1220) suggests three possible explanations: that the names are setups for the singing of *skolia* to follow, that Cleon is in fact rich enough to belong in such company,[69] and finally that Cleon is no longer a subject of dispute between father and son now that the old man has given up judging.

The first two explanations are plausible, but the third does not go far enough. Aristophanes expects his audience to be clever enough to see that the problems of the Athenian jury system are not simply solved by moving from the position of spectator to that of performer, if nothing else in the system changes. While Lincoln's dictum, "As I would not be a slave, so I would not be a master," would not have struck Aristophanes as sound social policy, he realizes that the problem of Philocleon's "slavery" within the jury system is not solved simply by making him one of the performers. His response, however, is to critique the kinds of performance the would-be leaders of Athenian society give—and now in their own elite gathering, the symposium.

The symposium is a traditional venue of poetic performance, and one linked in interesting ways to the theater.[70] While we have seen in *Knights* 529–530 how songs from the theater moved onto the symposium circuit, there were also songs native to this performance venue, the *skolia*.[71] The traditional means of singing them was for each performer to offer a line in turn.[72] When Bdelycleon attempts to teach his father this technique, however, Philocleon subverts the process by improvising verses to insult the previous singer. The first, since Bdelycleon begins by pretending to be Cleon, is a direct attack on Cleon as a thief and rogue (1226–1227), and Bdelycleon reacts with outrage. The next two attempts are subtler critiques which Bdelycleon allows to pass by, but the audience surely enjoyed them.

This episode demonstrates a number of inversions. The effect of parodying songs as familiar as these famous *skolia* is hard to recapture. We must emphasize, however, that there must have been a considerable emotional affect to these performances in their original contexts: they were a part of what generated the good feelings and emotional bond of the symposia. To parody them is not then just to make a verbal joke of popular entertainment, the equivalent of Weird Al Yankovic reworking a Michael Jackson song. It is also an attack on that emotive bond.

A further inversion is also present in this episode. The theme of the reversal of the generations, explicitly developed later on when Philocleon carries off a flute girl, begins here. Bdelycleon is now playing the father, tutoring a son who is about to attend his first symposium. Class and age become relatively interchangeable here, but it was certainly far more often the elite young, rather than the elderly lower class, who would need tutoring to prepare for taking a part in the symposium. Philocleon expresses some doubts about the violence-inducing effects of drinking,[73] but Bdelycleon reassures him that he can escape having to pay for any misbehavior by telling the outraged victims a witty story (1258). Philocleon finally expresses a desire to learn this skill (1262), so reminiscent of Strepsiades' desire to learn sophistic logic and thereby escape his debts, and the two leave the stage for the party.[74]

The chorus now sings the second parabasis. Such parabases are never on a unified theme but may have more relevance to their surroundings than is commonly supposed. The first section of this one echoes an insult from the rehearsal symposium (Ἀμυνίας ὁ Σέλλου, 1267; cf. Αἰσχίνης ὁ Σέλλου, 1243) and makes fun of another member of the elite traveling as an ambassador (1271). The chorus thus ranges itself alongside Philocleon in its disdain for the self-indulgence of the elite. The parabasis closes by speaking, somewhat surprisingly,[75] in the first person for the poet. He refers to an attack Cleon made on him, and this must refer not to events following *Babylonians* but to some incident subsequent to the *Knights*.[76] The details remain obscure, but two points are worth noting. Aristophanes pointedly refers to an audience observing this all and laughing at Cleon's attack (ἐγέλων . . . θεώμενοι, 1287), while waiting to see if Aristophanes will say anything entertaining (1299). Aristophanes structures these lines to focus attention on the outrageous behavior of Cleon, but I think we can sense here his considerable discomfort at having once again been put on display by his enemy. Second, he expresses his pleasure at having played a trick on Cleon (1291). As MacDowell rightly insists, this must be a reference to the present play: Aristophanes perhaps promised not to attack again, and then produced the *Wasps*. Indeed, the likeliest explanation would be that Aristophanes promised not to represent Cleon on stage again, as he certainly had done in *Knights*. Instead, by putting Bdelycleon and Philocleon on stage, he dramatized the division that Cleon was fomenting in Athenian society.[77] The verb ἐξηπάτησεν (1291) underscores the theatricality of this deception: Cleon thought he had put an end to such plays, but Aristophanes found a way to stage the tragicomedy of Athens without the prince. Perhaps *Wasps* is his *Rosencrantz and Guildenstern*.

The arrival of Xanthias on stage as a running slave messenger heralds the return of Philocleon. His lively, exclamatory account tells us that Philocleon has behaved outrageously at the symposium, becoming thoroughly drunk, beating Xanthias, and insulting his fellow guests.[78] It is also clear that Bdelycleon's instructions on how to tell stories at parties have gone for nothing, for Philocleon's jokes are derided as rustic and his stories inept (ἀμαθέστατ', 1321) and inapposite.

Xanthias hastily vacates the stage to make way for Philocleon, who arrives with flute-girl in tow and apparently pursued by angry citizens, played by silent extras, whom he threatens with a lit torch. He has now become explicitly a young man, for one of his pursuers notes that his youth will not excuse this behavior ("even if you are very young," κεἰ σφόδρ' εἶ νεανίας, 1333). When threatened with a summons for his outrageous behavior, Philocleon derides his accusers as old-fashioned and declares his contempt for the jury system in this succinct curse: βάλλε κημούς ("Damn the voting urns!" 1339). A more drastic reversal is hard to imagine, especially if the audience recalls that he originally was given to writing erotic graffiti about the κημός (at line 99)!

Now he has a new erotic interest, the flute-girl he has carried off from the party. They have entered from the side, and Philocleon now seeks to draw her into the house. His speech of persuasion is a comic masterpiece of inversion, for he depicts himself as a young man breaking away from the parental authority of his "little son," Bdelycleon (1356). As Angus Crichton has suggested, Philocleon has become his own grandson.[79] Bdelycleon has been throughout the play a somewhat colorless and repressive character compared to Philocleon, but this emphatic reversal here gives added zest to their confrontation. Bdelycleon arrives to try to control his father, only to be greeted with insults. Philocleon even refuses to admit that he has stolen the flute-girl he has his hands on, insisting with joyful Aristophanic fantasy that she is in fact just a torch, a conceit developed with cheerfully obscene comments on her naked form. When Bdelycleon tries to take her away, however, Philocleon turns the tables on his son both verbally and physically. He first tells the story that his son taught him in preparation for the symposium (at 1190ff.) about an older man who was nonetheless victorious at the Olympic games; then he knocks his son down. Striking his adult son is startling even by Greek standards, but there is an added frisson in that Philocleon has portrayed himself as the son: he has become in effect another Pheidippides (cf. *Clouds* 1321ff.), a πατραλοίας beating his own father.[80] As Bdelycleon ruefully notes, his father has at least learned that part of his teaching thoroughly (ἐξέμαθες, 1387).

The flute-girl presumably escapes at this point, and the scene turns more and more to physical comedy. Several more accusers show up in turn, accompanied by witnesses, to summon Philocleon to answer for damages to persons and property. The reformed juror answers them with more stories (about Aesop, Sybaris, and poets of the past)—and more violence. Bdelycleon's teaching has gone radically wrong: his father has indeed remembered the kind of stories his son tried to instruct him in but with the typical extremism of the Aristophanic hero uses them as "magic words," as though they could protect him from any retribution for his drunken violence. Bdelycleon must finally drag his father into the house in the midst of telling another Aesopic story.

The chorus sings a final interlude, giving the actor playing Philocleon time to rest before his final, particularly athletic display, as MacDowell observes. It claims to envy Philocleon for learning the opposite of his old ways (ἀντιμαθών, 1453) and praises Bdelycleon for his "gentleness" (ἀγανῷ, 1467) and for "adorning" (κατακοσμῆσαι, 1473) his father with better activities. This is surely ironic. At this point the play seems to have gotten precisely nowhere: the play began with Philocleon imprisoned in the house, and at this point it threatens to end with the same state of affairs While MacDowell rightly observes that Philocleon's "reeducation" is not yet complete, it is difficult to be sanguine about the prospects for success.[81] The irony may not solely or primarily be at the expense of the chorus, however.[82] This is surely another false ending, comparable to the victory of Agoracritus in *Knights*. Philocleon has been freed from his slavery to jury service, but it is also obvious that his violent and drunken behavior is not a satisfactory ending to the play either. The key irony here lies in the word κατακοσμῆσαι, whose root is κόσμος, meaning both beauty and order. Philocleon must be brought into some kind of order for the play to achieve a satisfactory resolution.

In the final scene Philocleon, heralded again by Xanthias, reemerges from the house and challenges the tragic dancers of the present, represented by Carcinus and his sons, to a competition in which he intends to prove the superiority of the work of Thespis and Phrynichus. The older view is that these scenes have nothing to do with the rest of the play, but the recent studies of Vaio, MacCary, and Bowie[83] have all attempted in various ways to elucidate the connections. Each has offered important insights, but I will suggest that Bowie points the way toward an interpretation of the ending as a satisfying and unifying solution to the problem of ordering the tremendous energy of Philocleon.

Both Vaio and MacCary emphasize the Dionysiac qualities of the ending. Vaio emphasizes the connection of Philocleon's wine-inspired dancing with the symposiastic motifs earlier in the play[84] but also sees most clearly the metatheatrical fusion of Philocleon's dancing contest within the play with the Dionysiac competition the play itself is engaged in. MacCary pays particular attention to the meter of this dance competition, connecting it with the songs of the *ithyphalloi* who carried the phallus-pole in processions in honor of Dionysus.[85] The play's finale with its particular musical and dance form carries us back to the beginnings of Dionysiac drama through the person of Philocleon:

That the dramatic context for [Philocleon's] recognition and rebirth should be an assimilation in rhythm and dance of comedy to tragedy is significant; he is getting back to Dionysos, who is originally both comedy and tragedy.[86]

For MacCary this ending celebrates the raw Dionysiac power still present in Old Comedy but in his view sadly lacking in the New Comedy which would succeed it.

Yet to demonstrate the Dionysiac qualities of this ending is not enough. Why should this dancing contest end this particular play? If it merely celebrates Dionysus, could it not be tacked on to the end of any Old Comedy, like the Euripidean tag lines which end a number of plays?[87] It is Bowie's insight into the ephebic theme running through the play, coupled with John Winkler's brilliant hypothesis that the chorus of tragedy was made up of ephebes,[88] which points the way to the solution. Bowie's view of the play as a "reversed ephebeia" has already been alluded to. He points out the introduction of the ephebic theme in Philocleon's failed attempts to escape from the house at the beginning of the play, then interprets the old man's subsequent failures in debate with his son and in his attempt to convict Labes as further rite of passage tests, but framed in terms of the further life stages of adult hoplite warrior and then aged juror. His successive failures strip him of his previous identity, as rites of passage are intended to do, and leave him ready to be reintegrated into society under the guidance of his son Bdelycleon (another element of reversal, of course, since fathers would normally guides sons through these rites of passage).

Bdelycleon is incapable of stage-managing that reintegration, and it is here where the ephebic plot of the play is comically modified. Putting the old man into the costume of elite society is not enough, nor will he learn his lines properly in order to take part in the elite symposium. Freed from his old life, Philocleon overflows with riotous, youthful energy that expresses itself in antisocial violence and hubris. More than the authority of his "parent" Bdelycleon is required to discipline him. It requires the power of the institutions of Athens as a whole to draw Philocleon back into the social order.

Winkler starts from the notable fact that tragedy and comedy are the only competitive forms at the Dionysia that are not tribally based, and plausibly connects this with the organization of these contests in the late Peisistratid period and their possible reorganization under Cleisthenes. Just as Cleisthenes' reforms aimed at breaking up previous loyalties to small, usually geographically based groups within the state and substituting a new identification with the city as a whole, Winkler suggests that the choruses of tragedy, composed purely on ability and not on the tribal basis of the dithyrambic competitions, were meant to foster a new civic identity. More controversially, Winkler used the limited visual evidence for choristers in rehearsal or putting on their roles to suggest that they were young men (as opposed to the adult actors) and indeed were ephebes. This is not the place to rehearse again the spotty and difficult evidence for dating the introduction of the ephebeia in Athens.[89] The case for an organized ephebeia in the fifth century cannot be definitively proved on our present historical sources alone, and Winkler himself in the second version of his article seems to step back from the claim that all tragic choristers were ephebes. I suggest, however, that the ending of the *Wasps* provides corroboration for his original view that state sponsorship of the tragic contests in honor of Dionysus was closely linked to the ephebeia.

The ending of the *Wasps* ties together the ephebic and metatheatrical themes of the play in a solution to the problem of Philocleon. Indeed this ending unites Aristophanes' criticisms of present tragic decadence and political corruption even more effectively than the brilliant critiques in the *Acharnians*. Bdelycleon succeeds in freeing his father from his spectator's role in the judicial drama of Athens, but he does so through means just as corrupt as those employed by his hated opponent Cleon. Therefore, just as in the *Knights*, the solution cannot simply be to transfer the old man's loyalty to a new leader (i.e., his son). Nor can the solution be simply to make Philocleon himself into a performer in this corrupt drama. It is here that Bowie's observations on the play's celebration of the waspish character of Philocleon and his fellow jurors are particularly apposite.[90] Many critics have seemed bothered by the fact that Philocleon is so much more appealing a character, even in his penultimate violent and destructive phase, than his son, Bdelycleon, who "ought" to represent Aristophanes' views, since he is the antagonist of Cleon. Aristophanes' real loyalty is always to the demos. His plays attack low politicians and oligarchic aristocrats alike. His real love is for the misled and misused Philocleons of Athens.

Philocleon must be weaned from pure spectatorship and made into a performer, but into a democratic performer, that is, into a rejuvenated choral performer. He returns to the stage in the finale as the reincarnation of Thespis and Phrynichus. His entrance is heralded as a paratragic event by Xanthias:

νὴ τὸν Διόνυσον, ἄπορά γ' ἡμῖν πράγματα
δαίμων τις εἰσκεκύκληκεν εἰς τὴν οἰκίαν. (1474–1475)

By Dionysus, some god has rolled
impossible difficulties into our house.

The point, however, is not parody *of* tragedy, but fusion of tragic with comic performance. A divinity has used the tragic device of the *ekkyklema* to introduce (εἰσκεκύκληκεν) astonishing things into the house and into the play. The result is a rejuvenation of dramatic form as well as of the hero himself: Philocleon will use the dances of Thespis to prove that modern tragic performers are as out of date as Cronuses (1479–1480).[91]

Philocleon arrives on stage performing dance figures of the tragedian Phrynichus. While there has been some controversy over the identity of this Phrynichus, in an article most important for our understanding of the play's ending, E. K. Borthwick has demonstrated that this is the tragedian.[92] Reconstruction of dance figures is of course a somewhat speculative procedure, but Borthwick makes an excellent case for Philocleon to be performing a crouching bird dance figure as he proclaims "Phrynichus bends like a cock" (πτήσσει Φρύνιχος ὥς τις ἀλέκτωρ, 1490).[93] More importantly, he contends that Philocleon follows this figure with a leap up from the ground, a pair of movements familiar from the pyrrhic dance.[94] Winkler again has argued for the close connection of pyrrhic and tragic dance,[95] so this opening figure performed by Philocleon invokes both Phrynichus himself and the origins of tragedy. Athenaeus (14. 628de) preserves a fragment of Chamaileon (fr. 42), which tells us that the older form of tragic dancing was "elegant" (εὔσχημον) and "imitative of military movements" (τὰς ἐν τοῖς ὅπλοις κινήσεις ἀπομιμούμενον).[96] Philocleon's rejuvenation then is expressed in his ability, not just to dance vigorously, but to dance the figures associated with tragedy of bygone days (Phrynichus and Thespis) and those associated with military dance, including on Borthwick's hypothesis one particular to the pyrrhic dance.

Philocleon dares any contemporary tragic performers to come out and dance against him (1497ff.). The challenge is taken up by the tragedian Carcinus and sons, that is, by dancers (possibly child performers) representing them.[97] The family were all notable for their short stature, the subject of several of the jokes which greet their arrival. One line in particular, with which Philocleon greets the third son, has long been a puzzle:

τουτὶ τί ἦν τὸ προσέρπον; ὀξίς, ἢ φάλαγξ; (1509)

What's this thing crawling towards us? A scorpion or a spider?
(trans. Henderson)

Sommerstein and Henderson accept this reading (that of the codices, except R). The real puzzle here is the word ὀξίς, which means literally a vinegar cruet. Sommerstein suggests *ad loc.* that ὀξίς is an otherwise unattested name for a spiny crustacean, while Henderson (citing Iamblicus *Protrepticus* 21θ) thinks of a poisonous scorpion. Borthwick proposes to read the following:

τουτὶ τί ἦν τὸ προσέρπον; ὦτος ἢ σφάλαξ;

What's this thing crawling on? A owl or a mole?

The reading of ὦτος or owl seems to me to be supported by Philocleon's later reference to all the dancers as a flock of birds (1513). The "'peering *schema*' of the owl dance" is well attested for earlier tragedy, and Borthwick argues that the final son of Carcinus appears in this posture. Here then is another reference to tragic dance or possibly satyric dance, with perhaps another joke at the short stature and therefore owl-like movements of Carcinus's offspring.[98]

We are far from having a satisfactory reconstruction of the precise nature of the dance competition between Philocleon and his opponents. There seems to be general agreement that the competitors do not dance the full tragic dances but simply use striking elements of those dance figures.[99] It is clear, however, that Philocleon descends into the orchestra (καταβατέον . . . μοι, 1514) to compete and eventually leads the chorus off dancing:

ἀλλ' ἐξάγετ', εἴ τι φιλεῖτ', ὀρχούμενοι θύραζε
ἡμᾶς ταχύ· τοῦτο γὰρ οὐδείς πω πάρος δέδρακεν,
ὀρχούμενος ὅστις ἀπήλλαξεν χορὸν τρυγῳδῶν.   (1535–1537)

But lead us out quickly, if you please, dancing
to the exit; no one's *ever* done this before:
dancing and sending the comic chorus off.

The final claim sounds a little curious. As Zimmermann notes, it seems unlikely that actors had never before led the chorus out or that choristers had never made a dancing exit; he suggests the novelty consists in the nature of Philocleon's dancing.[100] Perhaps, however, the surprise is that the actor joins the dance; indeed, the fact that Philocleon is dancing at all clearly identifies him as a chorister.[101]

There is another meaning to Philocleon joining the chorus as well. At the beginning of the play, Philocleon had to be prevented by physical force from joining the chorus, because his doing so would contribute to their destructive work in the law courts. Now he joins them freely—which implies that they too have been redeemed.[102] Their waspish nature also will be turned to good effect by merging into the Dionysiac dance.

The pseudo-Aristotelian *Problemeta* preserves the saying of the physician Alcmaeon of Croton that the reason human beings die is that they cannot join the end to the beginning.[103] Comedy is immortal because it can. Philocleon's renewal as an ephebe is a movement not just backward but forward as well.[104] His dancing exit takes us back not just to the play's beginning but to the origins of drama, from which both comedy and tragedy alike will be renewed.[105]

Appendix I. *Proagon* and the Lenaea of 422 B.C.

A lost play entitled *Proagon* competed against *Wasps* and defeated it in the contest at the Lenaea. Its existence, and the little we know of it, offer us a rare opportunity to study how one comedy positioned itself against another in the competition. An exceedingly puzzling complicating factor is that the *Proagon* was apparently also a play by Aristophanes.

The Hypothesis to *Wasps* states:

ἐδιδάχθη ἐπὶ ἄρχοντος Ἀμεινίου διὰ Φιλωνίδου ἐν τῇ πθ′ ὀλυμπιάδι. δεύτερος ἦν εἰς Λήναια. καὶ ἐνίκα πρῶτος Φιλωνίδης Προάγωνι, Λεύκων Πρέσβεσι τρίτος.

It was produced in the archonship of Ameinias [422 B.C.] by Philonides in the 89th Olympiad. It was second, at the Lenaea. And Philonides won first with *Proagon*, Leucon third with *Ambassadors*.

The record is therefore quite clear that Philonides, not Aristophanes, won the contest with the *Proagon*. The difficulty is that later writers record fragments of a play of this title only for Aristophanes, and Philonides, though a poet himself, later produced plays for Aristophanes. Since the work of Gröbl on the hypotheses, it has generally been assumed that Aristophanes was the author of *Proagon* as well as *Wasps*.[106]

At first glance it seems very odd that one poet should compete with two plays at the same festival, but that may only be a modern viewpoint. We tend to think of a play as the poetry, the story, the text—that is, those things the author alone contributes. No play can be reduced to its text, however, and this is peculiarly true of Old Comedy. While it is indeed unlikely at this period that a tragic poet would compete with two trilogies at the same contest, that may demonstrate simply the extent to which tragedy has already become literature, has, that is, become just the poetry in this period. Comedy remains the *komos*, to whose success elements of production (dance, costume, and spectacle) are still vitally important. Against this background we may note that the producer was the official competitor for the play. Technically then, if Aristophanes did write both plays, he was not competing against himself but against Philonides.[107] Though its evidentiary weight for the fifth century may be small, we may also note here that in 288 B.C. plays of the poet Diodorus placed both second and third at the Lenaea.[108] Moreover, the archon decided to which producer he would grant a chorus, and there was nothing to prevent two producers from putting forward plays of the same playwright.

It must have been somewhat out of the ordinary, nonetheless, and one wonders why Aristophanes chose to enter two plays for the same festival, or indeed why he had two plays ready at the same time. Gröbl was the first to connect it with the failure of the *Clouds* at the City Dionysia of 423: he suggested Aristophanes wanted to double his chances of a first prize and with it vindication after a humiliating defeat.[109] Mastromarco has offered a much more interesting suggestion: that there was a rule debarring the third-place finisher at the City Dionysia from competing at that contest the next year; Aristophanes then, who had two pieces in progress, intended for the Lenaea and City Dionysia of 422, respectively, was forced to put both forth at the Lenaea, if he did not want to delay one until the next year.[110] This seems a much more convincing explanation, though a number of fascinating questions remain. How would an author prepare to compete with himself? What relation would the two plays have to each other?

Though we can say relatively little about the plot of *Proagon*, it is clear that it dealt with that element of the tragic festival where the poets, on the day before the competition, appeared in the theater with their unmasked actors and probably announced the themes of their plays.[111] Euripides was certainly a character in the piece. Aristophanes seems, then, to have split the interests that were combined in *Acharnians*, making *Proagon* the play of literary parody and *Wasps* the overtly political play.[112] In one sense good tactics dictated that he differentiate the two plays strongly in the public mind, though he can hardly have had any great fear of the relatively obscure Leucon. It becomes all the more interesting to ask then why he chooses to list "Euripides being abused again" ($α\mathring{v}θις \, \mathring{α}νασελγαινόμενος \, Ε\mathring{v}ριπίδης$, 61) as an example of what *Wasps* will avoid, when his other play for the festival was on just this subject.[113] If *Wasps* was performed before *Proagon*, the audience will have no reason to connect this line with the latter, because they will not yet know the subject. If, however, *Proagon* went on first, this line in the later play will almost necessarily point a contrast between the two. Perhaps Aristophanes was so secure that he was willing to risk a little metatheatrical joke at his own expense.[114]

Appendix II. Staging Conflict in the *Clouds*

Any performance analysis of the *Clouds* is bedeviled by the question of revisions for the second version. One of the more famous problems is the appearance of the two Logoi of the *agon*, who according to Σ *Clouds* 889 appeared on stage as fighting cocks. Dover in his commentary has made a strong case for this being a feature of the original production, even though nothing in the present text unequivocally testifies to their representation as such.[115] More recently the issue has become entangled with Taplin's intriguing but ultimately unpersuasive suggestion that the Getty Birds vase represents, not the chorus of *Birds* as argued by J. R. Green, but the two Logoi from *Clouds*.[116]

In a note discussing the vase, Don Fowler has situated the costuming and therefore significance of the two fighting Logoi of the *Clouds* in an extremely interesting performative and cultural context.[117] Fowler suggests that these oversized cocks are meant to recall and invert an actual cockfight, held yearly in the theater as an example and instruction for Athens' fighting forces. The evidence for this is quite late and so may perhaps be doubted. Lucian's *Anacharsis* is a depiction of the lawgiver Solon explaining Athenian institutions and customs to the visiting Scythian of the title. Chapter 37 describes a cockfight to which men of every age must come, in order to accustom themselves to bloodshed. Aelian, *Varia Historia* 2.28 gives a colorful aetiology for this institution: Themistocles, leading the forces of Athens out against the Persians, saw two cocks fighting on the roadside. He stopped the army and harangued them on the courage of these animals who fought for nothing but dominance and reminded the Athenians that they were fighting instead for their fatherland, gods, and families. After the victory the yearly cockfight was established as an institution held ἐν τῷ θεάτρῳ.

As Fowler demonstrates, if we do accept the existence of an annual cockfight held in the theater to instruct the (male) audience in courage and virtue, the implications of Aristophanes' inversion of this institution in the *Clouds* are fascinating. Pheidippides, instead of being instructed in courage and made a better soldier for Athens, is taught sophistry with all its concomitant corruption of bodily strength and virtue. One spectacle knits young and old together in the common cause; the other equips the young to beat the old and overthrow their authority.

To compare the parody of this civic spectacle intended for the instruction of the Athenians with the parody of the law courts in *Wasps* may seem very much a case of great and small. After all, even Solon in *Anacharsis* sounds a little defensive about this Athenian custom as he explains it to his visitor. Perhaps Aristophanes' point was a little too subtle in *Clouds*, and no one would have thought that the courage of the Athenians in battle really *depended* on their attendance at the annual cockfight. The soundness of the democracy *did* depend, however, on the proper functioning of assembly and law courts. Bdelycleon's conversion of judicial process into a dogfight (even though he enters the fray on behalf of one of the dogs) makes the point much more obviously. Like the parody of the cockfight, it is also underlined by the coincidence of place, since the theater was also used on occasion as a law court.[118]

6

Making Peace—Or Dionysus in '21

I've come here tonight for three very important reasons.
The first of these reasons is to announce my divinity. I am a
god. The second of these reasons is to establish my rites and
rituals. As you can see, they've already started, and they're
coming along just fine. And the third reason is to be born, if
you'll excuse me.

—The Performance Group, *Dionysus in 69*

WITH THE *PEACE*, Aristophanes brings to a close his campaign against the
now dead Cleon, who had fallen in the battle of Amphipolis the previous summer. Despite some insincere protests (648ff.), Aristophanes clearly does not
subscribe to the view *de mortuis nil nisi bonum*. It is important for him in this
play to revisit some of his charges against Cleon and the danger he and other
demagogues (notably Hyperbolus) represent to the democracy. At the same
time he wishes to celebrate an Athens freed from their influence and freed
from war for the first time in ten years: indeed, the two (demagogues and war)
are often treated as two sides of the same coin.

As a result the *Peace* is paradoxically one of the most metatheatrical and
yet one of the least complex of Aristophanes' plays. While shot through with
direct address to the audience,[1] the decision to leave Cleon in Hades where
he belongs (lines 313–315; 649) means that no demagogic performance is put
on the stage to be critiqued, either directly (as in *Knights*) or indirectly (as in
Wasps). Instead, Aristophanes indulges freely in the kinds of metatheatrical
jokes we have become accustomed to, yet focuses attention tightly within the
theater space,[2] a space that, now cleansed of the corrupt performances of the
demagogues, can be rededicated to pure comic celebration (κῶμος).

Whether Aristophanes entirely succeeds in this enterprise is not our most
pressing concern. Judgments on the *Peace* have ranged widely, though few
would list it among his best plays.[3] In its own time it came second at the fes-

tival. I will argue that its virtues are more performative than purely textual. Although Aristophanes' rivals apparently satirized one part of his staging of this play, I believe that this staging contains much of the meaning of the *Peace*. Let us turn then to the details of its performance.

The play's induction bears some resemblance to that of the *Wasps*. Once again there is an offstage mystery, and a master who is afflicted with madness, but where *Wasps* began slowly with the two slaves drowsing on their night watch, here furious activity is already in progress, with one slave kneading in a trough and the other racing in and out of the *skene* (a dumbshow that could go on for some time before the beginning of the dialogue, thereby building tension and audience interest). It may even take a few lines for the joke to dawn on the audience, but when the hard-working slave at the trough appeals to the dung-collectors in the audience (or the whole audience *as* dung-collectors) to come and help him,[4] it now becomes obvious what they are feeding the beetle inside.

After further byplay continuing to build interest in the beetle, the second slave suddenly imagines some supposedly clever young man in the audience asking what a beetle has to do with the play, whereupon the man next to him allegorizes the beetle as Cleon eating excrement down in Hades (43–49).[5] This imagined exchange functions in two ways. While this allegory is never explicitly disavowed within the play, we will of course discover that the beetle has a function in the plot (as well as in Euripidean parody) and no obvious connection to Cleon. The attempted allegorical explanation, however, connects the play to Aristophanes' preceding work in which the audience *was* meant to see Cleon under other figures (most notably the Paphlagon, of course). Within the induction, the exchange functions like the guessing game in *Wasps* (71ff., "what disease does the master suffer from?") in drawing the audience further into the play's particular fictional world.

The slave now proceeds to explain that his master is mad ("not like you in the audience," οὐχ ὅνπερ ὑμεῖς, 55), but obsessed with Zeus' mismanagement of the world in allowing the war to continue. He rails at the heavens, and indeed we hear such an offstage cry (62–63), which the slave incorporates into his account. His narrative builds smoothly from the master's vain attempts to reach heaven by ladder to the introduction of the giant beetle, and he now glances through the door back into the house to see what is going on.

Trygaeus (whose name we will learn at line 190) has one of the great entrances of all time, swung aloft by the *mechane* on the back of his giant beetle. There is no way to determine whether he was the first writer of comedy to use this stage resource.[6] While his use of the device clearly parodies tragedy (most notably Euripides' *Bellerophon*), it is striking that tragic parody is subordinate here to the necessities of the comic plot. Aristophanes both mocks the pretensions of the tragic stage and demonstrates how comedy can exceed it in breadth of vision, as his hero takes wing to dispute the running of the universe with Zeus. The text also suggests Aristophanes has paid careful attention to the limitations of the device as well in the structuring of his scene. The first words of Trygaeus's song are an admonition to the beetle to fly gently, thereby covering the action as the giant prop beetle's pendulum motion slowly settles down.[7]

Suspended in mid-air, Trygaeus debates first with his servant and then with his daughter the wisdom of his plan to confront Zeus. He cites as his inspiration Aesop's tale of the dung beetle and the eagle,[8] thereby fixing the play primarily in the frame of fantasy. While numerous lines parody various bits of Euripides (including his *Aeolus* as well as *Bellerophon*), Trygaeus specifically rejects the tragic frame as impractical:

> {Θυ.} οὐκοῦν ἐχρῆν σε Πηγάσου ζεῦξαι πτερόν,
> ὅπως ἐφαίνου τοῖς θεοῖς τραγικώτερος.
> {Τρ.} ἀλλ', ὦ μέλ', ἄν μοι σιτίων διπλῶν ἔδει·
> νῦν δ' ἅττ' ἂν αὐτὸς καταφάγω τὰ σιτία,
> τούτοισι τοῖς αὐτοῖσι τοῦτον χορτάσω.   (135–139)

> Daughter. Shouldn't you have harnessed the wings of Pegasus,
> to look really tragic[9] to the gods?
> Trygaeus. But then, my dear, I'd have needed double rations;
> now whatever food I eat myself
> I can reuse to fatten this beetle.

Here Aristophanes subtly attempts to improve on his own past success. Dicaeopolis succeeded in his quest by rummaging through Euripides' collection of tragic characters, rejecting others in search of the most pitiable, Telephus (*Acharnians* 384). The daughter here suggests a similar procedure: go and find Pegasus in order to appear more authentically tragic. Trygaeus is above such expedients, however, and has a perfectly practical, if thoroughly scatological, reason for proceeding as he does. He so completely persuades his daughter that she then warns him against falling back into the tragedy mode:

> ἐκεῖνο τήρει, μὴ σφαλεὶς καταρρυῇς
> ἐντεῦθεν, εἶτα χωλὸς ὢν Εὐριπίδῃ
> λόγον παράσχῃς καὶ τραγῳδία γένῃ. (146–148)

Watch out for one thing: don't slip and fall
from there. Then you'll end up a cripple,
provide Euripides with a plot, and become a tragedy.

On one level this is simply the old gibe about Euripides' lame heroes, but
there are further implications as well. The daughter raises the possibility that
comedy could provide *tragedy* with its plots: the exchange need not always
be comedy parodying tragedy. This cheeky suggestion is quite in the spirit of
Aristophanes' claim that comedy can tell the city true things as well (*Acharnians* 500–501). Most interestingly, the last two words imply that the only difference between Aristophanes' comedy and a Euripidean tragedy is whether
the hero falls off his flying steed![10]

Trygaeus's flight, as the crane swings him from one side of the stage to
the other, proves less than smooth. Because the beetle is easily distracted by
the (to it) appetizing odors coming up from the earth below, Trygaeus appeals
directly to the audience not to emit any (150ff.). We should imagine the beetle
moving up and down as it swings across the open orchestra. Tragic parody is
marked by the opening allusion to Euripides' *Bellerophon* (154ff.; cf. Euripides
fr. 307) and the use of anapaestic meter. When he suddenly bursts out in iam-
bics (the meter of ordinary conversation), the sense that the actor is breaking
out of the play world and speaking directly as himself and not as the character
Trygaeus is therefore quite powerful:

οἴμ᾽ ὡς δέδοικα, κοὐκέτι σκώπτων λέγω.
ὦ μηχανοποιέ, πρόσεχε τὸν νοῦν, ὡς ἐμὲ
ἤδη στρέφει τι πνεῦμα περὶ τὸν ὀμφαλόν,
κεἰ μὴ φυλάξεις, χορτάσω τὸν κάνθαρον. (173–176)

Yipes! I'm terrified, and I'm not kidding now!
Hey, crane-man, pay attention!
Some wind's twisting up my insides,
and if you're not careful, I'll be fattening the beetle.

The direct address to the crane operator can be paralleled elsewhere in Aristophanes and was probably imitated by his competitor Strattis.[11] The notion
that the actor really was in some danger doubtless only increased the hilarity
of the audience (comedy is a cruel business at times), but Aristophanes does
not wish to distract his viewers from the plot for too long. Even before the
sentence appealing to the craneman is over, we are already being sutured back
into the fantasy frame by the joke about feeding the beetle.

Trygaeus now arrives at the other end of the stage, which functions as the house of Zeus.[12] It is not entirely clear to me when he dismounts from the beetle. Sommerstein assumes he does so immediately at line 179 and further that he knocks at the door. This is perhaps the most likely solution, although the comic possibilities seem considerable in beginning the dialogue while the mortal Trygaeus is still hovering midair above the god Hermes who then answers. All we know for certain is that when, several hundred lines later (at 720, to be precise) he looks for his beetle to take him back to earth, he is told that it has gone on to Zeus and will not be back.[13]

Hermes is appalled by both beetle and rider and roundly abuses Trygaeus for his outrageous invasion of heaven.[14] His bluster is all bluff, however, and easily appeased by a bribe. There is a larger problem confronting Trygaeus: Zeus and the rest of the gods are not there.

> {Ερ.} ἰὴ ἰὴ ἰή,
> ὅτ' οὐδὲ μέλλεις ἐγγὺς εἶναι τῶν θεῶν·
> φροῦδοι γάρ· ἐχθές εἰσιν ἐξῳκισμένοι. (195–197)

Hermes. Hee, hee, hee!
You won't get near the gods!
They're out of here: they decamped yesterday.

They have gotten so tired of the Greeks' disputes that they have moved far away, leaving behind Polemos, the embodiment of war, and Hermes to keep an eye on their bits of property (σκευάρια, 201). Leaving the god of thieves as one's night watchman is inherently comic, of course, and the fact that the gods gave up and moved out only "yesterday" (ἐχθές) may be meant simply as sadistic comedy. There is an echo here of a line in the *Iliad*, where Zeus is said to have left "the day before" for a banquet. Yet one wonders if a Homeric echo fully exhausts the comedy of "yesterday," especially given that it is brought up again in a few lines.[15] It is eminently possible that the gods in fact moved out of this "house" the day before the performance of the *Peace*—if a tragedy on the day before had had divine characters in its cast.[16] This notion is made more plausible by the reference to the gods' σκευάρια, which are enumerated as "little pots and boards and jars" (χυτρίδια καὶ σανίδια κἀμφορείδια, 202). Again, these diminutives are comic enough in themselves, for while it may not be necessarily humorous to the Greek mind for anthropomorphic gods to have possessions at all, one would expect their property to be a little more dignified than this kitchen equipment.[17] Most striking is the use of the term σκευάρια (rather than the more general σκευή), for this is the Greek technical term for stage properties—that is, just the sort of thing that stage divinities would leave behind.[18] The operation of this metatheatrical reference (if it is one) is quite in keeping with others in this play: it breaks the frame of illusion but continues to focus attention on the theater itself (i.e., what happened at the dramatic festival the day before).

The exposition proceeds expeditiously. Hermes tells Trygaeus that Polemos, having been left in charge by Zeus, has buried the goddess of Peace in a cave, heaping stones on her, and now is preparing to grind up the cities of Greece in a giant mortar (228ff.). At the sound of his approach, Hermes decamps with alacrity,[19] and Trygaeus finds a spot to hide and observe the scene.

What follows is the first preserved eavesdropping scene in the history of comedy. Reading this scene without being aware of the dynamics of its staging can give a misleading impression. Within it Polemos and his helper Kudoimos, figures embodying the fearsome reality that has plagued Athens and all of Greece for ten years,[20] make preparations for pounding all the Greeks into a hash. While doubtless both roles are played in a broad and burlesqued style, what holds the painful reality that the scene actually represents at a distance is the eavesdropping frame, which allows Trygaeus to comment on and make jokes about the action both he and the audience observe. Trygaeus's comments to the audience help shape and guide their reactions to what they see.[21] Polemos throws ingredients representing one city after another into the mortar. The first is a Spartan ally, and Trygaeus tells the audience explicitly they need not worry about it ("That's no problem for us, gentlemen," τουτὶ μέν, ἄνδρες, οὐδὲν ἡμῖν πρᾶγμά πω, 244). Megara and Sicily call forth more sympathy, although the former was also an enemy of Athens. Attic honey, though, is greeted with a joke about wartime prices rather than sympathy: Trygaeus says Polemos should use a cheaper kind, since Attic honey costs four obols a half pint!

Polemos has the ingredients for his hash, but no pestle to mix them with. He dispatches Kudoimos first to Athens to borrow one. The Athenians, however, have lost theirs with the death of Cleon. Thomas Hubbard has offered a particularly valuable account of how Aristophanes links one play to another through his development of images and metaphors.[22] Aristophanes had called Cleon a "pestle" in *Knights*.[23] Now by reusing the image in this "hell's kitchen" scene, Trygaeus can thank Athena that the city lost this "pestle" just when it needed to, without triumphing so openly over Cleon's death. Sparta too has lost its pestle with the death of Brasidas, and so Polemos in disgust goes off to manufacture his own.

Did the god say that just the young should dance? Or just the
old? Or just the whites? Or just the blacks? Or just the Ital-
ians? Or just the Greeks? Or just James Brown? No, he wants
his honor from all mankind. He wants no one excluded from
his worship. Not even The Performance Group.

—The Performance Group, *Dionysus in 69*

IN RESPONSE TO TRYGAEUS'S direct calls to the "men of Greece" (ἄνδρες
Ἕλληνες, 292) to come and help him in the task of rescuing Peace, the chorus
now enters—with great enthusiasm. The fundamental joke of this entrance is
that they arrive singing at the top of their voices and soon break into vigorous dance, while Trygaeus tries desperately to restrain them, first for fear of
rousing Polemos from within the *skene*, then for fear of waking Cleon / Cerberus down in the underworld (313–315), who also helped keep Peace imprisoned while he was alive.[24] In the historical context, this may be a warning
about premature celebration of a peace treaty not yet official, but in the context of the performance the dancing verges on pure farce. The effect is strikingly similar to the pirates' second act entrance in *Pirates of Penzance*, singing
"With cat-like tread" while shaking the boards with their voices and dances.
The comedy is obvious but effective and provides some dramatic tension between Trygaeus and chorus. Equally effective is the Bergsonian comedy of
their dancing. As Trygaeus struggles to restrain the chorus, they insist that
their legs are dancing on their own, in spite of their owners' promises and
attempts to stop (324–325). One could label this dancing ecstatic Dionysiac
possession, but that risks missing the fundamental comedy of the situation:
like Curly in a classic Three Stooges film, turned into a fighting machine when
he hears a certain tune, the chorus in this play are turned into dancing ma-
chines by the joyous prospect (ὑφ' ἡδονῆς, 324) of peace. The manic quality of
their entering performance recalls, indeed perhaps quotes, the dancing exit of
Philocleon and the chorus of *Wasps* at Aristophanes' last festival appearance.[25]
    The chorus appeals to Trygaeus to be the chief engineer or master plan-
ner (κἀρχιτεκτόνει, 305) of their project. Although this is certainly a theatrical metaphor in later Roman comedy, we cannot prove that the term would
have had clear theatrical associations for the fifth-century Greek audience[26].
Structurally, however, Trygaeus will assume the role of director of the play's
actions, just as the *architectus doli* of later Roman comedy does. On a more
mundane level, he proceeds to supervise work with ropes and tackle just as
Ictinus must have been doing on the Acropolis just a few years before. Trygaeus promises them a literally "sybaritic" life (συβαριάζειν, 340–344), if they

will only cooperate with him in rescuing Peace, and the chorus agrees, gladly renouncing their past life of military and jury service.[27]

Trygaeus moves toward the central stage opening to begin digging Peace out, but Hermes suddenly reemerges to oppose him, asserting that Zeus has proclaimed the death penalty for anyone who attempts to release Peace (371–372). When Hermes threatens to summon Zeus, Trygaeus enlists the aid of the chorus, instructing them to join in persuading Hermes. They employ both flattery and bribery not only to win his acquiescence but to enlist his aid. The offer of an eye-catching gold libation bowl does the trick (423–425), and Hermes agrees to help.

One is more than usually conscious in examining this play of the fact that we have only a libretto left to us, not full documentation of the original performance. Trygaeus instructs the chorus (or at least a portion of them) to enter the cave and begin removing the stones that cover Peace:

> ὑμέτερον ἐντεῦθεν ἔργον, ὦνδρες. ἀλλὰ ταῖς ἅμαις
> εἰσιόντες ὡς τάχιστα τοὺς λίθους ἀφέλκετε.   (426–427)

Your job's here, men. Go in with your mattocks
and drag the stones out as quickly as you can.

It seems best to assume with Sommerstein and Olson that some choristers do go inside, something that would be quite possible with the low stage of the fifth century.[28] It also seems possible that Trygaeus enters the cave briefly with them: this would explain why the chorus in 428–430 asks Hermes to preside over the enterprise, when back at 305 they asked Trygaeus to be in charge.[29] In any case Trygaeus is soon back on stage, joining Hermes in a libation and prayer to Dionysus. We presume that ropes have been run out from inside the central opening, and the choristers take up their positions along them.

At first their efforts are unavailing. Although various jokes and insults are scattered through this section, the humor and the interest must have been primarily physical, as the various choristers pull at cross purposes. Only when the chorus leader calls on the farmers to do the pulling alone (508) do they succeed in drawing the statue of Peace, accompanied by Opora ("Fullfruit") and Theoria ("Showtime") out of the cave on the *ekkyklema*.

A single scholium (Σ Plato *Apology* 19c) tells us that two of Aristophanes' competitors, Eupolis and Plato, made fun of him in their plays for using the device of the statue.[30] Although the statue is described as a κολοσσός, it need not have been gigantic.[31] Aristophanes is, however, evoking a very old understanding of the nature of divinity; Peace is identified with her statue, which has been treated like that of a dangerous power which can be controlled by confining the image.[32] Given that Aristophanes so often imagines the recreation of a lost era of the past, it seems highly likely that the figure was represented in an archaic or archaizing style. Naturally the image was not an actual statue in marble or bronze. One would need no more than a pole around which a peplos could be draped (as was done for cult statues in antiquity, most notably for the Athena on the Acropolis) and a mask placed on top.[33] It is worth remarking on the irony that Peace, the only divinity on Aristophanes' stage meant to be taken seriously, can only be represented as a representation. An actor inside the same mask and costume would render Peace, the peace for which Aristophanes and many of his fellow citizens had been longing for the past decade, a figure of fun rather than an object of desire. Only as an object, as stage property and not personality, can Peace have the dignity that the plot requires.[34]

While Trygaeus welcomes Peace as a sovereign deity (ὦ πότνια βοτρυόδωρε, 520) and struggles to find the right words to address her, his attention soon focuses on the more metatheatrical of her two companions, Showtime (Θεωρία). A. C. Cassio rightly emphasizes that the term θεωρία has particular associations with going to see the great panhellenic games at Olympia and elsewhere and therefore carries with it associations of freedom of movement long denied to those trapped in the city.[35] We should not, however, forget its fundamental meaning of spectatorship, a referent that has particular force in the theater at a performance. Trygaeus in fact specifies what Θεωρία entails:

> {Τρ.} ... ταύτης δ᾽ ὀπώρας, ὑποδοχῆς, Διονυσίων,
> αὐλῶν, τραγῳδῶν, Σοφοκλέους μελῶν, κιχλῶν,
> ἐπυλλίων Εὐριπίδου—
> {Ερ.}   κλαύσἄρα σὺ
> ταύτης καταψευδόμενος· οὐ γὰρ ἥδεται
> αὕτη ποιητῇ ῥηματίων δικανικῶν.
> {Τρ.} κιττοῦ, τρυγοίπου, προβατίων βληχωμένων,
> κόλπου γυναικῶν διατρεχουσῶν εἰς ἀγρόν,
> δούλης μεθυούσης, ἀνατετραμμένου χοῶς,
> ἄλλων τε πολλῶν κἀγαθῶν.   (530–538)

Tryg. ... she [smells of] fullfruit, partying, the Dionysia,
pipes, tragedies, Sophocles' songs, thrushes,
verselets of Euripides—
Hermes.   You'll be sorry,
slandering her like that. She doesn't enjoy

that poet's little lawcourt speeches.
Tryg.—ivy, wine-strainers, bleating herds,
the cleavage of women running to the field,
a drunken slave girl, an upturned jug,
and lots of other good things.

Note that Showtime even includes her other companion, Fullfruit or Opora
(ὀπώρας, 530). Ranking just after the fruits of the harvest are the pleasures
of the very festival the audience is now attending: the Dionysia, with its pipe
music, tragedies, and songs of Sophocles—even the little speeches that Euripides is famous for. Their mention allows Hermes to make a joke of the kind
we would expect from Aristophanes, but their inclusion at all in this list of
pleasures suggests the inclusiveness of Aristophanes' festival vision of peace.[36]
These spectatorial pleasures even precede (in importance or perhaps in actual
practice) those of wine and women. Without wishing to raise the shade of
Cornford or the *eniautos daimon*, I would nonetheless see in this passage a
clear indication that the pleasures of seeing were indeed understood by the
audience of the fifth-century theater to be Dionysiac.[37]

Hermes now invites Trygaeus to look at the cities talking and laughing (διαλλαγεῖσαι καὶ γελῶσιν, 540) with each other. Both are theoretically
still in heaven, as Trygaeus will explicitly make his way back to earth during
the parabasis (729ff.). One could therefore imagine with Sommerstein that
Hermes by some gesture indicates the earth below in his speech to Trygaeus.
We should remember, however, that this play is being produced at the City
Dionysia where (unlike the Lenaea) citizens of the allied cities were in the
audience as well. In his very next speech Hermes tells Trygaeus to look at
the faces of the spectators (τῶνδε . . . τῶν θεωμένων, 543) to observe how
those who prosper in time of peace are delighted while the war profiteers are
mocked and in despair. It seems better then to take Hermes' picture of the
cities talking and laughing with each other as a vision of the Aristophanic
audience, here and now, in the Theater of Dionysus. That unified audience is
precisely the spectacle that the play is attempting to stage.

After welcoming the goddess with loving hymns of praise,[38] the chorus
asks why she has been away so long. This allows Hermes to offer a much more
detailed explanation[39] than just her burial in the cave (which is perhaps to
be regarded only as a recent development, although notions of time are very
fluid in Aristophanes). We return once again to the Megarian decree—only
this time, the Megarian decree is explained as a stratagem of Pericles to distract
the demos after he became frightened that they would turn on him as they had
on his friend, the sculptor Pheidias. This improbable tale[40] is simply a setup

for the chorus's comment "That's why she's so beautiful—being a relative of his (i.e., Pheidias)" (ταῦτ᾽ ἄρ᾽ εὐπρόσωπος ἦν, / οὖσα συγγενὴς ἐκείνου, 617–618). The mention of Pheidias, however contrived, is nonetheless very important to the audience's reception of the statue of Peace. I believe it helps the audience accept Peace not only as a beautiful work of art (rather than the animate actor they may have expected), but more specifically as a *cult statue*. Pheidias was engaged in sculpting the statue of Athena Parthenos when he was charged and fled, later creating the cult statue of Zeus for the great temple at Olympia.[41] This superficially nonsensical story is actually part of the subliminal process of transforming Peace into a cult statue—and the Theater of Dionysus into her shrine.

Hermes' account lays the blame on the elite classes of both sides of the war but in particular on the orators (τοὺς λέγοντας, 635) who throve on the bribes and political power generated by the war, above all "the leathermonger" Cleon (although Cleon is in fact not named in the play—a small concession to his recent death, or a form of *damnatio memoriae*?). At this, Trygaeus pretends to be upset by this abuse of the dead and manages, in disavowing them, to repeat a number of insults against him.

When Trygaeus asks Peace to speak, Hermes says she is angry and therefore refuses to address the spectators (πρός γε τοὺς θεωμένους, 658). This tactic is of a piece with the original conception of Peace as a "real" divine image. Only Hermes and Trygaeus are on stage. The third actor could have been employed to give a voice to the statue. Instead Aristophanes chooses to abide by the conventions of "realism." Hermes pretends to hear her words whispered to him and conveys them to the audience (an appropriate task for the messenger of the gods, of course). She blames them for their earlier refusals to make peace, sets up a joke for Trygaeus against Cleonymus, and then asks who the power on the Pnyx is now. Here is Trygaeus's answer:

Ὑπέρβολος νῦν τοῦτ᾽ ἔχει τὸ χωρίον.
αὕτη, τί ποιεῖς; τὴν κεφαλὴν ποῖ περιάγεις; (681–682)

Hyperbolus now controls that spot.
Hey, what are you doing? Where are you turning your head?

There is no way to prove definitively that what Trygaeus describes was actually shown on stage, although Sommerstein, Halliwell, and Olson accept the idea that it was.[42] Ancient masks had the wig or headdress attached;[43] it would therefore be very easy, if I am correct in suggesting that the statue was put together out of costume and mask, to rig a mechanism to turn the mask to one side. The actor playing Hermes might even simply move it with his hand behind her "head."

Simple the mechanics may have been—but the effect would not have been simple. Aristophanes has done much to emphasize that the statue *is* a statue, fixed and immobile. For a statue, and indeed a cult statue, to move is more than startling—it is miraculous and a demonstration of divine power. The more serious in the audience might know stories such as that of the statue of Theagenes of Thasos (told in Pausanias 6. 11. 2–9), an athlete whose statue fell on and killed an envious rival who was whipping it. The statue was prosecuted for murder, convicted, and thrown in the sea, but a famine followed on Thasos. The Delphic oracle told the Thasians to restore the statue to its proper place, and thereafter they sacrificed to it as a god. Pseudo-Lucian in *de Dea Syria* 36–37, though a later source, gives an even closer parallel of a statue of Apollo, which prophesies by its sometime violent movements.[44] For most in the audience, the sheer surprise will simply move them to laughter. In either case, Aristophanes is sending a powerful message of rejection of the demagogic politics of the city as they are being continued by Hyperbolus.[45]

Peace then enquires about the cultural life of the city—and that means the state of tragedy and comedy, metonymically represented by Sophocles and Cratinus. Sophocles, we learn, is doing fine in his old age but getting greedy (696–699: the joke is obscure), and Cratinus is dead of shock over a wine jar smashed in the Spartan invasion (700–703). The details of these jokes are less important for us than their position in Peace's inquisition: the state of affairs in Athenian drama is second in importance only to the affairs of the assembly. Peace now hands Theoria and Opora over to Trygaeus, who, discovering his beetle has vanished, is instructed to go alongside the goddess (probably into the central stage opening) in order to get back to earth, thus leaving the chorus alone for the parabasis.

The choristers now divest themselves of some props, perhaps tools marking them as farmers,[46] to which Aristophanes adds a pointed joke:

ἀλλ' ἴθι χαίρων· ἡμεῖς δὲ τέως τάδε τὰ σκεύη παραδόντες
τοῖς ἀκολούθοις δῶμεν σῴζειν, ὡς εἰώθασι μάλιστα
περὶ τὰς σκηνὰς πλεῖστοι κλέπται κυπτάζειν καὶ κακοποιεῖν. (729–731)

Go then; farewell. But we must hand over our gear
to the attendants to keep, since a lot of thieves
like to skulk around the stage and make trouble.

The reference to the stage (σκηνάς) pulls us back to the here and now of the performance.[47] Once again the chorus speaks for Aristophanes and claims not only to have raised the standards of comedy above farce, buffoonery, and stock jokes about Heracles and slaves but also to have created a great art (τέχνην μεγάλην, 749),[48] which he has used not against ordinary citizens but to fight like Heracles against the great monster Cleon.[49]

Nor, the chorus claims, after his past successes did he use his fame to pick up boys in the gymnasia but instead went on as before. His phrase is somewhat curious: "I packed up my stuff and went on my way" (ἀράμενος τὴν σκευὴν εὐθὺς ἐχώρουν, 763). Although σκευή is more general than σκευάρια, in possession of a comic poet it may have a more theatrical meaning.[50] Could this be a reference to Aristophanes taking a production elsewhere, perhaps to the festivals of the Rural Dionysia? There were already deme theaters in the Peiraeus and elsewhere in Attica, although we have no attestations for the production of comedy there this early.[51] And despite the picture Aristophanes himself paints of the citizens being trapped within the walls by the war, in fact the Attic countryside was not continuously under Spartan control from 431 to 421. Some demes could have held their festivals. Aristophanes may then be saying in line 763 that, unlike some poets who used victory at the festivals to build their social careers in the city, he stuck to his art and continued to practice it wherever he could. After an invocation of the Muse (775),[52] parting shots at the playwrights Carcinus, Melanthius, and Morsimus conclude this abbreviated parabasis.[53]

Trygaeus reappears, perhaps limping,[54] bringing Opora and Theoria with him and joking that the audience who looked like scoundrels from the vantage point of heaven look even more rascally up close (819–823). He orders Opora taken inside to prepare for their wedding, banters with the chorus about his rejuvenation,[55] and then turns to the business of restoring Theoria to the *boule*. Again the staging is somewhat uncertain, but it looks as though Trygaeus displays Theoria on the stage as he asks for a volunteer to take charge of her and then hand her over to the *boule* (877ff.). At 881 he probably advances into the orchestra, leading her by the hand (δεῦρο σύ). This sets up a joke in which his slave, playing second banana, can pretend to recognize Ariphrades in the audience offering his services, allowing Trygaeus to make another joke about Ariphrades' addiction to oral sex (883–885).[56] Trygaeus then orders her to strip,[57] describes to the *prytaneis* their imminent sexual enjoyment of her in a joyous spate of metaphors,[58] and finally hands her over to a *prytanis* sitting in the *proedria*.[59] Nothing could more graphically demonstrate the benefits of peace. Stage and audience are physically united as Trygaeus hands Theoria over to someone sitting in the first row, with clear instructions that peace is then to be celebrated by Dionysiac sex after the performance.[60] While the play then focuses relentlessly on the here and now of the performance, Theoria looks forward to the opening out of peace to encompass the whole world at the end.[61]

Trygaeus proudly proclaims his benefits to the common people, then adds in almost throwaway fashion that he has "put a stop to Hyperbolus" (Ὑπέρβολόν τε παύσας, 921). This seems a bit of a non sequitur. One could say that, since all the demagogues have flourished during and from the war, its cessation will end their influence.[62] Yet why the specific mention of Hyperbolus? I would suggest that Trygaeus, here identifying himself with Aristophanes, is referring back to the response of the statue of Peace to Hyperbolus's name at 682, far too sanguinely suggesting that this play will both celebrate the restoration of peace and natural order at Athens and turn the public against Cleon's obvious successor.

The next order of business, according to Trygaeus, is to install the statue of Peace (ταύτην . . . ἱδρυτέον, 923). The term "install" implies recognition of what Aristophanes has been carefully building up since his introduction of the statue, its status as cult image and object of religious worship.[63] After some punning bickering over what sort of sacrifice to offer at this dedication, they decide on a sheep. Trygaeus sends the slave in to get the sheep and promises to provide an altar—which he then "discovers" as a permanent part of the stage setting ("In fact, the altar's right at the door!" ὁ γὰρ βωμὸς θύρασι καὶ δή, 942)![64] The effect, of course, is not to foster the illusion that the altar is the normal thing to find outside a house door but rather to call attention once again to the stage as stage.

The sacrifice is made the occasion for much broad comedy and even physical farce. After the slave returns with the sheep, Trygaeus instructs to throw barley to the audience (τοῖς θεαταῖς ῥῖπτε τῶν κριθῶν, 962). Sommerstein[65] pointedly notes the lack of evidence for this in religious practice and suggests a parody of the practice of throwing nuts and sweets into the audience (which Aristophanes accuses his rivals of). There is a strong element of visual comedy as well: while an actor could certainly throw compact objects such as large nuts or figs from the stage at least as far as the first rows, small grains would scatter ineffectually in the air, drifting down over the chorus. The slave's claim that "there isn't one of the spectators (τῶν θεωμένων, 964) who hasn't got barley" is laughably false on its face then but further sets up the following punning exchange:

{Τρ.} οὐχ αἱ γυναῖκές γ᾽ ἔλαβον.
{Οἰ.}   ἀλλ᾽ εἰς ἑσπέραν
δώσουσιν αὐταῖς ἄνδρες.   (966–967)

Tryg. The women didn't get any!
Slave.   Well, tonight
their husbands will give it to them.

The word κριθή means both "grain of barley" and in a slang sense "penis."[66] Again, the obscenity is not just an isolated joke but subliminally incorporates the audience, both men and women,[67] into the "sacrifice" and the play. They too, like the *prytaneis* with Theoria, will celebrate in Dionysiac fashion after the play.

The chorus is incorporated in an even more emphatic fashion: Trygaeus, instead of merely sprinkling lustral water over them as was normally done at a sacrifice, seems to have drenched some of them, which he then jokes about: they must be good because they have returned to their places after being soaked (970–972)! The feeling is quite improvisational: the actor playing Trygaeus cannot hit all twenty-four choristers with the water and may have varied his targets at rehearsal, making what happens at the performance a surprise.[68]

Trygaeus offers an appropriately theatrical prayer to Peace as "goddess of choruses" (δέσποινα χορῶν, 976), then instructs the slave to sacrifice the sheep. Now real animal sacrifice is never performed on the Attic stage. Although Aristophanes has done his best to create a religious atmosphere and represent Peace as a divine image being installed in a shrine, it seems that actual blood sacrifice could not fit comfortably inside the theatrical frame.[69] The same convention is observed at *Birds* 1056–1057, but here in *Peace* the avoidance of the actual sacrifice is turned into a joke: Trygaeus tells the slave to take the sheep inside and sacrifice it there, "in order to spare the producer (choregos) the loss of a sheep" (χοὔτω τὸ πρόβατον τῷ χορηγῷ σῴζεται, 1022)!

When the slave returns with the old bones that serve as the stage prop sacrifice, Trygaeus has prepared the altar. Despite their haste, they have not been quick enough, however. The chorus warned Trygaeus back at 950–955 to hurry, lest Chaeris the piper find out and force his way in for a share of the sacrifice. They may have avoided Chaeris, but the oracle-monger Hierocles shows up and proves just as greedy and disruptive. Nearly a hundred lines are occupied by rather broad and basic comedy, as Hierocles spouts his oracles and tries to cadge some food, while Trygaeus ignores and then resists him, finally ordering his slave to drive him off with a stick.[70]

The second parabasis follows (1127–1190), lyrically celebrating the joys of peace in the country contrasted with the corruption and oppression of the city in wartime. The theme is familiar from *Acharnians* on, but with one or two new twists. There are echoes of the symposium in the contrast of the delights of drinking and feasting with the hardships of battle.[71] These are contrasted with the arrogant but unnamed taxiarch (1172) who cavalierly juggles the call-up lists, mistreating the rank-and-file citizen soldiers.

The play now turns to the preparations for the wedding of Trygaeus and Opora. A sickle-maker (accompanied by a silent extra playing a potter) appears to thank Trygaeus for engineering the peace and brings a wedding present, presumably food (1197–1206). Various war profiteers, whose spokes-man is an arms dealer, arrive to complain, but Trygaeus turns them away with scatological mockery: swords are beaten, not into plowshares, but into toilet seats and laxative measuring cups.[72] The only resistance left is literally puerile: a boy comes out of the house to practice his song for the wedding feast, and it proves to be hexameter poetry on martial themes, which Trygaeus continu-ally interrupts and tries to rewrite. The boy turns out to be the son of Lama-chus, which explains all. Instead, Trygaeus asks for a song from the son of the much-mocked Cleonymus, who so notoriously abandoned his shield in battle, and he offers Archilochus's famous elegiacs on throwing his shield away. Thus even the world of private poetry is brought into alignment with the songs of peace being sung in the public theater. Correspondingly, the celebration in the open theater becomes an extension of the symposium celebration behind the scenes.

There is one remaining metatheatrical surprise, which helps make this point performatively. Trygaeus, just before leaving the stage to fetch out Opora, invites the chorus to partake of the gifts of food brought by the sickle-maker and potter. Sommerstein makes a strong case for the notion that the chorus in fact do eat some of these offerings.[73] That, however, entails an action on their part otherwise unparalleled in Greek theater. Greek masks covered the entire face (and indeed entire head). The only way to eat any of this food is for the choristers to push up their masks—and thereby step out of their roles in the play in order to become participants in the celebration of the "real" peace!

Trygaeus and Opora return, are greeted with the wedding hymn, and are finally carried off on the shoulders of the chorus. The invocation of food and wine is persistent throughout and culminates in the final line, an invitation to the audience ($ἄνδρες$, 1357) to join in the feasting and celebration, as the chorus dances off.

The use of metatheatre in *Peace* is then quite different from that in the three preceding plays, especially as they focus on Cleon and other dema-gogues. Those plays regularly shift audience attention from performance in the theater to performance in other venues, notably the assembly, but also the law courts (especially in *Wasps*). The movement in *Peace* is almost diametrically opposite. As A. C. Cassio has emphasized, the play constantly seeks to focus attention on the here and the now. As I have tried to show, that here and now emphatically means the theater itself, where the celebration of the Dionysia is now in progress. The celebration of the imminent return of peace, conceived as Peace, melts into that Dionysiac celebration. Thus, where Aristophanes employs metatheatre in the earlier plays to teach the audience to take a critical stance, to encourage them to resist the seductions of illusion, in this play he tries to suggest that behind the grandiloquent characters and fantastic plots of Old Comedy lies a bedrock celebration of wine and song, which he identifies as the natural state of man in time of peace.

The peace that *Peace* hymned so fulsomely proved short-lived. We are not, unfortunately, in the position to trace in details in those fragments of Aristophanes that might stem from the next few years his reaction to events as the general realization settled in that peace was not permanent. When next we can observe his metatheatrical games at work, the political world of Athens has changed radically.

7

Performing the City: *Birds*

November 18, 1967: Artaud is alive at the walls of the Pentagon. . . . The Pentagon vibrates and begins to rise in the air.
—Abbie Hoffman, *Revolution for the Hell of It*

ONE OF THE MOST ENTERTAINING moments of political theater during the
days of the Vietnam protests occurred when Abbie Hoffman and Co. rallied
round to levitate the Pentagon. Though no evidence exists, Hoffman swore
that around four in the morning they did succeed in lifting the building three
or four feet off the ground. The city of Nephelokokkugia in the *Birds*, which
soars so high in poetic imagination, hovered in actuality about the same distance above the ground, for it was a theatrical city, built to a surprisingly explicit degree on the stage of the Theater of Dionysus. Although the *Birds* is less
obviously metatheatrical than some of his earlier works, the play nonetheless
exploits its own performance situation both to increase its comic effects and
to literalize the metaphor of the "city in the air." Nephelokokkugia comes into
being through a series of enactments which are sometimes mimetic, sometimes self-consciously nonillusory stage performance. If the critique of spectator politics that Aristophanes launched in the *Acharnians* has become more
muted and diffuse in this play, he is still alive to its dangers, as a close performance reading of the play shows. He seems more intrigued, however, by
the creative powers of theatrical persuasion and the sheer intoxicating joy of
the liberated city of the Birds, into which he invites the war-weary citizens of
Athens.

The *Birds* begins precisely nowhere, a place characterized by its placelessness, an *outopia* as David Konstan has pointed out.[1] Two figures, whose names
we once again will not learn for some time, presumably arrive from one of the
parodoi into the orchestra but once there have no idea how to proceed. Nor
will the audience necessarily know whether they are comic warm-up charac-

ters, like the slaves in *Knights* or *Wasps*, or in fact main characters—as at least one proves to be.[2] The opening lines indicate they are wandering back and forth (and indeed the original production could easily have extended this into a long silent sequence of physical comedy):

> {Πι.} ὀρθὴν κελεύεις, ᾗ τὸ δένδρον φαίνεται;
> {Ευ.} διαρραγείης. ἥδε δ᾽ αὖ κρώζει "πάλιν."
> {Πι.} τί, ὦ πόνηρ᾽, ἄνω κάτω πλανύττομεν;
> ἀπολούμεθ᾽ ἄλλως τὴν ὁδὸν προφορουμένω. (1–4)

> Peisetaerus. Are you pointing straight on, where that tree is?
> Euelpides. Damn you! This one's croaking to go back again.
> Peis. You louse, why are we wandering up and down?
> We're going to die, shuttling back and forth on this road.

Their guidebirds eventually lead them to some cliffs (20), which are represented by the front of the stage.[3] Note too here the expression ἄνω κάτω. This anticipates the direction that the two will eventually locate: up, out of their current dilemma.

Before they find their way out, however, Peisetaerus (for so we will now name him) offers a remarkable direct address to the audience (27–48). The explicit form of his address indicates the audience's participation in the creation of the performance ("You gentlemen attending our story," ὦνδρες οἱ παρόντες ἐν λόγῳ, 30); the passage as a whole signals the political nature of the journey they have undertaken. Unlike the foreigners who are trying to squeeze their way into the *polis* and into Athenian citizenship, these two are trying to escape the city, escape from the oppressive operations of the democracy, especially the law courts. Almost as an afterthought, we learn that this journey has, if not a direction, a goal: to find Tereus the hoopoe.[4]

Suddenly we discover that the guidebirds *do* know one direction: up.

> {Ευ.} οὗτος.
> {Πι.}   τί ἐστιν;
> {Ευ.}   ἡ κορώνη μοι πάλαι
> ἄνω τι φράζει.
> {Πι.}   χὠ κολοιὸς οὑτοσὶ
> ἄνω κέχηνεν ὡσπερεὶ δεικνύς τί μοι,
> κοὐκ ἔσθ᾽ ὅπως οὐκ ἔστιν ἐνταῦθ᾽ ὄρνεα. (49–52)

> Euel. Hey, you!
> Peis.   What?
> Euel.   My crow's been trying to show
> something up there for quite awhile.

Peis.   And this jackdaw's
been gaping upward, as if to show me something:
there must be birds here.

As Sommerstein notes in his stage directions, Peisetaerus and Euelpides
mount the stage at this point[5]: ἄνω is the way one moves in Greek when
going on stage, κάτω the direction in which one exits. In other words, they
locate themselves, they find a place amid placelessness, by placing themselves
on stage, by assuming the proper place for actors in the differentiated space of
the theater and thereby begin the process of creating Nephelokokkugia.

The appearance of Tereus in response to the knocking of Peisetaerus and
Euelpides arguably provides another element of theatrical self-consciousness.
The bird who appears is in an advanced state of molting—and he is specifically
Sophocles' Tereus:

> τοιαῦτα μέντοι Σοφοκλέης λυμαίνεται
> ἐν ταῖς τραγῳδίαισιν ἐμέ, τὸν Τηρέα. (101–102)

Sophocles disfigured me this way
in his tragedies: I'm Tereus.

This is on its face a quite puzzling passage. To judge from his comments in
Frogs, Aristophanes admired Sophocles, and the great tragedian nowhere in
the fragments of Old Comedy comes in for the severity of criticism that Euripides does. I find very appealing the partial explanation offered by Gregory
Dobrov: Sophocles took the risk in his *Tereus* of showing us the title character
transformed, though probably only in tableau.[6] This would have been a daring
effect and perhaps not fully successful: there was doubtless a considerable danger that some members of the audience would find the transformation not
tragic but hilarious,[7] and so Aristophanes may simply be twitting Sophocles
with one of his unusual failures. But why is Tereus *shedding* his feathers? He
was certainly not represented this way in Sophocles' tragedy. The purported
explanation initially puzzles rather than illumines. When asked about his condition, Tereus says:

> {Πι.}   πότερον ὑπὸ νόσου τινός;
> {Τη.} οὔκ, ἀλλὰ τὸν χειμῶνα πάντα τὦρνεα
> πτερορρυεῖ, κᾆτ᾽ αὖθις ἕτερα φύομεν. (104–106)

Peis.   Because of some disease?
Ter. No, all birds molt in winter,
and then we grow new feathers.

This is wrong by 180 degrees. Winter is the least likely time for birds to molt, since they need the protection against cold. So why winter? Perhaps it is a reference to extradramatic time: but *Birds* was a City play, not a Lenaean one, so the season is almost spring rather than fully winter. I am tempted to believe, though I cannot of course prove, that Aristophanes or his producer bought Tereus' costume secondhand from the producer of *Tereus*—and perhaps quite cheaply because after a winter in storage the feathers were already beginning to fall off.[8] The joke makes a virtue of necessity and/or choregic parsimony. It is also, to judge from the Getty Birds vase, a joke that was carried through in the costumes of the chorus, once they appear.[9] In any case, comments on the costume as costume remind the audience forcefully that this character is just a shabbily outfitted refugee from the tragic competitions.

Peisetaerus and Euelpides inform Tereus that they are searching for a city—an anticity, in fact, characterized by its difference from the Athens they have left.[10] There *is* such a city, says Tereus, on the Red Sea—but Peisetaerus rejects that because it can be reached by sea from Athens (143–48). Some Greek cities are mentioned and quickly rejected.

Then comes Peisetaerus's great idea: to found a city among the birds.[11] This alone, he says, will transform the birds from archetypes of helplessness and idiocy[12] into a power to be reckoned with. And what gives this prospective city its potential for power? Its place, its location in the scheme of things, as Peisetaerus proceeds to demonstrate to Tereus (175–187):

{Πι.} βλέψον κάτω.
{Τη.}   καὶ δὴ βλέπω.
{Πι.}   βλέπε νυν ἄνω.
{Τη.} βλέπω.
{Πι.}   περίαγε τὸν τράχηλον.
{Τη.}   νὴ Δία
ἀπολαύσομαί τί γ᾽, εἰ διαστραφήσομαι
{Πι.} εἶδές τι;
{Τη.}   τὰς νεφέλας γε καὶ τὸν οὐρανόν.
{Πι.} οὐχ οὗτος οὖν δήπου 'στὶν ὀρνίθων πόλος;
{Τη.} πόλος; τίνα τρόπον;
{Πι.}   ὥσπερ ἂν εἴποι τις τόπος.
ὅτι δὲ πολεῖται τοῦτο καὶ διέρχεται
ἅπαντα διὰ τούτου, καλεῖται νῦν πόλος.
ἢν δ᾽ οἰκίσητε τοῦτο καὶ φράξηθ᾽ ἅπαξ,
ἐκ τοῦ πόλου τούτου κεκλήσεται πόλις.
ὥστ᾽ ἄρξετ᾽ ἀνθρώπων μὲν ὥσπερ παρνόπων,
τοὺς δ᾽ αὖ θεοὺς ἀπολεῖτε λιμῷ Μηλίῳ.
{Τη.} πῶς;
{Πι.}   ἐν μέσῳ δήπουθεν ἀήρ ἐστι γῆς.

Peis. Look down.
Ter.   I'm looking.
Peis.   Now look up.
Ter. I'm looking.
Peis.   Turn your head around.
Ter.   Zeus,
that'll do me good, if I twist my neck!
Peis. Did you see something?
Ter.   Yeah, clouds and sky.
Peis. Isn't this really the birds' sphere?
Ter. Sphere? How so?
Peis.   You could call it a way.
It's the way things travel and go
all through it, and it's called a sphere.
But once you inhabit and fortify this,
instead of just a sphere, you'll have a sphere of influence.
Then you'll rule men as though they were insects
and even destroy the gods with a Melian starvation.
Ter. How?
Peis.   This air is between earth and there.

The pun on πόλος (sky, heavenly sphere) and πόλις (city, state, political
sphere) in this passage is critical for the establishment of the bird city, as Konstan has seen. He emphasizes it as the establishment of hierarchy; the conversion of the unbounded sky into a bounded and delimited space by the wall
that the birds eventually build creates civilization: "It is not just a question of
the wall, but of a different way of conceiving space as territorial, a field marked
by limits of property."[13] Moreover, the vertical axis of the πόλος sets up a
social order, under which the two humans can now dominate the previously
unordered, unpoliticized birds.[14]

Yet there is another, less metaphorical way of looking at this critical passage. The terms κάτω and ἄνω have already been established as theatrical
terms by the opening. Peisetaerus's elaborate demonstration of where they are
establishes that the bird city will be built on stage.[15] It is a theatrical space
located midway between god and man, audience (βλέψον κάτω, 175) and
theologeion (βλέπε νυν ἄνω, 175), inhabited by the gods they plan to starve
into submission. And the point of looking around (176)? They will build their
city in the presence of the Athenian audience (whom they will eventually invite to join their anticity).

The building of the city begins with teaching the chorus, a process already
begun by Tereus, who has taught the birds the Greek language: ἐδίδαξα τὴν
φωνήν, 200. The teaching role is then assumed by Peisetaerus,[16] a role that is

always open to theatrical implication in Aristophanes (cf. Praxagora's "teaching" in *Ecclesiazusae*).

The entrance of the chorus displays some surprising features. A chorus of birds should of course arrive in flight, but such an effect was beyond the capabilities of the crane. When Euelpides looks upward for the birds to arrive from the sky (264), he begins a sequence that helps lift the stage from the ground. Startlingly, four birds appear, one by one, on the roof of the skene, their arrival described in lines which parody tragedy.[17] Then the twenty-four individually described birds of the actual chorus begin to arrive, in accelerating rhythm, into the orchestra. Eventually they are so numerous that they block the theater entrance—which Euelpides names, reminding us once again that this is a stage city set in a theater: "you can't see the wings for the winged hordes" (οὐδ' ἰδεῖν ἔτ' ἔσθ' ὑπ' αὐτῶν πετομένων τὴν εἴσοδον, 296).[18] The visual result, once the bird chorus fills the orchestra below the level on which the actors are situated, is that the stage and the city it represents are now airborne.

The chorus, as so often in Aristophanes, initially displays its hostility to the central figure(s). Peisetaerus and Euelpides are humans and therefore the birds' natural enemies. Their gaping beaks indicate at once their hostility and also their ultimate gullibility:

{Πι.}   οἴμοι, κεχήνασίν γέ τοι
καὶ βλέπουσιν εἰς σὲ κἀμέ.   (307–308)

Peis.   Uh-oh, they're gaping and
glaring and you and me.

The birds angrily accuse Tereus of violating their bonds of loyalty[19] and, though they may lack the unifying force of a city at this point, they nonetheless possess military organization enough to call upon their taxiarch (353) to lead the charge against the humans.[20] A pitched battle is about to be joined when Tereus intervenes, once again asserting that the birds have something to learn from humans (διδάξοντες, 372; διδάξειαν, 373) precisely because they are enemies: what one learns from enemies is the art of self-defence, more specifically the art of delimiting space by building walls (ἐκπονεῖν θ' ὑψηλὰ τείχη, 379), precisely what Peisetaerus will teach them. The question of how to decide whom to enclose along with the birds inside those walls is conveniently forgotten. Peisetaerus and Euelpides now enact the establishment of just such a defensive perimeter (and proleptically therefore of the bird city itself) on the stage, marking the boundary with a pot just used as a helmet (386–392).[21] Meanwhile the birds, behaving explicitly like hoplite warriors (ὥσπερ ὁπλίτης, 402), suspend hostilities in order to listen to the humans' proposals.[22]

Tereus invites Peisetaerus to "teach" (δίδαξον, 438) the chorus his new λόγοι, a process that describes equally well the *chorodidaskalos'* task and the process of political persuasion: by becoming *chorodidaskalos* and retraining the chorus, he incorporates them into his version of the new city. The metatheatrical dimensions of the scene are made clear by the terms of the treaty they now swear: if the chorus keeps its oath, it is to win the play competition by a unanimous approval of audience and judges, but if not, by a single vote margin:[23]

> {Πι.} κατόμοσόν νυν ταῦτά μοι.
> {Χο.} ὄμνυμ' ἐπὶ τούτοις, πᾶσι νικᾶν τοῖς κριταῖς
> καὶ τοῖς θεαταῖς πᾶσιν—
> {Πι.}   ἔσται ταυταγί.
> {Χο.} εἰ δὲ παραβαίην, ἑνὶ κριτῇ νικᾶν μόνον.   (444–447)

Peis. Now swear this to me.
Chor. I swear, by my hopes of winning
with all the judges' and spectators' approval—
Peis.   On these conditions.
Chor. And if I cheat, let me win by just one judge's vote.

The terms accepted, Peisetaerus can now disband his "troops", that is, Euelpides.[24] His preparations for his speech are still not complete: he calls for a garland, and Euelpides asks him whether he is getting ready for a banquet: a particularly meaningful question in light of the fact that at the end of the play Peisetaerus will be dining on birds who rebelled against the new democracy.[25]

Peisetaerus now unfolds his great idea: the birds were once kings of the universe and now have the opportunity to reclaim their realm from the gods. A curious feature of the presentation is that Euelpides is constantly interrupting his presentation. One might regard Euelpides' role as simply the traditional *bomolochos* figure, designed here simply to get any laughs he can, but we should not dismiss the effect of the presentation so quickly. Euelpides stands aside and apart from Peisetaerus's speech—and consequently the dramatic illusion he creates. Standing outside the dramatic space of persuasion, Euelpides can function as metatheatrical commentator. A key example of this is his comment at 479: "You'd really better grow a beak in the future" (πάνυ τοίνυν χρὴ ῥύγχος βόσκειν σε τὸ λοιπόν). As Sommerstein sees,[26] this functions as an aside to the audience in the theater, not to the birds themselves, since they already possess beaks: in this ironic fashion, Euelpides is inviting the audience to join the bird city Peisetaerus is proposing—an invitation that will become much more explicit later on. When Peisetaerus tries to use the birds on kings' scepters as part of his proof for their lost kingship, it is Euelpides who plants this firmly in a theatrical context: he has seen this in tragedies ("Some Priam holding a bird [sc. on his scepter] in those tragedies," Πρίαμός τις ἔχων ὄρνιν ἐν τοῖσι τραγῳδοῖς, 512). Other ironies or slips in logic go unremarked: a proof of the birds' divinity is that one can still swear by a bird, not a god: but the example is Lampon, who swears *in order to deceive* (ὅταν ἐξαπατᾷ τι, 521).[27] Peisetaerus's speech so overwhelms the chorus that they wish to become his slaves.[28]

Only then does he finally make his concrete suggestion: build a great, walled city. Once again, the languages of the theater and oratory converge as Peisetaerus teaches the chorus: "Well, then, I'll teach this bird city to be one" (καὶ δὴ τοίνυν πρῶτα διδάσκω μίαν ὀρνίθων πόλιν εἶναι, 550). Peisetaerus outlines the operations of the birds' power-sharing with the gods in great detail (554ff.). So enraptured with his words are the birds that they swear to join him in a "just, forthright, and holy" attack on the gods (δίκαιος ἄδολος ὅσιος ἐπὶ θεοὺς ἴῃς, 632)! Only once his persuasion has succeeded does Peisetaerus reveal his own significant name (644).

Much has been written about the motif of Eros in this play, especially about the anapaests of the parabasis beginning at 685.[29] Whether great poetry or not,[30] in performance it must have been ravishing—and that is the point. The Birds have become totally intoxicated with Peisetaerus's vision and want to enfold their audience into it as well. Their new theogony means to entice the spectators just as lovers use gifts of birds to persuade their reluctant beloveds (703–707).

It is after this ode that the invitation to the spectators to join the new bird city becomes explicit (753ff.). First that city is presented as an antinomia, in Konstan's terms, the place where normal moral categories are inverted. Most of these antinomian characteristics center around the fact that those who cannot be citizens in Athens (slaves, foreigners, and traitors) will be welcomed as citizens here. Then it is presented as the city of excess or megalonomy to use Konstan's term.[31] It is the source of wings that allow one to escape human limitations. In a superb parody of the common tragic choral theme of "I wish I were a bird and could fly away from here," the chorus now describes how wings would allow the *spectators* to fly away from the boring performances of tragedy (787), either for food or for sex with some woman whose husband is still stuck in the theater. The performance of tragedy, not the tragic situation itself, becomes the prison, comedy the world of escape—to which the spectators must return (789)![32]

Peisetaerus and Euelpides return wearing their newly acquired wings to inaugurate the new city. They are still in the process of adjusting to their new roles, however, and neither is all that pleased with his appearance. Peisetaerus compares Euelpides to a bird cheaply "painted" (γεγραμμένῳ, 805), which only underlines the theatricality rather than the reality of the transformation.[33]

Like any new city (e.g., a colony), theirs needs a name and a divine patron. Only one name, Sparta, is proposed and rejected (814) before they settle on Nephelokokkugia, and only one goddess, Athena Polias (828), who is rejected (in tragic parody) on the rather feeble grounds that a female deity cannot protect the city well enough. Instead they choose a bird, and Euelpides is immediately dispatched to begin the great wall around the city. In the most economical way possible, then, Aristophanes has assured his audience that his fantasy city is not a Spartan-sympathizer's construct and also (more disingenuously) that the city is not a satire on Athens.

What Nephelokokkugia remains, most obviously, is a city of performance, as Peisetaerus proceeds to demonstrate. He organizes a festival procession (πομπή, 849) and sacrifice in honor of the new avian gods—and includes a metatheatrical joke about the piper (858–861),[34] reminding us or perhaps reassuring us that this is only a representation of a religious ceremony.[35] Even that representation is never completed, since Peisetaerus first interrupts himself, turning on the priest for inviting too many and too rapacious birds to the sacrifice and taking over the ceremony, and then is in turn interrupted by the first of the usual series of *alazones* or imposters, all seeking wings.

Wings in the play function as markers of self-conscious theatricality. Peisetaerus and Euelpides acquired their wings through a magic herb off-stage. Now it transpires that Peisetaerus can disburse wings to would-be Nephelokokkugians from baskets—that is, as costumes or stage properties. Finally, wings can be bestowed simply by words, whether by Peisetaerus's original persuasion of the chorus to join his performance ("I take wing at your words," λόγων ἀνεπτέρωμαι, 433) or sarcastically, as he drives the informer away (1436ff.).

The first seeker after wings is a poet, continually (mis-) quoting Homer, and himself a teacher of choruses (912), which might make him a dangerous rival for Peisetaerus. He is a trainer of dithyrambic choruses (κύκλια, 918), however, and so no real threat to a dramatic composer such as Peisetaerus. His old-fashioned, Pindaric style is simply passé, and he comes off reasonably well in the encounter, successfully wheedling some clothes from Peisetaerus.

The next *alazon* receives much harsher treatment. He is a χρησμολόγος (960), an oracle-seller, a type of pest particularly prevalent in Athens as the war dragged on.[36] The most curious feature of his encounter with Peisetaerus is that it turns into a struggle between two textualities, between the oracle-seller's *written* collection of prophecies and another book, which Peisetaerus suddenly produces. Structurally, the joke works as a running gag: the oracle-seller reads an outrageous prophecy, Peisetaerus objects, and the oracle-seller replies simply "read the book" (λαβὲ τὸ βιβλίον, 974ff.). Peisetaerus produces his *own* written authority for hitting the oracle-seller and, when questioned, replies λαβὲ τὸ βιβλίον, hitting him with the book or scroll at the same time. On one level this is Three Stooges-style physical comedy, turning on a simple slippage in the meaning of λαβέ between "take (and read)" and "take that!" On another, one wonders what the audience thought when Peisetaerus pulled out his own scroll. Is this Harpo Marx, able to produce a burning blowtorch from his overcoat pocket when he needs one,[37] or might the audience see Peisetaerus's scroll as something more—perhaps even his script?

Meton the surveyor, an unnamed inspector, and a decree-seller all receive equally unceremonious treatment. We might pause a moment to consider the choice of Meton. His entrance is welcomed by Peisetaerus in a line now corrupt (994): τίς ἠπίνοια † τίς ὁ κόθορνος † τῆς ὁδοῦ, "what is the purpose, what the buskin of your journey?" Dunbar accepts the paradosis, but Sommerstein proposes τίς ἠπίνοια τῆς κοθορνωτῆς τῆς ὁδοῦ, "what is the purpose of your buskined journey?" In any case, the fact of an allusion to his footgear seems clear, though its purpose is obscure, unless it is a general allusion to effeminacy.[38] And why, if the power of the birds' city relies precisely in creating boundaries and enclosure where such did not exist before, would a surveyor be chosen as a particular enemy? Perhaps because he would potentially create boundaries and therefore divisions *within* the city. Konstan emphasizes the curious nature of the bird city which, while marked off from the rest of the universe by its boundary wall, nonetheless retains its "pre-civic" homogeneity of the populace.[39] Unlike the quarrelsome Athenians, the birds think and will one thing, unanimously. Note the revealing exchange between Meton and Peisetaerus at 1012ff.:

> {Πι.}　　　　　　ὥσπερ ἐν Λακεδαίμονι
> ξενηλατοῦνται καὶ κεκίνηνταί τινες
> πληγαὶ συχναὶ κατ᾽ ἄστυ.
> {Με.}　　　　　μῶν στασιάζετε;
> {Πι.} μὰ τὸν Δί᾽ οὐ δῆτ᾽.
> {Με.}　　　　　ἀλλὰ πῶς;
> {Πι.}　　　　　　ὁμοθυμαδὸν
> σποδεῖν ἅπαντας τοὺς ἀλαζόνας δοκεῖ.

Peis.   Just like in Sparta
aliens are being deported and there's an outbreak
of blows under way in town.
Meton.   A real revolution?
Peis. Zeus, no!
Met.   Then what?
Peis.   There's a unanimous agreement
to beat up all the con artists.

Peisetaerus warns Meton of possible violence against him. Is there a revolution ($\sigma\tau\alpha\sigma\iota\acute{\alpha}\zeta\epsilon\tau\epsilon$) brewing, Meton asks. No, there is a unanimous desire to get rid of frauds and shysters ($\dot{\alpha}\lambda\alpha\zeta\acute{o}\nu\alpha\varsigma$).[40]

A few blows convince Meton to depart, but he simply yields place to another representative and agent of Athenian textual order. The Inspector arrives, none too pleased at having been sent to this out-of-the-way place by a piece of writing ("a writ of Teleas" $\beta\iota\beta\lambda\acute{\iota}o\nu$ / $T\epsilon\lambda\acute{\epsilon}o\upsilon$, 1024–1025).[41] Peisetaerus accords him even shorter shrift before attacking him as well. The pace of the scene now accelerates, as a third dealer in words, the Decree-seller, also arrives with his wares in the form of a scroll (1037).[42] He joins forces with the Inspector, and the comedy becomes very physical until Peisetaerus succeeds in driving them both away.

Peisetaerus gives up his attempt to conduct the sacrifice onstage and carries it back into the skene (1057), leaving the chorus to perform the city in another way. The chorus now explicitly incorporates an element of the Dionysiac festival outside the play *within* its own performance and thereby seems to reach out and absorb the festival within itself. The City Dionysia, a major event at which the city displayed itself to the whole Greek world, contained much more than just the performance of the plays and choruses. In addition to the sacrifices, displays of tribute, and parade of orphans (well discussed by Goldhill[43]), there were also public proclamations. What we know of these suggests that decrees of public honors were more common,[44] but on the evidence of the following passage decrees of rewards for the punishment of state enemies were also included:

$\tau\hat{\eta}\delta\epsilon$ $\mu\acute{\epsilon}\nu\tau\omega\iota$ $\theta\acute{\eta}\mu\acute{\epsilon}\rho\alpha$ $\mu\acute{\alpha}\lambda\iota\sigma\tau$ ' $\dot{\epsilon}\pi\alpha\nu\alpha\gamma\omega\rho\epsilon\acute{\upsilon}\epsilon\tau\alpha\iota$·
"$\mathring{\eta}\nu$ $\dot{\alpha}\pi\omega\kappa\tau\epsilon\acute{\iota}\nu\eta$ $\tau\iota\varsigma$ $\mathring{\upsilon}\mu\hat{\omega}\nu$ $\Delta\iota\alpha\gamma\acute{o}\rho\alpha\nu$ $\tau\grave{o}\nu$ $M\acute{\eta}\lambda\iota\omega\nu$,
$\lambda\alpha\mu\beta\acute{\alpha}\nu\epsilon\iota\nu$ $\tau\acute{\alpha}\lambda\alpha\nu\tau\omega\nu$, $\mathring{\eta}\nu$ $\tau\epsilon$ $\tau\hat{\omega}\nu$ $\tau\upsilon\rho\acute{\alpha}\nu\nu\omega\nu$ $\tau\acute{\iota}\varsigma$ $\tau\iota\nu\alpha$
$\tau\hat{\omega}\nu$ $\tau\epsilon\theta\nu\eta\kappa\acute{o}\tau\omega\nu$ $\dot{\alpha}\pi\omega\kappa\tau\epsilon\acute{\iota}\nu\eta$, $\tau\acute{\alpha}\lambda\alpha\nu\tau\omega\nu$ $\lambda\alpha\mu\beta\acute{\alpha}\nu\epsilon\iota\nu$."
$\beta\omega\upsilon\lambda\acute{o}\mu\epsilon\sigma\theta$ ' $\omega\mathring{\upsilon}\nu$ $\nu\hat{\upsilon}\nu$ $\dot{\alpha}\nu\epsilon\iota\pi\epsilon\hat{\iota}\nu$ $\tau\alpha\hat{\upsilon}\tau\alpha$ $\chi\mathring{\eta}\mu\epsilon\hat{\iota}\varsigma$ $\dot{\epsilon}\nu\theta\acute{\alpha}\delta\epsilon$·
"$\mathring{\eta}\nu$ $\dot{\alpha}\pi\omega\kappa\tau\epsilon\acute{\iota}\nu\eta$ $\tau\iota\varsigma$ $\mathring{\upsilon}\mu\hat{\omega}\nu$ $\Phi\iota\lambda\omega\kappa\rho\acute{\alpha}\tau\eta$ $\tau\grave{o}\nu$ $\Sigma\tau\rho\omega\acute{\upsilon}\theta\iota\omega\nu$,
$\lambda\acute{\eta}\psi\epsilon\tau\alpha\iota$ $\tau\acute{\alpha}\lambda\alpha\nu\tau\omega\nu$, $\mathring{\eta}\nu$ $\delta\grave{\epsilon}$ $\zeta\hat{\omega}\nu\tau\alpha$ γ ' $\dot{\alpha}\gamma\acute{\alpha}\gamma\eta$, $\tau\acute{\epsilon}\tau\tau\alpha\rho\alpha$ (1072–1078)

> It's proclaimed on this day in particular:
> "If any of you kills Diagoras the Melian,
> he'll receive one talent, and if anyone kills
> one of the dead tyrants, he'll receive a talent."
> Now we want to make a proclamation too:
> "If any of you kills Philocrates the Sparrovian,
> he'll receive one talent—bring him in alive, and it's four . . .

The birds are in effect hijacking the Dionysia; it is *their* city, which, in addition to rewarding tyrant-slayers,[45] will also offer a bounty for the punishment of a cruel bird-seller. The city of Nephelokokkugia, at first a space limited by the very boundaries of the theater stage, defended by one soldier with a pot for a helmet against the chorus, now has grown so large that it swallows up the mere Athenian festival within itself.

Next the chorus makes an attempt in character to bribe the judges, a piece of business that should be jocular, but one element seems less than light-hearted. In addition to promising the "owls of Laureion" (that is, drachmas, 1106) and good luck, they promise the judges assistance in political peculation, in plundering from the demos when they happen to be allotted office (1111ff.). This seems less benign, perhaps even reminiscent of the chorus in *Clouds*, tempting the hearers with something they ought not to want. Since they turn immediately to threatening the judges with bird droppings, the point may slip by unnoticed by many, but the chorus has been encouraging the judges to fail in their duty to the demos.

A messenger arrives to recount the astonishing story of the building of the wall, a tour de force of fantasy—which Peisetaerus labels "truly a pack of lies" ($\dot{\alpha}\lambda\eta\theta\hat{\omega}s$ . . . $\psi\epsilon\acute{v}\delta\epsilon\sigma\iota\nu$, 1167). This openly admits that the bird city is built of words,[46] but they are none the less effective for all that. Hot on his heels enters another messenger with the news that the walls have already been breached by one of the gods. Sommerstein *ad loc.* notes the metatheatricality of the verb for his appearance, $\epsilon\dot{\iota}\sigma\theta\epsilon\hat{\iota}$ $\pi\rho\dot{o}s$ $\dot{\eta}\mu\hat{\alpha}s$ $\delta\epsilon\hat{v}\rho o$, 1169, which means "enter" in the sense of "come on stage." The messenger is also "glaring a war dance" ($\pi\upsilon\rho\rho\acute{\iota}\chi\eta\nu$ $\beta\lambda\acute{\epsilon}\pi\omega\nu$). This "war dance" is closely associated with tragic dance as well[47]: coupled with the verb $\epsilon\dot{\iota}\sigma\theta\epsilon\hat{\iota}$, it suggests that this messenger, not unlike the one before him, is a refugee from the tragic stage.[48] Peisetaerus promptly orders mobilization.

Heralded by a sound which is as likely to be the creaking of the *mechane* as it is music imitative of rushing wings,[49] Iris swings into view suspended from the crane. Here is an emphatically theatrical (and of course tragic) invasion of the theater space, showing us once more that the real location of Nephelokokkugia is the stage, the space beneath the theologeion. Peisetaerus under-standably defends his city with word games, demanding to know whether Iris is a "ship or a hat" (1203), trying to use language to redefine the intruder and therefore deal with the threat. One wonders if the pun is intended when Iris complains of Peisetaerus's behavior, ἄτοπόν γε τουτὶ πρᾶγμα, 1208. The business seems extraordinary (ἄτοπον) to Iris, precisely because she fails to recognize that there is a place now, a *topos*, where there was no place, no city before.[50] Nor should we miss the visual comedy of the arrested flight: one imagines that after years of practice the crane operator was capable of quite elegant effects in flying the gods (cf. the Foys in productions of *Peter Pan*), but once arrested in her flight Iris will dangle there quite obviously an actor on a rope. Peisetaerus charges her with a border violation, not merely for flying through the city but through chaos as well (διὰ τῆς πόλεως τῆς ἀλλοτρίας καὶ τοῦ χάους, 1218), not only reminding us of the great ode on the origin of Love from chaos but also suggesting that the city and chaos, the newly bounded space built in the essence of unboundedness, are one and the same.

Threatening this immortal with death and defying the usual divine blus-ter, Peisetaerus finally sends her back the way she came with a few threats of sexual violence to hasten her on her way. His response has a clearly metatheat-rical dimension too: his words parody Euripides' *Alcestis*, while his actions may well imitate satyrs in satyr play.[51]

A herald arrives from earth with the news that the riffraff of humanity (1280ff., those who took Sparta and Socrates as their models before) are now eager to become colonists (ἐποίκοις, 1307, a word suggestive of imperial-ism[52]) in Nephelokokkugia. Indeed this messenger babbles on so excitedly at first that he must appeal to Peisetaerus to "give me my cue" (1273)[53] to stop. Humans wish to imitate (ἐκμιμούμενοι, 1285) the birds, sing songs of bird in-spiration, and have already tried to use language to make themselves birds by giving themselves birds' names. The bird chorus is now so besotted with Pei-setaerus's vision that they do not detect the irony in their own statement that their city will now become "well-peopled" (πολυάνορα, 1313; cf. "good for a man to settle," καλὸν ἀνδρὶ μετοικεῖν, 1319). The city of the birds is losing its avian identity.

It remains a comic city, however, for while the chorus sings of the graces and wisdom that dwell within it, Peisetaerus is berating and abusing his slave Manes in typical comic fashion for being slow in bringing out the wings he will distribute to the new, would-be colonists. A young man who desires to beat up his father learns from Peisetaerus that he *can* do that here (the antino-mian theme) but at first is told he will still have to support his father. When

he expresses his disappointment, however, Peisetaerus seemingly relents, with
the following justification:

$$\epsilon\pi\epsilon\iota\delta\eta\pi\epsilon\rho\ \gamma\dot{\alpha}\rho\ \eta\lambda\theta\epsilon\varsigma,\ \mathring{\omega}\ \mu\acute{\epsilon}\lambda\epsilon,$$
$$\epsilon\mathring{\upsilon}\nu o\upsilon\varsigma,\ \pi\tau\epsilon\rho\acute{\omega}\sigma\omega\ \sigma'\ \mathring{\omega}\sigma\pi\epsilon\rho\ \mathring{o}\rho\nu\iota\nu\ \mathring{o}\rho\phi\alpha\nu\acute{o}\nu. \qquad (1360\text{–}1361)$$

> Since you've come with good intentions,
> friend, I'll wing you like an orphan bird.

The young man can become, as it were, an honorary orphan, which entitles
him to wings provided by the bird city. The allusion is a startling one: Peisetaerus imitates one of the most solemn and moving parts of the City Dionysia itself, the parade of the war orphans in their new, state-provided hoplite
armor, a ceremony fresh in the minds of the audience of *Birds*.[54] Peisetaerus's
gift of wings to this young man is a powerful move toward establishing the
bird city's independence.[55] The latter happily accepts this offer and flies off
to front-line service in Thrace (almost as good a way of getting away from
paternal control).[56]

The reception accorded Kinesias, the dithyrambic poet in search of ethe-
real inspiration, is much less cordial, even violent, and contrasts sharply with
the treatment given the first, unnamed poet (904ff.). Kinesias is a representative of the New Music, a particular Aristophanic target,[57] and so is soon
sent on his way with a blow or two. Although Peisetaerus offers him a place
as a trainer inside the city, he does so in a deliberately insulting way (1405),
designed to reinforce the message that he is not wanted.[58]

The climax of this particular series is an informer ($\sigma\upsilon\kappa o\phi\acute{\alpha}\nu\tau\eta\varsigma$, 1423)
seeking after wings, who instead is sent flying like a top with a whipping from
Peisetaerus. Just before that, however, in a passage of considerable significance
in this play about words, Peisetaerus says he will give him "wings through
speaking" ($\nu\hat{\upsilon}\nu\ \tau o\iota\ \lambda\acute{\epsilon}\gamma\omega\nu\ \pi\tau\epsilon\rho\hat{\omega}\ \sigma\epsilon$, 1437), a turn of phrase that puzzles the
informer. Peisetaerus explains through the analogies of a young man enticed
into hoping for a career as a chariot-driver through speech and another whose
mind is enthralled by tragedy. We are in danger of losing the point here, because the analogies do no justice to the radical conception Peisetaerus has proposed. He claims that his language is "performative" language,[59] and in doing
so he literalizes metaphor in a typically Aristophanic fashion: he has been creating citizens for the bird city by language, and the city is a city of language.
The chorus's invitation to the audience to join the city (discussed above, on
lines 753ff.) similarly offers to transform father-beaters and slaves into birds by
renaming them.

After the informer's flagellant dismissal, the chorus once again takes metaphorical flight. The opening lines seem very general:[60]

πολλὰ δὴ καὶ καινὰ καὶ θαυ-
μάστ᾽ ἐπεπτόμεσθα καὶ
δεινὰ πράγματ᾽ εἴδομεν.   (1470–1472)

Though he makes no explicit mention of it, Sommerstein's translation of these lines:

Many and unheard-of and marvelous
are the places we have overflown, and
strange the things we have seen.

captures the parody here (first noticed by Moulton[61]) of perhaps the most famous chorus in all of Sophocles, that from the *Antigone*, which begins:

πολλὰ τὰ δεινὰ κοὐδὲν ἀν-
θρώπου δεινότερον πέλει· (332–333)

Many are the world's wonders,
but none more marvelous than man.

The resemblances are few but nonetheless pointed: the same word to begin, and δεινά somewhere further along. The antistrophe in Sophocles does go on to speak of man's dominance over the race of birds (φῦλον ὀρνίθων, 342–343), and perhaps we should count this as a further resemblance. Parody of Sophoclean style it is not—but subversive use of Sophocles' ideas it may be. Has Peisetaerus so ensnared the birds in his noose of words that what they present as proof of their power and freedom, an ode on what they have seen flying over the vast world, becomes another demonstration of their subordination to man?

Prometheus now appears, comically muffled up and carrying a parasol. And why? So that the gods will not see him *from above* (ἄνωθεν, 1509).[62] As often in Aristophanes, we are in danger of taking this as natural and obvious when for the Greeks it may have been no such thing. Did the Greeks think the gods could see them only from above? Perhaps children literalized the process in this way, but this is surely a joke for adults.[63] In the theater, of course, the gods *can* see only from above, since they stand on the theologeion or swing from the crane. The unnecessary emphasis on the spatial dimension here, I suggest, is another reminder that the city is the stage, a platform poised not between heaven and earth but between theologeion and orchestra. Here and only here is Prometheus's parasol a very good defense against snooping gods. Mythologically Prometheus is a natural ally for subordinates (men or birds) turning on the gods.[64] He not only counsels Peisetaerus to demand Zeus' scepter but also Basileia[65] for his wife, since she is the keeper (ταμιεύει, 1538) of his powers. Prometheus expresses his hatred for the gods and further labels himself a Timon. One wonders if this is a theatrical reference too, for the character was already proverbial in Aristophanes' time (though the scholiasts thought he was historical), and the name turns up as a play title later.[66] Prometheus scuttles off, remarking that he hopes if Zeus *does* spot him, he will be taken for a parasol-carrier in a religious procession; Peisetaerus, with a good director's eye for the value of props in completing a stage picture, offers him a stool to carry to complete the disguise (1551–1552).[67]

After a very short choral interlude Poseidon appears, accompanied by the dim-witted Heracles and a Triballian god from "up-country," incapable of speaking clear Greek or of wearing his clothes in a dignified manner (1567–1569). The scene is broadly comic, turning largely on the voracious appetite of Heracles and the thick-headedness of the Triballian, but it has a political agenda as well. As Poseidon fusses over the Triballian, telling him to hold still as he adjusts the latter's cloak, we see the theatrical qualities of this embassy. Poseidon's doomed attempts through costume and instruction to turn the Triballian, whom divine democracy has put into office ("O Democracy, where on earth are you leading us, if the gods have elected this guy?" ὦ δημοκρατία, ποῖ προβιβᾷς ἡμᾶς ποτε, / εἰ τουτονὶ κεχειροτονήκασ' οἱ θεοί; 1570–1571), into an effective performer are in many ways the counterpart of Dicaeopolis's deconstruction of the costumed "ambassadors" in the opening of the *Acharnians*. Poseidon as director is no match for Peisetaerus, whose ability to persuade the birds now becomes starkly clear. In this scene we learn that the magnificent feast Peisetaerus is cooking up is (now that he himself has acquired wings, which he continues to wear) a cannibalistic one:

> {Ἡρ.} τὰ δὲ κρέα τοῦ ταῦτ' ἐστίν;
> {Πι.} ὄρνιθές τινες
> ἐπανιστάμενοι τοῖς δημοτικοῖσιν ὀρνέοις
> ἔδοξαν ἀδικεῖν.　　　　　(1582–1585)

Her. What sort of meat's that?
Peis. Some birds
convicted of rebelling against
the democratic birds.

Divine democracy is represented by a glutton and a dolt, while bird democracy devours its own.[68] It is hard to claim we have come very far from Athens after all.

Poseidon does his best to argue the case for the gods, despite his easily distracted companions, but he is hardly the ideal diplomat. He makes a serious faux pas in claiming that the gods will provide "halcyon days" (ἀλκυονίδας ... ἡμέρας, 1594), one thing they are surely capable of providing for themselves.[69] In short order Peisetaerus has reversed the situation, offering the birds' help to the gods (1606ff.) and, true to his name, persuading them to hand over Zeus' scepter.

Peisetaerus's demand for Basileia, however, produced only now when agreement seems at hand, is too much for Poseidon, who then tries to break off negotiations. Heracles, intent mainly on his dinner, is for peace at any price. When Poseidon tries to win him back, claiming that Heracles will be giving up his own expected inheritance from Zeus, the discussion demonstrates that Olympus is just one more version of Athens,[70] for Peisetaerus triumphantly demonstrates that Heracles is a bastard (νόθος, 1650) under Athenian law and therefore not entitled to inherit his father's property.[71] With no property interest in Zeus' continued rule, Heracles is more than willing to hand over sovereignty to the birds. Heracles browbeats the Triballian into agreement, Poseidon is outvoted, and Peisetaerus, grabbing a wedding cloak from a silent slave extra (1693), goes off to receive the scepter of Zeus and Basileia.

The finale, as Peisetaerus returns with his prizes, then dances off to his wedding to Basileia, is so splendid both visually and verbally that it seems almost impossible to question the "happiness" of this ending.[72] The Herald's announcement strains the boundaries of language, emphasizing that the birds' accomplishments (πράττοντες) are beyond telling (ὦ μείζω λόγου, 1706)[73] —just as the performance of the *Birds* surpasses any attempt to narrate its effects. As Peisetaerus brandishes his newly acquired thunderbolt, it seems likely that the thunder machine (the *bronteion*) sounds from offstage.[74] If so, Aristophanes, who elsewhere regularly mocks the resources of the tragic stage (such as the *mechane* and the *ekkyklema*) here employs another to enact his hero's power.

It is tempting to concede to a great artist such as Aristophanes a political foresight denied to most others in his society and therefore to look for warnings in this play against overweening imperial ambition in general and the forthcoming failure of the Sicilian expedition in particular.[75] Little in the present analysis of the play's metatheatrical devices will support such specific prescience. Peisetaerus is no Cleon figure, destroying the birds' city by factionalizing it, but a city founder creating order and power out of chaos. While to our modern sensibilities the bird city that devours its own may seem monstrous, it is monstrous in ways unlikely to trouble either Aristophanes or most of his fellow citizens,[76] and there are many pleasures (of language and otherwise) associated with this escape from the confines of besieged, imperial Athens. The bird city, built in a theater, becomes therefore a model of Aristophanes' own art. As long as he believed in the comedy that he practiced, his theatrical city in the air must be far more utopian than dystopian, a place of refuge and hope rather than a dire warning.

The *Birds* recreates an Athens in which the politics of persuasion have their proper place and only the parasitic enemies of the unified city practice a harmful deception. Now that Cleon is safely and long since dead, Aristophanes can again offer us a positive model of the theater and its power not just to teach but also to inspire the demos. In line with the ambitions implicit in his claim that "trugedy also knows about justice" (*Acharnians* 500), this theater proves to be his own comic theater.

Perhaps a modern analogy will be helpful. In Preston Sturges's brilliant film comedy, *Sullivan's Travels*, the eponymous hero, a filmmaker famous for his musical comedies during the Depression years, decides he must make socially relevant films instead and goes off to find that social relevance in America's underclass. Having experienced suffering even to the extent of being sentenced to a chain gang, the hero discovers, while watching a cartoon with his fellow prisoners, that comedy and the joy of laughter are gifts too precious ever to discard. The analogy is flawed is many ways: Aristophanes could not have written serious plays about the war, even if he had wanted to, because there was no serious, nonmythological medium in which to work. I think, though, that Aristophanes was a comic artist great enough to know, just as Sturges did, that even when there are serious points to be made, the artist does not abandon comedy's power not only to make us laugh but to console us with a vision of a better life. Neither Peisetaerus nor his play can be reduced to a statement for or against the continuing war, but together they count its costs, both in suffering and to the idea of democracy itself, even as they celebrate the improvisatory powers of the comic hero.

8

Cross-Dress for Success:
Thesmophoriazusae

"Daphne": "You don't understand, Osgood. I'm a man."
Osgood: "Well, nobody's perfect."
—*Some Like It Hot*

NOT SO MANY YEARS AGO one could lament how little work had been done on the *Thesmophoriazusae*. It was the neglected sister in the triad of plays about women. Lacking a strong heroine such as Lysistrata or even a political innovator such as Praxagora, it seemed to offer only a replay of the Euripides parody of the *Acharnians*, although it did provide the chance to try to reconstruct the lost *Andromeda*, based on its parodies. Beginning with Froma Zeitlin's brilliant treatment of the play, however, and a key essay by Helene Foley,[1] the play has moved to center stage, particularly in discussions of gender and representation. Its dizzying blend of parody and gender-bending raises peculiarly modern questions, such as whether any male writer, be it Euripides, Agathon, or Aristophanes himself, can actually say anything about female experience, or if all their attempts are simply what Elaine Showalter has so caustically dubbed "critical cross-dressing."[2] Such questions go to the heart of Aristophanes' relation to Euripides and to the claims of tragic illusion. I have no intention of denying the importance of any of these issues (indeed, they are essential to any understanding of this remarkable play), but I also want to bring some other issues of the play to the foreground as well. If the foregoing analyses of Aristophanes' earlier plays have merit in suggesting connections between those plays and the political practices of the demos, it seems unlikely that Aristophanes' concerns in this play should be purely aesthetic or theoretical, focused narrowly on the practices of one tragedian he has parodied before, nor more abstractly on the nature of representation alone (or even the relation of representation to femininity). It seems possible that the play's politics are not *only* sexual and might comment on the practices and not just the prejudices of the city as well. The timeless metatheatricality of the play has claimed a great deal of attention. In what follows let us also contemplate its time-bound comments on performance.

For at the center of this play lies once again a deliberative assembly. The historical gathering of women at the Thesmophoria was a religious rather than political gathering, of course, but Aristophanes *represents* it as functioning like an Athenian democratic body.[3] If Jeffrey Henderson is right to argue that the Athenian Thesmophoria was celebrated on the Pnyx, in or near the space of the male citizens' assembly,[4] the power of the play to parody and comment on the workings of the democracy is even greater. In a city where the rights of free and open deliberation were at peril, the play's political representations may have more significance than heretofore acknowledged.

Let me make clear at the outset that such a reading of the play does not depend intimately on the date of the play. The problem of dating the *Thesmophoriazusae* is tied to that of the *Lysistrata*. The consensus view is now that the *Lysistrata* was performed at the Lenaea of 411, the *Thesmophoriazusae* at the City Dionysia of the same year, although some still support a date of 410 for the *Thesmophoriazusae*.[5] Certainly one could say more about the nature of the play's comments on events if we could be absolutely, incontrovertibly certain that it barely preceded or shortly followed the oligarchic coup of 411. Whether the play foresees with alarm or reviews with regret, however, it should not be viewed as an escapist fantasy, utterly abstracted from the life of the polis that Aristophanes purported to teach through his works.

The play begins with two characters on a quest, much like Peisetaerus and Euelpides, one of whom is soon addressed as Euripides (4). The other figure, whose mask identifies him as an old man,[6] is never named in the play, but only described as being related by marriage to Euripides (74). Ancient commentators identified him as Mnesilochus, the father-in-law of Euripides, and while this name has no authority and is perhaps even improbable,[7] he is so fully realized and significant a character in the play that it seems to be better to use this personal name rather than a functional designation (such as the "Old Relative").

In this opening sequence Mnesilochus plays straight man or *eiron* to Euripides' *alazon*, as the latter plays word games about what they are going to see and hear. Mnesilochus, thoroughly confused by learning that he is not to hear and not to see, gets a good laugh with this riposte:

{*Κη.*}   νὴ τὸν Δί᾽ ἥδομαί γε τουτὶ προσμαθών.
οἷόν γέ πού ᾽στιν αἱ σοφαὶ ξυνουσίαι.
{*Ευ.*} πόλλ᾽ ἂν μάθοις τοιαῦτα παρ᾽ ἐμοῦ.
{*Κη.*}   πῶς ἂν οὖν
πρὸς τοῖς ἀγαθοῖς τούτοισιν ἐξεύροιμ᾽ ὅπως
ἔτι προσμάθοιμι χωλὸς εἶναι τὼ σκέλει;   (20–24)

Mnesilochus. By Zeus, I'm glad to learn that!
Intellectual conversation is really something.
Euripides. You could learn a lot like that from me.
Mnes.   So could I,
on top of these advantages, find out how
I could also be crippled in my legs?

On one level the joke is: "Since you've taught me to be deaf and blind, could you teach me to be lame too?" There may be more, however: what would it mean to learn to be lame from Euripides? As the daughter in *Peace* remarks (146–148), if her father falls and lames himself, he will become a tragedy of Euripides (τραγῳδία γένῃ). Euripides does not answer Mnesilochus's question, but in fact the old man is going to become, not just one, but several tragedies of Euripides. No one in the audience can know that at this point, of course, but Euripides' reputation (so carefully fostered by Aristophanes) for creating lame heroes is certainly a live resonance here and subliminally prepares the way for future action.

They arrive at Agathon's door, and the jokes immediately turn to the younger poet. The structure of this exchange is worth detailed consideration:

{*Ευ.*} ἐνταῦθ᾽ Ἀγάθων ὁ κλεινὸς οἰκῶν τυγχάνει
ὁ τραγῳδοποιός.
{*Κη.*}   ποῖος οὗτος Ἀγάθων;
{*Ευ.*} ἔστιν τις Ἀγάθων—
{*Κη.*}   μῶν ὁ μέλας, ὁ καρτερός;
{*Ευ.*} οὔκ, ἀλλ᾽ ἕτερός τις. οὐχ ἑόρακας πώποτε;
{*Κη.*} μῶν ὁ δασυπώγων;
{*Ευ.*}   οὐχ ἑόρακας πώποτε.
{*Κη.*} οὔτοι μὰ τὸν Δί᾽ ὥστε κἀμέ γ᾽ εἰδέναι.
{*Ευ.*} καὶ μὴν βεβίνηκας σύ γ᾽· ἀλλ᾽ οὐκ οἶσθ᾽ ἴσως.
ἀλλ᾽ ἐκποδὼν πτήξωμεν, ὡς ἐξέρχεται
θεράπων τις αὐτοῦ πῦρ ἔχων καὶ μυρρίνας,
προθυσόμενος, ἔοικε, τῆς ποήσεως.   (29–38)

Eur. Agathon happens to live here,
the famous tragedian.
Mnes.   Which Agathon's this?

Eur. There's an Agathon—
Mnes.   You mean the dark, husky one?
Eur. No, another one. You've never seen him?
Mnes. The bushy-bearded one?
Eur.   You've never seen him.
Mnes. Zeus, no, not that I know of.
Eur. And yet you've screwed him. But maybe you don't know him.
But let's duck out of the way, since some servant of his
is coming out with fire and myrtle branches,
to sacrifice, it seems, for poetry.

First a broad joke ("The famous Agathon . . ." "Agathon who?"), then a
series of increasing jokes attacking his masculinity follow, culminating with
the blunt statement that Mnesilochus has "screwed" the poet. All of this is
careful preparation for the dynamic of interaction between the two, once the
poet appears.

Lines 36–38 signal a convention so familiar from later drama that no one
to my knowledge has remarked how utterly unmotivated—within the plot—
they are at this point. Euripides and Mnesilochus step out of the way to eaves-
drop on Agathon's servant, who now appears from the house to offer a sacrifice and prayer. Now nothing in the play ever suggests that they should fear to
be detected by the servant or even that they can gain any useful information
by eavesdropping on the servant's prayer. Rather, the unmotivated eavesdropping form establishes a theatrical frame around both the servant and Agathon,
once he appears, and places Euripides and Mnesilochus in a position of apparently superior power.[8] Mnesilochus offers a series of ever louder comments
aside on the high-flown style of this poetical servant, culminating in more
crude insults against Agathon's masculinity, which finally bring him to the
servant's attention. A confrontation seems imminent, but Euripides hastily
smoothes things over. The servant retires, having announced Agathon is on
his way out.

In the ensuing interval[9] Euripides finally explains the reason for dragging
Mnesilochus out at first light: he is in fear for his life. Mnesilochus's response
is telling:

{Κη.} καὶ πῶς; ἐπεὶ νῦν γ᾽ οὔτε τὰ δικαστήρια
μέλλει δικάζειν οὔτε βουλῆς ἐσθ᾽ ἕδρα,
ἐπείπερ ἐστὶ Θεσμοφορίων ἡ μέση.
{Εὐ.} τοῦτ᾽ αὐτὸ γάρ τοι κἀπολεῖν με προσδοκῶ.
αἱ γὰρ γυναῖκες ἐπιβεβουλεύκασί μοι
κἂν Θεσμοφόροιν μέλλουσι περί μου τήμερον
ἐκκλησιάζειν ἐπ᾽ ὀλέθρῳ.   (78–84)

Mnes. How's that? Today the law courts
aren't in session, there's no sitting of the *boule*,
since it's day two of the Thesmophoria.
Eur. That's exactly why I'm afraid of extermination.
The women have plotted my destruction
and today they're going to hold an assembly
at the Thesmophorion to do me in.

Mnesilochus thinks that in the democracy a threat to a citizen's life could come
from only one of two sources: the law courts or the *boule*.[10] Since it is a holiday,
specifically the middle day of the Thesmophoria, notes Mnesilochus, it is not
legal for either of those bodies to be sitting. In the inverted world of comedy,
however, that is precisely what makes the threat possible: the women's anti-
assembly is about to deliberate on Euripides' destruction.[11] Euripides' desperate plan is to persuade Agathon, dressed as a woman, to infiltrate the assembly
and speak on his behalf.

At this point Agathon is wheeled out on the *ekkyklema* (οὐκκυκλούμενος,
96). The scene itself is both a parody of the influence of the New Music on contemporary tragedy and a delightful and visually striking self-parody of Aristophanes' first major attack on Euripides, the scene in the *Acharnians* where
Dicaeopolis begs for the costume and props of one of his ragged heroes.[12]
There Euripides was wheeled out, surrounded by the costumes of his ragged
heroes; here Agathon appears, already dressed in female clothing, and with
more scattered about him on the bed.[13] Agathon's facial appearance may be
equally striking. Lauren Taaffe, building on a suggestion of K. J. Dover, argues that Agathon "dresses . . . to be an object of vision and desire" and is
portrayed with a very close-trimmed beard.[14] If this is true, there is a further
striking visual association as well. One group of adult men in Athens needed
to cut their beards very close: professional actors, who wore the close-fitting
masks that covered the entire face and head. The best example of this is the
balding actor with close-cut stubble portrayed on the Würzburg fragments.[15]
Now no source tells us that Agathon acted in his own plays, and had he done
so at this late date, we might well have heard of it.[16] On the other hand, it is
not unlikely that he came to his own interest in theater through performing
in the chorus, for which he would have worn a mask. While the vases regularly
show unmasked choristers as beardless, some may well have had to trim their
beards in order to wear their masks.[17]

It looks as though Aristophanes is deliberately confusing his visual signals here, much as (to the consternation of commentators) he has confused his
verbal signals. Many are quite exercised about the precise nature of the theory

of poetic mimesis that Agathon adumbrates in this scene. Why, they ask, does Agathon need to dress in drag in order to compose women's parts for his plays? There may not be a precise answer to that question, in which everything Agathon does or says plays a logically coherent part. Rather, I think, Aristophanes is deliberately conflating the notions of poet and performer.[18] Remember that the original audience of this play had no idea where the plot was going. With multiple signals Aristophanes is setting up his audience to expect that Agathon will in fact do what Euripides asks of him, become a performer in a script devised by the older poet. Fifteen years before Dicaeopolis simply wanted the costume; now Euripides wants the costume with Agathon inside it. The theatrical precedent of the *Acharnians*, the framing of the scene here in *Thesmophoriazusae* as first eavesdropping and then therefore play-within-the-play, and the deliberate portrayal of Agathon as a performer himself and not just a poet all powerfully suggest that Agathon will volunteer.

These initial signals all prove to be wrong, because Agathon turns out to be much less manipulable than his reputation would suggest. At first Agathon is treated as spectacle. He performs a song in which he takes the parts of both chorus leader and chorus. Nothing allows us to reconstruct with certainty the manner of this performance, but there is ample scope for the actor to add physical or vocal comedy (exaggerated business as he leaps back and forth between the two roles) to the textual parody of Agathon's style. Agathon may well be using a falsetto voice to sing the role of the chorus of Trojan maidens.[19] Gender confusion even spreads to the nature of music itself, as the cithara is described as the "mother of hymns, outstanding for its masculine cry" (κίθαρίν τε ματέρ᾽ ὕμνων / ἄρσενι βοᾷ δοκίμων, 124–125).[20] The end of Agathon's performance is marked by one of the very few genuine stage directions in Greek drama: ὀλολύζει. Agathon gives a ritual female wailing cry, presumably as the chorus in the play he is composing. The effect must have been considerable and was no small tribute to the actor's vocal skills.

Mnesilochus's comments on this performance quickly bring it back to earth by describing the music's virtually physical (and lascivious) effects on him as a listener (130ff.). Lest anyone in the audience miss the parody, he specifically notes, before quizzing Agathon about his incongruous blend of masculine and feminine attributes, that he is using the words of Aeschylus's *Lycourgeia* trilogy (κατ᾽ Αἰσχύλον / ἐκ τῆς Λυκουργείας, 134–135). Such an explicit citation is surprising: Aristophanes rarely tells us precisely whom he is parodying. In the later fifth century revivals of Aeschylus are the likely source for general audience knowledge of his plays,[21] but perhaps it had been some time since *Lycourgeia* was revived. The reference is also subliminal preparation for the characters' interactions, not just parody of tragic rhetoric: Mnesilochus here takes on the part of Pentheus, mocking Agathon as Dionysus.²² Like Pentheus, Mnesilochus is soon to be tempted into the feminine disguise that he mocks—and into dire danger as a result.

Agathon's calm response to these jeers is his theory of mimesis, a discussion that, however comic, is the first technical use of this term.²³ His is a somatic theory: if one is writing masculine parts, says Agathon, the body of the male poet already has the wherewithal (154–155), but for writing female parts it must put on feminine garb and "ways" (τρόπους, 150). Mnesilochus quickly reduces this to its crudest meaning, "sexual position," accusing Agathon of "mounting astride" in order to write a *Phaedra*.²⁴ When Agathon says that mimesis must "hunt after" (συνθηρεύεται) the things the male body does not possess, Mnesilochus activates the potential pun on "wild beast" (θήρ) and by picking up the συν-prefix reverses the power relationship of hunter and hunted thus:

{Ἀγ.} ἀνδρεῖα δ᾿ ἢν ποῇ τις, ἐν τῷ σώματι
ἔνεσθ᾿ ὑπάρχον τοῦθ᾿. ἃ δ᾿ οὐ κεκτήμεθα,
μίμησις ἤδη ταῦτα συνθηρεύεται.
{Κη.} ὅταν σατύρους τοίνυν ποῇς, καλεῖν ἐμέ,
ἵνα συμποιῶ σοὔπισθεν ἐστυκὼς ἐγώ.   (154–158)

Agathon. If you're writing of masculinity, your body
is already equipped. What we don't possess
must be hunted down with imitation.
Mnes. Whenever you're writing a satyr play, call me:
I'll coauthor your rear nice and hard.

Mnesilochus now imagines a scene in which satyrs copulate with each other, leaving no doubt, however, that he will play the active role here.²⁵ Quick insults to three other tragedians, whose work resembles their characters (168–170), closes out the theme of poetry expressing the poet's character.

Character consistency and probability has very little to do with the practices of the Greek comic theater. After Mnesilochus has so extensively abused Agathon, Euripides now comes forward with no apparent embarrassment to ask Agathon for help. Agathon turns him down by turning Euripides' own poetry back on him:

{Ἀγ.} Εὐριπίδη—
{Εὐ.}   τί ἐστιν;
{Ἀγ.}   ἐπόησάς ποτε·
"χαίρεις ὁρῶν φῶς, πατέρα δ᾿ οὐ χαίρειν δοκεῖς;"

{*Ευ.*} ἔγωγε.
{*Αγ.*}   μή νυν ἐλπίσῃς τὸ σὸν κακὸν
ἡμᾶς ὑφέξειν. καὶ γὰρ ἂν μαινοίμεθ' ἄν.   (193–196)

Agathon. Euripides—
Eur.   What?
Ag.   Did you once write,
"You rejoice to see the light of day, but you think your father doesn't?"
Eur. I did.
Ag.   Don't expect me to bear
your fate. I'd have to be crazy too.

This is the line Pheres delivers to his son Admetus (*Alcestis* 691), when the latter abuses the old man for being unwilling to die for him.[26] Agathon uses Euripides' own words to escape from playing the role that he seems to have been destined for. The effect is all the more powerful for being direct quotation rather than parodic variation: he who lives by the epigram shall die by the epigram.

Agathon's refusal reduces Euripides to despair, from which he is rescued by Mnesilochus's offer of any help he wants. The action now moves into such high gear that neither Euripides nor Mnesilochus explicitly says that Mnesilochus is to play the role that Agathon was to have played. Instead the process of deconstructing Mnesilochus's masculinity and reconstructing a femininity on top of it begins at once. We have seen the end product in Agathon. Now in a dressing sequence far more elaborate than that in the parallel scene in the *Acharnians* we see how Euripidean femininity is assembled.

We begin with subtractions. After first divesting himself of his cloak, Mnesilochus must be shaved by Euripides. In a culture where men did not shave a razor is female equipment. Agathon has a whole case full and gladly lends Euripides one. A beard normally would have been part of the mask that covered the actor's entire head. Mnesilochus's mask was designed with a detachable beard that came off in two pieces.[27] During Mnesilochus's loud protests of pain, Euripides removes one half of the beard. Then Mnesilochus makes a break for freedom at 223, giving the whole audience a good view of his half-denuded mask before reluctantly returning for the rest of the treatment. Euripides offers him a mirror, and Mnesilochus is shocked to see, not the self he recognizes, but the effeminate Cleisthenes (235).[28] Next Euripides prepares to singe off the hair on Mnesilochus's posterior with a torch (238).[29] Again, realism has not the remotest thing to do with this procedure, as we shall see later in the play: if anything, hair removal will make his possession of the phallus even more visible. The routine exists primarily as the occasion for riotous slapstick comedy, secondarily as preparation for stripping off his costume later in the play.

Now the process of constructing the female version of Mnesilochus can begin. Mnesilochus is already wearing the padding of the comic actor, so the addition of female attributes on top is doubtless even more grotesque in the best pantomime tradition, with the "breastband" (στρόφιον, 251) he borrows from Agathon presumably already stuffed with exaggerated breasts and so forth. The rhythm of the dressing sequence seems very carefully calculated. For example, the hairnet and headband (κεκρυφάλου . . . καὶ μίτρας, 257), which would normally be put on separately, are here replaced by a unitary headpiece (κεφαλὴ περίθετος, 258),[30] either to sustain the comic rhythm or to obviate the technical difficulties of separate pieces. Agathon, having supplied all the costume pieces, is no longer needed and can be wheeled back inside (εἰσκυκλησάτω, 265). It remains only for Euripides to remind Mnesilochus to use a female voice (267–268) and to promise to rescue him, if need be. He then leaves Mnesilochus alone on the stage.

Lauren Taaffe has cogently analyzed the whole shaving and dressing sequence as a simultaneous transition of Mnesilochus from spectator to actor as well as from male to female.[31] From the secure position of normal comic spectator, mocking and laughing at the spectacle of Agathon, Mnesilochus has now become part of the spectacle himself, if anything an even more ridiculous comic version of femininity. For Taaffe a key moment is his glance into the mirror, whereby he becomes the object of the masculine gaze himself. At the same time she notes that, unlike Agathon, Mnesilochus does not become an object of desire. For all his sneering at Agathon, Mnesilochus also treated him as a possible object of desire. As the joke about helping him write satyr play shows, Mnesilochus seems quite willing to have sex with Agathon, so long as the act expresses Mnesilochus's superiority and Agathon's subordination. Taaffe acknowledges that no one will see Mnesilochus in drag as such an object of desire and that furthermore, despite his "feminization," we as audience will still identify to some degree with his male viewpoint in the coming scenes. As she rightly remarks, "Spectatorship is complicated here."[32]

Notions of spectatorship have been most carefully scrutinized in the area of film studies. Film theory of the 1970s developed a concept of spectatorship out of basic notions of classical Freudianism: the darkened film theater as voyeuristic vantage point, plots as standard Oedipal struggle, and rather straightforward identification of the viewer with the male desiring subject. Fissures soon developed in this rather tidy masterplot, not least because of feminism's challenges to such a strictly male conception of the gaze. Attempts to save the Freudian phenomena by shifting attention to sadism and masochism followed, to be challenged in turn by applications of Lacanian concepts of desire and even broader attempts to reshape psychoanalysis in ways that would not privilege male psychosexual development as normative. Finally the reception of films in discernibly distinctive ways by both racial and sexual minority communities further undermined the notion of a unitary spectatorship that could be invoked in studying the work of art.[33] After the sweeping certainties of the 1970s, the idea that multiple kinds of identification with the work of art are open to all kinds of spectators seems to be regaining a certain amount of respectability.

The spectators' relationship to Mnesilochus and other disguised performers yet to be encountered in this play therefore must indeed be complicated. We can neither dismiss drag comedy as "traditional" material needing no examination, simply another technique in the Aristophanic repertoire, nor suppress the possibility that such disguise might actually lead to "feminist" insight. Euripides is remarkably clear in his framing of Mnesilochus, however:

ἀνὴρ μὲν ἡμῖν οὑτοσὶ καὶ δὴ γυνὴ
τό γ᾽ εἶδος.   (266–267)

This one's a man to us but again a woman
in appearance

Agathon has already been wheeled inside on the *ekkyklema*. Therefore the "us" (ἡμῖν) he mentions can only be the audience and himself in their position of superior knowledge to the women and others who will only know Mnesilochus through outward appearance (εἶδος). It is precisely the effectiveness and durability of Euripidean εἶδος which the rest of the play will now test.

As Taaffe notes,[34] Mnesilochus's monologue in female character (279ff.) as he sets off to the Thesmophorion functions in itself as another prologue. It is an induction into a new play in which he will be a highly self-conscious performer, worried about exposure but generally keeping very well in character. It is in some ways a remarkably skillful performance, in which he expects the audience's complicity and participation. He begins by speaking to a nonexistent slave girl, Thratta. No silent extra appears to play this part, nor are we to see him as a definitely cracked Elwood P. Dowd talking with Harvey. Instead he improvises brilliantly to create the successful illusion, at least for the moment, of a well-to-do matron on her way to the Thesmophoria festival, who would of course not go out without her accompanying servant girl.[35] His parodic prayer that his "daughter" may find a rich but stupid husband

and his "son" have good sense may test the envelope of the illusion he is seeking to create (their names are obscene double entendres), but one petition is certainly heartfelt: "may I not get caught!" (ἀλλὰ νῦν λαθεῖν, 288). He then blends into the background of the scene, taking care also to "dismiss" Thratta (293–294).

Meanwhile the chorus finally appears, not with a parodos song, but rapidly streaming into the orchestra in no organized fashion.[36] The physical "blocking" of the chorus in this entrance is of considerable interest but hard to reconstruct with certainty. Mnesilochus seems to look for a place to sit (ποῦ ποῦ καθίζωμ', 292), and Sommerstein imagines that the chorus comes in and sits down in the orchestra as well, only to get up in order to sing their response to Critylla's opening announcement (312ff.), then sit again thereafter (372ff.) and apparently sing some of their following responses from this position. There would likely be some problems of both sound production and projection, were the chorus to try to sing from a seated position facing the stage, so I prefer to think that, while Mnesilochus may find a seat on the steps of the stage, probably at one side, thus remaining visible to the audience, the chorus remains standing.[37]

Critylla, presumably the priestess of the Thesmophoroi,[38] opens the assembly with prayers to the two tutelary divinities and others, to which the chorus responds.[39] Only when she then pronounces a ritual curse (331ff.) on those who plot against women by conspiring with Euripides or revealing their secrets does the parody of assembly formulae veer into open satire. The sendup of the language of assembly (which must have been very entertaining to all those citizens in the theater who had sat through it year after year on the Pnyx) concludes with the reading of the motion of the "boule of women" that the assembly should determine a punishment for Euripides, the boule having already found him guilty (372–379).[40] The motion is technically an open one, leaving the assembly free to debate proposed penalties, but in fact the boule has already made the determination of guilt.[41]

While bits of the Thesmophoriazusae have been used in debates about Athenian legal history, surprisingly little attention has been paid to procedures as represented and functioning within the world of the play. Although the term is not directly employed, it seems likely that Euripides has been the object of an eisangelia, a charge used to prosecute for treason or for plotting against the demos, here of course the demos of women.[42] The proof of this assertion is the fact that his fate is to be determined by the women in assembly (ἐκκλησίαν, 300 and passim), not by the women functioning as a court (*dikasterion*). As M. H. Hansen says in his very detailed study of *eisangelia*: "As far as we know, *eisangelia* was the only type of process in which the Assembly was qualified to pass sentence, all other trials being judged by the courts."[43] Many *eisangeliai*, particularly in the fourth century, were referred by the *boule* (which always plays some role in the process) directly to the law courts, but Hansen's statement about cases judged in the assembly seems clearly true.[44]

Beyond this point, things unfortunately grow more confused. Our evidence is largely from the fourth century, and the procedure in the fifth century may, perhaps more likely did, differ. Hansen believes that whether the cases were to be judged in the law courts or in the assembly in the fourth century (and perhaps earlier) was determined by whether the original charges were brought before the *boule* or the assembly, a distinction Rhodes sees as too rigid.[45] Related to this is Hansen's view that the *boule* made no preliminary judgment in cases that went to the assembly but did so in cases referred to the law courts.[46] No doubt this is true in the fourth century, but was it so in the fifth? The *boule* in this play has determined that Euripides is guilty but leaves his penalty to be debated in the assembly. The procedure may seem odd to us today, but it is a salutary reminder that in the Greek democracy there was no doctrine of separation of powers: the demos itself was sovereign and, while for certain judicial purposes that power might be instantiated in the juries, the full *ecclesia* might well deal with a threat to the demos as a whole. Either the conduct of *eisangeliai* in the fifth century were not so fully prescribed,[47] or Aristophanes is here deviating from reality for dramatic effect. For purposes of understanding the play, we need not decide this question: we need only see that Aristophanes portrays Euripides as a major threat to the demos of women who must be dealt with severely and swiftly, as *eisangelia* was designed to do.[48]

Mica rises to speak, beginning with a standard disclaimer of personal ambition (φιλοτιμίᾳ, 383).[49] The emotional structure of her speech is the same as that of the opening herald's announcement. She begins with complaints that can at least sound reasonable: widespread performance of Euripides' plays[50] has spread his slanders against women so effectively that husbands are constantly suspicious of their wives. They come straight from the theater benches (ἀπὸ τῶν ἰκρίων, 395) and start looking through the house for hidden adulterers, and even as simple an act as weaving a garland is used as evidence against the wife. Any sympathy these "reasonable" complaints might arouse, however, is soon overtaken by Mica's complaints that husbands now keep successful watch against the smuggling in of suppositious children, use watchdogs to frighten off adulterers, and keep much tighter control of household goods. Therefore the speaker proposes that they poison Euripides in punishment for his crimes.

Certainly many in the audience will only have heard these final jokes, built as they are on traditional comic concepts of women's randiness and thievery and traditional male fears about the paternity of their children. Whether Aristophanes meant at least some in the audience to detect the ironies of the situation depicted is another question, although the structure of the speech invites at least some reflection. After all, if the first half of the speech will get few laughs and generating laughter is the way to comic success, why bother to include those passages at all? The irony of course is that Euripides seems to have succeeded in the poet's task of teaching the people:[51] his crime is that he has modified male behavior in Athens in ways that, at least at first glance, will benefit male interests. It could be said, and indeed has been said, in dismissing the portrayals of female activities in this play, that they are simply male fantasy, a portrait of cultural anxieties rather than historical reality—and this is perfectly true, as far as it goes. Yet we cannot wholly dismiss the issue because of Aristophanes' explicit concern, from the *Acharnians* at least to the *Frogs*, with the power of the poet to teach, and of literature to move, an audience. The problem is the same one whereby the late Ayatollah Khomeini emerges as a more forceful advocate of the power of literature than Sir Philip Sidney: if Aristophanes is to claim that his own poetry can change minds, and therefore actions, and therefore benefit the city, he cannot dismiss Euripides' poetry as without effect. The question lingers, although we are not quite ready to answer it: why in this play does Aristophanes portray the effects of Euripides' poetry as benefitting the men of Athens, rather than, as in Pheidippides' use of Euripides in *Clouds*, a direct danger, undermining structures of authority within the city?

The chorus praises Mica's speech in no uncertain terms ("everything she says is right," πάντα γὰρ λέγει δίκαια, 436) and compares her favorably with the despised tragedian Xenocles.[52] The next speaker, a garland-seller, makes a more traditional charge against Euripides, that his tragedies have persuaded people there are no gods (450–451), therefore causing a drop in demand for her products. Leaving aside the probably anachronistic question of whether the purpose of religion is to sustain economic activity, we see that this potentially serious charge is undermined when the speaker announces she must leave to fill an order for twenty party garlands (the numeral is her last word, 458), since her own business seems to be booming.[53] When the chorus praises this woman's "complex intelligence" (πολύπλοκον νόημ', 463),[54] it is their own position as judges of assembly discourse which is ironized.

Mnesilochus rises to speak (466ff.). As various sources show, his address is modeled on Telephus's speech of defense while in disguise in Euripides' tragedy of so many years before. Aristophanes loved to parody this play and had in fact used this material before in the *Acharnians*. Malcolm Heath argues that the defense speech there combined in its parody two originally separate speeches in the Euripidean *Telephus* and that further only the speech to the assembled Greeks lies behind the speech of Mnesilochus here in *Thesmophoria-zusae*.[55] A basic methodological problem confronts us here and has particular bearing on how we will interpret Mnesilochus's speech. Can parody be used as a form of stemmatic criticism: that is, can we take the presence of a line or a form of a line in *both* the *Acharnians* and the *Thesmophoriazusae* scenes as sufficient proof to argue that the original of these lines stood in the *Telephus*? Or to cast the questions more broadly: do we assume that *only* the *Telephus* lies behind the speech in *Thesmophoriazusae*, or could Aristophanes wish to call to mind his own previous version in the *Acharnians*?

The problem is an interesting and significant one, for if Euripidean parody is the only association Aristophanes wishes his audience to hear, then Mnesilochus's "defense" of Euripides is a joke through and through and should elicit no sympathy from the audience. If, however, Aristophanes wishes us to recall Dicaeopolis speaking in defense of his separate peace as well, then the cause for which Mnesilochus speaks may not be so contemptible after all. The problem may be represented in microcosm by line 472:

αὐταὶ γάρ ἐσμεν, κοὐδεμί' ἐκφορὰ λόγου.

We're all alone, and there'll be no leak of information.

The first part of the line occurs in virtually identical form in the *Acharnians* at line 504:

αὐτοὶ γάρ ἐσμεν οὑπὶ Ληναίῳ τ' ἀγών

"We're all alone, and it's the Lenaean festival."

Now part of our problem is that while the scholia to the *Acharnians* helpfully point out some of the parodies of the *Telephus* and are indeed key sources for its fragments, the scholia to the *Thesmophoriazusae* seem to be generally unaware of the parody.[56] It is left to Heath, followed by Sommerstein, to conjecture that a line very much like *Thesmophoriazusae* 472 stood in the *Telephus*.[57] Without the coincidence, we would not necessarily look for a parody of *Telephus* in this particular line. True, it does not violate tragic metrical strictures, but Aristophanes was obviously capable of writing paratragic verse without a specific model in mind.

We might rather ask, is the phrase "we're all alone" consonant with the original tragic milieu? Would Euripides have indulged in the powerful irony of having Telephus, while trying to persuade the Greeks, make a point of saying "we're all alone, we're all by ourselves"? One might think that this veers too close to the comic mode even for that most ironic of tragedians. Nor is it clear why, within his characterization as a Greek, Telephus would need to make this point: the citizens of Argos would hardly expect to be reassured that no Trojans were present.[58] The phrase has the most obvious and understandable meaning in *Acharnians*, where a key element of Aristophanes' reply to Cleon's charges of slandering the city in front of the allies at the previous year's Dionysia is that now the festival is rather the Lenaea, and "we" Athenian citizens are now all alone. The phrase is almost as much at home in its context in *Thesmophoriazusae*, where the women's festival is as much an "in house" discussion in relation to Athenian society at large as the Lenaean festival was for Athenians, as opposed to the panhellenic audience of the City festival. Was Aristophanes so fortunate to find this phrase, so peculiarly appropriate to the situations in both his plays, already in *Telephus*? Or is Aristophanes quoting himself, and thereby invoking the spirit of Dicaeopolis in the later play's context? Conclusive proof is not possible unless a large chunk of *Telephus* turns up on papyrus somewhere. I would suggest, however, that we keep open the possibility of self-quotation on Aristophanes' part as well as the obvious notion of yet more Euripidean parody—and with it, the possibility that Mnesilochus deserves some sympathy from his audience beyond the audience of women of the chorus.

For certainly his defense of Euripides does nothing but enrage the women. His basic theme is that Euripides may have done wrong, telling some of the women's secrets, but at least he has not revealed the whole range of their other, even more vile crimes—which he now lists. He begins with a repetition and expansion of the traditional charges against women of lust and adultery. It soon becomes apparent, however, that women are superb performers and improvisers. Mnesilochus relates as personal experience a tale of sneaking out of the husband's bed and house at night to meet a lover and improvising a simple tale of illness when the husband wakes up. The deceptions become more elaborate, culminating in the story of a woman who fakes labor and, with the help of a midwife, smuggles a suppositious child into the house. They even know how to induce the baby to cry on cue, thereby convincing the husband it has just been born. Almost lost in these ever more outrageous tales is this intriguing and important contrast:

> εἰ δὲ Φαίδραν λοιδορεῖ,
> ἡμῖν τί τοῦτ᾽ ἔστ᾽;   (497–498)

We might almost translate this:

What's Phaedra to us, or we to Phaedra?

Mnesilochus is offering, somewhat clumsily, the Sidney defense of poesie: Euripides' plays do no harm to women because they are about the mythic past and do not deal with the actualities of contemporary life. The comedy is rather intricate here. The claim is ineffective, since Mica has offered evidence that Euripides' tragic models do influence the behavior of men in the audience, who are smart enough to realize that stories of Phaedra and other individuals of the mythic past actually relate to the contemporary world of Athens. At the same time, Aristophanes scores a point for comedy by demonstrating that it can talk directly, and not in mythic allegory, about the lives and foibles of present-day women and men.

This speech outrages the women of the chorus—although not one of them suggests it is false, only shameless in discussing these things openly (524–525). They parody the proverb, saying one should look under every stone, for fear of being bitten by a politician (ῥήτωρ, 528–530). This is a somewhat puzzling joke. Sommerstein explains it as referring to the notion that the orators, while professing devotion to the people, in fact worked against its interests and for their own. This is possible, but nothing in the context strongly reinforces the notion that the chorus thinks Mnesilochus is speaking in his own interest—unless we are to think of Mnesilochus still as representing Dicaeopolis and therefore still Aristophanes, for it would be in Aristophanes' personal interest to claim that tragedy is less effective in addressing the ills of Athens than comedy.

The violence of the women's reaction is somewhat startling. Mica accuses the women of being drugged for being willing to sit there and listen to such outrageous remarks.[59] She seems to look around for assistance in assaulting the speaker:

> εἰ μὲν οὖν τις ἔστιν —· εἰ δὲ μή, ἡμεῖς
> αὐταί τε καὶ τὰ δουλάρια τέφραν ποθὲν λαβοῦσαι

ταύτης ἀποψιλώσομεν τὸν χοῖρον, ἵνα διδαχθῇ[60]
γυνὴ γυναῖκας οὖσα μὴ κακῶς λέγειν τὸ λοιπόν. (536–539)

> Now if there's anybody—if not,
> we ourselves and our slave girls will get hot ash
> from somewhere and pluck her pussy, so she'll learn
> as a woman not to bad mouth other women in the future.

To whom is the incomplete question of line 536 directed? Rogers thinks the audience, although Sommerstein doubts this.[61] Those appealed to must contrast with αὐταί in 537. Mica is not a chorister and probably remains on stage after she speaks. Perhaps there are silent extras with her whom she can term αὐταί; there is no other proof of their existence. Sommerstein makes the reasonable point that the overwhelmingly male audience is not likely to be inclined to assist her—but perhaps that *is* the point. Mica speaks as though everyone within earshot were part of the assembly of women, sutured into the experience—but her appeal exposes the fact that they are not, that the male audience of citizens in the theater is not inclined to join in mob violence against the speaker.

Mica threatens Mnesilochus with painful sexual assault. Mnesilochus asks, he hopes rhetorically:

> εἰ γὰρ οὔσης
> παρρησίας κἀξὸν λέγειν ὅσαι πάρεσμεν ἀσταί,
> εἶτ᾽ εἶπον ἁγίγνωσκον ὑπὲρ Εὐριπίδου δίκαια,
> διὰ τοῦτο τιλλομένην με δεῖ δοῦναι δίκην ὑφ᾽ ὑμῶν; (540–542)

> If there's
> freedom of speech and we as citizens can speak freely,
> then is it justice for me, when I say what I think is right
> about Euripides, to be punished by plucking for this?

Note the key term παρρησία here: Mnesilochus points out that he is not just being outvoted by the majority but threatened with bodily harm for daring to use the Athenian right of free speech. This appeal to παρρησία sounds like the deliberate choice of a "hot-button issue" on Aristophanes' part.[62] He could easily show Mnesilochus simply being voted down by the women or cut straight to the brilliant send-up of the *Telephus* by having Mnesilochus snatch the "baby" at this point as an attempt to sway the assembly with threats instead of persuasion. Instead he deliberately shows us the assembly of women insisting that no woman should dare speak contrary to the views of all the rest.[63] The scene threatens to spiral out of control as Mnesilochus quotes ever more outrageous examples of female crime and Mica (and presumably the other women of the chorus) grow angrier and angrier until a physical brawl is clearly imminent.

A sudden intervention from Critylla and the running entrance of Cleisthenes aborts the confrontation, but we should not so quickly lose sight of the fact that an Athenian deliberative assembly was on the point of degenerating into mob violence because one of its members was exercising the right to "free speech," and that on behalf of another citizen whose life hung on the deliberations of that same assembly. While Mica may bluster at one point that Mnesilochus can have nothing left to say (554) and insists he is "babbling" ($\phi\lambda\nu\alpha\rho\epsilon\hat{\iota}s$, 559) at another, nowhere does she simply make the point that what Mnesilochus is saying is untrue. His crime is to speak of things that should not be spoken of. Now the Greeks did not have deeply emotional or Jeffersonian notions about freedom of speech, but the democracy was predicated on the necessity of the demos hearing advice freely given, in order to make informed choices between policies. Moreover, as the assembly here is functioning as the penalty phase of a trial, the refusal even to allow Mnesilochus to offer an alternative to the first speaker's proposed death penalty would certainly seem to violate Athenian norms of justice as well.

The arrival of the obviously effeminate Cleisthenes temporarily relieves the tension and confrontation. Because he is not identified for some time after his arrival, Sommerstein suggests that Cleisthenes was already a recognizable figure from the comic stage.[64] He simply labels himself, and is acknowledged by the women as, their *proxenus* ("agent, honorary consul") in the male political world of Athens (576, 602). If anyone in the audience even wonders why Cleisthenes can enter this all-female precinct, his appearance will give all the answer that is needed. He brings the disturbing (and disturbingly accurate) news that their assembly has been infiltrated by an agent of Euripides, whom the poet has "costumed" ($\dot{\epsilon}\sigma\kappa\epsilon\dot{\nu}\alpha\sigma\epsilon\nu$, 591) as a woman.[65] The women enlist Cleisthenes in the search for the spy. Mnesilochus tries to slip away but is stopped. Although Cleisthenes begins the interrogation, he is unable to penetrate even Mnesilochus's feeble disguise, and it requires the intervention of Critylla to establish that this "woman" does not know the secret rituals from last year. The scene turns to broad farce as Mnesilochus's femininity is deconstructed, his costume and accouterments stripped away. At last, despite his desperate efforts to conceal it from the women's view by moving it back and forth between his legs, his phallus is revealed, giving the final explanation (says Critylla, 649) for his defense of Euripides.

In another sense, though, Mnesilochus does *not* escape femininity by being stripped, particularly his status as object of the gaze. The jokes about his phallus render him erotic object rather than subject as well. Cleisthenes jokes about him shuttling his phallus back and forth like the Corinthians moving ships back and forth across their isthmus (647–648): Lauren Taaffe notes the resemblance between this and the scene at the end of the *Lysistrata* where personified Reconciliation (Διαλλαγή, 1114) is brought out and her body contended over like a map by the competing Athenian and Spartan delegations. Critylla even admires the color of his phallus (644).⁶⁶ Finally, either his female gown is never fully removed, or he resumes it again when Cleisthenes departs, for he is definitely wearing it (and complaining about it) later at line 939. Given his feelings there, it is perhaps more likely that the gown was never fully removed.

Cleisthenes departs to report this matter to the *prytaneis*, leaving Mnesilochus under guard by Mica and the others. The women of the chorus now proceed to search for *more* infiltrators. This is not particularly motivated within the fiction of the play: Cleisthenes reported only one spy, and one spy has been found. The effectiveness is purely theatrical and indeed should be somewhat threatening to the audience. The women are looking for spies, for men who have seen what they ought not to have seen—and the theater is full of them. The choristers light torches, dance in a circle, and conduct a vigorous search through "the whole Pnyx and the *skenai* and the aisles" (τὴν πύκνα πᾶσαν καὶ τὰς σκηνὰς καὶ τὰς διόδους διαθρῆσαι, 658) for any such criminals. This suggests that they actually search through theater cavea⁶⁷ and the stage area (the singular σκηνή) as well. The chorus members are all up on their feet and dancing, but they are hunting for a "seated" infiltrator (ἑδραῖος, 663; cf. ἐγκαθήμενον, 687) to be an example to all *men* (τοῖς ἄλλοις ἀνδράσιν ἔσται / παράδειγμ', 669–670) if caught.

In the past twenty years it has become almost de rigueur in certain kinds of broad farce to stage a chase through the audience, so much so that it has almost lost its power to surprise.⁶⁸ Nor does it disturb, since the audience sees and feels superior to the comic object of the chase. Aristophanes' effect here is bolder than that and resembles the famous finale of Peter Brook's production of *Marat/Sade*, where the bars across the stage opening, which had separated the on-stage as well as off-stage audiences of Marquis de Sade's play from the insane asylum inmate "actors," suddenly toppled out over the audience and the inmates swarmed forward, threatening the voyeuristic position that had seemed so secure. No physical barrier separated the orchestra of the Theater of Dionysus from the cavea, but the boundary of convention must normally have been quite solid: choristers entered and exited by the *parodoi*, and while they may have occasionally threatened or even gone on stage (see chapter 6, above, on *Peace*), the audience must normally have expected no more physical contact than a few nuts tossed their way or the occasional joke at the expense of the always vulnerable front row. The verses 655–687 describing their search for hidden men, verses entirely lacking in any of the jokes we might expect in Aristophanic song, suggest a much more disturbing effect—especially given the setting in the political space of the Pnyx.

The chorus's focus outward, on the audience, facilitates Mnesilochus's next move: they are presumably at the edge of the orchestra space. Although Telephus's first speech did no more good for him than its original speaker, he has recourse to another stratagem from the same play, snatching the baby from Mica's slave girl and dashing for refuge to the altar in the center of the orchestra, where he holds it hostage (689ff.).[69] The chorus is naturally out-raged again at this new crime; Mnesilochus claims it is vengeance for the women's "arrogant willfulness" ($\alpha\vartheta\theta\alpha\delta\acute{\iota}\alpha\nu$, 704).[70] Undeterred, the women prepare to burn him to death on the altar. Mnesilochus shouts his defiance, then unwraps the child to carry out his threat—only to discover that the "child" is a leather *askos* full of wine, complete with Persian baby slippers, which Mica has smuggled into the meeting!

This scene was clearly one of the great sensations of the play, as shown by a south Italian vase, illustrating Mnesilochus as Telephus, threatening the wineskin.[71] Moreover, it begins a series of four major performative parodies of Euripides, in which characters not only employ Euripidean language but play characters determined by the plots of Euripidean drama.[72] Note the con-tinuing theatricality of Mica's struggle: she does not admit her "baby" is a wineskin, despite the visual exposure. Instead, she continues to play the dis-traught mother, attempting to persuade Mnesilochus not to "kill" her child. In one sense it is no bad strategy: after all, someone in the Euripidean play *did* persuade Telephus not to kill the infant Orestes, or we would never have had all those plays starring him. Mnesilochus, however, insists that he will kill the child. Mica holds out a sacrificial bowl to catch the blood. Mnesilochus seems to indicate she may catch the wine as it flows out, but her next outraged reaction ($\kappa\alpha\kappa\hat{\omega}\varsigma \ \dot{\alpha}\pi\acute{o}\lambda o\iota$', 757) indicates that, in a gesture that destroys the *Telephus* parody by violating its premises,[73] Mnesilochus stabs the wineskin. I presume that, rather than waste the wine, Mnesilochus drinks it all as it spurts out himself. No self-respecting Aristophanic character would let a little thing like a Euripidean plot stand between him and a drink!

Without the prospect of rescuing the wine, the women lose interest in burning Mnesilochus on the altar. Critylla relieves Mica for guard duty, and Mnesilochus is left to look for another plan. Since Euripides has "rolled" him into these troubles (εἰσκυλίσας, 767, with a clear allusion to the *ekkyklema*[74]), he first looks for Euripides himself but then decides to borrow a device from the poet's play *Palamedes* (πόρον / ἐκ τοῦ Παλαμήδους, 769–770). He announces that, like Palamedes writing on oar-blades, he will write himself out of this dilemma by carving a message on wooden votive tablets that lie around in the sanctuary. Besides giving us more wonderful visual comedy, as the actor flings these fairly solid wooden boards around like frisbees (with the chorus doubtless ducking as best it can!), again Aristophanes literalizes a metaphor to demonstrate the futility of Euripidean written drama as opposed to comic improvisation.[75]

The chorus now turns to the audience and delivers a somewhat reduced parabasis in which they nonetheless retain their character as women (785ff.).[76] The primary joke here works through literalizing metaphor as well: why, they ask, if women are an "evil" (κακόν, 789 and passim), do men try to hold onto this evil and keep it at home? Then a different literalization follows, as the chorus compares the power and success inherent in women's names (*Aristomache*, "glorious battle," *Stratonice*, "army victory") to the failures of the men who now lead the demos.[77] In the alternative demos the women represent, there may be some minor thieves and failures, but they have kept their honor and ancestral weapons.[78] The chorus compare themselves favorably to "these" (τούτων, 814) in the third person, which Sommerstein interprets as the audience. Then whom are the women of the chorus addressing? One possibility would be that they are speaking over the heads of the male audience to other women, most likely seated at the back of the theater—but women are not really the intended audience of transvestite Aristophanic theater. More likely "these" refers to the leaders of the demos sitting in the front rows, those granted the right of *proedria*, a hypothesis reinforced when the chorus go on to propose that at their women's festivals such as the Stenia and Skira the mothers of those who serve the state well should be granted *proedria* (834) and the mothers of the cowardly, such as Hyperbolus, publicly disgraced. Spectatorship will thus map contribution to the demos—in mirror reverse of the present theater audience and present state of affairs in Athens!

Mnesilochus, seeing that *Palamedes* has not brought Euripides running, decides to try a new theatrical strategy:

τί δῆτ᾽ ἂν εἴη τοὐμποδών; οὐκ ἔσθ᾽ ὅπως
οὐ τὸν Παλαμήδη ψυχρὸν ὄντ᾽ αἰσχύνεται.
τῷ δῆτ᾽ ἂν αὐτὸν προσαγαγοίμην δράματι;

ἐγᾦδα· τὴν καινὴν Ἑλένην μιμήσομαι.
πάντως ὑπάρχει μοι γυναικεία στολή.   (847–851)

What could be keeping him? It must be
that he's ashamed of *Palamedes* being such a stiff.
What play can I use to lead him on?
I know! I'll imitate the new *Helen*.
My skirt's just right for it.

Euripides is ambiguously positioned here, as both author and spectator. Mnesilochus speculates that he may be ashamed of the *Palamedes* because it was ψυχρός, cold or emotionally unpersuasive. The solution then is to treat Euripides as a spectator and draw him to the scene by means of another play (τῷ . . . δράματι), last year's much more successful *Helen*.[79] Moreover, Mnesilochus realizes it is not enough simply to borrow a device (πόρον, 769) from a Euripidean play; he must throw himself into a complete part, and he chooses, on the grounds that he already has the costume, the *Helen*.

The send-up of Euripides' play which follows is brilliant, and we could easily immerse ourselves in the pleasure of its comic details. For Zeitlin it is central to the whole program of the *Thesmophoriazusae* and its critique of the femininity of illusion.[80] For Taaffe the failure of this parody to engage the female guard Critylla as willing spectator of its illusions demonstrates that women, in the Aristophanic theater at least, can be only the object, not the possessors, of an inherently male gaze.[81] I think issues of performance and persuasion are somewhat more complicated here and propose for the moment to concentrate on what the various acting strategies are trying to achieve.

Mnesilochus of course wants to be rescued before the law, in the form of the *prytaneis*, shows up. His survival strategy is role-playing, his instrument the *Helen*. He succeeds well enough to draw Euripides into the performance. We recall the ambiguity set up above: Euripides is in part spectator, in part subordinate player. Mnesilochus chooses the play and the protagonist's role. Euripides is drawn in and follows the script already laid out by Mnesilochus. Critylla, however, is not drawn in. She retains her superior position outside the tragic illusion, denying Mnesilochus's claim to be Helen and mocking his lines by resolutely and repeatedly moving back from his fictional framework to the historical reality of present-day Athens.[82]

When Euripides appears, playing the part of Menelaus to Mnesilochus's Helen, he seems on one level to be demonstrating his own vulnerability to the enchantments of his own tragedies. He accepts their fictions and makes himself part of the illusion, in contrast to Critylla, who does not suspend her disbelief in Mnesilochus's performance for a moment. On another level, however, there are *competing* illusions at work. Critylla is at least partly deceived: she does not recognize Euripides. Most likely he is costumed like Menelaus in some sort of rags.[83] I think it very unlikely, however, despite Sommerstein's suggestion, that he has in fact changed his mask; the whole point of the joke is for the audience to know that this is the same Euripides they have seen earlier in the play.[84] Critylla accepts this character as a stranger and a shipwrecked sailor; in fact, she tries to keep him from being "deceived" (ἐξαπατᾷς, 892) by Mnesilochus's performance. That very statement shows that she herself has succumbed at least temporarily to Euripides' performance at least.[85] At the same time Critylla demonstrates her own ability to be a deceptive performer with these lines:

οὗτος πανουργῶν δεῦρ᾽ ἀνῆλθεν, ὦ ξένε,
ὡς τὰς γυναῖκας ἐπὶ κλοπῇ τοῦ χρυσίου. (893–894)

This hoodlum came here, sir,
to steal the women's gold.

She accuses Mnesilochus of having violated the sanctity of the Themosphorion simply in order to steal from the women. Zeitlin points out that the motif may come from the *Palamedes*, where a false charge of stealing gold (planted in his tent) was the means for bringing about Palamedes' unjust conviction and execution,[86] but this kind of parody, far from explaining Critylla's actions, only shows her in a worse light. She knows very well the charge is false: she is seeking to deceive this stranger and conceal the fact that the demos of women has been plotting against the life of the poet Euripides. The result is a tragic draw: Euripides' performance cannot sway Critylla, nor hers him. Although Euripides forges on and Mnesilochus tries to enlist Critylla in their fiction by calling her "Theonoe," she resolutely resists the world of myth and locates herself by demotic and patronymic in the contemporary world of Athens: "Critylla, daughter of Antitheus, from Gargettus" (Κρίτυλλά γ᾽ Ἀντιθέου Γαργηττόθεν, 898).[87] Euripides and Mnesilochus are both stuck with the plot of the *Helen*, as line 906, quoted word for word from the *Helen* (line 558) shows: "Who are you? For the same tale holds you and me" (σὺ δ᾽ εἶ τίς; αὐτὸς γάρ σε κἄμ᾽ ἔχει λόγος).

When Euripides tries to lead Mnesilochus away, having "recognized" him as Helen, that provokes a threat of violence from Critylla and recognition that he is a fellow conspirator of Mnesilochus who has simply been playing a role (920ff.). At the sight of an approaching *prytanis* and archer, Euripides hastily retreats, only pausing to reassure Mnesilochus that he will not desert him so long as his stock of theatrical devices (αἱ μυρίαι . . . μηχαναί, 927) do not fail him. Critylla, quoting a proverbial expression ("that line caught no fish," 928) has the last word.[88]

At this point, the "real" Athenian *boule*, as opposed to the *boule* and demos of women in the play, takes over as the structure of authority. The *boule* has determined that Mnesilochus is to be fastened to a plank and put on display as a villain to all passersby (944). This moment in the play is unfortunately the subject of considerable historical controversy, which ties back into the question of the play's date. Could the fifth-century *boule* order the execution of an Athenian citizen on its own authority, as Aristophanes here seems to represent it doing? Or is this extraordinary action proof that the play dates to 410 and reflects the excesses of the *boule* under the short-lived oligarchic regime of 411? We can answer neither of these questions on the information of the play alone, and a full (and probably then still indeterminate) exploration of these issues would take us very far afield. I believe we can nonetheless say something about the effect of this action within the context of the play itself. The male Athenian *boule* has made its decision without ever hearing from Mnesilochus himself—just as the demos of women condemned Euripides without allowing any arguments to be made for him. They have made their judgment solely on the report of the effeminate politician Cleisthenes, as the *prytanis* acknowledges in his very first line (929). Mnesilochus will therefore have no opportunity to expose the plot against Euripides before he is punished. The Archer takes him away, and the scene is left to the chorus.

The chorus begins a circular dance, at the same time making reference to their holy and secret worship practices. Both the trochaic metre and the reference to "turning an eye in every direction" recall the earlier dance in which they searched the audience for spies.[89] Aristophanes does not repeat his effect there, however, but surprises the audience by having the chorus disavow abuse (963–965) and turn to hymns in praise of the gods, culminating in a celebration of Dionysus. This surprising disavowal of satire directed at members of the audience points the comedy in a new direction, and the play turns to the much more basic humor of the extended sequence with the Scythian archer which now closes the play.

> "We'll stoop to anything, if that's your bent."
> —The Player, *Rosencrantz and Guildenstern Are Dead*

THE ARCHER HAS ALREADY APPEARED briefly on stage—or rather his mask and costume have, worn by a nonspeaking extra. Only now, when he returns to the stage dragging Mnesilochus behind him, bound with an iron collar and shackles to a board, do we hear his voice, beginning the most extended scene of dialect comedy surviving from the Greek stage. His speech (as Sommerstein notes *ad* 1001) is characterized by a complete lack of aspiration and nearly as complete an absence of inflection of both nouns and verbs, although Aristophanes saves some comedy over uncertainty about noun gender for later in the scene. The Scythian archers at Athens were publicly owned slaves, used especially to keep order in the assembly. As such, they were the only slaves privileged, albeit under strictly controlled conditions, to use physical force against free citizens. To the democratic mind this was probably a better solution than using other citizens as a police force (from this point of view the slave was seen as an impersonal instrument of authority, not a being in his own right), but there must nonetheless have been considerable residual resentment, which finds expression in Aristophanes' caricature of the barbarian here.

The stage picture is extremely important here. The board to which Mnesilochus is so tightly bound indicates that he is to be executed by slow strangulation (*apotympanismus*). The result is that he is almost completely immobilized and becomes in effect a speaking statue. The inspiration for this may well lie in an early fragment of Euripides' *Andromeda*, where Perseus flying by at first thinks Andromeda is a *statue* ($\check{\alpha}\gamma\alpha\lambda\mu\alpha$).[90] In Euripides' tragedy this was probably meant to express Andromeda's beauty, as great as that of a work of art.[91] Aristophanes once again literalizes metaphor: his transvestite Andromeda is made a statue by being bound to an Athenian instrument of execution.

Mnesilochus's conscious inspiration comes from Euripides dashing out as Perseus ($\Pi\epsilon\rho\sigma\epsilon\grave{\upsilon}s$ $\check{\epsilon}\kappa\delta\rho\alpha\mu\acute{\omega}\nu$, 1011) while the Archer is temporarily absent from the stage. Just how this was staged is of necessity a matter of speculation, but I would agree with Sommerstein that the mechanics of the stage crane were such that it would have been very difficult to fly Euripides by in his Perseus costume in an apparently short interval of time (and would also detract from the effect of his later appearance on the *mechane*). Given that he is said to "buzz by" ($\pi\alpha\rho\acute{\epsilon}\pi\tau\alpha\tau o$, 1014), it may be that he dashes across the stage as though late for his cue to get into the necessary harness for using the flying machine. In any case, Mnesilochus sees enough to cue him in to his part—and, as he says in echo of his previous comment on the *Helen*, he has the shackles for it![92]

There is certainly some evidence that audiences found this motif of the bound woman disturbingly attractive. Sophocles' play on this theme seems to have produced a burst of vase paintings earlier in the century, and Euripides' play also had its effect on the visual arts.[93] This appeal to voyeurism and even sadism on the part of the male spectator is brilliantly satirized here by Aristophanes' use of the transvestite Mnesilochus as the object of vision. Verbally at least, he lets the masculine peep out from underneath the female costume, something not seen in the *Helen* parody. Who after all is the audience here? The Archer remains off stage, and the chorus, although addressed as the "maidens" (φίλαι παρθένοι, 1014) of the *Andromeda* chorus in a half-hearted attempt to enlist them in his performance, are not now likely to be taken in by Mnesilochus. In fact, Mnesilochus sounds not a little delirious as he wanders back and forth from his characterization as Andromeda, left as lunch for the sea monster, and himself, left in the lurch by Euripides.

His performance is nonetheless good enough, in perhaps the boldest invention of the play, to attract the character of Echo from Euripides' play! Sommerstein is surely right, despite the mistaken conclusions of the scholia, to see in Echo not Euripides (the character of the *Thesmophoriazusae*) playing a role, but the character herself from the previous play.[94] Note the initial exchange:

> {*ΗΧΩ*} χαῖρ᾿, ὦ φίλη παῖ· τὸν δὲ πατέρα Κηφέα
> ὅς σ᾿ ἐξέθηκεν ἀπολέσειαν οἱ θεοί.
> {*Κη.*} σὺ δ᾿ εἶ τίς ἥτις τοὐμὸν ᾤκτιρας πάθος;
> {*Ηχ.*} Ἠχώ, λόγων ἀντῳδὸς ἐπικοκκάστρια,
> ἥπερ πέρυσιν ἐν τῷδε ταὐτῷ χωρίῳ
> Εὐριπίδῃ καὐτὴ ξυνηγωνιζόμην.   (1056–1061)

Echo. Hail, dear child! As for your father, Cepheus,
who set you out here—may the gods destroy him.
Mnes. Who are you, who pity my suffering?
Echo. Echo, the chattering repeater of words,
who last year in this very place
myself competed along with Euripides.

Lacking the complete text of the Euripidean play, we often cannot be certain what is parody and what is free composition, but the only part of this exchange even suspected to come from the earlier play is line 1058, and it would obviously not have been spoken to Echo in the original. Mnesilochus seems genuinely puzzled as to who this person is, and I suspect the visual signals may be intentionally part of the confusion. When Euripides appeared playing Menelaus in the previous scene, we assume that he was still a typical comic actor, with the standard comic padding, over which he had thrown his shipwrecked sailor's costume. Echo, I suspect, appears in straightforward tragic costume, without the comic padding. Echo did not appear in the Euripidean play but was sung from backstage: now, it seems, she has been left at the theater all this past year since her last performance and has now wandered out to the front of the stage.

That this effect of a tragic character wandering into a comedy (a meta-theatrical device on a par with the use of Shakespearean versus newly invented characters in Stoppard's *Rosencrantz and Guildenstern Are Dead*) was actually used already in the Greek theater is attested by two vases showing comic and tragic characters together. One of the earliest phlyax vases, a calyx crater in New York, shows a youth in normal tragic costume (labeled simply *TPAΓΩI-ΔΟΣ*) observing a scene from a comedy.[95] It might be possible to argue that this is a "backstage snapshot," where we are to imagine the young tragic player as an actor hanging about to watch the comedy that followed his perfor-mance in a tragedy at the unknown drama festival, although I think a poten-tial encounter is quite possible. Far more compelling is a newly discovered bell crater, also from the beginning of the fourth century.[96] On it a character in tragic costume and normal facial features labeled "Aegisthus," having just entered through a stage door, confronts three padded and phallus-equipped comic players, two labeled "Choregus" and the third "Pyrrhias." Aegisthus's face presumably represents a mask that has "melted" into his own counte-nance, for it is represented quite realistically as opposed to the clear comic masks of the other three players (and their padding). One Choregus looks di-rectly at the tragic player and gestures toward him, while Aegisthus puts his hand to his head in a gesture that must surely indicate surprise or puzzlement: how, he asks himself, has he wandered into the wrong play?

Echo is a more self-conscious player here, but the effect on the audience must have been very similar. She identifies herself as Echo who "last year" in "this place" (i.e., the Theater of Dionysus) "competed along with Euripides." In doing so, of course, she demonstrates that she had not yet fully taken on her role, else she would not be able to speak independently (as we shall soon find out!). As a veteran of the previous production, she therefore feels well qualified to give Mnesilochus direction: he is to begin crying piteously, and Echo will chime in.

Both now assume their roles. Mnesilochus begins to sing as Andromeda again, but before long the echoes from Echo grow so frequent that they annoy him and distract him from his own performance. He soon addresses Echo as "old woman" (ὦ γραῦ, 1073) while expressing his annoyance at the interrup-tions, one of the few indications of her status and appearance, but an expres-sion which also suggests Mnesilochus accepts her as what she claims to be. When he grows more outraged, he addresses her as "my good man," a slip into the masculine gender, which indicates, as Sommerstein notes, that he is speaking actor to actor, for he is angry that his big solo is being chopped up: ὦγάθ', ἔασόν με μονῳδῆσαι (1077).[97]

The altercation is enough to attract the Archer back outside, where he gets to join in the fun. At first he thinks that Mnesilochus is the source of the echo, but he naturally denies it. Then, as the Archer's mispronunciations accumulate and are re-echoed, he tries to find the source of this annoying, mocking voice. Again, reconstruction of the stage action is somewhat uncertain, but it seems to take a while for the Archer to locate Echo, so she must somehow be concealing herself on the stage. To the pure Bergsonian comedy of mechanical repetition, which underlies Echo's original annoying repetitions of Mnesilochus's lines, are now added both ridicule of the Scythian's accent and (accepting a restoration in 1093) at least one joke based on repetition with a difference, where Echo can turn the Archer's threat into defiance of it:

> {*To.*} ποῖ ποῖ πεύγεις; ⟨οὐ καιρήσεις.⟩
> {*Ηχ.*} οὐκ αἱρήσεις.   (1093–1094)

> Ar. Where you runnin'? You no get free!
> Echo. You no get me!   (trans. Sommerstein)

A thoroughly slapstick chase is just on the point of developing when Aristophanes springs his great effect: the arrival of Euripides on the *mechane*, clad as Perseus and carrying the head of the Gorgon (1098). What is perhaps most surprising about this entrance is the lack of surprise on the part of the Archer.[98] To Euripides' announcement that he is Perseus, bringing back the head of the Gorgon, the Archer's only response is to wonder if he has the head of "Gorgo the secretary," perhaps one of the officials whom he has served.[99] The Archer seems capable of neither wonder nor illusion. He makes no reference to the *mechane*, points out to Euripides that despite what he thinks, Mnesilochus is no "maiden" (1110–1111), but when Euripides persists in his declaration of love, seems to find his taste bizarre but imaginable. When Euripides attempts to release Mnesilochus, however, the Archer prevents him. Euripides' conclusion deserves careful consideration:

> αἰαῖ· τί δράσω; πρὸς τίνας στρεφθῶ λόγους;
> ἀλλ' οὐκ ἂν ἐνδέξαιτο βάρβαρος φύσις.
> σκαιοῖσι γάρ τοι καινὰ προσφέρων σοφὰ
> μάτην ἀναλίσκοις ἄν. ἀλλ' ἄλλην τινὰ
> τούτῳ πρέπουσαν μηχανὴν προσοιστέον.   (1128–1132)

> Alas, what shall I do? To what speeches shall I turn?
> But his barbarian nature couldn't grasp them.
> To lavish strange ingenuities upon yokels
> would be in vain. Some other device,
> suitable for this man, must be brought out.

The Archer's "barbarian nature" simply will not grasp what Euripides is try-ing to do: untrained in the conventions of watching theater, he is therefore resistant to the spells of the *logos*.[100] Euripides' question in 1128 is despairing: there are no *logoi*, certainly none among his own compositions, to which he can now turn. Although he had at least been able to persuade Critylla to be-lieve in him as a shipwrecked foreigner, the Archer is utterly uninterested in who or what Euripides may be. He only knows how to do his duty. Euripi-des needs therefore, not one of his play scripts (λόγους) but a trick, a device (μηχανήν) suited to the barbarian's nature. He goes off in search of one, and the Archer apparently falls asleep on duty.

The chorus now briefly invokes Athena, specifically in her two aspects of "lover of choruses" (φιλόχορον, 1136) and "hater of tyrants" (ὦ τυράννους / στυγοῦσ', 1143–1144). Again, whether the *Thesmophoriazusae* proceeds or fol-lows the coup of 411, the theme is very timely—as it had not been over a de-cade before, when Aristophanes mocked such language in the *Wasps*.[101]

This brief ode prepares the way for the comically easy reconciliation now achieved between Euripides and the women of the chorus. He reappears to offer peace terms: he will stop satirizing women (a promise the real Euripi-des had already carried out, if we are right to see a significant change in dra-matic style after his defeat in the contest of 415[102]) if they will make peace. The women do precisely what they cursed in the opening of their assembly: they enter formal negotiations and accept his terms.[103] Euripides backs up his offer with a threat, if they fail to agree, that he will tell their husbands (pre-sumably in his plays, the only effective way to tell *all* their husbands) what the women *really* do: in other words, Euripides threatens to become Aristopha-nes, who has done just this in Mnesilochus's speech earlier in the play! The women agree but leave the problem of the barbarian Archer (simply called τὸν βάρβαρον, 1171) to Euripides.

Euripides proceeds to demonstrate that he has become Aristophanes al-ready, because his final "trick," though once more metatheatrical, is now a thoroughly comic and indeed improvisational one. Euripides is at last reduced to transvestitism himself, having dressed as an old procuress. He has brought along an aulos-player and a dancing girl named "Fawn." Like many a Plau-tine *poeta* character, he has rehearsed her along the way, for he admonishes her to remember her instructions ("Remember to do just what I told you on the road," ἅ σοι / καθ᾽ ὁδὸν ἔφραζον ταῦτα μεμνῆσθαι ποιεῖν, 1172–1173).[104] The flute wakes the Archer to this exchange:

{*To.*} τί τὸ βόμβο τοῦτο; κῶμό τις ἀνεγείρί μοι;
{*Eu.*} ἡ παῖς ἔμελλε προμελετᾶν, ὦ τοξότα.
ὀρχησομένη γὰρ ἔρχεθ᾽ ὡς ἄνδρας τινάς.   (1176–1178)

Ar. What's the buzz? What revel's rousin' me?
Eur. The girl was about to practice, officer.
She's going to dance for some men.

It may be a little grand to call one piper and one dancer a *komos* (which the Archer mispronounces κῶμό), but that is precisely what Euripides is staging —in the sense that the plays were still called in the official inscriptions the *komoi* in honor of Dionysus. Where high art has failed, lap dancing succeeds: at Euripides' instructions Fawn strips down, sits on the Archer's knee, then succeeds in arousing his considerable enthusiasm by her dancing.[105] When Euripides pretends to be leaving with Fawn, this persuades the Archer to enter negotiations for her attentions. They settle on a drachma for fee,[106] and Fawn leads the Archer offstage. In their absence, Euripides gives thanks to Hermes Dolios (god of thieves and deception) and releases Mnesilochus, whom he tells to "flee like a man" (ἀνδρικῶς . . . φεύξει, 1204–1205).

Euripides' final words to Mnesilochus contain an interesting textual problem, which relates very much to the poet's status in this final sequence. *Thesmophoriazusae*, except for a few papyri, depends entirely on one manuscript, R. At line 1208 the copyist of R originally wrote λέλυσον, which makes no sense.[107] He then corrected the text to read λέλυσο, the imperative, meaning "be free." Sommerstein opts for Bentley's proposal of λέλυσαι, "you are free," and argues that the imperative might be appropriate for a judge passing sentence but not for Euripides here. The issue is precisely one of performative language. A judge's language does not simply describe but in fact creates reality: within the society of which he is a representative, his spoken judgment makes a thing so. I believe that Euripides here, by adopting the plots and performances of comedy in place of his tragic *logoi*, has regained the power to create reality, and so should not just describe but create freedom for his long-suffering performer, Mnesilochus.

Once Euripides has made good his own escape, the Archer returns satisfied, but discovers he has lost his prisoner. The chorus of women does more than the bargain with Euripides calls for and thoroughly confuses the hapless barbarian before sending him running off in the wrong direction with a parting curse. Invoking the grace of the Thesmophoroi on themselves (and their play), they close by announcing that they have "played within measure" (πέπαισται μετρίως ἡμῖν, 1227), a somewhat curious expression. What is "measured" about the *Thesmophoriazusae*? Perhaps this expression looks back to the chorus's somewhat surprising disavowal of abuse of men at 962ff. Their response to men's hostility and suspicion turned out to be far more moderate and measured than their initial plot against Euripides' life would have led us to suspect.

Edith Hall's analysis of the Archer scene in this play shows how the Greeks, both men and women, unite together to dupe the barbarian, who has become their common enemy.[108] I suggest that this move is designed precisely to solve the problems of deep division among the citizens laid out in the first part of the play. The language of law, judgment, and hostility toward fair and open discussion that the women's assembly deploys in this play is not innocent. When the *boule* of women has already determined, without allowing the accused a hearing, that Euripides has done wrong to the demos of women and wishes the assembly to discuss only how, not if, he should be punished, that must have some relation to the political atmosphere of an Athens in which the threat of tyranny is very much in the air. The women of the play are not individually the oligarchs of 411 in drag. The threat to democracy is no longer personified in one identifiable leader such as Cleon, but the threat remains performative, in that some in the assembly were apparently trying to write the script for everyone else and allow no "improvisation" from unauthorized viewpoints.

If we allow ourselves a momentary glance forward to the end of the *Frogs*, the play whose advice earned Aristophanes a crown and the unique honor of a repeat performance of his comedy, we do not find there a detailed program of political reform, yet to classify that play as a "literary" comedy is to ignore the very immediate crisis occupying both poet and audience. Similarly, the crisis of 411 casts its shadow over the *Thesmophoriazusae* as well. Beneath the jokes about Agathon and Euripides lies a very real concern about the freedom of the democracy to hear all advice and all information necessary to make its decisions, a freedom threatened by the mutual hostility of the factions. Aristophanes' proposed solution is no more detailed than that he will offer the demos in the *Frogs*, but it anticipates the later play's gestures toward internal unity and external combat. Although at comic rather than tragic scale, Aristophanes proposes to turn the energy of internal hostility outward, against the barbarian, as Pericles once united Greece against the Persian threat.

9

Glorious Mud: *Frogs*

> Mud, mud, glorious mud—
> Nothing quite like it for cooling the blood.
> So follow me, follow
> Down to the hollow,
> And there let us wallow in glorious mud.
>
> —Flanders and Swann, "The Hippopotamos"

IN THE *FROGS* LITERARY AND POLITICAL criticism are blended inextricably together to a degree not seen in Aristophanes' work since the *Acharnians*. While the literary questions canvassed in the *Thesmophoriazusae* have considerable importance for contemporary political debates and issues of the degree of toleration of dissidence in Athens, the political issues of that play remain at a deep rather than a surface level. The *Frogs* presents itself initially as such a literary comedy: the god of theater goes to get a poet from Hades to save his choruses and keep them singing. In the play's second half, however, we discover that the frame of view is more encompassing—the choruses can be saved only if the city is saved, and that means saved in the war.

This blend of literature and politics is deeply incompatible with our modern notions of those categories. Given the apparent elements of formal innovation in the play, such a juxtaposition of literary taste and political peril has troubled not a few modern scholars, who have resorted to various explanations. Here we see how a little history is a dangerous thing: given that we know that Sophocles and Euripides both died not long before *Frogs* was produced, it has been tempting to try to reconstruct the impact of those events on the supposed "development" of Aristophanes' concept of the play and to explain structural "anomalies" as ad hoc solutions to the problems for the play created by these deaths. We could in good conscience simply bypass this whole debate: a script was performed at the Lenaea of 405 B.C. and whatever the series of events leading up to that performance, the reception of that performance event by the audience on that occasion constitutes the culturally interesting meaning of the play. *Ur-Frogs*, whether two or twenty in number, would be very interesting for Aristophanic compositional technique if they survived independently, but in fact can be no more than thought experiments. Of much more interest is the second performance which we know this play received, since that festival event may have employed a text differing in some particulars from that of 405, as Alan Sommerstein and many before have argued.[1] These points will be best dealt with as we progress through the text, for there is no evidence to suggest a massive rewrite of the text for that second performance.[2]

It might be useful nonetheless to examine very briefly one analysis of the play that posits substantial revision in the months leading up to the play's first performance. If we can show that the presuppositions about the nature of Aristophanic dramaturgy that underlie this view are less solid than they seem, we will be better able to appreciate the unity and effectiveness in performance of the script we have. In brief, J. T. Hooker argues that the original play concept was a satire of Euripides through verse parody and had the typical structure of a plotted first half, culminating in the *agon*, followed by illustrative episodes.[3] The original chorus was composed of Frogs, a raucous metaphor for Euripidean "music." Then Euripides, soon followed by Sophocles, died, and Aristophanes had to reset his play to the Underworld, with a consequent reversal of the overall structure: now episodes come first, followed by a second half containing the contest. The influence of Euripides' *Bacchae*, whether produced yet in Athens or only circulating in written form,[4] is seen in the new chorus of initiates, who now almost completely displace the original Frogs. This reconstructed *Ur-Frogs*, however, seems curiously undramatic: there is no "great idea" driving the satire of Euripides, nor is it even clear who his opponent would be: not Aeschylus, since on this view of the play he only comes into the picture once the action has been moved to the Underworld by the real Euripides' death; nor the chorus, since as embodiments of Euripidean music they would be his allies, not Acharnian-style opponents to be won over. Neither is it clear what consequences would follow from an *agon* satirizing Euripides in this *Ur-Frogs*. The most tempting part of Hooker's view is the account it gives for the apparent anomaly that the famous Frog chorus, which gives its name to the whole comedy, plays so little role in the finished piece. I will argue below, however, that the Frog chorus has a very specific and metatheatrical aetiology, and while we may regret the brevity of their contribution, we have no reason to assume that there was once more of this chorus in the play. They yield instead to more aptly human commentators on the later action.

The hypothesis of a radically different *Ur-Frogs*, then, satirizing a still living Euripides, creates more problems than it solves. As Dover observes, it seems peculiarly unjust to treat the "striking and successful innovation in plot-structure" of *Frogs* as the result of hasty revision of a much more standard original plot.[5] It does not seem so unlikely that, after twenty years of composing comedies for the festivals, Aristophanes was both capable of, and interested in, plot innovation.

The hypothesis of hasty revision also obscures the crucial role of Dionysus (a figure added on Hooker's view only once the play shifted to a *katabasis* plot), going in search of the dead Euripides. As Charles Segal has shown in a justly well-known article on the play's unity, Dionysus is essential to the structure of the *Frogs*.[6] As the embodiment of Athenian spectatorship, he grows in the course of the play. From idle shipboard slacker, filling his time reading Euripides, he is trained into a rower, tested as to his real identity, and finally proves himself a surprisingly capable judge of both tragic theater and democratic politics.

But we anticipate. Let us turn again to the play's unfolding in performance. From the very first moment, its theatrical self-consciousness is startling, even by the standards of earlier Aristophanic induction scenes. The god of theater, recognizable by his yellow robe even under the inappropriate attributes of the hero Heracles, which he has donned on top,[7] and a typical comic slave, riding a donkey but with his master's luggage nonetheless ludicrously piled on his own back, arrive discussing the question of what sort of jokes to tell the audience:

> {ΞΑΝΘΙΑΣ} εἴπω τι τῶν εἰωθότων, ὦ δέσποτα,
> ἐφ' οἷς ἀεὶ γελῶσιν οἱ θεώμενοι;
> {ΔΙΟΝΥΣΟΣ} νὴ τὸν Δί' ὅ τι βούλει γε, πλὴν "πιέζομαι."
> τοῦτο δὲ φύλαξαι· πάνυ γάρ ἐστ' ἤδη χολή.
> {Ξα.} μηδ' ἕτερον ἀστεῖόν τι;
> {Δι.}   πλήν γ' "ὡς θλίβομαι."
> {Ξα.} τί δαί; τὸ πάνυ γέλοιον εἴπω;
> {Δι.}   νὴ Δία
> θαρρῶν γε· μόνον ἐκεῖν' ὅπως μὴ 'ρεῖς—
> {Ξα.}   τὸ τί;
> {Δι.} μεταβαλλόμενος τἀνάφορον ὅτι χεζητιᾷς.   (1–8)

Xanthias. Shall I try one of the usual lines, master,
that the spectators always laugh at?
Dionysus. Anything you like, by Zeus—except "What a cramp!"
Watch out for that—it really makes me sick.

Xan. How about another clever line?
Dion.   Just not "Oh, my achin' back!"
Xan. What then? How about the show-stopper?
Dion.   Sure,
go for it—just don't use that one—
Xan.   Which?
Dion. Where you shift your load like you have to crap.

As has often been remarked, this opening allows Aristophanes to raise a laugh with old, familiar jokes, while at the same time disclaiming low-brow comedy.[8] The exchanges cast Dionysus as the by now somewhat jaded eternal audience of comedy and Xanthias as the hapless performer, trying to please him. Xanthias claims to be frustrated because he is forbidden to employ the typical jokes which writers such as Phrynichus, Lycis,[9] and Ameipsias would give a comic performer in his position. The irony of these remarks will have been even sharper if, as has been suggested, Aristophanes himself played Xanthias in this opening.[10] Dionysus's reply underscores his role as performer—and makes a point about the festival setting as well:

μή νυν ποιήσῃς· ὡς ἐγὼ θεώμενος,
ὅταν τι τούτων τῶν σοφισμάτων ἴδω,
πλεῖν ἢ 'νιαυτῷ πρεσβύτερος ἀπέρχομαι. (16–18)

Don't do it! When I'm in the audience
and see one of these routines,
I go away a year older.

The joke relies on the fact that the festival comes around once a year—but when the jokes are so bad, Dionysus ages *more* than a year in the process. We are told that the statue of Dionysus was carried into the theater for the City Dionysia festival and given a place of honor in the front row; while we cannot prove the same true for the Lenaea, an equation between the figure of Dionysus in the performance and the spectator as everyman watching from the audience (θεώμενος . . . ἴδω) is eminently clear.

Dionysus and Xanthias, having presumably entered via a parodos, now arrive at the central portal of the *skene*.[11] In answer to Dionysus's violent knocking[12] Heracles appears, giving us a mirror scene, for the hero is surely dressed in precisely the same lion skin and carrying the same club as Dionysus.[13] There would be ample scope here for the performers to imitate each other's gestures (compare Groucho and Harpo in the famous mirror scene in *Duck Soup*). If they initially leap back in horror from each other, it gives all the more point to Xanthias's comment that Heracles is afraid that Dionysus is out of his mind (41).

The introduction of Heracles allows Aristophanes to pursue the same double-edged comic game we saw in the initial discussion of jokes. The scene lays out Dionysus's purpose in seeking a way to the Underworld: the experience of reading the *Andromeda* has awakened in him a great desire[14] for its dead author, Euripides. Heracles is incapable of understanding desire other than in physical terms: he thinks Dionysus has been afflicted with sexual desire. Dionysus explains rather that he has a yearning for Euripides just like the yearning Heracles has for soup. Aristophanes, who in *Peace* 741 disclaims the use of the "hungry Heracles" as a source of comedy, is not above exploiting it here, as he did in *Birds*.

The ensuing discussion of the state of tragedy has an elegiac tone to it. With Euripides and Sophocles both dead and Agathon departed from Athens, tragedy is left in the hands of *epigonoi* and nobodies. Line 94 tellingly refers to poets who manage to obtain one chorus, then are never heard from again. The introduction of tragic performances at the Lenaea c. 440–430 B.C. had increased from three to five the number of poets who could be heard in the city in a given year, but many more strove for performance slots. Comedy was in the same state, and perhaps that is a subtext here too: just as Sophocles and Euripides had dominated tragedy together from the 440s onward, so too Aristophanes, Eupolis, and until his death Cratinus had ruled the comic stage, but now there was a flood of new entrants.

Dionysus explains that his props (τήνδε τὴν σκευήν, 108) and disguise as Heracles (κατὰ σὴν μίμησιν, 109) have a purpose: he wants to pass as the hero in the Underworld, but he needs good traveler's advice for the journey. Heracles offers various ways to kill himself; Dionysus prefers the longer, non-lethal route. For that he needs two obols, says Heracles, to pay the ferryman's fee. The joke here has been thought obscure, but it may repay some attention. Charon's standard fee was one obol.[15] Why must Dionysus pay two? Suggestions of a reference to various state subsidies are inapposite: Dionysus is not *receiving* two obols, as impoverished Athenians sometimes did, but *paying* two obols for something—and the something is admission, here to the Underworld. Given Dionysus's role as typical Athenian spectator, the allusion seems likely to be to the two-obol fee for admission to the theater.[16] This then becomes the first in a series of jokes equating the theater itself with Hades (and the audience, as we shall see, with its denizens).

Heracles details the path via Charon's boat across a great swamp, past sinners lying in the mud (the worst of whom are guilty of theatrical crimes, such writing out a speech of Morsimus![17]), past bands of the blessed who will give further directions, and finally to Pluto's door. This is more than simply a preview of the play's action: it is, as G. T. W. Hooker saw,[18] a recognizable path through the contemporary Athenian landscape, from the shrine of Heracles outside the Diomeian Gate (= the house of Heracles here), through the marshes along the Ilissos River, and past the fields just beginning to flower (350–352, etc.) where the initiates of the lesser mysteries at Agrai celebrated at just this time of year.[19] As I have argued elsewhere at length, that path leads quite specifically to the Lenaean Theater, near the Ilissos and the shrine of the Dionysion in Limnais.[20] Dionysus's travels, then, will lead the god of the theater to the very theater in which his worship is even now being celebrated by the play in which he is appearing.

Dionysus tries unsuccessfully to hire a passing corpse to help Xanthias with the luggage but refuses to pay the going rate. This encounter probably takes place on the stage (allowing a quick entrance and exit for the corpse and his bearers), but as Charon, heralded by his own offstage cry, now heaves into view in his ferry, Dionysus must descend from the stage to meet it. The boat is presumably on partially concealed wheels and can be dragged out of one *parodos*, across the orchestra, and into the other *parodos*, whether by means of a rope put in place before the performance begins or by men concealed behind the boat.[21]

The scene may offer a strong visual reminisce of a key scene in Eupolis's *Taxiarchs*, showing Dionysus being instructed in rowing by the admiral Phormio.[22] Here Charon tries to make an oarsman of the hapless Dionysus. As they set out across the orchestra, with Dionysus rowing vigorously if inexpertly, the chorus begins its famous chant of βρεκεκεκὲξ κοὰξ κοάξ (209ff.). If the ancient scholia had not suggested such a thing, we would never have dreamt that this chorus might not have appeared in the orchestra, since the visual appeal of green-clad choristers hopping about the orchestra as they sing is so obvious. As MacDowell and Dover note, the advantages in audibility of a visible chorus are equally overwhelming.[23] It is also, as C. W. Marshall eloquently demonstrates, vastly funnier than the alternative.[24] I shall assume here that the chorus of frogs do appear in the orchestra and compete directly with Dionysus in Charon's boat.

The scene's power in performance is not to be doubted: even when read, it is one of the parts most likely to stick in memory, and its humor is obvious. What is the impact of the reminisce of Eupolis, however? While we cannot date his *Taxiarchs* too closely, it probably lies at least twenty years back—and comedies seem not to have been restaged at this period. Unless a song or two from the production had remained active in public memory, then, any visual allusion is alive only for an older generation in the audience. It seems most unlikely that Aristophanes' purpose was to mock Eupolis; any appeal beyond the immediate visual comedy of the scene presumably lies in the theme Segal sees in the play: the gradual development of Dionysus toward discipline and self-confidence.

Having had the last word in his singing contest with the frogs, Dionysus now disembarks on the other side of the orchestra. He explicitly notes that he is paying his two obol fare: ἔχε δὴ τὠβολώ (270). This renewed reference to the price of theater admission helps set up the following jokes, for Dionysus and Xanthias now peer out into the audience, attempting to determine where they are. Recognition comes when they spot the parricides and perjurers—in the audience (274–276)!

In this imaginary darkness, Xanthias proceeds to have a little fun with his cowardly master. He hears noises, then claims to spot the monster Empusa. Dionysus is so frightened that he appeals to his priest, presumably sitting in the front row (297): "Priest, save me—so I can go drinking with you!" Note the *do ut des* basis of this metatheatrical appeal: he asks his priest to save him so that the priest will have the company of the god of wine at his party after the performance. The signal that the danger is past is a theatrical joke as well: Xanthias quotes the unfortunate mispronunciation of the protagonist at the performance of Euripides' *Orestes* in 408[25]:

ἔξεστί θ' ὥσπερ Ἡγέλοχος ἡμῖν λέγειν·
"ἐκ κυμάτων γὰρ αὖθις αὖ γαλῆν ὁρῶ." (303–304)

And, like Hegelochus, we can say:
"After the storm, how weasily we sail!"[26]

The message that Dionysus and Xanthias have arrived in the theater is thus hammered home.

The chorus arrives, singing in praise of Iacchus. It is an unusual chorus in representing both men and women, a choice not insignificant in a play that works so hard to forge a unified Athens in the face of the direst circumstances. Also unusual is their use of anapaests, which traditionally belong to the parabasis. No particularly cogent explanation of this formal innovation has been offered. The verses do call attention to the performance's status as a comedy, invoking the memory of Cratinus (357), rejecting low-class comic devices (βωμολόχοις ἔπεσιν, 358), and reviling an unnamed politician for a vengeful attempt to cut the comic poets' pay (367–368). When they tell themselves to advance in a "manly" fashion (ἀνδρείως, 371), we are reminded that these are all male performers, whatever their costumes and masks, who have just been fed a good lunch for their afternoon performance (376).[27] They call on Demeter to save her chorus and ask for victory in the contest (392–393). They also refer to their tattered clothing, which, while it may have a ritual explanation, also reflects a considerable saving in expense for the choregus of this production![28] In response to Dionysus's question, the chorus assures him he has arrived at the door of Hades.

Xanthias overcomes Dionysus's hesitation to knock by reminding him that he has the costume (σχῆμα, 463)[29] to play Heracles. Costume and its problematic relationship to the wearer are in fact at the center of the superb comic scene that follows. When the doorkeeper Aeacus[30] answers his knock with violent abuse and threats, Dionysus is left prostrate with terror. Stung by mockery from his slave, he dares Xanthias to put on the costume of Heracles. The result, of course, is that the next person they encounter[31] welcomes this Heracleoxanthias and invites him in to a feast—whereupon Dionysus asks for his costume and role back. He insists that he was just joking (παίζων, 523) when he handed over the costume and succeeds in reclaiming costume and role from Xanthias in this striking exchange:

{Δι.} . . . κατάθου τὸ δέρμα.
{Ξα.}   ταῦτ᾽ ἐγὼ μαρτύρομαι
καὶ τοῖς θεοῖσιν ἐπιτρέπω.
{Δι.}   ποίοις θεοῖς;
τὸ δὲ προσδοκῆσαί σ᾽ οὐκ ἀνόητον καὶ κενὸν
ὡς δοῦλος ὢν καὶ θνητὸς Ἀλκμήνης ἔσει;   (528–531)

Dion. Unhand that lion skin.
Xan.   I call everyone to witness
and appeal to the gods.
Dion.   What gods?
Witless and vain it is for you to suppose,
slave and mortal that you are, to be Alcmene's son.

Even as Dionysus propounds a theory of an inherent connection between the performer's nature and the role he plays, the whole situation casts such a theory into grave doubt. It is not just the deep irony of Dionysus the god dismissing Xanthias's appeal to the gods with the scornful question "what gods?" Dionysus is insisting that the ontological categories of "slave" and "mortal" are ineradicable, even as events prove precisely the opposite. Nor is a certain metatheatrical vertigo far from the surface here: even as these two trade lion skin and club back and forth, we are reminded that under the masks and padded costumes are two Athenian actors, who are neither slaves nor gods but perfectly capable of playing either in rapid succession.[32]

Before Aristophanes develops this same joke through repetition, there is an extremely interesting, albeit brief, choral comment on the politician Theramenes. Theramenes of course was notorious for his role after the battle of Arginusae, where he succeeded in turning public anger against his fellow generals, who were condemned en masse for failing to rescue survivors, thereby saving his own skin. Several years later I believe Aristophanes alludes even more specifically to Theramenes' ability to stage-manage the assembly when he shows the women packing it with costumed supporters in the *Ecclesiazusae*.[33] In 405 as the war came to its desperate conclusion, Theramenes was still a power to be reckoned with, so Aristophanes' comment is rather brief, but I think still tellingly theatrical. The chorus comments on Theramenes' ability to stay on the fortunate side of events:

> μετακυλίνδειν αὐτὸν ἀεὶ
> πρὸς τὸν εὖ πράττοντα τοῖχον
> μᾶλλον ἢ γεγραμμένην
> εἰκόν᾿ ἑστάναι, λαβόνθ᾿ ἓν
> σχῆμα·   (536–539)

> He always rolls
> to the lucky side
> rather than standing
> like a painted image, keeping
>   a single guise.

Note the extremely unusual word μετακυλίνδειν, which Rogers translates "shift." Despite the specific reference to the side or wall of a ship (τοῖχον),[34] the notion of rolling does not seem to fit in with a ship metaphor: objects rolling about inside a ship are dangerous, not fortunate. I suspect that a reference to the *ekkyklema* underlies the term here: Theramenes knows how to roll or shift himself into a new part when need be in order to survive.[35] He also knows *not* to be a γεγραμμένην / εἰκόν᾿.[36] Painting and writing metaphors are not fundamentally separable at this point: Aristophanes is (ironically) praising Theramenes for his refusal to play a part scripted for him by others, wearing the single costume (ἓν / σχῆμα) they would place on him. Declining to be the villain of Arginusae, Theramenes wrote himself a new part as heroic defender of the victims of the disaster and righteous persecutor of the other generals. Just in case this all cuts too close, Aristophanes quickly lightens the mood by

giving Dionysus a passage in responsion to that on Theramenes, devoted to
a fantasy of revenge on, and abuse of, the unfortunate Xanthias.

Aristophanes now replays the game of musical costumes. An outraged
hostess or tavern-keeper and her helper Planthane confront and terrify the
newly recostumed Dionysus. The hostess even claims to see through "Heracles'" disguise of tragic costume: the κόθορνοι (557) he is wearing give him
away.[37] After roundly abusing poor Dionysus, she goes off to fetch her pro-
tector Cleon (one last joke at the expense of Aristophanes' long-dead enemy),
leaving Dionysus to undertake the difficult task of persuading Xanthias into
the Heracles costume again. Xanthias throws the theory of an inherent connection between performer and role back in Dionysus's face (582–583)[38] but
once again agrees to the exchange. The chorus encourages Xanthias with virtually a method theory of acting, advising him to remember the god he is
performing (593) in order to keep up the role.

Xanthias proves to know more about behaving like a master than Dionysus does, for when the Doorkeeper comes storming out again, ready to take
"Heracles" into custody, Xanthias coolly (and truthfully!) swears that he has
never been to Hades before and offers his "slave" to be tortured in order to testify to the truth of this assertion. Dionysus discovers he has not been so clever
after all. His protest that he is in fact a god, Dionysus son of Zeus (631), while
Xanthias is the slave, is far from immediately convincing. Xanthias proposes
they flog Dionysus anyway, since if he is a god, he will not perceive it and
thereby demonstrate his divinity. Dionysus counters with the same challenge
to Xanthias, and the puzzled Doorkeeper agrees to test them both.

Whether it was yet popular belief in the fifth century that the gods were
immune from pain as well as immortal (unlike the Homeric gods, who could
be wounded and suffer) is scarcely the point. The comedy of the ensuing contest relies on a certain metatheatrical Schadenfreude. Although blows can be
partially faked on stage, the audience is quite well aware of the danger that
the actor playing the part will suffer real pain: this is a significant part of
the audience's enjoyment.[39] Both Dionysus and Xanthias prove far from immune to pain. In fact, as they both attempt to improvise explanations for
their increasingly obvious reactions to pain, their "real" natures do emerge,
although the Doorkeeper is not the right audience to recognize the difference.
Both brush off their first exclamations as reactions to common, if interesting
events: thinking of a feast of Heracles, seeing some passing horsemen, feeling a thorn (650–657).[40] Xanthias then contrives that the Doorkeeper strike
Dionysus twice in succession. His more violent reactions he now ascribes to
thinking of verses of poetry: first a (spoken) verse of Hipponax (659), then a

passage of Sophocles sung out even more forcefully (664–667 = Sophocles fr. 371). Thus the god of theater finally resorts to tragic quotation to express his severest pain—whereupon the Doorkeeper remembers that Hades and Persephone will know which one their fellow divinity is!

Once the three actors have departed, the chorus sings a passage remarkable for its immediacy to the moment of performance.

> Μοῦσα, χορῶν ἱερῶν ἐπίβηθι καὶ ἔλθ᾿ ἐπὶ τέρψιν
> ἀοιδᾶς ἐμᾶς,
> τὸν πολὺν ὀψομένη λαῶν ὄχλον, οὗ σοφίαι
> μυρίαι κάθηνται   (674–677)

Muse, begin the sacred dances and come to the pleasure
of my song,
to see the great throng of people, where the sophisticated
thousands sit.

They invoke the Muse of choruses as she looks out at the thronged audience seated (κάθηνται) in the theater.[41] The spectators are flattered as "sophisticated" and promised pleasure (τέρψιν) from the song. We must take one step away from the occasion of first performance here to note that this passage is the famous parabasis on account of which, according to the play's hypothesis, the *Frogs* was accorded the then unique honor of a second performance.[42]

The theme of their advice to the city is reconciliation, a plea to restore the disenfranchised. The verses are carefully structured in responsion to mix comedy in with serious advice. After the flattery and a hit at Cleophon in the ode, the chorus in the epirrheme reasserts its traditional role as advisor and teacher of the city (ξυμπαραινεῖν καὶ διδάσκειν, 687). The crimes of those disenfranchised are portrayed passively: they were tripped up (σφαλεῖς, 689) by Phrynichus. The contrast of old and new is introduced here: these men, whose ancestors served the city with distinction, are cut off from political life, while slaves who fought in one battle are received into the citizen body.[43] The chorus even suggests that posterity will judge that the city has acted wrongly toward the disenfranchised (703–705). The antode relieves the mood with another personal attack, on the obscure bath proprietor Cleigenes.[44] The antepirrheme transmutes the contrast of old and new into the famous and potentially subversive metaphor of debased coinage. The city's current leaders are likened to the new silver-coated copper coinage which Athens in her desperation had issued.[45] In this early demonstration of Gresham's law, the new fiat coinage had driven out the old, tested Attic silver (722–724), just as the new, worthless political class had driven out the traditional leadership of Athens.

One wonders whether Aristophanes realized how potentially revolutionary this metaphor was. Money was still to some extent a novelty rather than
a given in this society. While the urban population handled money regularly,
rural life retained much of the barter economy.⁴⁶ The power of money to make
virtually everything fungible was still rather new. In precisely this sense coins
are the perfect metaphor for citizens in the radical democracy, for its fundamental principle was that citizens were as interchangeable as honest coinage.
Just as there was no reason to prefer one drachma to another, so long as Athens
kept an honest weight standard, so no citizen was to be preferred to another in
filling most offices and functions in the democracy—until now. Silver-coated
coppers and short-weight politicians had driven the authentic exemplars from
the market. Did Aristophanes know and follow through the economic logic
of this situation? Standards can only be restored by eliminating the debased
coinage from circulation—and this was the chilling logic of the various oligarchic revolutions against the democracy in Athens, soon to begin again with
the elimination of Cleophon.⁴⁷

Xanthias returns with the Doorkeeper one last time, recapitulating the
gesture toward the traditional comedy of the play's beginning. Jokes about
beatings, spying on their masters, and general trouble-making gradually yield
to exposition of the background to the second half of the play in what
amounts to a new prologue.⁴⁸ If we needed any further assurance that Hades
is just another version of Athens, this dialogue provides it, for not only do
Xanthias and the Doorkeeper recognize each other as blood brothers who love
and do the same things, but the uproar behind the *skene* (θόρυβος καὶ βοὴ / χὠ
λοιδορησμός, 757–758)⁴⁹ prompts the Doorkeeper to fill in the background of
a Hades riven by strife between the partisans of old and new tragedy. Aeschylus, honored with a throne as the best tragedian,⁵⁰ is now being challenged by
Euripides, who since his arrival has been canvassing support among the dregs
of underworld society.⁵¹ Few of the infernal public are supporters of Aeschylus, "just like here" (ὥσπερ ἐνθάδε, 783), says the Doorkeeper with a gesture
to the audience, and the public have demanded that the issue be settled by
a contest (ἀγῶνα, 785),⁵² to which Pluto has agreed. The Doorkeeper even
foreshadows the device of the weighing scale (797–798), noting that Euripides will fight over every word. The biggest surprise is saved for last: lacking
fair and competent judges of drama in Hades, Pluto has appointed Dionysus
to decide the contest!

The servants depart, the chorus offers a short lyric as build-up (814–829),
and the combatants enter, Euripides chattering and Aeschylus glowering silently. Dionysus is trying to persuade Aeschylus to reply, and Pluto must be

present as well, probably seating himself on a throne center stage.[53] He and Dionysus will function as the onstage audience, mirroring the one watching from across the orchestra.[54] Euripides accuses his opponent of maintaining an "Aeschylean silence" for effect and eventually goads him into replying. Aeschylus's countercharges mix the familiar complaints about indecent subject matter with newer stylistic criticisms: Euripides is not only the familiar "maker of beggars, a rag-stitcher, . . . a creator of cripples" (πτωχοποιὲ καὶ ῥακιοσυρραπτάδη . . . χωλοποιόν, 842- 846) who puts incest in his plays (850), he also is guilty of such musical innovations as "Cretan monodies" (849).

Although Aeschylus eventually agrees to the contest, he pleads one telling handicap: he claims the contest is not equal (οὐκ ἐξ ἴσου . . . ἀγών, 867) because, while Euripides' plays died with him, his own did not and are therefore not available to him in the underworld! Once again, Aristophanes literalizes a metaphor. As Hubbard has pointed out, Aeschylus's plays *were* alive in contemporary performance, as Euripides' in theory should not be.[55]

The chorus calls the Muses to witness the contest, and Dionysus orders both combatants to pray before the contest. Aeschylus's invocation of Demeter is much what one would expect, but Euripides announces he will pray to "other gods," which include Aether and the "hinge of the tongue" (Αἰθήρ . . . καὶ γλώττης στρόφιγξ, 892). Dionysus appropriately labels these a "new coinage" (κόμμα καινόν, 890), picking up not only the chorus's reference to poets as "coiners of opinions" (γνωμοτύπων, 877)[56] but the earlier image of the city's new leaders as debased coinage (725–726). The disturbing quality of this image must be, if anything, even greater here. What will it mean if new gods can be coined like new money and circulate freely in a system of exchange? How will one tell the old, genuine articles from the new? We have just seen the problem enacted on this stage where the Doorkeeper was quite unable on his own to distinguish the "real" god from the play-acting one in the scene with Xanthias and Dionysus. Comic instability of identity begins to have more radical implications.

Euripides' first attack on Aeschylus is more complex than usually acknowledged. He begins, as Dover notes (*ad* 908), in Gorgianic fashion, outlining the shape of his speech. This echo of Gorgias in turn gives a particular coloration to the substance of his first charge: Aeschylus *deceived* the spectators (τοὺς θεατὰς / ἐξηπάτα, 909–910) through his famous silent characters into thinking there was more going on the play than there really was. The language of deception in such a context must remind us once again of Gorgias' *bon mot* on the value of deception in spectators' experience in the theater.[57] Yet

Euripides, in direct opposition to Gorgianic teaching, is claiming that Aeschylean deception is a *bad* thing. How can this be?

Euripides is not attacking the illusionism of Aeschylean tragedy (or Attic tragedy, for that matter) per se. His charge is that Aeschylus promised more than he delivered and gave the *impression* of tragedy (πρόσχημα τῆς τραγῳδίας, 913) without the actual substance. Euripides must tread carefully here in describing Dionysus's role, which embodies that of the Athenian spectator. The spectators knew nothing more than Phrynichus in those days (910). When Dionysus says he liked the old Aeschylean silences, Euripides accuses him of being naive or childish (ἠλίθιος, 917)—a strong charge, yet imputing more blame to the one who deceived him—and Dionysus then admits that he was![58] The echo of Demos's description of his deception by Paphlagon is disturbing, and all the more so because Aristophanes is there being careful not to place the sole blame on Demos: he too behaved like a young fool (ἠλιθιάζω, *Knights* 1124) while under Paphlagon's influence but by the play's end has regained control of himself and his perceptions.[59]

Euripides' theory of tragedy, it seems, is that the spectator is the measure of all things. Aeschylus's plays keep the spectators waiting for a great revelation (919), but when it comes, it is so wrapped in monstrous compound words unknown to them (ἄγνωτα τοῖς θεωμένοις, 926) that they cannot understand it. Euripides for his part claims to have put tragedy on a diet to purge it of swollen language but then added monodies (944) and, although he does not use our term, expository prologues (946–947). His proudest achievement, however, is that he has made tragedy "democratic" (δημοκρατικόν, 952), allowing everyone from master to slave to speak in his plays.[60]

Euripides now introduces the theme central to his dispute with Aeschylus. While they will develop it at length in the next section of the *agon*, its appearance here merits our close attention, especially for its form. Euripides gestures to the audience and says:

{Εὐ.} ἔπειτα τουτουσὶ λαλεῖν ἐδίδαξα—
{Αἰ.}   φημὶ κἀγώ·
ὡς πρὶν διδάξαι γ' ὤφελες μέσος διαρραγῆναι.
{Εὐ.} λεπτῶν τε κανόνων εἰσβολὰς ἐπῶν τε γωνιασμούς,
νοεῖν, ὁρᾶν, ξυνιέναι, στρέφειν, ἐρᾶν,[61] τεχνάζειν,
κἄχ' ὑποτοπεῖσθαι, περινοεῖν ἅπαντα—
{Αἰ.}   φημὶ κἀγώ.   (954–958)

Eur. Then I taught these people to speak—
Aes.   You did indeed;
you should have been ripped in half before you taught them so.

Eur.—how to insert subtle rules and square off sayings,
to think, to see, to understand, to twist, to love, to contrive,
to suspect tricks and think "outside the box" always—
Aes.   You did indeed!

Aeschylus twice agrees with the claim—but not its moral merits. Euripides *has* taught the spectators (τουτουσί) by training actors in roles and behavior which the audience then imitates, but to Aeschylus's mind that teaching has corrupted the Athenian populace. Euripides concludes with exemplars of their respective teachings, and it is notable that the "followers" (μαθητάς, 964) he attributes to both himself and Aeschylus are not contemporary poets but politicians. Taken at face value, Euripides is claiming that his plays have taught these politicians to perform their roles in the democracy, especially as speakers before the assembly. His own prize specimens are Cleitophon—and Theramenes.

Again, as with the chorus's earlier reference to Theramenes' theatrical abilities (533–541), the topic is touched upon lightly, then turned quickly to laughter as Dionysus ironically compliments him as a σοφός γ' ἀνήρ (968).[62] The comedy becomes even broader as Euripides claims the reasoning skills he taught the audience (again τούτοισιν, 972) were useful at home. Dionysus burlesques the notion, imagining a man coming home and asking after lost or consumed goods in broadly paratragic tones. Thus the treatment of Theramenes, while criticizing his performative politics, is much more cautious than the all-out attack on Cleon two decades before, suggesting that even Aristophanes had to be careful what he said in these final months before the fall of Athens.[63]

Aeschylus replies. He begins in surprisingly Socratic fashion by quizzing Euripides on the proper role of the poet, getting his opponent to articulate the poet's duty thus:

$$\beta\epsilon\lambda\tau\acute{\iota}ους \; τε \; ποιοῦμεν$$
τοὺς ἀνθρώπους ἐν ταῖς πόλεσιν.   (1009–1010)

We make men better citizens.

The principle seems the same as that Euripides himself just expounded, but the language has been, at least temporarily, detheatricalized. Aeschylus prefers to speak of "making" men better, not teaching them roles; he is an essentialist, not a behaviorist. He shifts the comparison of results from the political classes (Phormisios vs. Theramenes) to the rank and file: he claims to have made men into dedicated warriors, while Euripides made them into shirkers who prefer hanging around the Agora.[64] In an aside Euripides acknowledges the force of

this hit (1018),[65] but he subtly subverts the course of the argument when he
demands to know how Aeschylus did this:

καὶ δὴ χωρεῖ τουτὶ τὸ κακόν· κρανοποιῶν αὖ μ᾽ ἐπιτρίψει.
καὶ τί σὺ δράσας οὕτως αὐτοὺς γενναίους ἐξεδίδαξας;   (1018–1019)

This is really going badly; he'll wear me down with his helmet-making.
And what did you do to teach them to be so noble?

At first Euripides here continues to use the language of making (Aeschylus's
style is "helmet-making"), but he quickly shifts ground to his preferred language of "teaching." Aeschylus apparently does not deign to reply immediately, occasioning a prompt from Dionysos, but then cites his *Seven Against
Thebes* and *Persians*. He claims his plays inspired every spectator with immediate martial ardor (1022)—"see the play, take the hill." He tries to reassert the
language of making ("writing a play full of Ares,"[66] δρᾶμα ποιήσας Ἄρεως
μεστόν, 1021), but Dionysus, conflating representation and audience, turns
this against him, accusing Aeschylus of making (πεπόιηκας, 1023) the *The-
bans*, rather than the Athenian audience, more valiant in war. Aeschylus then
seems to slip unconsciously, via the technical usage of διδάξω for "produce a
play, rehearse the chorus" into the more general language of teaching:

εἶτα διδάξας Πέρσας μετὰ τοῦτ᾽ ἐπιθυμεῖν ἐξεδίδαξα
νικᾶν ἀεὶ τοὺς ἀντιπάλους, κοσμήσας ἔργον ἄριστον.   (1026–1027)

Then after that I produced *The Persians* and taught them
to want always to conquer their rivals, polishing them off.

This jingoistic Aeschylus is so far from our current concept that it is customary to ascribe it to Aristophanes' love of exaggeration and the demands
of dramatic conflict here in the *agon*. Yet was Aristophanes free to construct
any Aeschylus he liked? Perhaps not entirely so: scarcely any of his audience
had seen Aeschylus's original productions—but most of them had seen Aeschylean revivals. The Aeschylus of the Athenian audience's repertoire is composed of the productions they had seen in the theater, not the school edition
Aeschylus we moderns read. The explicit references here argue for fairly recent
or at least very memorable restagings of *Persians* and the *Seven*—and perhaps
Myrmidons as well.[67]

The notion that Attic tragedy intended to convey political messages now
seems rather dubious.[68] Contemporary tragedians did not write to shift votes
in the assembly. A dead tragedian, however, might be more amenable to politi-

cal appropriation. While we may not be able to answer the question definitively, we ought at least to ask whether some kind of reappropriation or at least reinterpretation occurred in the restaging of Aeschylean works in the last decades of the fifth century. Pleasant as it would be to believe that citizens volunteered for the liturgy of putting on a play of Aeschylus for the sheer aesthetic love of his poetry, it is quite possible the *choregoi* had more immediate purposes in mind. Was Aeschylus already being deployed in a "culture war" against modernism and Euripidean despair even before the production of the *Frogs*? Even more specifically, were those responsible for recent restagings of the *Persians* and the *Seven* trying to raise public morale and even encourage defense of the homeland? The analogy of Olivier's *Henry V* beckons. Aristophanes may not be the onlie begetter of this hypermilitaristic Aeschylus.

In any case, Aeschylus portrays himself as the logical extension of a tradition of poetic didacticism, flowing from Orpheus on through Hesiod and Homer. If the tribute to Homer as instructor in military tactics rings a little odd now,[69] we need not doubt that some tried to use Homer in this way. In fact, Aeschylus makes the analogy of theater and classroom quite clear, when he insists it is the poet's duty to select what to put before the public. He repeats the familiar charge that Euripides has put disgraceful women on the stage. Truth is no defense: the poet should conceal vice, not parade it (1053–1055).[70]

In a fresh variation on a familiar charge, Aeschylus claims that Euripides' ragged heroes are not only a disgrace in themselves but have taught the rich how to pretend to be poor and therefore unable to fulfill their duties as trierarchs to equip state ships for the war (1065–66). Dionysus labels this deception (ἐξαπατήσῃ, 1068), a charge picked up and broadened by Aeschylus, who claims that the rhetorical tricks taught by Euripides have sown sedition in the fleet (1071–1072) and enabled demagogues to deceive the demos ("clowning chimpanzee politicians . . . ," βωμολόχων δημοπιθήκων / ἐξαπατώντων τὸν δῆμον, 1085–1086).[71]

For all the sound and fury, this opening section of the *agon* in fact establishes an agreed framework for the debate. Both poets maintain that their role is to teach the people. Their disagreements lie in the supposed effects of their teaching. Both insist their own work has a good effect. Aeschylus is given the more rhetorically colorful argument that Euripides' plays have evil effects, destructive of social and military order. Euripides' argument is principally that, since no one can understand what Aeschylus is going on about anyway, his plays have essentially no effect. The charges of deception are also rather unequal in seriousness: Aeschylus may deceive the audience into thinking a silent character is waiting to produce a great revelation—which proves incomprehensible—but Euripides teaches active skills of role-playing, disguise, and deception, which can further financial fraud and form a basis for leadership in the assembly. Already interwoven into the discussion is one contrast that will persist throughout the debate: while both engage in a contest over wisdom (882), Euripides' special concern is for clarity (918, 927).

The chorus responds to this rather theoretical preliminary skirmish by asking for more, assuring both combatants they need not fear an unlearned public (1109–1110) because the audience are all the book-reading sort (1114)[72] who will get the jokes (θεατῶν . . . σοφῶν, 1118). They need to be such, at least at first, as Euripides proposes to begin by testing Aeschylus's prologues, a term he now uses explicitly (where earlier he paraphrased its function, lines 946–947), although Aristophanes makes sure he slips in a definition of this technical term in the process: "the first part of the tragedy" (τὸ πρῶτον τῆς τραγῳδίας μέρος, 1120).[73] With deft word-parsing sophistry, Euripides demonstrates the redundancy and frequent incomprehensibility of the opening of Aeschylus's Choephoroi. Dionysus, although a representative book-reading audience member (recall his original experience of reading the Andromeda!), finds himself unequal to the intellectual pressure of the discussion, requesting instruction (δίδαξον γάρ με καθ' ὅτι δὴ λέγεις, 1162)[74] and then protesting he still cannot comprehend (ὅ τι λέγεις δ' οὐ μανθάνω, 1169), but Euripides' point has been made. Aeschylus briefly counterattacks in the same sophistic vein (1183ff.) but then resorts to a more concrete weapon.

Aeschylus proposes to destroy Euripides' prologues with "a little bottle of oil" (ληκύθιον, 1200ff.). On one level the joke mocks the metrical monotony of Euripidean verse while simultaneously juxtaposing triviality with tragic solemnity. In effect, Aeschylus does to Euripides what he accuses Euripides of doing to the art of tragedy as a whole: he deflates its dignity by substituting a minor mishap for the great deeds of tragic heroes past. The incongruity is devastating and, as Dover suggests, builds with the rhythm of a repeated joke in children's pantomime. Perhaps a modern American analogy can capture both the sense of metrical parody and the trivialization of serious material: someone once pointed out to me that Emily Dickinson's most common poetic form was American ballad meter and that therefore most of her poems, including the famous "Because I could not stop for Death," could actually be sung to the tune of "The Yellow Rose of Texas." Think about it.

Whether there is another level to the joke has been debated for more than twenty-five years, beginning with Cedric Whitman.[75] The term λήκυθος comprehended several types of vases, one of which is long and distinctly phallic in shape. If we assume a sexual *double entendre*, the joke could mean simply "lost his erection" or, more sinisterly, "was castrated." The problems with this view are that the joke does not then seem to fit every situation perfectly, there is no contemporary evidence for ληκύθιον as a sexual euphemism,[76] and one might have expected Aristophanes to elaborate the sexual implications of the joke, if there were any. All these lead to Dover's cautious verdict of "not proven." E. K. Borthwick, however, has recently strengthened the case for a sexual meaning to the word λήκυθος when used by Demosthenes in the next century, and M. F. Kilmer has argued that the λήκυθος is a visual signal for impending sexual activity in vase painting.[77] Finally, we must reckon with the possibilities of the actor's delivery of the lines: as a famous Monty Python sketch demonstrates, by using the repeated refrain "Nudge, nudge, wink, wink, say no more, say no more," it is quite possible to imply a sexual meaning to items and phrases that have none to begin with. The joke does therefore seem to be energized by more than metrical parody.

Aeschylus proceeds to do just as he promised, tacking the phrase "lost his little bottle of oil" onto prologue after prologue of Euripides with devastating effect.[78] The assaults quickly become personal for Dionysus, since he himself is the subject of the second of the prologues (from the *Hypsipyle*) that Aeschylus attacks.[79] His response is a parody of the Aeschylean Agamemnon's death cry ("Alas, we are stricken again by the bottle of oil," οἴμοι πεπλήγμεθ᾽ αὖθις ὑπὸ τῆς ληκύθου, 1214), and he later speaks of "our prologues" (1228), thus identifying himself with Euripides' discomfiture. Aeschylus even demonstrates that the ληκύθιον can be put into both the first *and* the second lines of Euripides' *Oineus* (1238–1241). Dionysos, observing that the ληκύθιον is popping out all over his prologues like sties on the eyes,[80] advises Euripides to turn to the subject of lyric verse (τὰ μέλη) instead.

This is Euripides' opportunity to turn the tables on Aeschylus, but Aristophanes structures the performance in a way to turn the deck against him. In the first place, Euripides recites the Aeschylean lyrics himself. Not only is this dramatically less effective than interrupting one's opponent, as Aeschylus was able to do, but it illustrates the cultural dominance of Aeschylus: even though he may despise the older poet's work, Euripides has nonetheless memorized these lyrics. They are part of the cultural baggage he has inherited, like it or not. Euripides' criticism is structurally not all that different from the "little bottle of oil." It essentially amounts to the tendency of Aeschylus's lyrics toward repetitive dactylic rhythm, but tacking on an obscure phrase (1265 etc.) or even the onomatopoetic syllables φλαττοθρατ τοφλαττοθρατ does not have quite the same comic bite.

A puzzled question from Dionysus[81] sets up Aeschylus's counterattack. He claims Euripides' lyric passages come from "whores' songs, scolia of Meletus, Carian flute tunes" (πορνῳδιῶν, / σκολίων Μελήτου, Καρικῶν αὐλημάτων, 1301–1302) and such. Once again, the charge is that Euripides has breached the barriers that once separated tragedy from other realms, and tawdry popular music has slipped in along with the characters dressed in rags and the other impedimenta of daily life.

Aristophanes brilliantly demonstrates just what that means. When Aeschylus calls forth the "Muse of Euripides" (1306), a mute performer appears to dance in accompaniment to the parody of Euripidean lyrics. Her appearance appalls Dionysus, either because she is so ugly and decrepit or because she is dressed as, and behaves like, a prostitute—or both.[82] Her makeshift castanets (1305–1306) seems to allude visually to Euripides' recent *Hypsipyle*, in which the title character, now an old woman, entertains a baby with a rattle or castanets. Given Aeschylus's reference to prostitutes' songs (1301), it seems most likely that Aristophanes has taken the humble but sweet domestic stage picture from the Euripidean play and turned it into a burlesque and lascivious dance, made all the more comic by the apparent age of the performer.[83]

The Euripidean pastiche that Aeschylus sings, while the "Muse" pantomimes to his lyrics, draws heavily on the *Hypsipyle* as well. A *lanx satura* of gobbets which make no particular sense together, the verses also offer a wild exaggeration of the style of the "New Music" and in particular the dragging out of one syllable over many notes in the grotesquely elongated εἰειειειειλίσσετε (1314).[84] At the dance's climax, the "Muse" embraces Euripides, and Aeschylus demands of someone "Do you see this foot?" (ὁρᾷς τὸν πόδα τοῦτον; 1323), followed by virtually the same question in the next line. Both questions are answered "Yes." Speaker assignments are a considerable problem here, but I follow Dover in giving the first answer to Euripides, the second to Dionysus, although the reverse may be just as likely. In any case, as Borthwick has compellingly argued, the point is not any metrical anomaly in line 1322 the audience might have heard but something they can *see*: a physical foot, that of the "Muse," which is then matched to the foot of Euripides in a simultaneous parody of *Hypsipyle* and *Electra*.[85] The "Muse" is both Hypsipyle recognizing her sons and Electra recognizing her brother Orestes. In a brilliant bit of metatheatrical vengeance, Aeschylus forces Euripides to recognize the "family resemblance" between himself and his "Muse" because her foot is just as big as his—precisely the kind of identity proof for which Euripides had dared to twit Aeschylus by having his Electra reject such evidence! As Euripides squirms in his "Muse's" embrace, Aeschylus drives the point home:

you criticize my μέλη, while your own songs are written in the style of the "twelve tricks of [the prostitute] Cyrene" (τὸ δωδεκαμήχανον / Κυρήνης, 1327–1328).[86] Presumably she releases him at 1329 and departs.

Aeschylus now targets Euripides' monodies, a particular source of pride as we remember. These too were classified as μέλη, but their use by individual characters rather than the chorus was indeed an innovation. While tragic repetition of words and syllables comes in for mockery again, the principal humor seems to be derived from the mismatch of style and substance, for this elaborate lament turns out to come from a woman searching for a stolen chicken.

A sudden shift from verbal to visual follows, as Aeschylus calls for the scales and challenges Euripides to a weighing contest (1365). There is assuredly a visual reminisce of the weighing scene in Aeschylus's own *Psychostasia*, in which Zeus balances the fates of Achilles and Memnon, but painfully little is known for certain about this play, of which only three disconnected words survive.[87] Taplin has pointed out that we know even less about this lost play than has been commonly assumed; Zeus may not have appeared in the play and the famous weighing of fates could in fact be reported or perhaps more likely represented with Hermes holding the scales.[88] The scene in *Frogs* seems to me evidence for the original representation on stage, and we would very much like to know whether there had been a recent revival of this production. Although there is a danger of circular argument, the potential contrasts between the two scenes are striking and rich. We must not forget the presence of Pluto presiding over this weighing scene, even though he has not spoken: as Zeus' brother and king of the counterpart kingdom to Olympus, he offers a central visual counterpoint to Zeus in the original scene. The mothers of Achilles and Hector at the scales are replaced by the male poets and their winged words. Dionysus's flippant reference to "weighing art like cheese" (τυροπωλῆσαι τέχνην, 1369) points toward continuing comedy, but the visual dimension signals a new direction. A choral lyric covers the action of bringing the scale onto the stage.

The very location of the stage picture may exemplify the most comprehensive reversal, that of life and death which Dionysus will soon taunt Euripides for imagining: τίς δ' οἶδεν εἰ τὸ ζῆν μέν ἐστι κατθανεῖν (1477), "Who knows if life be death . . . ?"[89] Aeschylus's weighing scene may have played on the theologeion, while that in Aristophanes takes place on the stage.[90] The meaning of the weighing is reversed as well: in both Homer and Aeschylus, the balance pan that sinks toward the ground indicates death and proleptically the movement to the underworld.[91] Aristophanes reverses that. Three times both poets speak their lines into the balance—and three times the pan of Aeschylus sinks. But here the sinking balance beam points toward life, toward the realm of the living—that is, the direction down from the stage and into the orchestra, whence the chorus will lead Aeschylus away at play's end. Even those of the audience who do not follow the sophistical explanations of why one line is "weightier" than the other will see in the movement of the balance which the winner is.[92]

It is all the more surprising, therefore, that Dionysus professes himself unable to decide between the two (though perhaps no more surprising that Demos's continual inability to decide in *Knights* between the two contenders). Although Charles Segal suggests that Dionysus matures as an audience member in the course of the play,[93] he has not yet reached the point where he can make this decision on his own. Pluto, present on the stage since the beginning of the contest, suddenly intervenes (1414). The surprise is like that of the thitherto silent Pylades to Orestes in *Choephoroi* 900–902—and I wonder if deliberately and deeply ironically so. Pylades speaks to remind Orestes of the "faithful oaths" (πιστὰ δ᾽ εὐορκώματα) they must keep. Pluto tells Dionysus he may take with him the poet he considers the better—which allows him to break the oath that he swore.[94]

Much has been made of the supposed inconsistency of Dionysus coming down specifically to fetch Euripides from Hades and now choosing to take the winner of the contest. Although swiftly handled, his words take us back to the theme laid out in considerable detail at the beginning of the contest: the need for a poet to teach the city. Dionysos states this in appropriately theatrical terms:

> φέρε, πύθεσθέ μου ταδί.
> ἐγὼ κατῆλθον ἐπὶ ποιητήν. τοῦ χάριν;
> ἵν᾽ ἡ πόλις σωθεῖσα τοὺς χοροὺς ἄγῃ. (1417–1419)

> Now, listen to me.
> I came here for a poet. Why?
> So that the city, once save, may continue my choruses.

Even though his desire for Euripides may have been aroused by reading, Dionysus has been thinking all along of tragedy as something performed in his honor. His choruses must be kept going—and that can only be accomplished by saving the city.

The issue returns to the here and now with startling force. In this theater where Dionysus's journey has brought us, the poets debate in direct terms what advice is best for the city. In rich metatheatrical irony, tragedy can only give its advice when quoted by comedy, for only then can the audience know that aphorisms or metaphors are meant to be applied specifically to a policy decision.

Characteristically, Aristophanes does not endorse one policy decision over the other, although he leans in one direction. The first test question is: what do we do about Alcibiades? Dionysus asks each poet to give his γνώμη, and we are reminded of the chorus's introductory praise of poets as coiners of γνῶμαι (γνωμοτύπων, 877). Euripides fences and asks first what the city's γνώμη about Alcibiades is. Told it is divided (the city both loves and hates him), Euripides offers an aphorism, carefully generalized as befits tragic utterance:

μισῶ πολίτην, ὅστις ὠφελεῖν πάτραν
βραδὺς φανεῖται, μεγάλα δὲ βλάπτειν ταχύς,
καὶ πόριμον αὑτῷ, τῇ πόλει δ᾽ ἀμήχανον.   (1427–1429)

I hate a citizen who'll prove slow
to help his country, but quick to harm her greatly,
useful to himself indeed, but useless to the city.

Aeschylus's advice employs the metaphor of the lion cub to say that Athens, since it is saddled with Alcibiades, had better adapt to him (1431a–1432).

Dionysus declares that one poet has spoken σοφῶς, the other σαφῶς (1434)—and he is still confused.[95] It is far from clear which is which.[96] While Dover is certainly right to say that a gesture could have resolved any doubt as to who spoke σοφῶς and who σαφῶς, need we assume such a gesture? Without one, the audience may well be in some doubt.

There are definitely problems with the transmitted text of the next exchange, and this contributes to our confusion, although it may have been quite clear in the original performance. Dionysus asks both poets for direct advice about the salvation of the city (1436). Presumably both must answer him—but we seem to have more text than that. Dover has reordered the lines based on the assumption, going back to Dindorf and Hermann, that the text we have is a conflation of the two Athenian performances of the play, the original in 405, and the repetition ordered by the state. In Dover's version, Dionysus asks for their plans, and Euripides responds with a wild piece of fantasy, a plan for aerial bombardment of the enemy (lines 1437–1441, followed immediately by 1451–1462), while Aeschylus, having first asked how the city employs its useful citizens (τοῖς χρηστοῖς, 1455), momentarily re-

fuses to answer here in the underworld. When pressed, Aeschylus yields and
does answer, but the answers differ for Dover in the 405 and 404 versions.
In 405, he gives a Periclean but epigrammatic answer which implies a naval
strategy (1461–1466); the next year, Athens having in large part lost any effective fleet, the answer is more general but still epigrammatic: change those the
city puts her trust in and pursue a course opposite to the present one (1442–
1450). The phrasing of 1443–1444 with its elaborate play on alpha-privatives
sounds highly Euripidean, however:

> ὅταν τὰ νῦν ἄπιστα πίσθ' ἡγώμεθα,
> τὰ δ' ὄντα πίστ' ἄπιστα—

> When we regard the faithless as faithful
> and the faithful as faithless—

Probably to be preferred is the arrangement proposed by Sommerstein,
in large part anticipated by Tucker.[97] In this view, lines 1437–1441, spoken by
Euripides and Dionysus and immediately followed by 1451–1453, represent
the original script of 405. Lines 1442–1450 are the alternative version prepared
for a performance in 404, displacing the first version, and therefore constitute
Euripides' answer (and *only* answer, in this version) to Dionysus' request for
a plan. Sommerstein also makes a good case for regarding these new lines as
part of a stronger emphasis on changing the city's leaders, an issue of even
greater urgency (for some parties!) in 404. It is still somewhat of a puzzle,
however, why Euripides should be the one to give this good advice, if good
advice it was, instead of the poet destined to win the contest,[98] but undeniably this is a simpler solution than Dover's and one that gives 1443–1444 to
the poet Aristophanes has so often caricatured for using just such a style.

Pluto politely presses for a decision, and Dionysus, still unable to make
up his mind, decides to entrust the decision to his ψυχή (1468). Its decision
quotes one of Euripides' most famous lines against him: "My tongue swore
—but I'll choose Aeschylus" (ἡ γλῶττ' ὀμώμοκ', Αἰσχύλον δ' αἱρήσομαι,
1471). Euripides' rage is boundless, but his attempts to shame Dionysus into
changing his mind[99] only provoke further parodies: "What's shameful, unless it seems so to the spectators (τί δ' αἰσχρόν, ἢν μὴ τοῖς θεωμένοις δοκῇ;
1475). Aeschylus turns Euripides' own standards against him, fusing a parody
of an infamous line from his *Aeolus* (fr. 19) with his views as laid out at the
beginning of the debate. Euripides' last words are a question: literally, "will
you look upon me dead?" (περιόψει με δὴ τεθνηκότα; 1476). The implicit

and blackly comic answer is, yes—because that is precisely what we all have been doing since Euripides came on stage. For him there is no escape.

The actors clear the stage, allowing the chorus to draw a more explicit moral than usual (1482ff.), before Pluto returns to dispatch Aeschylus on his mission to save "our city" (πόλιν τὴν ἡμετέραν, 1501). Some consider the possessive a compliment to Athens, but it may be a dire warning: Pluto was not a divinity much honored with worship or gladly acknowledged in ancient Greece. He even gives Aeschylus instruments of suicide to deliver to a few Athenian politicians![100] Aeschylus is to save the city with good advice and to educate the large number of "idiots" (ἀνοήτους, 1503) in Athens.[101] Of particular significance is the term Pluto chooses here for "educate": παίδευσον, not δίδαξον. At issue is not so much the hierarchical emphasis of the former, teaching as a schoolmaster does his pupils, but the careful avoidance of the notion of any theatrical, deceptive teaching. Aeschylus must restore the pre-Euripidean teaching function of the theater. That teaching may in fact begin even as the play ends. Aeschylus bequeaths his newly secured chair of tragedy to Sophocles to keep and departs, even as Pluto orders the chorus to accompany him with his own songs (τοῖσιν τούτου τοῦτον μέλεσιν, 1526). The final six verses of our play text are Aristophanes', with allusions to Aeschylus, but these would not be enough to cover the full departure of the chorus from the orchestra. As Radermacher and Dover both suggest, the chorus may have taken departed to a genuine Aeschylean song, thereby returning Aeschylus in the most emphatic fashion to the world of the living.

The *Frogs* is the most metatheatrical of Aristophanes' plays in the sense that it deals on both a theoretical and practical level with the problems of creating tragedy and comedy. It begins by reexamining the state of comedy and ends by proposing a revival (in the original sense of that word) of Aeschylean tragedy. Yet it would be profoundly wrong to treat it as a meditation on aesthetics alone, an extended lament on decline from a literary golden age. The political issues that become evident at the end of the play are implicit in its concerns from the beginning.

If we cast an eye back now to the play's more "comic" first half, we see matters of identity, role-playing, and "teaching" at the heart of all its routines. Dionysus begins with a purely instrumental view of role-playing. He costumes himself as Heracles in the simple-minded belief that this will prove advantageous to him and a protection against the dangers of the journey to the underworld. That journey turns out to be far more complicated than he expects. For one thing, he has to work to get there. Whether the rowing scene invokes in the audience's memory a similar training regimen in Eupolis's *Taxi-archs*, the implication is clear: Dionysus can no longer be a layabout on ship-board, whiling his time away in the self-absorbed pastime of reading, but has to learn the fundamental Athenian skill of rowing. Once he gets to the under-world, he also learns that a costume is not itself a role: without learning how to behave like Heracles, it is no good simply disguising himself as Heracles. Xanthias takes the lead at improvising dialogue in character with his role as Heracles, and Dionysus must learn to do the same—and does so, at least well enough to achieve a draw in the contest with his slave.

In the second half of the play, we learn that Dionysus has two faces—not just those of tragedy and comedy, but also as spectator, judging others' competitive displays, as well as performer himself. Moreover, spectatorship, as Aristophanes has been arguing from the *Acharnians* on, is not a purely pas-sive pursuit, but one that requires the right kind of active contribution. One can hardly say that Dionysus becomes a successful performer in the first half of the play, although he does improve his skills. In the second half, however, he does finally master what is required of him to become a successful tragic *spectator*, and in doing so he models that behavior for the rest of Athens.

It was in fact too late—too late for even the best tragedian's γνῶμαι to save Athens from the situation into which her performing politicians had led her, and too late also in the longer view to establish a revived Aeschylean tragic theater as "the" proper tragic theater.[102] Tragedy, like Old Comedy itself, was losing that immediate connection to the life and imagination of a single city, Athens, and becoming internationalized.

The irony of the *Frogs*' immediate reception is sharp. From the broad and developed critique of spectator politics laid out in this play, the Athenians seem to have received primarily the almost unique bit of policy advice Aris-tophanes here proffers: take back the exiles. They did—but that alone was not enough to rebuild the participatory democracy Aristophanes dreamed of.

The irony is tempered by the continuing presence of the play itself. If *Frogs* failed to rebuild the proper relationship of theatrical performance and spectators in its own time, its meditations on these subjects and its view of two great tragedians have decisively shaped their later reception. It is no mean achievement to come out of the wreck of a great culture.

IO

Waiting in the Wings:
Ecclesiazusae

> Walk like a man, talk like a man,
> Walk like a man, my son. . . .
> —Frankie Valli and the Four Seasons

OUR STORY DRAWS TO A CLOSE—but that is not the spirit in which to approach this playful and revolutionary comedy. We know, as Aristophanes did not, that the second Athenian empire was to be only a shadow of the first and eventually fall victim to Macedonian expansionism. We know too that the playwright was approaching the end of his life. The ancient tradition that divides comedy into Old, Middle, and New and the cataclysm of 404 loom so large in our historical consciousness that the assumption that these must have been of equal significance for Aristophanes in his art insinuates itself easily.[1] The temptation to classify the *Ecclesiazusae* as a minor piece before we even experience it is powerful, and a view of it as a diminished, merely "ironic" comedy has until recently been widespread. The *Lysistrata* has always commanded an admiring audience. More recently the gleeful intertextual games of the *Thesmophoriazusae* have captured much attention. The *Ecclesiazusae*, more revolutionary than either of its predecessors, has nonetheless trailed along in their shadow. This comedy's opening scene, however, plays with the nature of the performance in ways quite as interesting as Aristophanes' earlier metatheatrical experiments and suggests consequently a more purely comic interpretation of this play than that now generally held.

More than most plays, the *Ecclesiazusae* negotiates the conditions of its own reception with its audience and only gradually articulates its particular vision. If we already know the nature of Praxagora's plan, we must put our anachronistic knowledge aside and reenvision the performance as it unfolds through time. Where the metatheatricality of early Aristophanes has com-

manded increasing attention,[2] the surprising innovations of the *Ecclesiazusae*
and particularly their implications for the theatricalization of politics have
been read in a distinctly antitheatrical way. Most current interpretations of the
play insist, primarily by reading backward from one scene near the end, that
the play must be ironic or satiric in intention; feminist scholarship in particular has been curiously insistent that the women's attempt to create a utopia
yields instead a dystopia. Let us, however, sit back and watch the *Ecclesiazusae*
create its own category before we attempt to devise one for it.

One fine spring morning in perhaps 393 B.C.,[3] a strange figure strode onto
an Athenian stage. Like Dionysus in the opening of the *Frogs*, this performer
enacts a cognitive dissonance: the mask and body outlines are those of a female
figure, but one who has thrown a distinctively male cloak over herself. Praxagora (only named later) comes forward and begins the play by apostrophizing
the lamp she carries:

> Ὦ λαμπρὸν ὄμμα τοῦ τροχηλάτου λύχνου,
> κάλλιστ᾽ ἐν εὐστόχοισιν ἐξηυρημένον   (1–2)

O bright eye of the wheel-thrown lamp,
loveliest invention of skilled artists

She goes on to discuss the lamp's lineage and experience of women's secrets.
The lines are paratragic (the lamp as substitute for the sun), perhaps a mockery
of Euripides, perhaps not;[4] in any case, the joke seems miniature and flat,
perhaps paradigmatic for what has happened to Aristophanes' comedy in the
fourth century. Other than to mock the style of some obscure tragedian, what
is Aristophanes' purpose here?

Recovering the impact of this moment in performance is a key to a better
interpretation of the whole. The joke lies not just in word play: Aristophanes
is here trying to turn a natural disadvantage into a comic asset. At the end of
this play, the chorus will appeal to the judges not to forget them, even though
they have the disadvantage of coming on first among the day's five comedies
(1154ff.).[5] We know therefore that these opening lines of *Ecclesiazusae* were the
very first played in the day's competition, and I suspect that they were written
or rewritten once Aristophanes was allotted first position on the program.

Here and throughout the play we must be aware of how the physical
realities of production shape dramatic meaning. The actor playing Praxagora
is carrying a real, lit lamp. Greek household lamps were not large. On its own
in the vast Theater of Dionysus, this small stage property would be nearly invisible. In the bright light of full day, it would be virtually impossible even

for front row spectators to tell whether such a lamp was lit. A tiny household lamp would only be visible in the vast Theater of Dionysus in the pale light of dawn, where Praxagora now unfolds the women's plot to seize control of the Athenian assembly—and she does so with a visual parody of such scenes as the signal fires in the *Agamemnon*.[6] The joke is not just a parody of Euripidean or pseudo-Euripidean language, but a subversion through performance of a long tragic tradition. It also effects a key spatial reversal, bringing the private indoor world of women out into the public world of the open air, a move that anticipates much in the play to follow.[7]

I do not suggest that the whole idea for the predawn meeting of the women in this play came to Aristophanes after he was allotted first position at the festival; some such plotting and rehearsal session as we are about to witness was necessary to the overall design of the play. Nonetheless, I suspect that the use of the lamp as focus in the scene, as confidante to whom Praxagora can begin to pour out the necessary exposition of the plot, was a last-minute inspiration of Aristophanes, who realized he could use it to fuse the actual time of production with the fictional time of his play. Paradoxically, this touch of "reality" can be used to highlight the "fictionality" of later parts of the play.

Praxagora's opening soliloquy contains, in addition to tragic parody, important hints of what is to come. She tells us that a plot was set in motion at the festival of the Skira and employs language appropriate to the political sphere to describe it ("the proposals seemed good to my friends," βουλεύματα . . . ἔδοξε ταῖς ἐμαῖς φίλαις, 17–18). We learn that the women are going to take their seats at the assembly, disguised as men.[8] Women are about to seize the government.

Just after this startling bit of information, another lamp appears to close and frame Praxagora's opening soliloquy. She breaks off and steps back out of the way (27–28), for she does not yet know whether it is carried by a female coconspirator or a man. Her own lamp and that carried by the approaching (but unnamed) First Woman quite literally fade away as the real dawn begins to light the scene. Moments later, Praxagora summons the Second Woman with a stealthy scratch at her door (34), and the three of them then watch and comment (41–53) as the chorus filters silently in. With the chorus's arrival the serious preparations for the women's takeover of Athens can begin.

What follows is the earliest developed rehearsal scene in comedy: the women gradually work themselves into the masculine roles they must play in order to persuade/rig the assembly so as to institute rule by women in Athens.[9] This inductive quality of the scene accounts for the otherwise puzzling and highly unusual feature: the chorus enters silently, not in character, because they have not yet put on their characters. They are a cast assembling for the final dress rehearsal in one sense: the scene gives us the illusion that the process of illusion-making has not yet begun.

The play with the nature of theater that takes place in this scene is wonderfully rich and dense. Male choristers in female costumes reenact and simultaneously invert the process of learning to portray the other sex, which they themselves have now mastered.[10] Ancient Greek society enjoined a strong differentiation of the sexes in outward appearance. These women must learn to wear the clothes of men, to walk like them, talk (and especially swear) like them, and finally to act politically as men do.

They have already made some preparations. As Suzanne Saïd has pointed out,[11] the present scene is an assembly manqué, poised between a religiously sanctioned assembly of women, their gathering at the festival of the Skira where they concocted the idea of disguising themselves as men, and the Athenian assembly where they will force their proposal through. They have employed the time since the Skira to transform their own bodies by ceasing to shave their body hair and sunning themselves to acquire a tan (60–64)![12] Their masks undoubtedly would be light-colored, just as those of any other women on the Attic stage: their tan is a matter of imagination.[13]

The women arrive carrying men's cloaks, walking sticks, Laconian shoes, and false beards (68–75). It is not entirely clear when they put these all on. No doubt there is a certain amount of horseplay with these props from the beginning,[14] but Praxagora's words at the close of this scene to the chorus (268ff.) imply that they at least do not put on their beards and masculine costumes until they are ready to depart for the Pnyx. Probably the actors on stage costume themselves before they begin individually to rehearse their assembly speeches (e.g., Praxagora to the First Woman, "You there, put your beard on—hurry up and become a man," ἴθι δὴ σὺ περιδοῦ καὶ ταχέως ἀνὴρ γενοῦ, 121).

Aristophanes does not dwell much on the simple comedy of transvestism in the women's first scene, saving such jokes for their return from the assembly. If this seems strange, it should not: throughout the history of comedy, female transvestism has seemed far less funny than male, in large part because female transvestism is usually empowering (from Shakespeare's disguised heroines to *Victor/Victoria*) and therefore somewhat threatening, while male transvestism is portrayed as adding one more restriction to those the male comic body is always heir to (the old relative in *Thesmophoriazusae*, Babs in *Charley's Aunt*, Jack Lemmon and Tony Curtis in *Some Like It Hot*).[15]

Instead, the scene concentrates rather on the women's attempts to speak and act politically. It takes some time for them to master their parts. The First Woman never even begins her speech, for having put on the speaker's crown, she assumes that its significance is that she is about to drink, not speak (132–146). This takes the stock joke on women's bibulousness[16] and turns it into an occasion for jokes about the apparently drunken behavior of the male assembly: *they* pass laws so wild they must be drunk at the time (137–139) and quarrel with such drunken violence in the assembly that the constabulary must drag them away (142–143).

The Second Woman volunteers to speak, and Praxagora coaches her in both speech and deportment:

ἄγε νυν ὅπως ἀνδριστὶ καὶ καλῶς ἐρεῖς
διερεισαμένη τὸ σχῆμα τῇ βακτηρίᾳ.   (149–150)

Come now, speak like a man and well,
resting yourself on your walking stick.

An essential part of her role-playing, says Praxagora, is to speak ἀνδριστί, a very rare word: the only other occurrence we know of in comedy is Crates fr. 24 K-A., ἀνδριστὶ μιμεῖσθαι φωνήν.[17] The male actors might have been using a falsetto voice up until now in their portrayal of these women, but most would find it exceedingly difficult to project a falsetto to the back of the vast Theater of Dionysus. On the other hand, the later specialization of certain actors in female parts suggests at least the possibility that certain vocal qualities were considered more "feminine."[18] If the actor playing the Second Woman, perhaps chosen with an eye to his natural vocal timbre, forces his voice lower to sound more "masculine" at the beginning of his speech, the point will have been made, and a quick reversion to his natural timbre will not be remarked.[19]

Praxagora also exhorts the Second Woman to adopt a masculine posture. Praxagora has the instincts of a good director and knows that beards and male clothing are not enough; the women must master the art of putting these various elements together. The word σχῆμα here betokens not "weight" so much as "pose": she is to lean heavily yet easily on her stick as they have seen men do (and not tentatively, as women, unused to walking with sticks, might).[20] This she manages and launches her speech with the customary "unaccustomed as I am to public speaking" clichés (151ff.).

Though she has mastered voice and posture, the Second Woman has not yet internalized her part. Within five lines she swears by the two goddesses, Demeter and Persephone (155), a gender-specific oath no man would use.[21] Praxagora gives her one more chance, but she fails again: she begins by addressing her assembled "fellow women" (165, ὦ γυναῖκες αἱ καθήμεναι). She improvises an excuse from a stock joke: she claims she saw Epigonos among her hearers and therefore thought she was addressing women (167–168). Praxagora nonetheless waves her down and takes the rostrum herself to rehearse the speech she will give.

We must be careful not to misinterpret the scene until now. It is tempting to praise Praxagora's speech by denigrating the other women's attempts up to this point. The analogy of Lysistrata may mislead us. Lysistrata in her play is a unique figure, the only woman capable of organizing and maintaining the sex strike. Aristophanes deliberately tells us very little about Lysistrata, in part to set her off: it is unclear whether she has a husband, for example,[22] and thereby participates in the strike herself. Praxagora is by no means unique, nor is she the sole originator of the plot.[23] Though we cannot yet know that she has a husband, she is simply different in degree, not kind, from the women who have spoken before her. *All* the women are slowly mastering their acting skills, learning to wear their masculine garb properly, move, and speak not only in a masculine voice but also from a masculine mental architecture.[24] The sequence builds to Praxagora, who has learned to speak by observing the orators on the Pnyx.[25] Practice has made perfect.

Nor should we devalue Praxagora's speech because it is a rehearsal, not the real performance in the assembly (of which we only hear reports later).[26] Something quite extraordinary has happened in the theater, which gives added weight to her address: the unparalleled behavior of the chorus has transformed the theatrical space into an even better imitation of the political space on the Pnyx than that achieved in the *Acharnians*.

We noted above that the chorus entered without a parodos song, which while unusual is not unparalleled. What *is* completely unparalleled and astonishing is the fact that, having entered, they then sit down.[27] Moreover, they sit down facing the stage, with their backs to the audience. They become at once the front rows of the Theater of Dionysus and simultaneously and proleptically the front rows of the assembly on the Pnyx. Just as in the assembly, Praxagora orders them to sit down as soon as they enter (57), and her further instructions to the would-be speakers to sit down (130, 144, 169) also echo the herald in *Acharnians* 123.[28] Both the First Woman and Praxagora emphasize that the women must sit up front in the assembly, right below the speakers' bema (87, 98)—just as they are now seated at the front of the theater.

The theater of the fifth century was fundamentally a choral space, especially for comedy, in which the chorus acted as bridge between the story en-

acted by the actors and the reactions of the audience.[29] As the importance
of the chorus declined toward the end of the century,[30] however, this unified
space began to break up. A gap opened up between stage and chorus—and
between chorus and audience. The extraordinarily modern effect that Aristophanes achieves here is possible only because this division of the theatrical
space has progressed substantially. The chorus seems to shed its specifically
choral role by sitting down. At the same time it does not shed its role in the
fiction of the play; by attaching itself to the vast body of citizens seated in
the theater, the chorus transforms theatrical spectators into assembly participants. The audience at this point is still a theatrical audience in that it is watching a theatrical rehearsal (as do the poet and producer on a well-known vase
showing Perseus dancing on a low stage[31]), but it also becomes a political
audience.

Kenneth Rothwell's discussion of the title of the play has some particular
relevance here. He argues that the verb ἐκκλησιάζειν may mean "to address
the assembly" in this period, not merely to attend it.[32] If so, there is a further
deduction to be drawn, although apparent only in retrospect: ultimately only
one woman, Praxagora, addresses the actual assembly. The play's title, however, is plural, and the only time more than one woman addresses the populace
is *here*, in the rehearsal scene. The title itself indicates the transformation of
theatrical space.

A modern parallel may perhaps illuminate Aristophanes' technique here.
Such a parallel is harder to find than one might suspect, given the plethora
of entrances from, and chases staged through, the audience in many performances now. Tom Stoppard's *The Real Inspector Hound*, while designed especially for a proscenium theater, shows us the same play with fiction/audience
boundaries, though to an opposite result. When the curtain rises on Stoppard's play we see, beyond the stage setting for a stock English murder mystery, an apparent reflection of ourselves: another (though shadowy) audience,
with two theater critics seated down front. These two, Moon and Birdboot,
begin by commenting on the play but are gradually swallowed up in its action
(and one is in fact killed by the action). Stoppard's mirror solution is dictated
by the sight lines in a proscenium house: we want to watch Moon and Birdboot's faces, not the backs of their heads. The same shifting boundary is at
work, though, as in *Ecclesiazusae*.

Perhaps an even better parallel, though a directorial innovation rather
than a necessary consequence of the script, is a production a few years ago
by Britain's National Theater of Shakespeare's *Coriolanus*. The Olivier Theater
was transformed into an open, Greek-style space with a sand-filled orchestra

circle occupying most of the stage. Upstage center were great doors, to the right and left of which were two or three rows of brick benches, hugging the curve of the orchestra. These benches were the day-of-performance seats. The spectators on them, however, were used (one might almost say, exploited) for the crowd scenes in the play. A few actors, deputized to speak the few crowd lines, would herd them out into the orchestra whenever a crowd scene occurred and encourage them to cheer or jeer, as appropriate. The somewhat heavy-handed point: the Roman *populus* in *Coriolanus* is simply manipulated by senators and tribunes in turn for political ends, just as this segment of the audience was manipulated by the actors and director for their own artistic ends.

Other plays of Aristophanes have hinted at the equation of the theater audience and the assembly. In our very first surviving play, the *Acharnians*, the theater audience is used as the assembly for the purposes of the fiction. Aristophanes' point in *Ecclesiazusae*, though, is subtler and more damning: the boisterous audience of 425 were participants in both the theater and the assembly. Now, as the theater space breaks up, we see that both bodies become spectators primarily, divided from the action by an invisible but growing gap. Though as long ago as *Knights*, Aristophanes' criticism of spectator politics was clear, he has never before conceded, as in effect he does here, that the gap cannot be closed again.

Praxagora's speech, like much in Aristophanes, is carefully balanced between seriousness and comedy. It opens on a note of sincerity and perhaps pathos:

ἐμοὶ δ᾽ ἴσον μὲν τῆσδε τῆς χώρας μέτα
ὅσονπερ ὑμῖν· ἄχθομαι δὲ καὶ φέρω
τὰ τῆς πόλεως ἅπαντα βαρέως πράγματα. (173–175)

I have just as much share in this country
as you; I suffer and grieve over
all the ills of the city.

This is basic democratic doctrine: every citizen has an equal share in the fate of the city. It is also the same sentiment we heard when the women of the *Lysistrata* lamented their share in the losses of the city in war. So too the women of *Ecclesiazusae* suffer with their city.

Praxagora's speech is a rehearsal not only of her own presentation but a chance for the other women to practice the proper reactions, which will help them carry their point in the assembly. Her speech is divided into four sections by interruptions from the listening women. The length and humor of these interjections diminishes as both Praxagora and her hearers warm to their roles and the proposal. She begins with a denunciation of Athens' present leaders and the corruption of the political process produced by the introduction of pay for assembly attendance (173–188). The First Woman interrupts with an approving oath—but unfortunately swearing by Aphrodite (189), as only women do. Praxagora coaches her on staying in character, then gives a brief and somewhat confusing account of Athens' recent vacillations in policy (193–203). By now the First Woman has mastered her part: she exclaims "what a clever fellow!" (ὡς ξυνετὸς ἀνήρ, 204) and wins approval from Praxagora for praising her "properly." Praxagora again denounces assembly pay and offers her revolutionary proposal: to turn control of the state over to the women (205–212). Both her companions cry out their approval, using the proper gender (ὦγαθε, 214). By now Praxagora takes no notice: both she and her hearers are fully absorbed in their roles.

Praxagora concludes with a demonstration that Athens needs the conservatism of women. The fusion of assembly and theater we have seen in the staging of this scene is crystallized by the verb she uses to launch this final section of her speech: ἐγὼ διδάξω, "I will teach" (215). Both poet and orator teach their audiences—but with the added echo of "rehearse," for the play's producer/director "teaches" the chorus their parts. Praxagora's teaching, however, quickly consumes itself: her praise of women for keeping the old ways turns first into a slogan, ὥσπερ καὶ πρὸ τοῦ. Nine lines (221–228) end with this catchphrase. The first few are serious enough, praising women's work and traditional religious duties, though the very repetition is ironizing. Soon, though, the traditional jokes about women take over, and Praxagora praises them for their consistent adultery, tippling, and voracious sexual appetites. She concludes with the paradoxical demonstration that, as women are themselves mistresses of deception, no one else will be able to deceive them (ἐξαπατηθείη ... ἐξαπατᾶν εἰθισμέναι ... , 237–238).

We would do well to meditate for a moment upon the femininity of illusion, as here proclaimed by Praxagora. Saïd, in her perceptive analysis of this play, insists that "La transformation des femmes en hommes dans *l'Assemblée des femmes* ne fait donc à aucun moment illusion."[33] It is true that we have, not the actual assembly, but the rehearsal for the assembly; nonetheless, we have participated in the growing power of the illusion these women wish to create. At first awkward and unrehearsed in their parts both as speakers and listeners, they have gradually mastered them and at the same time transformed the theater itself into the assembly, their audience into the voters. Saïd is troubled by the self-reflexive sexual jokes put in the mouths of these characters. The incantatory repetition of Praxagora's slogan culminates in the proud proclamation that "they'll enjoy screwing just as before" (βινούμεναι χαίρουσιν ὥσπερ καὶ πρὸ τοῦ, 228). In the next section, the women praise Praxagora for her speech and then ask her how she will deal with insults and even physical attempts to drag her away in the assembly. She takes the word they use for "drag away" (ὑποκρούωσιν, 256) and converts it to a sexual meaning with her reply: she will do what the women of the *Lysistrata* are pledged not to do, προσκινήσομαι (literally, "move in response"). Saïd insists that this all shows that "femmes qui ne triomphent dans le jeu politique qu'en le dénaturant et en le transformant en un jeu sexuel, où elles excellent."[34] But in the world of Aristophanic values is that a bad thing? Is it truly Aristophanic to separate the political from the sexual and value the former above the latter? We should perhaps at this point reserve judgment.

Praxagora instructs the chorus to costume themselves and put on their masculine characterizations. The actors withdraw, leaving the chorus to practice their roles (278, μιμούμεναι) and get into character as old rustics by singing appropriately. Note the combination: song and acting, the formula for theater. Their language emphasizes they must remember their parts and practice addressing each other as "gentlemen" (285, 289), with only the occasional, hastily corrected slip into the feminine gender (298–299). This chorus rehearsal is the inversion of the scene on a well-known Boston pelike.[35] There the young men of the chorus are shown in the process of donning their female costumes and trying out the gestures for their new roles. Here the women of the chorus undergo a similar transformation into men.

The departure of the chorus carries this inversion one step further. Choruses usually do not leave during the course of a play. These entered silently but depart singing, giving the audience a curious "backstage" feeling: we have in effect witnessed the final dress rehearsal for their performance in the assembly. As with modern backstage comedies, however, the effect is to increase the reality of what we have just witnessed.[36] What the women have just done is real; the upcoming assembly is the illusion.

The next scene has a backstage feeling as well. Notorious for its scatological humor (compare the opening scene of the *Peace* and the jokes Dionysus rejects at the beginning of the *Frogs*), the scene not only brings onstage what would normally be left off but, in the absence of the chorus, gives us the feeling that the play is beginning over. Praxagora's husband, Blepyrus, driven by necessity, comes out of his house to relieve himself in the "dark." By now it is fully light in the theater, and when he moves to a position where "no one will see" (322), he is doubtless down center in full view of the audience. Since his wife has taken his cloak and shoes, he has donned her yellow gown and slippers. The sexual inversion of the new state is thus demonstrated even before it is proclaimed. Women in men's clothes rule in the assembly, while the men are left at home in female garb.[37] Blepyrus is soon detected by an unnamed neighbor, then by his other neighbor Chremes as the latter returns from the assembly. Blepyrus is thus twice humiliated by being found in his feminine attire. His nightmare is that he will become a subject for the comic stage (371)—which is precisely what is happening to him.

The first concern of all the men is the loss of their assembly pay. Even Chremes, who was able to attend, arrived too late to be among the first six thousand who were paid. For Blepyrus, the loss of his three obols of pay is tragic—and inspires him to tragic misquotation of Aeschylus (391–393).[38] We see why Praxagora's plan was needed: every citizen's concern is first for himself. So too Blepyrus objects to all the charges against men reported by Chremes, so long as he thinks they are directed solely at him, but when Chremes indicts the whole audience with a gesture ("this crowd," τωνδὶ τὸ πλῆθος, 440), Blepyrus quite readily agrees that they are guilty.[39] When Chremes reports that the state has been handed over to the women, though he makes no mention of the theme of sexual communism, Blepyrus's first fear is that he will be compelled to perform sexually (465–468). Chremes concludes with the hope that the new regime will be the golden age of which the old tales tell (473), and both depart the stage.

The women now return stealthily, fearful of detection before they can shed their disguises (482, σχῆμα, cf. 503). Taking care to tread masculinely (483), the chorus enters the orchestra and then gathers under the shadow of a wall (in fact, the front edge of the stage) to divest themselves.[40] Praxagora appears on stage to supervise this operation (504–516), but before she herself can slip into her house, she is intercepted by her husband Blepyrus.

Her first task is to explain what she was doing out of the house at so early an hour. Effortlessly, she improvises a friend in childbirth to whom she was called. When Blepyrus demands to know why she took his cloak and stick (and incidentally left him dressed like a corpse[41]), she claims she took the one for warmth and the other to defend her husband's property from thieves (i.e., the cloak, though her own honor is also her husband's property in the Greek view). When informed that women now rule, she first pretends astonishment, then warms to the theme.

Up until this point, we have heard only that women will rule, not how. Now the chorus calls on Praxagora to lay out her new program:

δεῖται γάρ τοι σοφοῦ τινος ἐξευρήματος ἡ πόλις ἡμῶν.
ἀλλὰ πέραινε μόνον
μήτε δεδραμένα μήτ᾽ εἰρημένα πω πρότερον.
μισοῦσι γὰρ ἢν τὰ παλαιὰ πολλάκις θεῶνται.
ἀλλ᾽ οὐ μέλλειν, ἀλλ᾽ ἅπτεσθαι καὶ δὴ χρῆν ταῖς διανοίαις,
ὡς τὸ ταχύνειν χαρίτων μετέχει πλεῖστον παρὰ τοῖσι θεαταῖς.
{Πρ.} καὶ μὴν ὅτι μὲν χρηστὰ διδάξω πιστεύω· τοὺς δὲ θεατάς,
εἰ καινοτομεῖν ἐθελήσουσιν καὶ μὴ τοῖς ἤθάσι λίαν
τοῖς τ᾽ ἀρχαίοις ἐνδιατρίβειν, τοῦτ᾽ ἔσθ᾽ ὃ μάλιστα δέδοικα.   (577–585)

Our city needs some clever new plan.
Just one thing: don't do
what's been done or suggested before.
People hate the old stuff they've seen so often.
No more delay—get on with your ideas,
since speed is what the spectators like most.
Prax. Yes, I believe I'll teach you something useful. As for
the spectators, my main worry is if they want to carve
a new path and not wear out the old, familiar ruts.

The language acknowledges openly that this is a theatrical situation, with
spectators (580, 582–583) who demand novelty in entertainment.[42] Praxagora
proposes to "teach" (διδάξω) this theater audience as she has already taught
the assembly (cf. 215). This is the great dividing point within the play. The
political work is already accomplished: the women now rule. The theatrical
work, teaching the people as comedy should teach them, remains to be done.

It is the second half of *Ecclesiazusae* (from this point on) that has generated the most reaction from succeeding centuries. Many readers insist that the
communal state which Praxagora now outlines, and aspects of whose operations we later see, is meant to satirize utopianism, possibly even a specific
philosophic utopia.[43] A strong moralistic tone echoes through much written
on the *Ecclesiazusae*: one scholar speaks of "the idler's paradise," another de-
plores the "drone-like life of pleasure,"[44] which Praxagora's state engenders.
Feminist scholars are among those most offended by Praxagora's nurturing,
maternal state, which they have so well described. But is Aristophanes truly a
secret Thatcherite, who will allow us a good party tonight, only on condition
that, come Monday morning, we all put our shoulders to the wheel and get
down to the business of building a better Athens? Let us see.

Praxagora's great, new idea is that all property will be held in common,
as in a single household. Recent work on the *Ecclesiazusae* has made it clear
that the women of Athens will wield their newly acquired power, not by the

inversion suggested by the opening scenes (i.e., by masculinizing themselves to fit the power structure that exists in Athens), but by domesticating public space.[45] The space outside this new, encompassing home is left to the slaves, who will perform the real work of agriculture (651). Thus women retain much of their traditional role and character as the custodians and dispensers of property within the household. Just as within the household (at least in the days before separate bank accounts or even the Married Woman's Property Act) resources are held in common, so too in the new state. Blepyrus interrupts Praxagora with a number of objections to her scheme. First, he points to the distinction between real estate and movable property (602). No one can hide land, but a citizen who chooses to resist the new order can easily conceal gold and silver. Praxagora's answer is simple and devastating: she abolishes monetary exchange.[46] If the state dispenses all goods, money will be worthless because there will be nothing to buy. Ah, replies Blepyrus, but what about sex? One needs money for presents and so forth (611–613). Now Praxagora reveals her truly revolutionary concept: all women will be held in common.[47] To Blepyrus's objection that then all men will choose the beautiful women, she replies that there will be a rationing system, or perhaps one might call it a National Service Scheme: men who wish the favors of the beautiful women must first take care of the needs of the ugly or lower class, and the same will be true for women pursuing handsome men.

Praxagora proclaims her system a thoroughly democratic idea and a good joke on the σεμνοτέρων:

νὴ τὸν Ἀπόλλω καὶ δημοτική γ᾽ ἡ γνώμη καὶ καταχήνη
τῶν σεμνοτέρων ἔσται πολλὴ καὶ τῶν σφραγῖδας ἐχόντων (631–632)

By Apollo it's a democratic notion and a great joke
on the upper crust and the guys with pinkie rings.

We should not gloss over the Schadenfreude of this passage, which Aristophanes clearly expects his audience to share. It is one of the enduring facts of life that the young, beautiful, and fashionable do better in the on-going sexual competition than their opposites. In almost any audience, the vast majority will not be the young and the beautiful, and the spectacle of such being forced to earn their sexual pleasure has an obvious appeal.[48]

Praxagora ends by describing the domestication of public, civic space under the new regime. No mention is made of the assembly—which has already been turned into a form of theater by the rehearsal scene. The sovereign demos of Athens assembles in three forms: the assembly on the Pnyx, the theater, and (representatively) the law courts. In the new state these law courts become dining halls. This public space, however, is not merely domesticated by being turned into ἀνδρῶνας (676); it is also theatricalized. Note that poetry in the new order takes on part of the function of dispensing justice and punishing wrong-doers: poetic recitals by the young (678)[49] of martial deeds will make the cowardly so ashamed of themselves that they will not be able to eat. Apparently poetry's the thing wherein to catch the conscience of the scoundrel. We already know that having one's rations cut is the only possible punishment, since actions at law are abolished in the new Athens (657–667). Poetry will punish those whom no one else has detected. All three gatherings of the people (assembly, law courts, and theater) meld into one.

Blepyrus declares himself completely satisfied with the scheme (710), but one detail remains. Praxagora closes a loophole in her original declaration of sexual communism by excluding all the prostitutes from the new household: they will be classed with slaves, outside the pale, and therefore not competitors with free citizen women (represented by the chorus, whom Praxagora indicates with the deictic αὗται, 720) for the attentions of young men (718–724). Both Praxagora and Blepyrus now depart.

It is here that the problems of the staging of the *Ecclesiazusae* become acute. Between lines 729 and 730, the Ravenna manuscript has the notation *XOPOY* ("Chorus," also at 876). If this is evidence that a chorus once filled this spot, then Chremes leaves the stage with a declaration of his intention to contribute his goods to the common fund before this choral performance, and returns after it. If not, he leaves the stage and reenters immediately, a curious procedure.[50] In fact, we have no further word from the chorus until line 1127, a very long time for them to remain silently standing in the orchestra. Lacking direct evidence, we can only speculate. The later use of interpolated choral interludes in comedy suggests that such essentially detached songs were also possible this early. Ussher rightly notes that the *Ecclesiazusae* chorus has character and participates in the plot, just like earlier Aristophanic choruses. Aristophanes has been playing very complex games with its nature, showing us how a chorus puts on character and removes it. Not all comic choruses, however, foreground their character throughout. Aristophanes might here have reused material from his earlier plays or simply fallen back on the use of popular songs in the remainder of the performance.[51]

In another way, the absence of further metatheatrical gamesmanship with the chorus suggests that Aristophanes no longer wishes his audience to view the play's action through a frame, to keep an emotional distance, indeed to see the play's action as implausible and therefore ridiculous. Instead much of the humor becomes more farcical and more physical, while the play's fiction is accepted.

The humor of the next scene, a dialogue between Chremes the good citizen, who agrees to turn his goods over to the state, and his unnamed neighbor, who urges him to wait and see whether the new state is a success, works through the contrast of great and small. Chremes organizes a mock Panathenaic procession of his household goods (such as pots and tripods). We cannot say with certainty how this was staged, but surely the visual dimension is of great importance. If we imagine a procession of slaves (any supernumeraries would be so interpreted) carrying these small items, the humor will lie in a contrast of size: it takes the labor of one slave to carry a single kitchen utensil to the new common storehouse.[52] The obvious temptation for a modern staging would be to use actors inside giant papier-mâché representations of these household goods, which would "read" much better in a huge outdoor theater. Quite probably Aristophanes had a better solution to this problem of staging than either of these.

Another reason to imagine considerable visual comedy is that, frankly, the verbal humor of the bickering between Chremes and his unnamed selfish neighbor is of limited appeal. It is brought to an end by the appearance of the female herald, who issues the invitation to the feast:

> ὦ πάντες ἀστοί, νῦν γὰρ οὕτω ταῦτ' ἔχει,
> χωρεῖτ'   (834–835)

All you citizens, since that's the way it is now,
come on in

Just what is the force of νῦν γὰρ οὕτω ταῦτ' ἔχει? Rogers and Ussher (*ad loc.*) take this to mean that now, for the first time, *all* citizens are invited to a public banquet. Yet such banquets were scarcely unknown in Greece; all citizens feasted together at the Panathenaia, for example. I take it to mean rather that all who hear are now citizens: the slaves, the prostitutes, and presumably any foreigners have now all been removed, so that now only the household of citizens remains. The herald paints a scene of abundant food, wine, and sex, through which a rejuvenated Geron strides laughing with another "youngster" (848–849). The neighbor attempts to find a way to slip into this feast without surrendering his goods, to which Chremes rejoins with a jingling series of derisive questions, culminating in "if they laugh at you, what then?" (ἢν δὲ καταγελῶσι, τί; 864).[53] Comedy, then, is the ultimate defense of the new state against such parasites as this neighbor.

It is peculiarly frustrating for the understanding of the whole play that we have no stage directions at the end of this scene. The neighbor schemes to carry in some of Chremes' goods and represent them as his own in order to slip into the feast. Chremes says that he understands what the neighbor has in mind, packs up, and departs. The neighbor's final speech is this:

νὴ τὸν Δία, δεῖ γοῦν μηχανήματός τινος,
ὅπως τὰ μὲν ὄντα χρήμαθ' ἔξω, τοῖσδέ τε
τῶν ματτομένων κοινῇ μεθέξω πως ἐγώ.
ὀρθῶς, ἔμοιγε φαίνεται· βαδιστέον
ὁμόσ' ἐστὶ δειπνήσοντα κοὐ μελλητέον.   (872–876)

By Zeus, I need some scheme,
so I can keep what I have now, and still
get a share in the goodies with the rest.
Right, I've got it! I must head
where the banquet is, and no dawdling.

What great idea comes to his mind in the last two lines? Does he find something accidentally left behind on the stage by Chremes, as one translator has imagined?[54] One wonders at the lack of a deictic pronoun then. Or does he simply come up with one more harebrained scheme, which will work no better than his proposals simply to batter his way in past the doorkeepers?

The question is one of both tone and fact: is the scene just played a classic one between Aristophanic *eiron* and *alazon*, with Chremes a Dicaeopolis or Peisetaerus figure, fending off a greedy fraud who deserves no share in the results of the good idea? Or is this a demonstration of the satiric nature of the *Ecclesiazusae*, a proof that the frauds and cheats can and will destroy this attempt at a comic utopia which is not off in a Neverland but enacted within the walls of Athens? The problems must be faced squarely. First there is the character of Chremes. Since he is a virtual cipher, used only as a foil for Blepyrus and to report the results of the assembly, it is difficult to cast him as a traditional Aristophanic hero.[55] What, however, are the alternatives? Blepyrus is no better a choice, since the great idea belongs to Praxagora. Yet any dispute over the new idea must be among males; despite the testing of boundaries in this play, it is difficult to imagine Praxagora herself fending off *alazones* (which often requires physical force) after the fashion of a Dicaeopolis.

One very intriguing suggestion about characterization (which would also clarify the play's structure) deserves a hearing: Douglas Olson has proposed that the unnamed neighbor of this scene may be the young man who appears in the next. This would go a great way toward establishing the necessary balance in the subsequent scene. As Sommerstein notes of the former, his "opportunism . . . is contemptible . . . and he is given no positive qualities whatsoever."[56] If he does cheat his way into the feast and return in the next scene, his "punishment" is all the more just—and will be seen to be so by the audience.

There follows a scene (in two parts) that has appalled modern critics almost to a man—or a woman. As Chremes and neighbor have shown us economic communism at work, so this episode shows us the workings of sexual communism. An old woman waits for the men to appear, so that she can claim her rights under the new law. She hopes to attract one by her singing and invokes the help of the Muses (877–883). A young girl appears, to challenge her to a singing contest in rather specific terms:

νῦν μέν με παρακύψασα προὔφθης, ὦ σαπρά.
ᾤου δ' ἐρήμας οὐ παρούσης ἐνθάδε
ἐμοῦ τρυγήσειν καὶ προσάξεσθαί τινα
ᾄδουσ'· ἐγὼ δ' ἢν τοῦτο δρᾷς ἀντᾴσομαι.
κεἰ γὰρ δι' ὄχλου τοῦτ' ἐστὶ τοῖς θεωμένοις,
ὅμως ἔχει τερπνόν τι καὶ κωμῳδικόν.   (884–889)

So you peeped out and got ahead of me, you old bag.
You thought you'd strip my vines while I wasn't here
and snag some guy with your singing.
If you do, I'll sing a counter melody.
And if this is boring for the spectators,
still it has something pleasant and comic to it.

The contest then is staged with full knowledge of the audience (888) and in the hopes that it will have something pleasantly comic to offer. To judge by the stomach-churning reactions of most critics, Aristophanes has failed completely.[57]

The singing contest itself consists of three exchanges. As two others will appear, it is conventional to speak here of the First Old Woman. She calls on the piper for assistance,[58] then sings a verse on the theme "there is beauty in extreme old age." The girl accuses her of envy and makes the first of a series of love-and-death jokes, calling the First Old Woman the "darling of death" (905).[59] The most obvious reference is to the First Old Woman's mask, which is painted a stark white to imitate the use of white lead cosmetics. When she first appears on stage, the First Old Woman notes that she has liberally painted her face with such makeup (878). The women continue to exchange insults as the girl both laments and expounds her lonely state: her mother has gone out, and she is all alone in the house (911–917).[60]

The naming of names has a great deal to do with our interpretation of the ensuing scene. Do we know the name of the young man who eventually appears? Rogers and Ussher simply call him the "young man," while Douglas Parker, Sommerstein,[61] and Henderson all opt for "Epigenes," whom the First Old Woman names as the one she is waiting for (931). Many critics assume that the girl is waiting for the specific young man who eventually appears,[62] although she never names anyone but a "friend, companion" (ἑταῖρος, 912), while the old woman knows she is waiting for Epigenes. Though the young girl responds to his name by saying the old woman's only lover should be "Oldster" (literally, Geres), it is worth noting that she does *not* say "But Epigenes is *my* boyfriend!" The armchair critic, skilled at counting Lady Macbeth's children, can generate an entire Harlequin romance for this unnamed girl and an unnamed boy in an instant, while simultaneously turning the First Old Woman into a raving Messalina: on this view, the girl is waiting specifically for him, "her" lover, while the First Old Woman is waiting for the first man that walks by. If on the other hand, the young man who does appear is indeed Epigenes—and we have no specific evidence to the contrary—the First Old Woman knows him individually, while the girl need not in fact be waiting for any particular young man. In any case, the old woman's erotic desires are comparable to those of the young girl, and we have no reason to assume that they are automatically to be ridiculed or despised.

We must recall that this young girl is a citizen[63] (for any professional courtesans such as young men might have visited regularly before the institution of Praxagora's state are classed among the πόρναι, and therefore have already been excluded from the new communism). As such, she has been carefully guarded all her life—until today, under Praxagora's new dispensation. We should not imagine that Epigenes has ever visited her before,[64] nor that they have any strong "emotional" attachment (an aberration in the ancient view in any case).[65] Thus the girl and the First Old Woman are not respectively love and lust personified, but merely inexperienced and experienced lust.

Many of the staging techniques in the ensuing scene anticipate the conventions of New Comedy. Both the girl and the First Old Woman withdraw (Νε[ις]. . . . ἀπέρχομαι. Γρ.[α] κἄγωγ᾽ . . . , 936–937) to await the arrival of the young man.[66] In any case, the dynamics are those of the eavesdropping scene, here with two competing eavesdroppers standing outside the action (which contains only the young man, when he first appears) and attempting to control that action.

We should also not make the mistake of seeing this young man (whatever

his name is) as an innocent surprised by the demands of the First Old Woman
when she appears. His very first words (938–941) make it clear that he knows
what his duty is under the new law. He hopes somehow to evade that duty.
Strictly interpreted, he intends to be a scofflaw just like the unnamed citizen
in the previous scene with Chremes.

A duet between the newly arrived young man and the girl now ensues.
Its putative charms and relations to other love lyrics need not detain us. It
has a simple dramatic purpose in Aristophanes: to induce the girl to open the
door and let the young man in. By the end, the young man is clearly tiring of
words and wants to get on with things.[67]

A fascinating role-playing contest between the old woman (who suddenly reappears) and the young man ensues. Both try by turns to fictional-
ize and therefore theatricalize the situation in ways that will ensure control
over the other (977ff.). First she claims that the young man knocked at her
door; he denies it. She demands to know why he carries a torch (a conventional prop for a reveler in search of entertainment); he produces the old excuse about looking for a man from Anaphlystos. Now he tries to seize the
initiative (knowing very well what she wants) by classifying her as a sixty-
year-old legal case, which the courts are not yet dealing with. This produces
a straightforward claim under the new law from the First Old Woman: since
he attended the banquet of the new state, it is now time to pay up. She does
try one more fantasy: she attempts to interpret the young man's reluctance as
surprise at finding her alone out of doors (992–993) as no respectable young
woman would be. He counters with a fantasy in which he fears her "lover"
(994), a painter of white-ground *lekythoi* for the dead (and another hit at her
dead-white face or mask).

After further wrangling[68] the First Old Woman finally produces a text of
the new law under which she claims his services. The deictic pronouns ($\tau o v \tau \iota'$,
$\tau o \hat{v} \tau o$, 1012) show that she has a papyrus or some written copy from which
she reads (1015–1020). Legal quibbling and more insults ensue, but the law
licenses the First Old Woman to use force, and she begins dragging the young
man away. The girl now emerges from her hiding place (or her house). She
charges that what the old woman has in mind is virtually incestuous and, if
generally practiced, will people the land with Oedipuses (1038–1042).

Two kinds of writing, or if you will two linguistic orders, are struggling
for possession of the stage: the legal and the mythopoeic. The latter wins instantly. Just as the recital of heroic poetry at the public feasts (noted above) is
enough to punish the cowards with such shame that they cannot eat, so here

the vision of herself as Jocasta is enough to drive the First Old Woman from the stage. Though she reviles the girl for finding such a narrative weapon ("this story," τόνδε τὸν λόγον, 1043), she cannot resist its power and departs.

This victory, however, proves astonishingly temporary. The young man speaks but four lines of thanks to the girl before the Second Old Woman, even more unappealing than the First, appears to claim him. The girl apparently flees.[69] Another voice calls from behind the young man, demanding to know where the Second Old Woman is taking him (1065–1066). Anticipating the stage techniques of New Comedy, the young man responds with thanks before he turns back to see who is speaking. It turns out to be the Third Old Woman, the ugliest of all, and a virtual tug-of-war ensues (with the young man playing the rope). Various rowing metaphors highlight the physical action as he is dragged back and forth between the two (1086ff.). Both the rowing comparisons and the *lekythos*/death images reach a climax together as, in his final soliloquy, the young man imagine himself being buried at the harbor's mouth, with one of the old women erected over him as a *lekythos* grave marker.[70]

Is this all the tragedy the young man imagines it to be? The imagery of death comes from the mouth of the young man only. Why should we then read this imagery as the author's "true" view of the situation rather than one character's reaction to it? I have given my reasons above for questioning whether the First Old Woman is trying to separate Romeo and Juliet. We must further ask: why should we accept the young man's statement that complying with the new law is going to kill him? After all, he is not to be the permanent possession of either of the old women: after he performs his duty under the law, he will be free to return to the young girl he desires. It is possible, in fact, to take this scene "not as a critique of the women's communist experiment but as its most glorious expression" and a "triumph of comic energy."[71]

Nor is it clear that we should automatically detest these old women, who after all merely fight for their fair share in the new state, for the basic democratic right of *isonomia*. One wonders if the scene is, at some level, a parody of similar male struggles over female entertainers. The pseudo-Aristotelian *Constitution of Athens* records a law that not only set maximum prices for flute-girls (*auletrides*) but provided for city officials to conduct a lottery if more than one customer wanted to hire these sexual as well as musical entertainers at the official price.[72] True, these old women represent a sexuality no longer associated with child-bearing, but this "sterility" can as easily represent pleasure without consequences.[73] The old in Old Comedy, both men and women, are generally viewed in a positive light and eventually triumph in their struggles with the young.[74] If the image of rejuvenated old men such as Philocleon or

Dicaeopolis who win young girls for their pleasure is meant to be a comic celebration, why should we assume that the reverse is satiric? Perhaps Old Comedy celebrates the recovery of youth by the old of both sexes.[75]

Praxagora's servant girl now enters, praising the glories of the feast (where she has had more than a little to drink) and searching for Blepyrus.[76] She greets the chorus (1114), then the rest of the citizens (in effect, the theater audience beyond). She finally asks the chorus directly (1125) where Blepyrus is—just as he appears. She calls him a most happy man (and the chorus agrees: 1129, 1134), because he alone out of thirty thousand citizens has not yet dined. On one level this is certainly the joke about the shoemaker's children: Praxagora (whom we have not seen since she outlined the new state) has been so busy caring for this new household of all the citizens that she has neglected her own husband. It is not meant as a sneer at Blepyrus (who shows no signs of taking it this way).[77] Blepyrus is apparently accompanied by some female attendants, perhaps the beautiful girls to whom he as an old man is entitled first opportunity under the new law.[78] Thus we would have a studied visual contrast between the young man who feels oppressed by the new law, and the old man who (like so many older figures in Aristophanes) revels in the new state of things.

The maid invites everyone to the party, including the spectators and the judges who favor them:[79]

> καὶ τῶν θεατῶν εἴ τις εὔνους τυγχάνει,
> καὶ τῶν κριτῶν εἰ μή τις ἑτέρωσε βλέπει,
> ἴτω μεθ' ἡμῶν·   (1141–1143)

> If any spectators happen to favor us,
> and if any of the judges aren't looking elsewhere,
> come on with us!

Blepyrus pretends to extend it even wider, to everyone—if only they go home for dinner (1148)! Though many take this as a nasty joke at the audience's expense, it is in fact quite traditional in ancient comedy and not at all offensive;[80] however much Aristophanes plays with the dividing line between fact and illusion, his audience will hardly have expected a free meal.

Nor is it likely that Aristophanes would wish to alienate the judges just before he makes a remarkable appeal to them. The chorus teases the audience with the promise of a dinner song (1153), but then makes a small request:

> σμικρὸν δ' ὑποθέσθαι τοῖς κριταῖσι βούλομαι,
> τοῖς σοφοῖς μὲν τῶν σοφῶν μεμνημένοις κρίνειν ἐμέ,

τοῖς γελῶσι δ' ἡδέως διὰ τὸν γέλων κρίνειν ἐμέ—
σχεδὸν ἅπαντας οὖν κελεύω δηλαδὴ κρίνειν ἐμέ—
μηδὲ τὸν κλῆρον γενέσθαι μηδὲν ἡμῖν αἴτιον,
ὅτι προείληχ'· ἀλλὰ πάντα ταῦτα χρὴ μεμνημένους
μὴ 'πιορκεῖν, ἀλλὰ κρίνειν τοὺς χοροὺς ὀρθῶς ἀεί,
μηδὲ ταῖς κακαῖς ἑταίραις τὸν τρόπον προσεικέναι,
αἳ μόνον μνήμην ἔχουσι τῶν τελευταίων ἀεί.   (1154–1162)

I want to make a little request of the judges:
that the clever ones, remembering our cleverness, vote for me;
those who like a good laugh, because of our jokes, vote for me—
in fact, I want just about everybody to vote for me—
and don't blame us for the fact that we were allotted
first slot on the program, but always judge the choruses fairly,
and don't behave like those cheap trollops
who always only remember their last customers.

Though he has flattered the spectators above by naming them first, Aristophanes knows that in fact the judges are unusually important today, because he has been allotted the first position. There will be four more comedies played that day, before the voting begins. Given the theme of the *Ecclesiazusae*, the phrasing of his appeal is more than usually pointed: Aristophanes asks the judges not to allow themselves to be feminized through the process of watching the rest of the day's plays, but to retain their own proper natures. If they do, they will naturally vote the prize to him. The chorus now dances off with Blepyrus, at the same time invoking the wondrous dish (the longest word in Greek: lines 1169–1175) on which they will all feast.[81]

We have now experienced the whole of the *Ecclesiazusae* in the same linear way its original spectators did. We are finally prepared to confront the question that has dominated the scholarship on this play: is it a straightforward wish-fulfillment fantasy in the mold of earlier Aristophanic plays, or is it ironic, a subtle satire of the communistic ideas on which Praxagora's state is based? The ironic interpretation, dominant on the continent at least since Wilamowitz,[82] holds that, despite the apparent celebration on stage at the end of the play, Praxagora's state is a failure and perhaps morally repellent as well. Let us then consider whether the new state succeeds in functioning as Praxagora intends, and then whether its results are desirable.

Arguments for a satiric interpretation of the *Ecclesiazusae* usually ask different questions of the scenes that illustrate the workings of the new state. The question posed of the scene between Chremes and his neighbor is: will common ownership of property work, or will it be defeated by private self-ishness? The question asked of the scene illustrating the new sexual communism, however, is usually: is this a good/admirable idea? I suggest we apply the same standards to both scenes. Certainly Chremes' neighbor resists the notion of contributing his own property to the common stock, but just because he calls Chremes a fool for cooperating with the new law, that does not prove the latter is one. Chremes sees his neighbors contributing their property to the common fund (805–806); he is therefore not an isolated idealist, the one fool in Athens who actually does obey the law. Does the unnamed neighbor succeed in retaining his property and yet drawing benefits from the new state? We know neither the details of his idea for cheating the state nor whether he succeeds, but we have been given no particular reason to expect he will.[83] Moreover, it is not clear how he would be better off if he does gain admission to the banquet while retaining his own property: since Praxagora has abolished private exchange, he cannot use his property to purchase anything in any case.

No one has questioned whether sexual communism works efficiently in the play; the usual complaint is that it works far too well. We should not allow the young man's emotional rhetoric to distract us from the fact that Praxagora's state functions in this regard precisely as it was intended. This young man hopes to cheat the new law by having access to the young girl before he performs his duty to the old.[84] Nor is he being "raped" by the old women. Their claim to him is contingent on his desire for the young girl; under the terms of the law, if he were to abandon his pursuit of the young girl, the old women would have no further claim upon him—but this possibility is never raised. The fact that this young scofflaw fails in his attempt to reap the benefits of the new state (not only the banquet but free sexual access to young citizen women, which he never would have had in the real or rather pre-Praxagoran Athens) without paying the price is further evidence that the unnamed neighbor will not succeed in his similar attempt, either.

The most curious claim of the ironic interpretation is that the final banquet of the play is not "real," that we are meant instead to understand that the city is unable to provide food and wine to the citizens as it claims. This is based on a serious misreading of the joke that the spectators can join the play's banquet—by going home to eat. As noted above, this is by no means unparalleled in ancient comedy in general or Aristophanes in particular. It is typical of a whole complex of jokes about the nature of theatrical illusion, but there is nothing to suggest that this single occurrence has a substantially different meaning from any other occurrences in Aristophanes. Are we to imagine that the maid's drunkenness is not "real" since she has not been drinking "real" wine?[85]

Saïd's claim that selfishness causes the new state to fail[86] thus falls to the ground. The notion that the *Ecclesiazusae* is an indictment of a value system based on individual selfishness has always seemed dubious, since self-gratification is the goal of every Aristophanic hero. Food, wine, and sex are *the* comic goods. A modern reader of the plays may be disturbed by the vision of Peisetaerus roasting jailbirds at the end of the *Birds* to provide for the feast that closes that play or may fail to appreciate the humor of starvation represented by the Megarian in the *Acharnians*, but the original Greek audience seems to have had no such qualms. The victorious have a perfect right to self-gratification in comedy, even at the expense of others. We should therefore not let modern sentimentality betray us into an undeserved sympathy for the young man in this play, who despite his protestations suffers much less than the Megarian or the jailbirds.

A further claim may still trouble us: the notion that the political life of Athens has been suppressed or abolished by the new nurturing, or perhaps smothering maternal state. This is, I submit, to look at the play with the eyes of Aristotle rather than those of a comic writer or his audience. Though Aristotle believed that the function of leisure was to provide the opportunity for a man to pursue politics, it does not follow that Aristophanes thought the same, nor that the abolition of politics in favor of endless feasting in the new state is a bad thing.[87] Dicaeopolis's goal in the *Acharnians* is hardly to participate in properly run assemblies: he wants peace, and the good things peace entails. The rejuvenation of Demos and Philocleon in their respective plays includes festivity and celebration as well as the restoration of healthy politics. If the golden age returns in the *Ecclesiazusae*, what is the need for politics?

It is precisely this utopian element in the play that Froma Zeitlin confronts in an important recent essay, arguing that the play enacts a reversal of a fundamental patriarchal myth.[88] Under King Cecrops the Athenians had to decide between Athena and Poseidon as patron deity of the city. Women were then voting citizens, and all voted along strict gender lines; because there was one more woman than man in the population, Athena was chosen. The defeated Poseidon caused enough problems that Cecrops abolished the vote for women (and instituted marriage, to keep them home and subordinate). Zeitlin argues that the *Ecclesiazusae* reverses all this: women regain the vote, the private becomes the public, the *polis* dissolves, and marriage is abolished in favor of the indiscriminate sexuality of the age of Kronos. For Zeitlin, the existence of this mythic paradigm suffices to render ambiguous the celebration at the end of the play. As with the utopian vision at the end of *Birds*, however, the performance must strongly inflect any possible mythic meanings, and the golden age of sensual fulfillment the play offers would have a powerful appeal to the largely male audience.

We return then to the function of theatrical self-consciousness in the *Ecclesiazusae* and consider whether its purpose is to devalue or satirize Praxagora's program. Such a function would be unparalleled: no one suggests that when Trygaeus calls out to the crane operator to save him in the *Peace* that this is intended to satirize his quest for peace. Why should games with the nature of illusion in this play be any different? Saïd has made much of the point that we have, not an actual session of the assembly, as in *Acharnians*, but rather a rehearsal for the assembly.[89] She takes all the traditional jokes about women's bibulousness and sexual voracity as the settled opinion of Aristophanes and most Greek males on the nature of women. She can then suggest that the takeover of the government by the women would be a virtual castration of the essential maleness of politics; the very mutability of women, like the effeminates who speak in the assembly and already run Athens, becomes a judgment on the essential corruption of the democracy.[90]

Saïd sees the *Ecclesiazusae* as the culmination of a trend, going back as far as the *Birds*, of turning the attack from the would-be leaders of the democracy to the functioning of the democracy itself; it is "une mise en question du peuple lui-même."[91] It is true that there are fewer attacks on named individuals in the *Ecclesiazusae* than in past plays, but some remain. It may be that there simply were no more villains on the scale of Cleon.[92] Comedy was, moreover, an important element of democratic control in the city (and so perceived at the time); for Aristophanes to use comedy to criticize the demos itself would be both difficult and dangerous.[93]

This is an unnecessarily complicated view. If Aristophanes had wished to attack the corruption of the demagogic politicians, he had at hand the traditional accusations of sexual submission employed with such glee in the past. An attack on the "effeminacy" of the audience for being willing to listen to such leaders, however, has no place here. Simply to *be* a spectator is not a feminizing experience;[94] the issue remains the nature of the spectators' response. An ironic interpretation of the *Ecclesiazusae* risks reading the later antitheatrical prejudice of the philosophers back into Aristophanes.

If we simply continue to assume that Aristophanes thought the art that he practiced a good one, the theatrical self-consciousness of this play in general and the function of the rehearsal assembly in particular take on quite a different meaning. His ambition of winning the prize "worthily of the festival" (as the chorus of initiates in *Frogs* 389ff. puts it) continues to imply a belief in the power of his art to benefit the citizens. Instead of functioning to keep the shocking notion of rule by women at a safe distance, then, the rehearsal assembly acts as an induction, drawing the audience into the process of creating (if only temporarily) the theatrical illusion. Aristophanes rehearses both performers and audience in their roles and paradoxically increases the "reality" of what we see on stage by placing the costumed performance in the assembly off stage. The transmutation of the assembly and the law courts of Athens into theatrical venues themselves is not a collapse of all political activity into a hollow mimesis of a lost reality (à la Plato) but a liberation of the power of theater to re-imagine its world.

It is not necessary (and perhaps not possible) to prove that the *Ecclesiazusae* is a great play. Its structure is more haphazard, its characters less engaging than many of Aristophanes' earlier plays. If we now conclude by remembering that which we began by forgetting, it is eminently possible to see the marks of its time upon this play. Since the fall of Athens in 404, the political world of Aristophanic comedy has contracted. The stage is no longer the whole universe, as in *Birds*, but simply the city itself.

We should not, however, exaggerate this decline. The essential celebration of the sensual is still the heart of this comedy. Comedy remembers, recovers, and recollects. If old women as well as old men reap the benefits of this new state, that is not sufficient reason to conclude the play is a bitter satire of Athens' present condition. Nor does the fact that Aristophanes shows us the creation of theatrical illusion in this play satirize the power of illusion, any more than does his use of metatheatrical techniques in his earlier plays. Aristophanes is the kind of magician who can show us how some of the tricks work and nonetheless entice us into the world of his imagination. Within that world, role-playing and theatrical manipulations demonstrate the power of the dramatic imagination to transform reality, to build a new, comic city in the shell of the old.

Appendix: On Theatrical Assemblies

Lauren Taaffe calls our attention to a remarkable theatricalization of the assembly attested about a decade and a half before the performance of the *Ecclesiazusae*.[95] The situation is the tempestuous aftermath to the battle of Arginusae in 406 B.C. where the Athenian generals commanding the fleet, although victorious in the battle itself, failed to pick up all the wounded from their own side. The assembly had met once to debate taking action against the generals but had adjourned without a final vote due to encroaching darkness. Theramenes, worried that the blame might fall on him,[96] devised a counter-strategy, recorded by Xenophon, *Hellenica* 1.7.8.

Μετὰ δὲ ταῦτα ἐγίνετο Ἀπατούρια, ἐν οἷς οἵ τε πατέρες καὶ οἱ συγγενεῖς σύνεισι σφίσιν αὑτοῖς. οἱ οὖν περὶ τὸν Θηραμένη παρεσκεύασαν ἀνθρώπους μέλανα ἱμάτια ἔχοντας καὶ ἐν χρῷ κεκαρμένους πολλοὺς ἐν ταύτῃ τῇ ἑορτῇ, ἵνα πρὸς τὴν ἐκκλησίαν ἥκοιεν, ὡς δὴ συγγενεῖς ὄντες τῶν ἀπολωλότων. . . .

After these things came the Apaturia, where fathers and relatives meet together. Then Theramenes' followers at this festival enlisted men with black cloaks and many with their hair cut, to come to the assembly, as though they were relatives of the battle casualties. . . .

There is much this brief account does not tell us, of course. A minimalist reading would suggest that Theramenes and his supporters simply sought out those who were already in mourning (and clearly not just those mourning for the dead of Arginusae) and persuaded the men to come to the assembly in a body. Perhaps those in mourning were likely to come to the Apaturia, although we are nowhere told this. The Apaturia was a phratry festival, celebrating the enrollment of children, ephebes, and newly married women, hence apparently the emphasis in the phrasing on "fathers and their relatives." One sacrifice at the festival celebrated the cutting of the ephebes' hair.[97] Now anyone can put on the costume of dark mourning garments and as easily put them off again. Cutting one's hair close was a more dramatic step whose evidence was not easily erased thereafter. A bolder reading of this passage might speculate that Theramenes and his party persuaded some of the ephebes whose hair was being cut for the festival to take advantage of their shorn condition and undertake the role of mourners in the assembly.

In any case it is clear that Theramenes saw the opportunity for a new kind of audience participation in the theater of politics and used it brilliantly. We can assume that many leaders or would-be leaders in the assembly had a group of followers who would coalesce around them on a certain issue and would strive to turn those supporters out at key meetings.[98] Yet such supporters could be and were swayed by the performances given by the leaders in their speeches to the assembly; turn-out did not guarantee success. Theramenes saw a way to move the performance off the speaker's bema and into the audience itself. In doing so he collapsed any emotional distance assembly members might have had from a speaker and his speech. Most citizens knew at some level that the regular speakers in the assembly represented a point of view, shifting though it might be, and not a pure reflection of "truth." A citizen could therefore judge speakers to some extent by past performance and results. They could read the speeches as performance. This is the very skill that Aristophanes claims to be teaching the demos in the *Acharnians*. By contrast there is no expectation of emotional distance from other citizens simply seated in the body of the assembly; there is no natural assumption that they too are giving a performance. Yet that is precisely what Theramenes' followers did, to brilliant effect. By taking persons who were not in fact family of the casualties of Arginusae and casting them in that role, he succeeded in creating a firestorm of public opinion against the generals, resulting in their ultimate and unconstitutional condemnation over the bootless resistance of Socrates, then serving among the *prytaneis*.[99]

Nothing specifically connects this historical event with Aristophanes' portrayal of an audience giving a performance in the *Ecclesiazusae*. The parallel is nonetheless deeply suggestive. The plot for the assembly takeover is hatched at a religious festival: the Skira and the Apaturia. The plot takes some little time to mature. The women in the *Ecclesiazusae* must tan themselves and practice their parts. Theramenes and company must arrange for an indictment in the boule, followed by the actual assembly. Finally, the point is won not simply by packing the assembly with enough supporters to win by brute force of numbers but also by the persuasive force of the illusion those disguised supporters present.

Reprise—And Coming Attractions

Something familiar, something peculiar,
Something for everyone, a comedy tonight!

—Stephen Sondheim, *A Funny Thing Happened
on the Way to the Forum*

ARISTOPHANES HAD, not just a talent to amuse, but a talent to make his audiences think. Nor was this talent confined to occasional criticisms of individual politicians or policies. His concerns went much deeper, to issues of communication, persuasion, the nature of leadership, and the nature of democratic participation, all of which in fifth-century Athens do not sort themselves neatly into boxes labeled "politics" and "literature" respectively. Aristophanes saw in the thousands of spectators gathered together to celebrate the Dionysiac festivals the same citizens who gathered together to operate as a demos elsewhere. In many areas of the life of Athens, assembled masses of citizens embodied the demos where most would observe only, while others spoke—until those who had heretofore been only spectators were called upon to render final judgments, either by actual vote or in the form of acclamation.

Aristophanes chose to practice his art as a poet in a form that would reach the maximum number of citizens. Perhaps as many or more listened to the recitals of Homer at the Panathenaic festivals and elsewhere—but the texts to be recited on such occasions were already a closed canon. To compose epic in the fifth century was to be a marginal figure. Two poetic careers were open to him through which he might regularly be heard by thousands of his fellow citizens at some of the most elaborate, expensive, and prestigious celebrations his city could muster. In one mode, he would be confined to the world of myth and to an already hardening canon of stories about a limited number of families and their misadventures. In the other, he would be able to depict both individuals great and small from his own city and time, as well as animals, creatures of fantasy, and also a selection of divinities and heroes.[1] Whether Aristophanes formulated the choice to himself this way—indeed, whether he could have articulated categories such as the mythic and historical apart from their embodiment in the city's festivals—in any case he chose to practice the form of poetry that most directly addressed his fellow citizens and their mental world.

The conventions and practices of that form of poetry as he took it up in the 420s included political satire and mockery embedded in plots, though the plots seem to have been relatively recent additions to the repertoire. We are told they were brought in by Crates, and what evidence we have for Cratinus's art suggests that his political plays were more a feature of the end, rather than the beginning, of his career.[2] Our evidence further suggests that narrative plots brought with them the notion of sustained, individualized characterizations. In short, Aristophanes both chose the poetic art that could most directly speak to his fellow citizens and their lives and did so in a time when comedy was the growing and changing art form.

His first plays appeared when the Athenian democracy was facing its greatest internal challenge since Ephialtes and greatest external challenge since the Persian Wars. It may be arguable how clear this was at the time, but the combination of a lengthening war with Sparta and the internal political struggle following the death of Pericles in the plague would have left most citizens well aware that their city faced very important choices.

It is clear that for Aristophanes one of the key questions was how to deal with the challenge of Cleon for political leadership at Athens. Scholars have given varying assessments of how "personal" Aristophanes' dislike of Cleon was. Given the savagery of his treatment of the dead Cleon in *Peace* and even *Frogs*, it seems clear to me that Aristophanes disliked Cleon intensely. His plays are much more than personal mockery, however. The early plays about Cleon are united not just by their detestation but by a common strategy they propose for dealing with Cleon. *Acharnians* propounds the theory which *Knights* and *Wasps* put into practice: together they aim to school the audience in performance criticism, to teach them how to see persuasive performances, whether in the assembly or in the lawcourts, as *constructed*. Aristophanes both assembles and disassembles persuasive speeches and their speakers in an attempt to teach the audience how the tricks are performed. The audience that apparently appreciated *Acharnians* so much that it won first prize then went on to elect Cleon general at the next election; this has often been cited as a demonstration that the world of comedy had nothing to do with the real world of politics.[3] The failure of a strategy, however, is hardly proof that no strategy was intended. Sometimes it *is* possible to persuade the audience to "pay no attention to that man behind the curtain," as Peisistratus did when Solon attempted to expose his performance.[4]

In our first surviving play Aristophanes chose to teach this kind of performance criticism both directly, through the exposure of the fake ambassadors, and indirectly, through tragic parody. Tragic parody was not, and could not be, purely instrumental: it is not just a trope for politics. It is clear that Aristophanes also objected to the kind of sophistic "social performance" that Euripides appeared to be teaching through his tragedies. Few today, and very few who are ever likely to read this book, are sympathetic to the notion that experiences of performance and literature are capable of "corrupting" their audiences. We may worry about what children might see in films or on the Internet, but we are serenely confident there is nothing whatever that *we* should be protected from seeing. Perhaps Aristophanes felt the same dilemma as well. It has often been suggested that such detailed parody of Euripides suggests a certain admiration, indeed envy on Aristophanes' part. At times, as when in *Thesmophoriazusae* a garland-seller complains that Euripides' atheism has undermined belief in the gods and therefore her business (yet seems to have plenty of customers to attend to), Aristophanes may even satirize some of the opposition to Euripides. Yet his tragic parodies in *Acharnians* and later evince genuine concern about sophistic thought and persuasive techniques and their potential to do harm in the democracy. This split focus on both political performance and tragic performance may have allowed audience members to mistake vehicle for tenor and treat all of Aristophanic metatheatre as aesthetic criticism—and the history of Aristophanic criticism shows they were not alone.

Self-consciousness about performance in Aristophanes, however, whether political or aesthetic, is not just a matter of mockery. His plays do not just criticize the way things are but offers alternative, preferable comic visions. Because he criticizes deception of the spectators by others, Aristophanes cannot just unveil a utopian mythos before his audience and tell them to believe in it. To do so would be to become a Sausage-seller himself, elbowing others aside in the scramble for honors, but ultimately doing nothing different himself. Instead, he must show us the tricks *and* make us believe in the vision at the same time. This is the challenge of *Peace, Birds*, and even *Ecclesiazusae*.

The first may seem the least successful. The peace he attempted to enact into existence at the festival of 421 did in fact come into being a short time later—but it did not last. Events and the powers of hindsight turned his *Peace* from a Dionysiac celebration into an awkward stage property mocked by his competitors. Perhaps also, however, we should not expect one of his earliest essays in fashioning a positive vision in the theater to have been as easy, or as zestful, as his mockery of the long-time opponent both of peace and himself, Cleon.

The later plays are much more successful. *Birds* builds an enticing utopia, even while reminding us of its theatrical nature. Its alternate city, while formulated comically through its mockery of those who try to horn in on the vision, is nonetheless politically unified and poetically entrancing. Peisetaerus may be a one-man state, like Dicaeopolis before him, but his political and theatrical skills together elevate him to the position of ruler of the universe. *Frogs*, on the eve of political and military disaster, stages just the prologue to a renewed and restored city, in large part through the renewal of Dionysus as the proper kind of spectator. Only at play's end is he ready to chose correctly. The *Ecclesiazusae* is still pursuing this renewal of spectatorship more than a decade later, though its vision of utopia is more material in the aftermath of the near-extermination of the city.

Metatheatre is thus both a means of political (and theatrical) criticism and a means of building political and theatrical alternative worlds. If these alternative worlds are at times less than fully embodied or articulated, this need not surprise: the less detailed the political utopia, the more comprehensive its appeal. It is no less sincere, nor less effective in the theater. We may not know at the end of *Frogs* what Aeschylus will do back in Athens—but despite the wisdom of historical hindsight, an audience will still hope that he can save it.

The *Ecclesiazusae* presents the last real political utopia. *Wealth* has a metatheatrical sequence as well, where the slave Carion takes on the role of the Cyclops briefly, but here comedy becomes parasitic on another form, and one no longer purely theatrical: the dithyramb. This brief sequence is neither a critique (even of literary form) nor an alternate vision. It would be an easy platitude of biographical criticism to argue that Aristophanes was growing old and less inspired. It is equally possible to say that he was still capable of reading judges' and audiences' reactions. *Ecclesiazusae* had not won first prize, and he may have been trying vigorously at the end of his career to adapt himself to a new audience and its tastes. Perhaps it was his audience, and not Aristophanes, who first turned emphatically away from political comedy.

Aristophanes did not ultimately win his battle against the performing politicians of his day. The masters of synthetic emotions and staged political events continue to plague democratic cultures, even as the venues for their performances change. Yet Aristophanes' attempt to teach the demos of Athens to be critics as well as connoisseurs of performance deserves to be remembered and appreciated. In the absence of enough remnants of his competitors, it is hard to be certain what their plays were capable of. Certainly other poets of Old Comedy, especially Cratinus, employed metatheatrical elements and techniques in their plays, but it is doubtful whether any of them achieved Aristophanes' sustained critique of theatrical manipulation of the political life of Athens. It would be many centuries indeed before anything remotely resembling his skillful disassembly of political performance would be seen on the stage or elsewhere in literature again.

Nor is political performance criticism, however innovative, his sole theatrical legacy. Equally remarkable is his ability to entice viewers into the various alternate theatrical worlds that he created, even as he joked about the means for creating them. It was not inevitable that an illusionistic style of comedy should triumph over the heady and nonillusory mixture of insults, farce, fantasy, and parody that compounded and recompounded in Old Comedy. Walter Kerr in a book that still repays close reading has made a strong case that the vitality of comedy depends in significant measure on the health of tragedy and on a culture's confidence in the significance of human action and choice.[5] Old Comedy may have faded from the scene not through the triumph of Euripides and tragedy's capacity to suture its spectators into its illusion, but rather through the diminution of any present tragic vision. Tragedy became classicized, distant in style and moral assumptions as well as narrative and characters from the world of contemporary experience. With it faded comedy's capacity for direct challenge to tragedy's assumptions.

It is hard to avoid a valedictory, if not epitaphic, tone in summing up the achievements of Aristophanes within the form of Old Comedy. Yet the anarchic comedy at the expense of theatrical form itself which we have termed metatheatre does not vanish permanently from the ancient stage. Flashes of it resurface in Menander, and Plautus will once again make his own plays and players the object of metatheatrical jokes, even as he resynthesizes such self-conscious play with a new conception of comic heroism. To trace an identifiable Aristophanic influence on either of these manifestations would exceed our evidence, although continuing finds of visual evidence for fourth and third century performances of comedy in Italy may yet suggest some possible avenues. The spirit of comic mischief that Aristophanes embodies, however, the enemy of anything that takes itself too seriously, whether politician or playwright, reappears again and again, from Plautus to Pirandello, a laughing ghost within the machine to remind us to listen to the gears clanking. It is no small thing to have been the first practitioner of such an art.

Notes

Chapter 1. The Naming of Parts

1. Abel 1963, 83.

2. Calderwood 1971, Hornby 1986.

3. Hornby 1986, 32.

4. Larson 1994 is an illuminating example of this pattern in the field of Spanish Golden Age drama, only now being corrected. One should note that Calderwood 1971 included discussion of Shakespearean comedy, as does Hubert 1991.

5. Styan 1977 offers a fascinating account of the "Shakespeare Revolution" and its influence on other theatrical practice.

6. Taplin 1977.

7. Seale 1982, Halleran 1985.

8. Ringer 1998, 7–19, gives an excellent overview of metatheatrical criticism and its reception in classics, though he deemphasizes some of the conflicts. Cf. Wiles 1987, Goldhill 1989, and Slater 1993b.

9. Segal 1982.

10. See also, for example, Zeitlin 1980.

11. Ringer 1998, 7–8. My second ellipsis excises a reference to "illusion," which I do not find helpful for the reasons given hereafter.

12. For a critique of this evolutionary view, see Slater 1995.

13. Kerr 1967, 269–273, is a more thoughtful response to Abel 1963 than most but still claims that all metatheatre can ultimately be reduced to a form of comedy.

14. An image I borrow from Zeitlin 1980.

15. de Ste. Croix 1972, 370–371, and passim. Konstan 1995 and Cartledge 1990 represent valuable and interesting developments from his positions.

16. To be fair, Heath 1987a, 41–43, explicitly rejects the label of "aestheticist" for his view, claiming that he believes political comedy is possible: Aristophanes was just not attempting such a thing. His insistence, however, that any contradiction within the political statements of the plays proves that Aristophanes was "opportunistic" in his comedy and could not possibly have expected any expression of political views by his characters to be taken seriously does reduce all of comedy to a quest for nothing but the experience of laughter. Cf. MacDowell 1995, 5.

17. Unsurprisingly, many previous treatments of metatheatre are inclined to view it as one more technique in the endless quest for audience laughter.

18. Goldhill 1991, 167–222.

19. Goldhill 1991, 184–185.

20. Goldhill 1991, 171–174 and passim.

21. Note that Goldhill's fascinating chapter does not claim to give a full account of Aristophanic comedy but rather focuses on *Acharnians* and *Frogs* as examples of comedy's contribution to the contemporary struggle over the poet's *sophia* and his role in society.

22. Abel 1963, 83.

23. An example from the American television sitcom emerged a few years ago: a pattern in which the last few minutes of the program are reserved for outtakes, showing the actors failing to maintain illusion, or even for performers to appear and interact in their own supposedly "real" personas.

24. Slater 1985c and 2000.

25. *Poetics* 5 (1449b); cf. Pickard-Cambridge 1962, 132–162.

26. The traditional chronology dates the foundation of tragedy at the City Dionysia to 534 B.C., while comedies were introduced in 486. Connor 1989 shows clearly the shakiness of readings of the Marmor Parium that purport to prove that Thespis's performance in 534 was the beginning of the City Dionysia and offers intriguing arguments for dating the actual organization of the state festival after the fall of the Peisistratids. Even if his dramatically lower beginning date for tragedy of 501 is accepted, however, comedy still comes almost a generation later.

27. νῦν οὖν Ἠλέκτραν κατ᾽ ἐκείνην ἥδ᾽ ἡ κωμῳδία / ζητοῦσ᾽ ἦλθ᾽. . . . Aristophanes here seems to use "Electra" ambiguously as both the character of that name and the play, perhaps in fact the second play of the *Oresteia*, which we know as *Choephoroi*. Newiger 1961 attractively suggests that Aristophanes here plays on audience knowledge of a recent Aeschylean revival.

28. See Taplin 1983. LSJ records the traditional grammarians' explanations for the source of the pun: that actors used wine lees as makeup, that the dramatic contest took place at the vintage or time of new wine, or that new wine was given as a contest prize. In new wine the lees have not yet settled out. Uncomplimentary as the image of lees may seem, one wonders if the term recognizes the secondary, reactive nature of comedy, formed as a by-product to tragedy. As Kerr 1967, 20, says, "comedy never has come first. It is something like the royal twin that is born five minutes later, astonishing everyone and deeply threatening the orderly succession of the house."

29. E.g., *Acharnians* 499, 500, 886; *Clouds* 296; *Wasps* 650, 1537; Aristophanes *Gerytades* fr. 156 K-A. and Aristophanes fr. 347 K-A. (from the lost "Second" *Thesmophoriazusae*—presumably first in actual chronological order).

30. See below, chapter 3 and n. 79.

31. Plutarch, *On Listening to Lectures* 46b (Csapo and Slater 1995, 360 [IV. 305]).

32. Tragic and comic poets, naturally, but also others ranging from Homer and Simonides (*Clouds* 1362) to the contemporary dithyrambists. Note that while there is inscriptional evidence for the form ποητής, used by Dover in his editions of *Clouds* and *Frogs*, I have with Sommerstein and others preferred the traditional form.

33. The term ποιητής occurs frequently in the early parabases: cf., for example, *Clouds* 545, *Wasps* 1016, 1018, 1049, 1051, *Peace* 773, 799.

34. Cf. the description in Alexis fr. 184 K-A. of something being "colder than [Aristophanes' son] Araros."

35. Cf. *Frogs* 868, 907, 1366. Euripides' own poetic activity is described in the *Thesmophoriazusae* as "making": ἡνίκ᾽ ἠρχόμην ποιεῖν, 174; ἐποίησάς ποτε, 193.

36. Heath 1990 persuasively reconstructs this play; cf. now Luppe 2000b; Rosen 2000.

37. Gilula 1994 suggests (see below, chapter 7 n. 23) that *Birds* 448 can even pun on the terminology of parabasis.

38. The standard study of the epirrhematic *agon* is Gelzer 1960. See also the very perceptive discussion in Reckford 1987, 239–250 and passim.

39. There may be a subtly metatheatrical joke at work as well. The speaker describes the confrontation as "*old-fashioned* single combat" (μονομάχου πάλης), which distances us from the world of the mythic action: single combat is outdated only from the perspective of the fifth-century spectator. If the reference is to the play's formal *agon* as well, it may be further an ironic comment playing on audience awareness of the formal and traditional structure of the *agon*. By contrast, fr. 543 K-A. (*Telemessians*) promises that the *agon* there will not be "the same sort as formerly, but full of new material" (οὐ . . . τὸν ἀγῶνα τόνδε τὸν τρόπον / ὥσπερ τέως ἦν, ἀλλὰ καινῶν πραγμάτων). Fr. 349 K-A. (*Thesmophoriazusae β*), though, seems just to use *agon* in a proverb.

40. Cf. *Frogs* 1410, where Aeschylus's taunting δύ' ἔπη probably means "two words" and 358, βωμολόχοις ἔπεσιν, "buffoonish words," a characteristic of (others') comedy.

41. Cf. Cratinus fr. 211 K-A. and Eupolis fr. 392 K-A.

42. There is a textual problem here, in that the mss. say Pheidippides "sang" the speech (ᾖσ' . . . ῥῆσιν). Dover *ad loc.*, following a suggestion of Borthwick, emends to ἦγ', Sommerstein to ᾖκ'.

43. See Borthwick 1994 on "rope-twisting songs" (ἱμονιοστρόφου μέλη, *Frogs* 1297).

44. Dover *ad* 245.

45. Whereas the chorus in the *Alcestis* speaks of future hymns that will honor the dead queen (ἀλύροις . . . ὕμνοις, 447). Compare the metaphorical reference to the ὕμνος Ἅιδου in Phrynichus fr. 74 K-A.

46. Probably his own play, although Aristophanes may mock two poets at once by having him quote Morsimus: see Sommerstein *ad loc.* for critique of the latter view.

47. The noun also appears in *Frogs* 849, 944, and 1330.

48. The nearest thing to an exception would seem to be the famous remark of the chorus of the *Œdipus Tyrannus*, where the chorus asks, if these things are true, "why should I dance in the chorus?" (τί δεῖ με χορεύειν; 896).

49. Using the word θρεττανελό for the sound; cf. the word τήνελλα, *Acharnians* 1227ff. (Sommerstein *ad loc.*), which imitates a flourish on lyre or flute.

50. Zimmermann 1993b, with particular reference to Pherecrates fr. 155 K-A. (and further bibliography).

51. Note also *Wealth* 289 (where the chorus explicitly dances ὑφ' ἡδονῆς) and 761; Zimmermann 1995, 122–125, has a valuable discussion of the change in theatrical conception between these two passages. One can tire of dancing as well (Aristophanes fr. 618 K-A.), even though the chorus of the *Lysistrata* claims they never will (541–542).

52. E.g., *Peace* 1319, *Lysistrata* 1246, 1277.

53. *Skeuai* fr. 138 K-A.:

ὥστ᾽ εἴ τις ὀρχοῖτ᾽ εὖ, θέαμ᾽ ἦν· νῦν δὲ δρῶσιν οὐδέν,
ἀλλ᾽ ὥσπερ ἀπόληκτοι στάδην, ἑστῶτες ὠρύονται.

54. In the tragedians, the term in this sense occurs only in Eur. *Cyclops* 221 (see Olson *ad Peace* 323), which suggests that explicit mention of dance figures is metatheatrical. At *Bacchae* 832, Euripides' most metatheatrical play, σχῆμα τοῦ κόσμου seems to mean "costume," but otherwise the word in tragedy is much more general.

55. Kerr 1967, esp. 144–209, eloquently discusses the comedy of materiality, the ways in which the comic body is bounded, limited, or indeed tripped up by things in the world around it.

56. Dionysus at *Frogs* 523 tells Xanthias it was only a joke (παίζων) when he costumes the latter as Heracles. The women of the *Ecclesiazusae* chorus remind themselves to change back from their masculine disguises when they return from the assembly: πάλιν μετασκεύαζε σαυτὴν αὖθις ἥπερ ἦσθα (499).

57. Frr. 136–142 K-A., though fr. 141, quoted in Σ *Frogs* 367, refers to cutting the pay of the comic poets.

58. The definitive study of costume in Aristophanes is Stone 1981.

59. There may not be a mask as such, though she probably has a bird's crest while her double aulos functions as her beak: see Romer 1983. 137–138 and Sommerstein and Dunbar *ad Birds* 672.

60. Slater 1989a and below, pp. 225–26.

61. On this scene and its metatheatricality, see most recently Zeitlin 1994, 138–139, with references to major previous discussions.

62. Compare Dicaeopolis's exit at *Acharnians* 408.

63. Cf. Aristophanes frr. 160 K-A. and 192 K-A., Strattis fr. 4 K-A., and the reference to the μηχανοδίφας at *Peace* 790.

64. I follow Sommerstein's speaker attribution; Dunbar gives this to Euelpides.

65. Cf. Eupolis fr. 205 K-A. (attributed by Koch to Cratinus as fr. 306K), Pherecrates fr. 101 K-A.

66. Cf. Eupolis *Maricas* fr. 192 K-A., πρὸς τὸ θέατρον. and Metagenes fr. 15 K-A.

67. Sommerstein *ad loc.*

68. *Birds* 1106ff. Perhaps the fact that the chorus remains in character keeps such bribery comic; the chorus in *Clouds* 1115ff. similarly offers advantages to the judges. Note also the Birds' earlier oath to keep the peace treaty with the newly arrived humans, in reward for which they are to win by the unanimous vote of the judges (πᾶσι νικᾶν τοῖς κριταῖς, 444; cf. in Eupolis fr. 192 K-A., ἅπασι τοῖς κ[ριταῖς).

69. Cf. Pherecrates fr. 102 K-A.

70. Slater 1985a.

71. Disputed by Luppe 1972 and Luppe 2000a (with intervening bibliography); see also below, chapter 7 n. 45.

72. Kolb 1981; Schnurr 1995a and 1995b; Robertson 1992, 43–48.

73. *Pace* Pickard-Cambridge 1946, 10–15, who gives all the relevant evidence.

74. Slater 1986. See also below, p. 186.

75. Camp 1971; Rosen 1989.

76. Pickard-Cambridge 1988, 41.

77. Sifakis 1971, 7; cf. Dedousi 1995, esp. 129–131. On nonillusory drama, see Styan 1975, 180–223.

Chapter 2. The Emergence of the Actor

1. My translation is adapted from both Perrin's Loeb and that of Csapo and Slater 1995, 224 (2B). Gauly 1991, 269 n. 12, suggests a connection with the famous Gorgias fr. Diels-Kranz 82 [76] B 23 (see chapter 3, pp. 60–61, below).

2. Ringer 1998, 24–26, also connects these two anecdotes but points out further that Solon himself engages in acting: when a law forbids discussion of resuming the war for Salamis, Solon according to Plutarch (*Life* 8.1–3 and Solon fr. 1 Bergk) adopts the pretence of madness in order safely to recite his poem, urging the renewal of the war. This anecdote is followed by yet more role-playing, as Solon sends a man pretending to be a deserter to Salamis. The fake deserter lures the occupying Megarians into an ambush manned by beardless young Athenians pretending to be women. Tempting as it is to see the ur-chorus of ephebes here, it is probably not possible to reconcile Solon the opponent of Peisistratid performance and Solon the impresario of war performance here. I simply take the earlier anecdote to be representative of more general Greek suspicion of performance in politics.

3. There were certainly reperformances in the deme theater of the Peiraeus before the end of the fifth century. The theater at Thorikos dates from the end of the sixth century but may well have been built for assemblies rather than theater (Whitehead 1986, 16). I believe it was originally suggested that the still unpublished deme theater at Trachones was late fifth century, but it is now considered mid-fourth century (see the useful discussion of what little has been made public in Wiles 1997, 29–30). Taplin 1993, 91 (relying largely on Whitehead 1986, 212–222, discussing primarily fourth-century and later evidence for deme theaters) has argued for a significant amount of reperformance at the Rural Dionysia in the late fifth century, but positive evidence is lacking. Even if more archaeological evidence for fifth-century theaters is found, this would not necessarily prove the existence of dramatic performances: theaters could be used for assemblies, courts, and a wealth of nondramatic musical, dance, and poetic events. I have briefly suggested elsewhere that a very interesting relief sculpture showing tragic, comic, and satyr masks from the very late fifth or early fourth century from Dioniso (Athens NM 4531: beautifully illustrated in Green 1994, 82, fig. 3.19) may mark the introduction of dramatic performances in that deme: Slater 1985b, esp. nn. 27, 46. I believe the real flowering of formal dramatic performance at the Rural Dionysia is a post-Peloponnesian War phenomenon.

4. It does not remain so: when acting styles themselves become classicized, acting becomes one of the most conservative elements in theater performance. See Csapo and Slater 1995, 257 and passim.

5. See Sutton 1987, 10. One possible exception (but later) occurs in the family of Eugeiton III; see Sutton, p. 25. Change between generations may have been possible: Rothwell 1994.

6. On the three actor rule and role distribution in tragedy, see most recently Sifakis 1995 and Dedoussi 1995. On the possibility that Aristophanic comedy used four actors in some plays, see MacDowell 1994 and Marshall 1997.

7. Pavlovskis 1977 argues that the voices of actors allowed the audience to identify them behind their masks and even appreciate certain ironies through the combination of roles.

8. Lefkowitz 1981, viii.

9. Pickard-Cambridge 1988, 130.

10. On the sharp differentiation between the protagonist and his assistants, see Sifakis 1995.

11. He may have been the first victor ever in 449: Csapo and Slater 1995, 227 (IV. 12 = I.G. ii^2 2325). He was still acting in 422 B.C.: Pickard-Cambridge 1988, 131 and I.G. ii^2 2318. He was also mocked by Plato Comicus, fr. 175 K-A.

12. On the dominance of the protagonist in the performances, see Sifakis 1995.

13. Ringer 1998, 5–6, draws the further inference that Sophocles was among the first to experience a separation between his dramatic poetry and his own performance.

14. Winkler 1985, 20–23, 42–58.

15. Owen 1936. Cf. Jouan 1983, 75 on *Phoenissae*. On allotment of actors see below on νεμήσεις ὑποκριτῶν: cf. Csapo and Slater 1995, 228 (IV. 15).

16. Pickard-Cambridge 1988, 93–94.

17. Slater 1988c. I argue there for restoring a famous comic actor named Hermon (Pollux 4, 88) as the winner of an actor's contest over Aristophanes' protagonist, Apollodorus.

18. Csapo and Slater 1995, 136 (III. 74 = I.G. ii^2 2319): Callippides, of whom we shall hear more, was the winning actor in the Lenaean competition for tragic actors. A new fragment of the Lenaean victory lists for the year 364 seems to indicate that Hephaistion won the actors' contest that year, while the play he acted in placed second: Camp 1971, 305, and Pickard-Cambridge 1988, 359–360. If we could trust the later scholia on the *Clouds*, we might have evidence of a third instance. Σ *Clouds* 524 says that the actor (ὁ ὑποκριτὴς, but this must mean the protagonist) who played in the *Banqueters* was beaten (ἡττήθη); it has often been claimed that Aristophanes won first prize with this, his first venture. Unfortunately the *Clouds* scholion is an erroneous explanation of a line which in fact refers to the failure of the *Clouds*. In 311 B.C., Asclepiodorus won the actor's contest, having performed in both the winning and the third place plays (Csapo and Slater 1995, 228 [IV. 14 = I.G. ii^2 2323a]).

19. Sutton 1987 discusses "theatrical families." Sifakis 1979 suggests a system of apprenticeship already in the fifth century.

20. Pickard-Cambridge's account, 1988, 279–305, despite the criticisms here raised, remains the standard.

21. But [Aristotle] *Problems* 30.10 (956b) shows that the *technitai* of his day derived their living from their craft, since part of his explanation for why the *technitai* are depraved (πονηροί) is their necessity of working at their craft for their living (διὰ τὸ περὶ τὰς ἀναγκαίας τέχνας τὸ πολὺ μέρος τοῦ βίου).

22. Pickard-Cambridge 1988, 281 n. 2. The issue for our purposes is not whether the *technitai* were yet legally organized into a σύνοδος, but whether they had a group self-consciousness.

23. Chamaeleon is difficult to date. Wendling 1899 opts for a floruit around 280 B.C. and suggests he belonged to the older Peripatetics. See also Koepke 1856, esp. 26–27, who suggests that Chamaeleon's works περὶ κωμῳδίας, περὶ Σατύρων, περὶ Θέσπιδος and περὶ Αἰσχύλου formed in effect a "historia" of the Dionysiac competitions, that these works "videntur ii igitur non tam singulares quaestiones quam maioris voluminis partes fuisse."

24. Poland 1934, 2497, rejects the story, but Shear 1995, 172 and 189, establishes that

it is quite consistent with the recent establishment of the public archive at the Metroon and dates Alcibiades' action to 407/6. Lefkowitz's approach, which would presume a scene from a comedy mocking Alcibiades lies behind the story, would not invalidate its evidence for our purposes. Whether the *technitai* here are real or stage representations, they are evidence for theater professionals behaving as, and being understood by spectators to be, a group with a group self-consciousness.

25. Spyropoulos 1975.

26. Aristotle, *Poetics* 5 (1449b); Σ *Knights* 537: οἵας δὲ Κράτης ὀργάς· οὗτος κωμῳδίας ποιητής, ὃς πρῶτον ὑπεκρίνατο ⟨τὰ⟩ Κρατίνου, καὶ αὐτὸς ποιητὴς ὕστερον ἐγένετο, καὶ ἐξωνεῖτο τοὺς θεατὰς καὶ τὴν τούτων εὔνοιαν. See also below, chapter 4, pp. 76–77, for a discussion of the poetic strategy that shapes the brief history of comedy that Aristophanes gives in the *Knights*.

27. Bailey 1936; Sutton 1988; Slater 1989b.

28. Seeberg 1995, 8; cf. Green 1991, 30–31.

29. Seeberg 1995, 6–7; some inscriptions suggest that the Corinthian padded dancers sang as well, but we need not assume that they rehearsed a new song or set of songs for a given performance.

30. Seeberg 1995, 8 and n. 40, takes singulars in Magnes fr. 6 K-A. as evidence for an individualized actor.

31. A comparison with earlier film comedy may be apt: neither the Marx Brothers nor even a somewhat later performer such as Bob Hope are actors in the same sense as their dramatic counterparts: rather, they are skilled comic performers who partially assume a role in an action, but their audience welcomes, indeed expects, assertion of their independent comic personas in the midst of the action.

32. See the remarks of Trendall and Webster 1971 in their introduction, especially the distinction they draw between a representation and an illustration. Also Pickard-Cambridge 1988, 362–364.

33. Green 1991 gives an illuminating account of the generic distinctions. For a fuller account, see Green 1994, 16–48.

34. Green 1991, 40.

35. Fragments of an oinochoe from the Agora show a mask carried in a performer's hand: see Talcott 1939, also illustrated in Pickard-Cambridge 1988, fig. 32. For choristers rehearsing, see for example Pickard-Cambridge 1988, figs. 33, 34, 85.

36. Green 1991, 41.

37. Green 1991, 24.

38. Berlin amphora (F 1930): Ghiron-Bistagne 1976, fig. 114; London oinochoe (BM B509): Ghiron-Bistagne 1976, fig. 115, Green 1994, fig. 2.10, Green and Handley 1995, fig. 3 (in color). Dating c. 480, the latter could illustrate an official state-sponsored comedy, since the contests began in 486.

39. Taplin 1993, 55–60, 66, and pl. 9.1; Green 1994, fig. 2.21. See also chapter 8, p. 176 and n. 95, below.

40. I leave aside for the moment the very difficult question of a few vases that name Euaion, the son of Aeschylus, who may have acted in his father's plays (in revival?) and those of Sophocles; see Trendall and Webster 1971, 62 n.; III. 1, 28; III. 2, 1; and III. 2, 9.

41. Slater 1985b; also illustrated in Pickard-Cambridge 1988, fig. 51.

42. On Aeschylean revivals, see below, ch. 3, p. 44 and n. 6. Attempts have been made to solve discrepancies in the reported number of his victories by arguing that some were posthumous, but the evidence is not decisive. The *Life of Aeschylus* 13 claims that he won "not a few victories" (οὐκ ὀλίγας . . . νίκας) after his death, but we cannot verify this. Revivals of old plays were first formally organized in the fourth century; see Pickard-Cambridge 1988, 99–101.

43. One exception may be *Clouds* 541, where the scholia tell us the joke is against the comic actor Hermon, whom we know from Pollux 4, 88. The tradition is somewhat confused, and in any case Aristophanes does not refer to the actor by name.

44. See Slater 1989b and below, pp. 56–57 on the evidence of *Acharnians*.

45. Cf. comments in Csapo and Slater 1995, 16 [I. 29].

46. Edmonds 1957, 817 note c and 1000; given a victory for the poet in 418, thirty years more of professional activity would be a reasonable upper estimate.

47. Edmonds 1957 places it around 416, Sommerstein in the general introduction to his *Acharnians* edition, p. 5, suggests "after c. 420." Gelzer 1971, 1411, more cautiously concludes that it is "undatierbar."

48. Braund 2000, an entertaining but highly speculative discussion of Strattis's play and the public persona of Callipides, opts for the reading ἐν Καλλιππίδῃ, but does not acknowledge how unusual such a reference to a competitor's work would be in Aristophanes.

49. Even if we accept Kassel-Austin's text, the speaker is comparing himself to *some-one* in the *Callipides* who behaved in this way, and the title character is surely the likeliest suspect.

50. It is now customary, however, to identify the poet Aristotle refers to in *Poetics* 1458a as Sthenelus. In Slater 1985a, I simply accepted the identification of Sthenelus as a poet, but now I wonder if there may not be two figures, one an actor and another a poet, or if perhaps the poet, despite the late date, also acted. I suspect some influence of the memorable picture of Euripides in the *Acharnians*, surrounded by the props of his tragedies, on the interpretations that see Sthenelus only as a poet. Just what could it mean for a tragic poet to lose his stage equipment? If, however, actors either supplied or were given after the performance some of their own costumes, the figure of an actor forced to sell these to live would be an obvious target of Aristophanic humor.

51. The subject must be the choregus, since it seems not to be Euripides himself, and it is quite interesting to note that the poet himself did not (at least in this case) make the decision on whom to employ as protagonist.

52. I quote the fragment from K-A. The text Edmonds translates included his own supplements in the first two lines, thus: τί οὖν γενόμενος εἰς ⟨τίν'⟩ ὀπὴν ἐνδύσομαι; / ζητητέον. φέρ' εἰ γενοίμην ⟨μυ⟩ γαλῆ.

53. While actors are clearly present by name in Old Comedy, their activity may well not be named. Buttrey 1977, 19, suggests that when Dicaepolis comments at *Achar-nians* 401 on Euripides' servant, ὁ δοῦλος οὑτωσὶ σοφῶς ὑποκρίνεται, the verb ὑπο-κρίνεται may have a conscious theatrical association: i.e., it means that the servant here "performs, acts" in Euripidean style. Perhaps we could even extend this argument to a curious fragment of an unknown Aristophanes play, fr. 602 K-A. (585K):

"ἄκων κτενῶ σε, τέκνον." ὁ δ' ὑπεκρίνατο,
"ἐπὶ Παλλαδίῳ τἄρ', ὦ πάτερ, δώσεις δίκην."

The two characters whose dialogue is reported here speak from different worlds, the first in tragic diction, the second in the flat reportage of everyday Athens. They are arguably the worlds of tragedy and comedy. Is the second not just answering (see Buttrey 1977 for this meaning of ὑποκρίνομαι), but playing his role (in a comic fashion)? Other than these passages, I know of no use of a verb for an actor playing a role in Aristophanes.

54. Antiphanes fr. 189 K-A; cf. Lowe 2000.

Chapter 3. Euripides' Rag and Bone Shop: Acharnians

A previous version of this chapter appeared as "Space, Character, and *ΑΠΑΤΗ*: Transformation and Transvaluation in the *Acharnians*," in *Tragedy, Comedy and the Polis*, ed. Alan H. Sommerstein et al. (Levante Editore, Bari, 1993), pp. 397–415. Reprinted by permission.

1. *Acharnians* was a Lenaean play. I have argued in Slater 1986 that there was in the fifth century a separate Lenaean theater down near the banks of the Ilissos. Even if that argument is not accepted, however, the process of defining the theatrical space here outlined will have proceeded in the same fashion in the Theater of Dionysus on the south slopes of the Acropolis.

2. Martin Hose first suggested to me that he may have been seated in the front row of the theater audience; I very much regret having missed the same suggestion first published by MacDowell 1983, 147, which I ought to have cited in Slater 1993a; cf. now Henderson's Loeb. This staging is the most effective for a modern production, underlining the equation of theater and assembly, which I argue for hereafter. Would it be possible in the ancient theater? It might be objected that actors in the ancient theater were masked and padded and that therefore this figure would be instantly recognizable in the audience. A mask can be put on in an instant, however, and could simply be stored out of sight. Moreover, the sight lines in the ancient theater were such that a costumed figure (and the costume, with the exception of the padding, would have been normal Athenian attire) seated in the front row would be visible only to those immediately around him—until he rose and began to speak. If the suggestion offered below on this actor's identity is correct, it will have been perfectly natural for him to have a front-row seat. The staging here suggested remains only a possibility and is not essential to the interpretation that follows.

3. For a general treatment of this topic, see Slater 1987 with further references. Those involved in modern productions (e.g., Ley and Ewans 1985; Rehm 1988; Rehm 1992, esp. 31–42) have been more inclined to see actors in the orchestra. There is now a very helpful review of changing twentieth century views of stage and orchestra in Wiles 1997, 63–65. Against Wiles, however, I would see a considerable technical advantage in the existence of a low stage on acoustic grounds (Hunningher 1956) and think that the audience gradually comes to perceive a difference in theatrical space between stage and orchestra.

4. Dale 1969b, 285, believed in a row of steps (apparently continuous) across the front of the skene. In her reconstruction of *Acharnians*' staging she has Dicaeopolis seated on these steps at the play's opening. This presents considerable problems of staging once the Herald enters. Dale's essential understanding of how the actor shapes

the space around him is admirable, however, and does not succumb to artificial strictures on movement within the theater space. Cf. Handley 1993a, 99–104.

5. The number of doors in the fifth-century *skene* has been fiercely disputed. Dale
1969a, 267–268, in a splendidly reasoned piece on problems of staging, argues forcefully for a single door into the *skene*. The problem is bound up with our understanding
of the demands placed on the imagination of the audience in the course of performance. An audience can be induced to imagine anything, given sufficient clues and
practice of how to do so, as minimalist stagings in this century have proved time
and again. Characters may mime climbing steps and have the audience accept that the
action is now being played on two levels, or a small number of stylized gestures may be
accepted by the audience as a complete (and emotionally gripping) rendition of a mad
scene or a battle. To ask an audience to accept that a single door actually represents
three different doors is by no means unimaginable. On the other hand, our texts do
not speak as though they asked the audience to imagine many things that were clearly
beyond the capabilities of the the stage to represent, such as full-scale battle scenes (the
exceptions being such rare effects as the earthquake in the *Bacchae*, though Hammond
1988, 33 n. 90, believes that even the thunderclaps, smoke, and fire that ended the *Prometheus Bound* were within the technical grasp of the Aeschylean theater). Aristophanes' parodies of the *mechane* are proof that attempts were made to show characters as
flying or appearing from above. The implication is that, where technical resources suf-
ficed, the Greek theater tried for as naturalistic a representation as possible (rather than
the highly coded and conventionalized representations of the Far Eastern theater, for
example). While definitive proof is impossible, the position of Dover 1966 that some
comedies require at least two doors is certainly preferable; cf. now Handley 1993a, 109–
111.

6. Webster 1967, 13, assumes that lines 10–11 mean only that the order of performance was changed, with Theognis coming on before the Aeschylean revival; on the
other hand, Dicaeopolis could simply have been expecting an Aeschylus play again, because there had been a revival at the previous year's festival. Taplin 1993, 65 n. 25, speculates that the occasion may not have been the actual day of performance but rather
the proagon; this is attractive, because one would assume that after the proagon, most
citizens would know what plays and playwrights were competing at the festival. On
revivals of Aeschylus, see Newiger 1961 and Cantarella 1974 [1965].

7. Though real political conflict between Cleon and the Knights doubtless lay
behind the original theatrical event. On the reference to Cleon here, see Sommerstein *ad loc*. The reconstruction of *Babylonians* is far from certain; its chorus were not
Knights but the Babylonian slaves of the title. A trial scene was likely, but there is no
proof that Cleon appeared in person. Carawan 1990 makes an interesting case for a
historical attack on Cleon, not in the law courts but in the assembly through the procedure of προβολή, an ingenious proposal relying on references in Theopompus to
enmity between Cleon and the knights. There are three possibilities: first, that Aristophanes refers to a stage event; second, that he refers to a historical event; and third,
that Aristophanes here refers back to his own comment on, or representation of, a
historical event within his previous play. In such cases, the argument from silence is
very hard to weigh: would we be more likely to have independent corroboration of
a προβολή against Cleon or of a scene in a lost play? Carawan's attempt to discount
the argument from context (that Cleon's discomfiture is a theatrical pleasure because

the others are), claiming it is "a familiar mode of comic logic to connect the most disparate examples, *modus absurdus*, throwing together figures of the theater and politics" fundamentally misses the point: these pleasures are *not* disparate examples but are all connected through spectatorship. In my view the evidence still favors a theatrical representation of Cleon as the primary referent, with or without a concomitant historical basis. Even if Carawan is correct and Dicaeopolis witnessed Cleon's plight only in the assembly, his pleasure remains one of *theoria* and prepares us for the play's critique of spectator politics (for which see below).

8. Aristotle, *Ath. Pol.* 42.4; Demosthenes *Meid.* 8–10; Thucydides 8. 93–94 (the theater in the Peiraeus); Pickard-Cambridge 1988, 64 and 68–70; Ober 1989, 132 and n. 70, with further references; Goldhill 1991, 186.

9. On similarities of the two institutions, see Henderson 1990, esp. 271–284, and in general his explication of the "Old Oligarch's" [= ps.-Xenophon] treatment of the operations of the radical democracy.

10. I take Sommerstein's stage directions to be general helps to the reader or for a modern staging. Thus when he writes at line 40 "[Enter Herald, Prytaneis, and Archers, followed by a crowd of citizens.]" I do not take this to be his judgment on the original staging.

11. Olson 1992, esp. 304 and 319 on the distortion.

12. It is unlikely that the orchestra of the Theater of Dionysus in the fifth century was circular. Dinsmoor 1951 noted that the remains of the blocks supporting the fifth-century seats were rectilinear and tried to restore a polygonal cavea around a circular orchestra, but Gebhard 1974 better accounts for the evidence by dispensing with the imaginary circle (contra Wiles 1997, 44–55). The contour of the hillside on the south slope of the Acropolis does suggest that the audience was to some degree wrapped around the dancing space of the orchestra. I use the term "horseshoe" to indicate this loose configuration.

13. Kannicht 1971, 579, takes it as self-evident that "verwandeln sich die Zuschauer in Ekklesiasten und damit zugleich in Mitspieler ihres eigenen Schauspiels." Kannicht's evidence from modern performance is invaluable, but it has also been worth our effort to test this against the performance conditions in the fifth-century Theater of Dionysus. Cf. Perusino 1986, 29: "Nel 'popolo' convinto dagli argomenti di Diceopoli non saranno da identificare solo i giudici acarnesi, ossia il coro, ma il popolo ateniese, impersonato dagli spettatori seduti in teatro."

14. There was a historical Amphitheus, a fellow demesman of Aristophanes (Dow 1969). On his role here as a literalization of his name, see Edmunds 1980, 3–4.

15. Sommerstein translates "Stay seated and keep silence."

16. Redfield 1990, 321, suggests that a similar breakdown of the barriers between performance and audience in the political assembly takes place after the reforms of Cleisthenes, and as a result "the moral authority of the assembly began to decline. As the audience began to vote they were drawn into the play, and the Assembly came to be conceived as a place of contest between warring interests."

17. Such as his comment on the ambassadors' costumes: ᾿Ωκβάτανα τοῦ σχήμα-τος, 65. For σχῆμα as costume, compare *Frogs* 463, 523; *Knights* 1331; and Menander *Sikyonios* fr. 2 Sandbach (= 439 K). He critiques what he sees like a spectator in the theater. Cf. his reaction to the King's Eye himself, 94ff.

18. Where his seat was in relation to the *prytaneis* is unclear. He may simply have

sat on the orchestra floor, as most citizens would have on the Pnyx. When he turns and faces the stage, he becomes part of the audience. When he wishes to interrupt, he can simply rise and face the audience again, as any citizen seated toward the front on the Pnyx would have done in order to be heard.

In March 1989, thanks to the kindness of the Ephoreia of the Acropolis, I was able to test various possible movements for Dicaeopolis in the Theater of Dionysus. While the theater has been greatly changed since the fifth century, the relative spatial relationships of stage and orchestra can still provide some useful information. I take the maximum distance that the actor playing Dicaeopolis would have to cross, if he were seated in the front row around the orchestra, to be roughly that between the throne of the priest of Dionysus and the present front line of the remains of the stage (P-P in the plans of Pickard-Cambridge 1946). One can cover this distance easily in 13–15 seconds. Probably the actor started from a position closer to the stage, either in the orchestra or further along the side of the orchestra toward the stage. We should not imagine the actor as speaking while crossing to and mounting the stage; speech would distract from the emphatic movement and, since the actor would be moving toward the stage, would be almost impossible to hear.

19. If there were benches at the edge of the orchestra, they could be cleared away by stage hands or simply left. Unoccupied, they are essentially invisible. This flexible, redefinable use of space (or change of scene) tends to trouble those who interpret all Greek plays as though they were late fifth-century tragedies. Pöhlmann 1989, 48–49, on the one hand defends the change of location as a lingering legacy of earlier tragedy while at the same time carving up the space in front of the stage into small areas apparently permanently allotted to the Pnyx or Euripides' house. Both he and Landfester 1977, 38–42, believe that Dicaeopolis must have *two* separate houses in the play, one in the country where he celebrates the Rural Dionysia, and one in the city, from which he departs for the Choes festival. There is no evidence whatsoever for these two houses.

20. Esp. Newiger 1957, 52–53, 104–105 and Newiger 1980, 220–221.

21. Perhaps with an obscene pun on πέος: Edmunds 1980, 6 and n. 15.

22. On the effect of this entrance, see particularly Zimmermann 1985[2], 34–41.

23. Zimmermann 1985[2], 35–36 sees a visual and theatrical reminisce in the Acharnians' pursuit of Dicaeopolis of a "Suchmotiv" from tragedy and satyr play, most notably in the *Eumenides* of Aeschylus. The comparison captures exactly the dynamic of the stage action; demonstration of a direct Aeschylean influence probably demands more evidence for the restaging of the plays in the 420s (for which line 10 of this play is an essential starting place).

24. Cf. Slater 1987.

25. One wants to find an echo here of the audience's experience in the theater which on the occasion of the City Dionysia would have witnessed the arrival of just such a phallic procession, but the evidence is maddeningly evanescent. Our only proof of a phallic procession before the City Dionysia consists of one substantially restored inscription, I.G. i[2]. 46, a decree of 446/5 concerning the Athenian colony of Brea. Pickard-Cambridge 1988, 36, says "there is no evidence of any phallic elements in the procession or the festival" of the Lenaea—but given how little we know of the City Dionysia, silence may not be decisive. Claims for a phallic procession at the Rural Dionysia rest entirely on this passage of the *Acharnians*. For another view, see Cole 1993.

26. Taaffe 1993, 26–27, even suggests that with this procession "Dicaeopolis has . . . imitated, in miniature and in parody, the beginnings of the dramatic genre in which he exists." Thus the progression through the Dionysiac festivals of the Athenian year within the play (on which, see below) would begin with a metatheatrical refoundation of comedy.

27. The actor playing the daughter is presumably wearing the elaborate festival mantle characteristic of the κανηφόρος: see Roccos 1995, with illustrations. Dicaeopolis is thus first a costumer and director of other performers, before he takes up a new costume and role himself.

28. Probably imaginary, primarily for reasons of the actor's safety. Stones large enough actually to be seen by the audience would be very dangerous indeed, and actions miming the throwing and Dicaeopolis's dodging of the stones would read quite well, given the lines. Nonetheless, the audience is expected to imagine physical interaction between orchestra and stage, which argues against those who believe that these spaces were hermetically sealed off from each other, with no interaction allowed.

29. Of some interest here is the first reference to Cleon, as the chorus declares "I hate you even more than Cleon, whom I'll cut up as shoe soles for the knights" (ὡς μεμίσηκά σε Κλέωνος ἔτι μᾶλλον, ὃν / ἐγὼ τεμῶ τοῖσιν ἱππεῦσι καττύματα, 299–302). It has been suggested (e.g., by Starkie, ad loc) that this is a hint of "coming attractions," advertising the forthcoming Knights; cf. Carawan 1990, 145, and n. 23, Hubbard 1991, 34, 53 n. 34. It is likely to be a part of Aristophanes' testing of the waters for the reception of further attacks on Cleon, given Cleon's recent attempt to strike back (see further below).

30. Was this shocking scene represented on stage in the Euripidean Telephus or only reported by a messenger speech? Handley and Rea 1957, 24, incline to the latter view. It seems to me that the case here is rather different from the literalization of metaphor so liberally practiced by Aristophanes. Perhaps Aristophanes practices an interesting metatheatrical inversion here, placing offstage events onstage (cf. this device in Tom Stoppard's Rosencrantz and Guildenstern Are Dead, for example, which gives us the action of Hamlet as seen by the two minor characters of the title), but at this distance in time from the original, this simply threatens to be too subtle, unsupported by textual parody. I prefer to believe that Telephus's seizure of the baby Orestes and subsequent speech were represented onstage, as argued by Heath 1987b, 275–276, 279; cf. MacDowell 1995, 54–56.

31. Here Aristophanes literalizes a Euripidean metaphor; on this phenomenon in Aristophanes see Newiger 1957. Its primary function, of course, is as an outrageous parody of the danger involved in attacking Cleon and speaking in favor of peace.

32. On this scene, see Rau 1967, 37–42.

33. Bowie 1988 argues, against the common consensus, that Dicaeopolis here adopts the character, not of the comic poet Aristophanes, but of the comic poet Eupolis. The most attractive part of this suggestion is the explanation it gives for the character's name, Dicaeopolis. Bowie argues that compounds ending in -polis usually have a verbal first element (e.g., Sosipolis) and, given the rarity of adjectival bases, the name Dicaeopolis will make us think of its virtual synonym, Eupolis. This is quite clever, and Bowie makes a possible case for Eupolis too having been prosecuted by Cleon for an attack in a comedy (which Bowie speculates was the Astrateutoi) in the previous

year. The problem is that "too." Bowie must admit that Aristophanes (or at least Callistratus) was prosecuted as well. It seems odd that the Aristophanes who proclaims his pride in the *Wasps* at having attacked Cleon would wish to hide behind Eupolis here. The character name has proved troublesome to some who wish to etymologize Dicaeopolis as the personification of a "just city" and yet have difficulties with the private nature of Dicaeopolis's peace (e.g., Foley 1988). For Dicaeopolis as a personification of justice opposed to that of the city, see Perusino 1986, 17–33. Yet the "utopian" element in *Acharnians* (Zimmermann 1983) in all its possible meanings is very much a part of the appeal of comedy. That a poet of Old Comedy should choose to parody or borrow from another poet of Old Comedy (as opposed to tragic parody), as Bowie postulates for some lines of *Acharnians*, seems to me most unlikely (cf. Slater 1985a). Finally, the argument from silence has some weight here. If Dicaeopolis were really recognizable as Eupolis, if Eupolis had also been prosecuted by Cleon, indeed if there were any cogent parodies of Eupolidean lines in the *Acharnians*, we would expect to learn that from the scholia. Bowie's suggestion could be made to accord with the interpretation advanced here of the general metatheatrical tone of this scene, but I think it is unpersuasive. Cf. now Parker 1991 and Sidwell 1994.

34. Halliwell 1980, 34–41, shows that this was Aristophanes himself and not Callistratus, his producer; cf. Perusino 1986 on "I registi di Aristophane," esp. 55–57. MacDowell 1982b has attempted to answer Halliwell's case by a very literal reading of several Aristophanic metaphors that may not have been chosen to convey legal niceties; his portrait of Aristophanes as a poet who had to be instructed from the ground up by Callistratus also seems doubtful. The real objection, though, is the notion that Aristophanes' identity as author of three successive plays could have been kept secret in the close-knit society of late fifth-century Athens. We also have a fragmentary commentary on the *Acharnians* preserved in a third-century A.D. papyrus, P. Oxy. 6. 856. Line 27 of the papyrus reads: [. . . . . υ]πο Κλεωνος δικην εφυ[γε. While I regret my previous over-translation of this (Slater 1989b, 73 n. 11, corrected by MacDowell 1995, 44 n. 35), the subject of this prosecution is clearly Aristophanes, not Callistratus. MacDowell 1995, 40–45, now takes the view that it does not really matter whether the "secret" of Aristophanes' authorship was known or not (despite the emphatic κρύβδην, *Wasps* 1018; cf. Sommerstein *ad loc.*); the archon gave the chorus to Callistratus, and if there was trouble, Callistratus alone had to answer for it. It is this "alone" which I find so doubtful; it seems most unlikely that the legal nicety that Callistratus was the only producer of record would protect Aristophanes from Cleon's prosecution. Surely they both would have been prosecuted together—if Callistratus was felt to have any real responsibility for the content of the play at all. Since he believes that Dicaeopolis speaks for Callistratus (and only Callistratus) here, it is curious that MacDowell does not pursue this to its logical end and conclude that Callistratus *wrote* these lines—since this too is a joint production.

35. Atkinson 1992, 56–61, suggest *eisangelia*.

36. Halliwell 1980, 35 n. 11. At Slater 1989b, 73 and 76, I appeared to attribute the view that this was an attack on Cleon *personally* to Prof. Halliwell, which he informs me (private correspondence) is *not* his belief, and on the question of slander he refers me to Halliwell 1991. I regret the error. It does seem to me, however, exceeding difficult to discriminate between political attack and personal slander in Athens of this

period: see the brilliant explication of comedy's function in the radical democracy by Henderson 1990.

37. Sifakis 1971, 7–14; Bain 1977, 1–12; Dedoussi 1995.

38. Styan 1975, 180–223.

39. I have argued this point in full in Slater 1989b.

40. The allusion is complicated (see Sommerstein *ad* 388, 390). Hieronymus is certainly a tragic poet, known for his horrifying masks, among other things, although the "cap of Hades" which confers invisibility is drawn from *Iliad* 5. 844–845.

41. Were I staging the play today, I would use precisely this effect, but one cannot of course prove that Aristophanes did so in the original production.

42. There is a pattern of characters revealing their names to doorkeepers: see Olson 1992. 308.

43. The papyrus commentary on *Acharnians*, P. Oxy. 6. 856 provides some evidence, though it is hard to interpret. Line 33 seems to refer to the rags and such around Euripides: [..τα ρα]κη κ(αι) τα σχισματα: It seems very likely then that line 32 refers to the costumes and/or props as well and specifies where they are in relation to Euripides: [......]ται παρ αυτωι υπο δ(ε) χειρων[. One may indeed wonder whether a third-century A.D. commentator knew anything about staging at all, especially of an Aristophanic comedy, but we should not dismiss this evidence without thought. That the costumes and props should be *by* Euripides is no surprise, but what are we to make of υπο δ(ε) χειρων? The comment falls somewhere between line 419 and 444 of the text; it could well be specifying the original position of the props.

44. One problem is the demonstrative with the name of Oineus in line 418. Starkie suggested this indicated a book roll. I would prefer to see the mask here; see Slater 1988b. Fowler 1989a has kindly called my attention to Macleod 1974 and 1980 (reprinted in his *Collected Essays*), which argue for possible visual associations between the rags Euripides has lying about and book rolls. Macleod may well be right in general, but he does not to my mind solve the problem of όδί in line 418. Euripides says to Dicaeopolis:

τὰ ποῖα τρύχη; μῶν ἐν οἷς Οἰνεὺς όδὶ
ὁ δύσποτμος γεραιὸς ἠγωνίζετο;

The demonstrative cannot refer, I think, simply to the rags themselves which are already present in the prepositional phrase ἐν οἷς. όδί and ἐν οἷς must be two different things, and we are left again with the question, what object pointed to with όδί could be seen and appreciated by the whole audience. I think the mask most likely.

45. Sommerstein translates "And why are you *wearing* those tragic rags . . . ?" (my emphasis). The lines are also so interpreted by Muecke 1977, 63, for example. This is a possible meaning of ἔχεις, of course, but otherwise there is no evidence that Euripides is *wearing* the costumes at all, though Macleod 1980 suggests that he is using them as a bed cover. This is possible, but they cannot all be on the bed, and a joke that Euripides is so poor and/or cold that he used costumes as coverlets seems out of place. The fragmentary scholion noted above (n. 43) does suggest that the costumes are by, not on, Euripides. We must not allow any anachronistic memories of Agathon clad in female garb in the *Thesmophoriazusae* to influence our interpretation here.

André Laks has suggested to me there may be considerable significance to the singular in ἐκ τραγῳδίας. Dicaeopolis asks, not "why do you have the rags of your tragedies" (i.e., considered as individual pieces), but rather, "why do you have rags/scraps from tragedy" (considered perhaps as a genre, or as Euripides' peculiar conception of the genre). The question seems almost to imply that it is not so surprising that Euripides has rags, but it is surprising that the source of these is tragedy. Laks further suggests that the phrase ἐσθῆτ᾽ ἐλεινήν (413) may be chosen with an eye toward current philosophical discussions of tragedy (later of course culminating in Aristotle's discussion of ἔλεος), which thus prepares us for some of the philosophical implications of Aristophanes' self-defense in the parabasis (for which see below).

46. See LSJ s.v. and Olson *ad Peace* 177; it is often used in Aristophanes, certainly not always to express surprise (for which, compare *Clouds* 30). Bernhard Zimmermann has suggested to me that ἀτάρ may be used for its tragic ring; LSJ do note that it is more frequent in poetry (especially in epic), but it is also found in Plato and the fragments of comedy (e.g., Cratinus 200 K-A., Leucon 1 K-A., Eupolis 56 K-A.). The effect is to separate the two jokes emphatically; the first is purely a joke about style (visually concretized), while the second suggests a referent in theatrical praxis as well as a point about style.

47. Pickard-Cambridge 1988, 90.

48. And the mockery of the poets themselves; see below on Aristophanes' reference in this play to the miserly choregus Antimachus, who stinted on the banquet for the choristers after last year's Lenaean production, lines 1154–1155. The role of choregic liturgies in competition for status in the democratic state is quite complex and well explored in Wilson 1997 and 2000.

49. Pickard-Cambridge 1988, 88 states "It was possible to hire second-hand costumes . . . ," a view that rests entirely on one quotation from Pollux 8. 78, which distinguishes between new and secondhand costumes:

τοὺς δὲ τὰς ἐσθῆτας ἀπομισθοῦντας τοῖς χορηγοῖς οἱ μὲν νέοι ἱματιομίσθας ἐκάλουν, οἱ δὲ παλαιοὶ ἱματιομισθωτάς.

Like much of Pollux, this is quite undateable. I find the notion of any established form of costume rental in the fifth century simply unimaginable, though isolated transactions between one choregus and another (assuming the choregus retained ownership of the costumes) are not out of the question.

50. We hear of some plays in the fifth century being reperformed at the theater in the Peiraeus. While it is not inconceivable that the costumes were then reused, it still seems unlikely, for the new choregus would wish to demonstrate his own public spirit, and the visual display of "his" production was essential.

51. Such expense, as well as changing taste, might explain the relative scarcity of animal choruses in later fifth-century comedy.

52. It could conceivably have been part of the actor's remuneration, but we should not assume so in all cases. Such costumes certainly could have been sold to others. Greek clothing was not exactly made to measure; there were no size 39 Long chitons. We might also wonder whether the young men of the chorus would have that much use for captive maiden costumes—although they could give them to family members.

53. Such costumes are simply luxury clothing, *not* status-specific robes such as a king's coronation robes today. It is interesting to speculate about the gorgeously embroidered robe of the flute-player displayed on the Getty *Birds* krater (published in Green 1985). It is possible that flute-players needed elaborate costumes for other performances and therefore had their own, but I would incline to think that the flute-player's costume here was paid for by the choregus as part of his choregeia and was intended to display his wealth and civic pride.

54. We do not know before this moment that Dicaeopolis is going to get a *costume*, only that he needs to "equip" himself theatrically (ἐνσκευάσασθαί, 384) to evoke pity.

55. This is what differentiates Euripides' ragged heroes from Xerxes in his tattered Persian robes in Aeschylus's *Persians* ("the remains of my garments," τὸ λοιπὸν τόδε τᾶς ἐμᾶς στολᾶς, 1018); see Hall 1996 *ad loc*. The most reasonable reconstruction is that the actor playing Xerxes wears a once valuable Persian robe, now heavily damaged, making the powerful visual point of the destruction of wealth and splendor. Telephus' were never anything more than the cheapest of clothing to begin with.

56. ῥάκιόν τι τοῦ παλαιοῦ δράματος, line 415. Euripides does something similar with the whole history of Attic tragedy at the end of his career. See the analysis of the *Orestes* in Zeitlin 1980.

57. It may be a little deceptive to speak of "reduction" here. Plays in this period were naturally evanescent; apart from a reading public whose existence, let alone size, is highly disputable, the plays simply had no existence after their one-time production, save as some of the poetry was remembered and reperformed at parties and such; cf. Strepsiades' request for performance from his son in *Clouds* 1364ff. and the stories of Athenian prisoners from the Sicilian disaster who were released from slavery or accorded better treatment because they could perform Euripides (Satyrus, *Life of Euripides*, Plutarch, *Life of Nicias* 29 [= Csapo and Slater 1995 9A and B]).

58. It is interesting that there is no explicit discussion of masks. I believe that Euripides gestures to a mask of Oineus at line 418 (see Slater 1988b), but thereafter nothing suggests that masks continue to be discussed. We may have here evidence for the limits of nonillusionism in Old Comedy. While the obvious way to change characters in masked theater is to put on the mask as well as the costume of the character to be assumed, Aristophanes apparently thought that would be too confusing for his audience (and perhaps too dangerous for himself, if the argument below about the political implications of the *Acharnians* is correct).

59. Muecke 1982a, 21–22, sees Dicaeopolis's begging for a seemingly endless series of props as the result of his having put on the *beggar* Telephus's costume. This is a pleasant conceit but doubtful, for it assumes that the character, through the costume, takes over Dicaeopolis's whole personality. In fact, one key point of this scene is to demonstrate how the actor can reuse Euripidean props and costumes for other purposes; he remains throughout superior to the character he plays.

60. See Sommerstein's note, which points out that if Triclinius is right in attributing these lines to the *Telephus* (440–441):

δεῖ γάρ με δόξαι πτωχὸν εἶναι τήμερον,
εἶναι μὲν ὅσπερ εἰμί, φαίνεσθαι δὲ μή·

Aristophanes must have altered at least the ending of a line, doubtless to sharpen his metatheatrical point. Cf. Rau 1967, 33 n. 37, and a discussion of the lines as addressing two aspects of the Athenian audience in Lada 1993, 120.

61. The *Telephus* parody adds a resonance here. Handley and Rea 1957, 32–33 note, "To fulfill his mission, Telephus had not only to be recognized, but to be recognized as a Greek." The audience must know that the player speaking here not only is *not* who he claims to be (Telephus), but is in fact the actor behind the mask (Aristophanes). Only then does the joke have its full dimensions.

62. Bailey 1936, citing brief suggestions in the editions of both Rennie and Starkie. Sutton 1988 makes the same case within an analysis of the metatheatrical nature of the *Acharnians*. The suggestion has generally not won favor, and Foley 1988 is typical of those who dismiss it. The following summarizes my case for Aristophanes as actor; the full argument is in Slater 1989b.

63. The one likely exception is Cratinus, who presumably spoke in trimeters in his *Wineflask*, as an anonymous referee reminds me. Sutton 1988 points out one possible parallel in trimeters from Aristophanes, *Skenas Katalambanousae*, fr. 488 K-A.:

$$\chi\rho\hat{\omega}\mu\alpha\iota \ \gamma\grave{\alpha}\rho \ \alpha\mathring{v}\tau o\hat{v} \ \tau o\hat{v} \ \sigma\tau\acute{o}\mu\alpha\tau os \ \tau\hat{\omega} \ \sigma\tau\rho o\gamma\gamma\acute{v}\lambda\omega,$$
$$\tau o\grave{v}s \ \nu o\hat{v}s \ \delta' \ \mathring{a}\gamma o\rho\alpha\acute{\iota}ovs \ \mathring{\eta}\tau\tau o\nu \ \mathring{\eta} \ '\kappa\epsilon\hat{\iota}\nu os \ \pi o\iota\hat{\omega}.$$

We know from the scholion to Plato's *Apology* in which this is preserved that the speaker here is talking about Euripides, and the scholiast interprets the passage as though Aristophanes were speaking in his own person. Kaibel thought this was a tragic poet portrayed as a character speaking about Euripides, since "suo enim nomine non loquitur comicus trimetris usus" (cited in Kassel-Austin), but that is only the assumption based on the practice of the surviving plays.

Bailey (following Kock) cites another possible parallel for the poet speaking directly to the audience in trimeters, Plato fr. 115 K-A., from the *Perialges*: $\mathring{o}s \ \pi\rho\hat{\omega}\tau\alpha$ $\mu\grave{\epsilon}\nu \ K\lambda\acute{\epsilon}\omega\nu\iota \ \pi\acute{o}\lambda\epsilon\mu o\nu \ \mathring{\eta}\rho\acute{a}\mu\eta\nu$. Again, this could be a character, or it could be chorus-leader speaking, but as with fr. 488 K-A., this could also be the poet speaking for himself. We simply know too little in the case of Plato Comicus to speculate.

64. For what the audience might be expected to know of the legend and the play, see Foley 1988. 34–36 and n. 9. Aristophanes of course returned to parody this play even later in the *Thesmophoriazusae*, by which point, however, the play had probably become the archetypal example of Euripidean dramaturgy.

65. For a full account, see Handley and Rea 1957. A full list of tragic lines parodied in the *Acharnians* is given by Rau 1967, 185–187. The extent of parody troubles Fisher 1993, 38, who then discounts the possibility that a "serious" argument underlies Dicaeopolis' shifting stances, but see below (pp. 60–61) for the notion that Aristophanes is teaching the audience how to "read" performance.

66. Not in fact a completely honest defense, if Brown 1974 and Worthington 1990 are right to see a caricature of Cleon on a Corinthian cup: see the discussion of Demosthenes and Nicias in the opening of the *Knights*, pp. 68–70 below.

67. See his note *ad* 509.

68. And *not* in favor of the Spartans, as Foley 1988 quite properly points out. This is not the place to address the whole question of the morality and/or moral exemplarity

of Dicaeopolis's private peace with Sparta. That this is a private peace and not shared by the city as a whole (most emphatically not by Lamachus and his ilk) has disturbed a number of modern commentators, who agonize over how this isolated pocket of rural peace can be a "just city" as Dicaeopolis's name seems to promise. Comedy, unlike tragedy, is not afflicted with a conscience; I find this no more troubling than the cannibal city that devours its criminals in the *Birds*.

69. See Sommerstein *ad loc*. and Dover. Retraction of the foreskin of the passive partner is not a necessary concomitant to the act of anal intercourse which Sommerstein suggests is here meant. I think it more likely that Dicaeopolis is suggesting an act in which Lamachus will be the passive or at least subordinate partner.

70. Again, see Sommerstein *ad loc*. Opinions will differ as to whether Lamachus's phallus should be unusually large (grotesque, according to Greek aesthetics) or unusually small (the obvious choice for a modern production). It is in any case quite clear that *hopla* has in Greek a sexual connotation.

71. Line 598. Aristophanes must tread very carefully here and so moves quickly. He claims Lamachus was elected "by three cuckoos" and immediately changes the subject to who gets to go on embassies and thus profit from the state. The exchange in 618–619 functions in the same way; the appeal to democracy is answered by another attack on Lamachus's personal financial motivations.

72. We learned from Amphitheus at line 184 that the chorus wears τρίβωνας. The best discussion is Dale 1969b, 289–290. Sifakis 1971, 103–108 places this reference in context but reaches no firm conclusion. Philocleon in the *Wasps* (1131ff.) must also be persuaded to give up his *tribon* and with it his old life as a juror.

73. Ketterer 1980.

74. Dale 1969b, 289–290 is right to maintain that in general masks, not costumes, are the signifiers of character, but that is less true of the chorus, who, despite Dicaeopolis's use of a few individual names (609ff.—and of course no one in the audience asks how Dicaeopolis happens to know the names of these individuals he presumably has never met before), simply share a general character. The gesture of discarding the cloaks also helps carry the audience over the fact that Dicaeopolis has not defeated Lamachus with argument (a fact that tends to trouble modern commentators) but with theatrical de-mythologizing. Nothing in the text indicates that the chorus members put their cloaks back on. Presumably they wore tunics underneath (unlike Socrates in life or Philocleon on stage: see MacDowell *ad Wasps* 1123).

75. Bowie 1982 is an excellent discussion of how the parabasis is tied to the foregoing action but curiously, however, makes no mention of the fact that Dicaeopolis's speech as Aristophanes, which is central to the connection, is unique.

76. The commentator in P. Oxy. 6. 856 (lines 69–79) glosses line 647 thus: υ]περ εαυτου λεγων οτ(ε) ᵏᵃⁱ βασιλε[υς. The word εαυτου must refer to Aristophanes and not Callistratus.

77. See Taplin 1983 for a succinct demonstration of the fact that Aristophanes in this play is claiming the salutary moral teaching function traditionally associated with tragedy.

78. From MacDowell 1982a, to which I am indebted on many points. His translation implies that he regards both sentences to be Gorgias, whereas Diels-Kranz take only the first (which I have given in bold type) to be so. The explanation sounds a little

flat for Gorgias and is more likely to be Plutarch, but we should not doubt that Gorgias's epigram applied to deception in the theater. See also Garzya 1987, 154 and now Lada 1993, 99.

79. This comment is attributed to no particular work of Gorgias and is undateable. Gorgias first came to Athens in 427 as an ambassador from Leontinoi in Sicily. A good general treatment of Gorgianic deception is Verdenius 1981; on Gorgias and traditional poetic ἀπάτη, see Segal 1962, esp. 112–114 and 130–131. His encomium on Helen is traditionally dated later, though some have put it before his first visit to Athens (on chronology, see Segal's n. 11). See also Ringer 1998, 27–30. The discussion in the *Acharnians* suggests strongly to me that this remark about tragedy was made during his first visit or very early on in his encounter with the Athenian dramatic festivals. I must emphasize, however, that Aristophanes' use of a theatrical model to critique ἀπάτη in political discourse stands, whether this particular saying of Gorgias was its occasion or not.

80. It is of course in one sense impossible to establish what Aristophanes "really" thought of Euripides, i.e., whether the particular form of attack he chose represented a personal conviction that Euripides himself was dangerous or simply that his plays could serve the audience as a familiar embodiment of sophistic reasoning and moral instability. He could certainly presume that more in his audience has seen a Euripides play than had attended any given assembly or jury trial in which Cleon appeared.

81. Lines 652–654 must refer to the poet of the play, Aristophanes, but as Sommerstein rightly remarks, everything that comes down to us from antiquity about possible Aeginetan connections or heritage for Aristophanes derives from this passage; there is no independent evidence. The third-century A.D. commentator of P. Oxy. 856, line 74, already contains such speculations. Perusino 1986, 22–23 makes the very interesting suggestion that this is an answer on Aristophanes' part to charges by Cleon (made in heated exchange following *Babylonians*) that Aristophanes was not an Athenian citizen but merely masquerading as one; cf. Storey 1998, 126–127.

82. Aristophanes makes the claim that comedy, just like tragedy, can exercise the traditional didactic function of poetry; indeed, he is almost saying that comedy (his, at least) can replace tragedy (Euripides', that is) in this regard. For a succinct demonstration of Aristophanes' didactic claims for comedy, see Taplin 1983.

83. Accepting Hamaker's conjecture here; see Sommerstein's note *ad loc.*

84. Aristophanes treads very carefully here. By making very cruel jokes about Megarian starvation and diverting all animosity toward those who profited from the decree, i.e., informers, he appeases those in the audience who still support the Megarian blockade.

85. *Mechane* in the context of a play can easily have the connotation "theatrical device," and the Megarians were famous for low theatrical comedy; see Sommerstein *ad loc.*, Taaffe 1993. 28, and *Wasps* 57.

86. Note the metatheatrical comment on the choruses: this may be a much subtler version of Aristophanes' jokes which open *Frogs*, commenting on the banality of (others') comic chorus, eternally singing about luxury foods—and yet including such a reference in his own comedy.

87. Pickard-Cambridge 1988. 25–29.

88. Pickard-Cambridge 1988. 42–43. There is some minor controversy about

whether the date was the same throughout Attica. The evidence for a date in Poseideon includes Theophrastus *Characters* iii and I.G. ii² 1183 and 1496.

89. The Anthesteria took place on 11, 12, and 13 Anthesterion (roughly the end of February), the feast of Choes falling on the 12th and Chutroi on the 13th.

90. And specifically back to area of the theater itself, if I am correct in arguing (Slater 1986) that there was a separate Lenaean theater next to the Dionysion in Limnais. The first day of the Anthesteria, called Pithoigia, took place near but not in the sanctuary itself (πρὸς τῷ ἱερῷ, Phanodemos 325 F 12 Jacoby = passage 20 in Pickard-Cambridge 1988, 6), which was only open on Chutroi. Drinking contests on Choes took place all over the city, but the official contest took place in the θεσμοθετεῖον, location unknown. Thus the Anthesteria festival itself moves geographically from the whole city into the shrine itself in the progress from Choes to Chutroi. Compton-Engle 1999, 367–368 argues that the play already returns to the city when Dicaeopolis opens his private market; I think that the space is deliberately ambiguous in that scene, though it facilitate the movement back to the city.

91. For use of the ekkyklema here, see Dale 1969, 291–292, and Sommerstein *ad loc*. Its use best explains the order to "close up the house" in 1096: σύγκληιε.

92. MacDowell 1983, 158–160. The name Derketes is rare but attested at fourth century Phyle: MacDowell is surely right to see a joke at the expense of a historical individual here. *Pace* Fisher 1993, 39–40, Dicaeopolis's "selfishness" is quite reasonable in Greek terms. Carey 1993, 248 n. 10, suggests (*ad* 1024) that the farmer may be a fraud.

93. This suggests that the motif of a warrior's face reflected in his own shield, most famous from the fallen Persian on the Alexander mosaic, a composition dating from the late fourth century, goes back at least to the fifth century in the visual arts, for the complex visual parody here seems to imply a type scene of a warrior gazing at a reflection in his shield with which the audience should already be familiar.

94. The humor may be increased, if we follow Sommerstein 1993b and reorder the lines thus: 1108, 1113–1117, 1109–1112, 1118. It is perhaps pushing things too far to suggest that reverse peristalsis (Dicaeopolis's threat to regurgitate, using Lamachus's helmet feather) is now turned into the joys of eating.

95. See Sommerstein *ad loc.*, who compares *Knights* 1274–1289, 1300–1315; *Wasps* 1265–1283; *Peace* 781–795, 801–814; *Frogs* 678–685, 706–717.

96. On this strophic pair as poetry and its relations to the rest of the play see Moulton 1981, 18–24.

97. Halliwell 1980, 44–45. One assumes that Aristophanes did not win first prize on that occasion and may have held the miserly attitude of Antimachus to be the proximate cause.

98. For an unduly pessimistic answer, arguing for a radically ironic view of the festivities that close the play, see Fisher 1993, 41–44.

99. Pickard-Cambridge 1988, 14–15, with discussion. There is also a reference to ἀγῶνες αὐτόθι οἱ Χύτρινοι καλούμενοι in Σ *Frogs* 218, in a statement attributed to Philochorus (328 F 57 Jacoby = passage 8 Pickard-Cambridge 1988, 4).

100. Slater 1990, 389 and n. 11; cf. also above, p. 28.

101. There are a number of other questions. Who determined which poet would enjoy the services of the winner of this contest? Presumably the contest winner was a valuable asset. Was he allowed to determine for which poet he would act? And what

about the rather short rehearsal time? There are only a few weeks between 13 Antheste-rion and the City Dionysia. The chorus presumably began rehearsing well before that. Were the actors brought in only at the last minute?

102. It may be objected that all the emphasis is on Choes and not Chutroi (though the latter is mentioned by Lamachus, 1076), but that is explained by the focus on the drinking contest, and Chutroi, on which drinking vessels from the day before were deposited in the shrine, is obviously closely connected. Pickard-Cambridge notes that the drinking, begun on Choes, seems to have continued past sundown, when the day of Chutroi technically started. One wonders if the ἀγῶνες χύτρινοι were in fact held after sunset on that evening.

103. Cf. Henderson 1990, 276–177 and passim, on "competitive displays for the *dêmos.*"

Chapter 4. The Politics of Performance: Knights

1. See Hubbard 1991, 70–71, and passim on role-playing in the play. Costas Pana-yotakis has suggested to me (personal communication) that sausage-sellers may be familiar stock figures from the subliterary mime even this early, although our evidence for this type in mime comes from a very late source, Choricius (*Apol. Mim.* 110). On Cleon, see MacDowell 1995, 80–83; more fully Lind 1990.

2. Edmunds 1987b, vii–viii, conveniently summarizes earlier views; cf. Reinders 1995.

3. See Sommerstein, *Knights* 3. Worthington 1990 discusses a Corinthian cup showing a masturbating Sphinx, previously identified by Brown 1974 as Cleon. Wor-thington identifies the other figure, over whom the Sphinx triumphs, as Demosthenes and sees the specific influence of the *Knights* on the Corinthian artist's representation. He also identifies another Cleon caricature in this group of cups. This suggests that Cleon was right to worry about how Aristophanes portrayed him in his plays!

4. Henderson, *Knights* introduction III, which he very kindly shared with me in draft.

5. Hubbard 1991, 64–66, on the use of language in this opening.

6. On the image of Demos as a character in the play, see Newiger 1957, 13–17 and 33–49.

7. Littlefield 1968, 10, notes that the wine helps transform him into "the efficient stage-manager of the drama."

8. One wonders if the Sausage-seller could actually be working the audience, sell-ing his wares as the play begins; this would certainly be an effective modern staging.

9. Neil *ad* 151 convincingly defends this meaning of ἀναβαίνω against the objec-tions of John Williams White and others; cf. Landfester 1967, 13 n. 9. An anonymous referee kindly called my attention to the force of καί in line 169, where Demosthenes asks the Sausage-seller: "Get up *also* on that table," (ἐπανάβηθι κἀπὶ τοὐλεὸν τοδί), implying that he is already on a raised surface. S/he also cites *Clouds* 1487, "getting up further onto the Thinkery" (ἐπαναβὰς ἐπὶ τὸ φροντιστήριον) and Thucydides 3.23.1, men climbing further up towers (ἐπαναβιβάσαντες).

10. As well as the harbors and the merchant ships (τἀμπόρια καὶ τὰς ὁλκάδας,

171). Hubbard 1991, 34, sees an allusion forward to Aristophanes' forthcoming *Merchant Ships* (Ὁλκάδες), often dated to the succeeding Lenaea of 423, in the conversation of ships in the so-called second parabasis of *Knights* (1300–1315). Could there also be another such allusion, especially in the actor's survey of them from a height, to Aristophanes' *Islands* (Νῆσοι) here? There was ancient doubt on the ascription of *Islands* to Aristophanes (apparently shared by Sommerstein: see his general introduction in the *Acharnians* volume), but K-A. accept it in *PCG*. It could conceivably have preceded *Knights*. It certainly displayed metatheatrical features as well, notably in fr. 403 K-A's reference to the chorus entering through the parodos: {A.} τί σὺ λέγεις; εἰσὶν δὲ ποῦ; / {B.} αἰδὶ κατ' αὐτὴν ἣν βλέπεις τὴν εἴσοδον. Someone comments, probably during this entrance, on the appearance of one of the islands: ὡς ἐς τὴν γῆν κύψασα κάτω καὶ ξυννενοφυῖα βαδίζει (fr. 410 K-A.). Cf. Wilson 1977.

11. Neil *ad* 169–70, with references, and Pickard-Cambridge 1962, 86–88. Cf. the story of Hippocleides (Herodotus 6. 129), Athenian suitor for the daughter of Cleisthenes of Sicyon, who "danced his marriage away." Having been chosen over all the other suitors for his ἀνδραγαθίη, he offended his prospective father-in-law by dancing at his marriage feast. The final straw was when Hippocleides called for a table to be brought, on which he performed. While Herodotus specifies that Hippocleides danced on a τράπεζα rather than an ἐλεός, there may nonetheless be a prototheatrical scene recognizable here, which of course exacerbated the offense.

12. He is a πονηρός (181) and descended from πονηρῶν (186). His momentary hesitation (182) worries Demosthenes, who thinks he might have something καλόν on his conscience (184; cf. Cairns 1993, 353), but is soon reassured.

13. The Sausage-seller is only marginally literate (188–189), which in part explains why he must be instructed in what the oracle says. Svenbro 1993, 193, suggests that to be poor at reading was to be resistant to the domination of others' texts, so this detail may foreshadow the Sausage-seller's role in leading Demos out of the position of dominated *eromenos*: see below, pp. 82–83.

14. Sommerstein's stage direction; cf. Neil *ad loc.* on οὑτοσί, although he thinks this means that Paphlagon is now visible inside the house from the stage, improbable in a theater as large as the Attic. For Cleon's right of *proedria*, cf. lines 575, 702–704.

15. Dover 1967 argues attractively that Aristophanes is suggesting Cleon's face was so hideous the prop-makers (σκευοποιῶν covers other stage props as well as masks) could not bear to look; Sommerstein *ad loc.* suggests political caution on Aristophanes' part. In any case, the setup allows Aristophanes to have his cake and eat it too: the audience is told in no uncertain terms that Paphlagon equals Cleon and gets a good laugh out of the fact that it is not a (potentially actionable) portrait.

16. Bowie 1993, 58ff., finds a deliberate emphasis on succession myths and gigantomachic motifs in the portrayal of Paphlagon. Such associations are certainly present, although perhaps not as systematic as Bowie believes. While the Sausage-seller is fated to succeed the three previous politicians, as Zeus succeeds Uranos and Cronos, the *Knights* does not end with the permanent ascendancy of the Sausage-seller but rather with the restoration of Demos.

17. Lines 299–302. See previous chapter, n. 28.

18. See Green 1985, 98–108, and Seeberg 1995, 7, on characterized *komoi* in the period before state sponsorship began in 484. It is possible, perhaps even likely, that

such early groups that went to the trouble of acquiring character or animal costumes would use them for more than one "performance." The pantomime Knights on Berlin F 1697 [= Green 1985, fig. 6] may represent a much larger tradition.

19. The cavalry seems to have been carrying the burden of the defense of the city and home territory at this period and thus presumably enjoyed public favor: Spence 1990, esp. 106–107, and 1993, 211–212, 215.

20. See Edmunds 1987a and 1987b, 5–16, for the tradition of this theme in political poetry.

21. Compare a similar joke about learning the dramas of Dionysius in Ephippus fr. 16 K-A.

22. As Paphlagon himself does, for his appeal to ὦ γέροντες ἡλιασταί at 255 is over the heads of the chorus to the audience—but it is unlikely to win him any sympathy.

23. Neil attributes both of these interjections to the chorus (also 451 and 453), while Sommerstein assigns them to Demosthenes. The decision is not easy: the use of κρέας as a term of address to the Sausage-seller in 421 is unusual but repeated in line 457, a line both Neil and Sommerstein give to the chorus. Uncertainties over the division of parts here contributes to problems in assessing Demosthenes' role. It is worth noting that the device being complimented at 421 is a theatrical one, however simple: the old gag of "look there: the first swallows of the season!" enables the Sausage-seller to distract some butchers long enough to steal their meat (cf. below, n. 43). Pickard-Cambridge 1962, 136, even sees the ghostly presence of the fruit-stealer of Epicharmean comedy hovering behind the Sausage-seller here. Perhaps Demosthenes is the right one to admire this technique.

24. Hubbard 1991, 23–33, including a review of earlier criticisms of the ritualists' views.

25. T. Bergk (quoted in PCG ad loc.) interprets Cratinus fr. 361b K-A. to be a chorus complaining about the works they have to sing: πάντα φορητά, πάντα τολμητὰ τῷδε τῷ χορῷ. This too implies an ongoing existence for the chorus.

26. Winkler's view (1985 and 1990) that the tragic choristers were ephebes remains very intriguing but has no bearing on the comic choruses.

27. Bowie 1993. 63–64.

28. See Σ Knights 537 on Crates, who is probably dead but may simply no longer be composing, and Slater 1996. Aristophanes may also have alluded to Cratinus as an old-fashioned poet, suitable only for the symposium, at Acharnians 850: Neri 1997.

29. See Winkler 1990, 37–42, on seating and its political significance in the theater.

30. The chorus has criticized the whole present generation of political leadership for striving after such honors as προεδρία at line 575. Neil ad 703–4 cites Alexis fr. 42 K-A., indicating that those outside the citizen body sat at the edge of the theater: ἐνταῦθα περὶ τὴν ἐσχάτην δεῖ κερκίδα / ὑμᾶς καθιζούσας θεωρεῖν ὡς ξένας. Pickard-Cambridge 1988, 268–270, discusses seating. Conceivably the Sausage-seller is even expressing the wish here that Paphlagon be deprived of his citizen rights and thereby banished to the outer limits of the theater.

31. Sommerstein ad loc. argues for the existence of this rock and against the use of the ekkyklema in the staging of this judgment scene. An anonymous referee notes that the deictic at 754 ("on this rock," ἐπὶ ταυτησὶ ... τῆς πέτρας) clearly shows that something represented the Pnyx here.

32. Henderson 1990, 286 and passim; cf. Ober 1989, 152–155.

33. The parabasis of this play *is* the primary evidence for such circulation: i.e., the success Cratinus's song had on the private symposium circuit (lines 526–530); cf. further Slater 1996, and for tragic songs, Lai 1997. We learn from Σ *Knights* 973 that the opening of this chorus parodies Euripides, but no particular play is specified, and parody would not exclude the attempt to create a popular and repeatable song. George Robertson has suggested to me (personal communication) that there may be an echo of Simonides' epigram for the base of the tyrrancides' statues (Page, *Epigrammata Graeca* 1 = *CEG* 430), which uses the image of light in a similar way: ἦ μέγ᾽ Ἀθηναίοισι φόως γένεθ᾽, ἡνίκ᾽ Ἀριστογείτων Ἵππαρχον κτεῖνε καὶ Ἁρμόδιος.

34. A similar, much briefer oracle contest takes place in the *Birds*. See below, pp. 140–41, where I argue it is much clearer that the audience is meant to understand that Peisetaerus is making up his oracles on the spot to counter those of the oracle-monger.

35. It is beyond our scope here to reopen the vexed questions of the origins of comedy, but ritual insult does seem a plausible origin for some elements of comedy: Pickard-Cambridge 1962, 144–147 and passim. Cf. the so-called Fescennine verses in the tradition of Roman comedy: Duckworth 1952, 7–8.

36. In fact, both reeducation and old-age supervision: γεροντἀγωγεῖν κἀναπαιδεύειν πάλιν, 1099; see Landfester 1967, 66–68. Demos paradoxically portrays himself as both too old and too young to look after himself, a passivity of which he must be cured. The verb γεροντἀγωγεῖν is sufficiently rare that Brock 1991, 161 n. 4, suggests it too, like the image of Paphlagon as a lover of Demos, parodies a remark of Cleon.

37. On this scene and its importance for the whole structure of the play see now Reinders 1995, with exhaustive review of previous discussions. While he is correct to insist (esp. p. 17) that the scene does criticize Demos and makes the contrast with the rejuvenated Demos of the play's end meaningful, I suggest that criticism is couched in a way that carefully differentiates Demos from his role-playing servants.

38. In discussion following a version of this chapter in Leeds, it was suggested to me that there may be a pun on Demos's name in the chorus's final accusation, ὁ νοῦς δέ σου / παρὼν ἀποδημεῖ (1119–1120): i.e., that sense has wandered away from the body of the demos. It is an intriguing suggestion, especially in light of Aristophanes' immediately preceding use of the image of the public gaping in awe at the speakers who deceive them, but we cannot be certain.

39. The verb ἡλιθιάζω is not that common. Cratinus fr. 200 K-A. from the *Wine-flask* offers an interesting but unfortunately corrupt parallel, where Cratinus, presumably speaking *in propria persona*, acknowledges τῆς †ἡλιθιότητος τῆς ἐμῆς. Second childhood images include the references to his readiness for "reeducation" at 1099 and later to the two "lovers" (ἐραστῶν, 1163) competing for him—which implies that he, Demos, is the "beloved" and therefore younger partner in the relationship.

40. The imagery of forced vomiting (1148, ἐξεμεῖν) has made Neil *ad loc.* and others think of *Acharnians* 6 (see above, pp. 44–45). Here (and in line 404) the focus seems more on Cleon's future fate than on what has already happened to him, but the image was obviously one Aristophanes liked.

41. Brock 1986, 25; cf. the detailed study of the Old Oligarch in Henderson 1990.

42. Although we should not exaggerate the effects of the seige on all Athenians outside the city walls: Spence 1990.

43. Landfester 1967, 73–74, finds the gift of a hare typically erotic (though also a noteworthy delicacy at *Acharnians* 1110): this picks up a sequence of imagery going back at least to 732, when Paphlagon declares himself Demos's lover (ὦ Δῆμ᾽, ἐραστής τ᾽ εἰμὶ σός), and concluding at 1341, when Demos finally repudiates this subordinate role. One of the best points for Bowie 1993 in arguing for an interpretation of the Sausage-seller as an ephebic figure in this play is his use of this trick (p. 55): "Especially noteworthy in the context of the ephebe are the two occasions on which the Sausage-Seller employs the same 'Look behind you' trick that brought Melanthus victory in the Apaturia myth." Bowie is quite right to point out that the Sausage-seller is often cast as an ephebic figure. It is worth noting, however, that the use of the trick here to steal the hare's meat is not decisive: the appeal to Demos to examine the baskets (and thereby see for himself what a thief Paphlagon) is what seals the final victory. On theft of food, cf. Wilkins 1997, 260–261.

44. Greenblatt 1980, 228.

45. In fact, the audience has only seen and heard the part of the oracle foretelling the coming of a sausage-seller (195–212). Paphlagon asks the Sausage-seller four questions (1232–1246), the third of which is "what trade did you take up?" His reaction shows that this is the decisive question. Few in the audience will remember, and none will care, that we have not seen the Sausage-seller instructed in the other answers. We simply assume that he somehow learned them from the stolen oracle.

46. *Pace* Neil, Paphlagon is certainly carried in on the *ekkyklema* at the end of this speech: see Sommerstein *ad loc.*

47. *Alcestis* 181–182: σὲ δ᾽ ἄλλη τις γυνὴ κεκτήσεται, / σώφρων μὲν οὐκ ἂν μᾶλλον, εὐτυχὴς δ᾽ ἴσως.

48. One can surmise he found the public response to *Alcestis* rather excessive, but he must in fact rely on the strength of that response in order for his joke to have punch. *Alcestis* was presented in 438, along with Aristophanes' favorite Euripidean target, the *Telephus*, and so like it clearly remained surprisingly fresh in the audience's memory. Landfester 1967, 26 and 75–78, also detects an imitation of Sophocles' *Oedipus Tyrannus* in Paphlagon's downfall as foretold by the oracle, wherein reversal and recognition coincide in the best Aristotelian fashion. Landfester does note, however, that Paphlagon is really the Sphinx in this imitation, and Agoracritus more of an Oedipus figure. Sophocles may well be the deep structure here, but the parody is focused by the quotation on Euripides and Cleon alike.

49. Landfester 1967, 98–100, argues the audience is meant to hear positive associations ("chosen by the people") here as well.

50. Brock 1986, 23, compares the false endings in Sophocles.

51. Landfester 1967, 24: "Gesucht wird nicht ein rechter oder schlecter Demagoge, sondern ein Demos, der keines Demagogen bedarf." Cf. also Bowie 1993, 77, acknowledging the limits of his ephebic interpretation of the play's action: "The ephebic mythos is ultimately not one that offers a practical solution to the problem of politicians whose nature one does not approve of."

52. Totaro 1999, 40–47.

53. Hubbard 1991, 34, suggests this may be, among other things, an advertisement of the "coming attraction" of Aristophanes' forthcoming play, *Merchant Ships* (Ὁλκάδες). See above, n. 10.

54. Edmunds 1987a, 256 [= 1987b, 43], thinks Demos has simply undergone cosmetic changes, but Olson 1990 argues persuasively that the rejuvenation is meant to be "real."

55. See Sommerstein *ad loc.* Aristophanes thus claims the *ekkyklema* for the comic theater in its own right, not just as a parody of tragic usage.

56. He has been changed from an old man not into an adolescent but into a fully active, self-controlled *adult* citizen. He is no longer the passive object of the erotic attentions of the politicians but himself the active lover, as is marked not only by his acquisition of the female embodiments of the thirty-year peace treaties (see below), but also by the gift of the boy who can both carry his campstool and be the properly passive object of Demos's active homosexual attentions:

{Ἀλ.} ἔχε νυν ἐπὶ τούτοις τουτονὶ τὸν ὀκλαδίαν
καὶ παῖδ᾽ ἐνόρχην, ὅσπερ οἴσει τόνδε σοι·
κἄν που δοκῇ σοι, τοῦτον ὀκλαδίαν πόει.   (1384–1386)

On these erotic themes, see Landfester 1967, 50–55 and 103–104. An example of such a boy with a stool appears on an amphora by Exekias, *ABV* 145. 13 (Vatican 344), a reference I owe to Professor Anne Mackay.

57. Cairns 1993, 352, on this convention for the expression of shame.

58. Lind 1990, 172–184, argues that Aristophanes alludes specifically to the area of the Cerameicus and the Dipylon Gate. See Bennett and Tyrrell 1990 on the the scapegoat theme here. Schmitt Pantel 1992, 225–226, notes the opposition between the Prytaneum, the center of order where Paphlagon used to dine, and this marginal realm of sexual license and distance from the city center. Note also that Agoracritus will take over the seat once held by Paphlagon: εἰς τὴν ἕδραν, 1405; *Σ Knights* 1405 explains: εἰς τὴν προεδρίαν.

59. Sommerstein *ad loc.*

60. Landfester 1977, 62: "so gibt es doch auch schon außerhalb dieser Szenen entsprechende Andeutungen, die, *freilich nur wenn man den Schluß kennt*, die Doppelfunktion des Wursthändlers deutlich erkennen lassen" (emphasis mine). These indications include the praise of the Sausage-seller as savior of the city (457ff.). See also Kraus 1985, 190 n. 265, who points to the Sausage-seller's claim at 903 that Athena ordered him to vanquish Paphlagon.

61. εἰς τοὺς ἀγρούς, 1394; cf. the reference in 805. Spence 1990, 92, suggests that use of the cavalry as a mobile defense force had in fact greatly lessened the impact of the annual invasions on the Athenians.

62. E.g., Carey 1993.

Chapter 5. Bringing Up Father: Wasps

A previous version of this chapter appeared as "Bringing Up Father: *Paideia* and *Ephebeia* in the *Wasps*," *Nottingham Classical Literature Studies* 4 (1996): 27–52. Reprinted by permission.

1. Hubbard 1991, 126, discusses intertextual reinforcement of this division: the

first part of the play recycles elements of *Babylonians*, *Acharnians*, and *Knights*, while the second half attempts to improve on *Clouds*.

2. They may even be nodding during the first few lines (Borthwick 1992), a sequence of physical comedy that could begin well before the lines themselves.

3. Note the surprisingly modern interpretation given, however. When Sosias tells Xanthias not to worry, insisting the dream portends nothing δεινόν, Xanthias replies δεινόν γέ πού 'στ' ἄνθρωπος ἀποβαλὼν ὅπλα (27), the pun on ὅπλα playing on castration anxiety. Cf. Reckford 1987, 221–222; Brillante 1987.

4. The figure simply indicates a minimal payment (for a minimally valuable service): MacDowell *ad loc*. Does it allude to the recent increase in jury pay from two to three obols, a measure authored by Cleon? The pay is clearly set at three obols by the time of *Wasps*: see below, lines 788–791. The increase may come soon after *Knights*, since *Knights* 798 suggests a proposal to raise the jurors' pay (there outlandishly to five obols) is in the air.

5. Like the politician that he is, Aristophanes always seeks out the middle ground. The strategy is to isolate other poets and other audiences on the fringes, either too high-brow or too low-brow; compare *Clouds* 537–562 and *Peace* 748–750.

6. The distribution of parts is much disputed here. I follow MacDowell, though Sommerstein's arrangement has much to commend it, too (notably no need to postulate a lacuna after 76, as MacDowell must). The basic dynamic of the scene (one slave reports audience comments, the other responds) is clear, whatever the part distribution.

7. It indeed increases the joke, if those whose comments Sosias claims to report were known to be seated in the *proedria*. In the present state of the Theater of Dionysus, with its Roman semicircular orchestra, the actor playing Sosias would have time to walk only about half of the orchestra edge on the lines, according to my own attempts (see chapter 3 n. 18 on *Acharnians* above), but that is ample time to establish the effect, and the original staging was probably more varied than a simple curved walk.

8. Boegehold 1995, 28–29, and illus. 1, reconstructs a κημός.

9. A century before this, one can find a cup describing itself as *kalos* (on *ABV* 162.1): ΚΑΛΟΝ ΕΙΜΙ ΠΟΤΕΡΙΟΝ. A wonderfully self-conscious red-figure cup by Apollodorus, *ARV*² 120, 12 (see "Addenda I," p. 1627), shows two cups within a symposium scene, one inscribed ΚΑΛΟΣ, the other ΚΑΛΟΝ, as does a cantharus shown on his *ARV*² 121, 22 [Florence 4211]. By Aristophanes' time, however, a *kalos* inscription is unambiguously erotic. Is there then a sexual (i.e., anal) connotation to κημός? Henderson 1975 records none, and indeed a *kalos* inscription referring to a body part certainly is not easy to find. The unattributed cup Villa Guilia 50404 (*ARV*² 1565), illustrated in L. Deubner, *Attische Feste* (Berlin 1877) pl. 4,1, shows a large standing phallus, inscribed ΚΑΛΗ. Martin Kilmer, who kindly called my attention to this vase, reports the suggestion of Eric Csapo that this feminine form might be meant to be understood with ψωλή (Kilmer 1993, 217, and his illustration R607). The inscription ΨΟΛΩΝ appears on a bell crater, *ARV*² 1607; Shapiro 1987, 117 n. 37, takes this to be a satyr name. A satyr named ΦΣΟΛΑΣ (for Ψωλάς) appears on an aryballos, *ABV* 83.4. If κημὸς καλός, were understood to be obscene, one would not be surprised to find no record of it in vase painting.

10. Demos (*PA* 3573), son of Pyrilampes; Sommerstein *ad loc*. No *kalos* inscrip-

tions are recorded on vases for this individual in *ARV* ^{2}. On the other hand, *kalos* inscriptions become quite rare after about 440 B.C. (Shapiro 1987, 117 and n. 37, notes a handful of examples); Philocleon may be showing how old-fashioned he is by writing a *kalos* inscription at all. Sommerstein's translation of 98 is slightly misleading: we are not to understand that the original graffito contained the patronymic, for while Shapiro 1987 gives examples of this rare form of *kalos* inscription, it had surely disappeared by the time of *Wasps*. On the dynamics of *kalos* inscriptions, see now Slater 1999; Lissarague 1999.

    11. Cleon's divisive role in Athens emerges in an earlier pun on the word *demos*. The sea monster in Sosias's dream was dividing and weighing out fat (δημόν . . . βούλεται διστάναι, 40), interpreted as dividing the people (δῆμον, 41, simply a change of accent); cf. *Knights* 954, also a charge of dividing the people (818).

    12. The visual comedy of this is obvious; the joke that follows seems rather feeble by contrast. When Bdelycleon defeats his father's attempt to escape via the chimney, he laments that people will now call him the "son of old Smoky" (Καπνίου κεκλήσομαι, 151). Sommerstein *ad loc.* and others interpret Καπνίας as a general nickname for a boastful fellow; why this should be particularly humorous at this point is hard to see. The scholia tell us that Καπνίας could be applied to wine that was clouded or turning and go on to note that this was the nickname of the (probably recently deceased) comic playwright Ecphantides. Perhaps this is more than irrelevant erudition from the scholiast: the patronymic here in *Wasps* may be Aristophanes' nod to a comic predecessor. At this point in his career he is very concerned to reestablish his credentials as a popular comedian after the failure of *Clouds* the year before (cf. lines 65–66); also, he is more likely to refer favorably to a comic poet who is now dead and therefore no longer a competitor (cf. the praises of Magnes and Crates in *Knights* 514–540). Cratinus's quotation of one of the older poet's songs in fr. 361a K-A. (= Ecphantides fr. 4 K-A.) suggests that Ecphantides was still popular and therefore worth Aristophanes associating himself with. Sommerstein cites Wilson 1973 on the dates of Ecphantides, wherein Wilson suggests that the playwright referred to in I.G. Urb. Rom. 216. 1–6 [= Callias test. 4 *PCG*; Mette 1977, VI A 2.1–6], no part of whose name survives in the inscription, might not be Callias but rather Ecphantides, on the grounds that Ecphantides was the only known author of a play called Σάτυροι which could have been produced in 437 B.C., the date given in this inscription. The traditional ascription relies on the fact that Callias is known to be the author of a Κύκλωπες, the play title partially preserved in line one of this entry in the inscription. If Wilson is right about Σάτυροι, however, Ecphantides was also then the author of a play called Κύκλωπες. Aristophanes' mention of "old Smoky" may indicate that some elements of the Odysseus parody here in *Wasps* allude to Ecphantides' Κύκλωπες.

    13. Scenes of Odysseus clinging to a ram are popular in black-figure vase painting (e.g., *ABV* 528, 38, London, British Museum B 502 = Boardman 1974, fig. 255), rarer in red-figure (Boardman 1975, 233), but were doubtless still familiar to Athenian audiences, perhaps in other media. The parody with the ass may not be merely ridiculous but also obscene. The ass in vase painting (especially the Return of Hephaestus) often has a disproportionately large phallus, and Philocleon may resemble a phallus in the initial stage picture. If so, there is even more when he is separated from the ass: the ass becomes female, and he becomes its foal (188–189). Davidson 1997, 140, briefly

labels the Odysseus parody "obscene" but does not explain how he visualizes it; other commentators focus only on the foal image.

14. Aristophanes uses this kind of obvious comedy of the elderly elsewhere: fr. 591 K-A., 93: ἐλαφρὸν οἶά τις μόλυβδος, referring to a chorus of old men (γερόντων ὁ χορός), possibly in his play Γῆρας.

15. The chorus, with the young leading the old, also points forward to the play's central theme of education: see Long 1976 and Lenz 1980, 32–35.

16. MacDowell ad 302.

17. Cf. the same theme in the aria "A Tenor All Singers Above" in Gilbert and Sullivan's Utopia Ltd., where the tenor lead insists his real emotions prevent him from singing his high notes. Philocleon follows up here with a request to the chorus not to shout (μὴ βοᾶτε, 336, 371) and wake his son, suggesting that the chorus are singing at the top of their voices, rather like the chorus of Pirates singing "With Catlike Tread" in Pirates of Penzance.

18. Sommerstein ad loc. on these movements. MacDowell ad 395 is also reminded of the Major General's "I thought I heard a noise."

19. The consensus of opinion now seems to hold that these stings are secured to their posteriors and therefore separate from the phalloi which the actors also wear. It is somewhat unclear how they then manoeuver and attack, as they probably do not charge backward. Perhaps the stings are flexibly mounted and can be bent forward for these attacks.

20. This scene, like that in Peace (see below, pp. 121–22), demonstrates that the stage of the fifth century must have been low enough to make this assault seem plausible.

21. The noun ekkyklema does not occur in Aristophanes; rather, its operation is indicated by verbs using the κυλίνδ- root. See above, chapter 1, pp. 17–18. LSJ cite this line and Plato, Phaedrus 275e s.v. κυλίνδω for the meaning "bandy about." The root meaning, however, may be more active in the Phaedrus passage than LSJ allow: Socrates says that once something is written down, it can "roll around" everywhere, out of the original author's control. A pun on the book roll used for writing seems likely here.

22. Father and son agree to make "these men" (τούτοισί γ', 521) judges between them, which Σ Wasps 521 glosses as τοῖς θεαταῖς. Sommerstein ad loc. takes this to mean just the chorus, but the legal framework already implies a jury, which like the audience in the democracy represents the demos as a whole.

23. See MacDowell ad 538 on the middle form γράψομαι, although he takes the probabilities to lie in the other direction; cf. Stanford ad Frogs 151, citing Tucker on the force of the middle in ἐξεγράψατο. MacDowell ad 559 thinks Bdelycleon writes "with a flourish," but I take the imperative ἔστω to be directed to the slave. Reckford 1987, 247–248, thinks the technology of writing is meant to seem new and comic here.

24. Fig. 76 in Pickard-Cambridge 1988, 210, dating it c. 420 B.C.; Csapo and Slater 1995, pl. 4B. Richard Green (personal communication) has made the excellent point that some if not all of the proedria in the fifth-century theater would have been wooden chairs, rather than the stone ones preserved today. Thus the vase could portray the actual performance rather than a rehearsal. One spectator looks rather young to be

honored with official proedria, pointing toward a rehearsal situation, but both possibilities should be borne in mind.

25. A forensic association is not ruled out, but the evidence for note-taking at trials is considerably later than the 420s (e.g., Demosthenes 46.11; cf. Boegehold 1991, 169). There was considerable emphasis on speeches appearing spontaneous and unrehearsed. Olson 1995, 144, argues the note-taking characterizes Bdelycleon "as a writer," thus identifying him (and his point of view) with Aristophanes. Bdelycleon, however, *fails* as a writer. I suggest the visual picture here emphasizes Philocleon as a performer, whose performance is to be critiqued by his son.

26. To my knowledge no one (not even Goldhill 1994, 357–360, a ferocious assault on the notion that women could appear in court) has questioned the historicity of this description of an Athenian trial, although given elite Athenian notions about protecting women from the public gaze (their names are normally not mentioned in court, but indicated only by periphrasis, for example) it seems rather extraordinary that a man would drag his daughters into court for these appeals to pity, thereby exposing them to the lascivious gaze of such as Philocleon. Goldhill rightly notes that the text of the *In Neairam* and the doubtful anecdotes about the courtesan Phryne appearing in court are no evidence for whether women of the citizen class would appear. None of the parallels cited by Sommerstein *ad* 568 from the Attic orators indicates the introduction of female children into court. [Lys.] 20.34, Andoc. 1.148, and Dem. 21.188 all speak of παῖδας, Dem. 21.99 of παιδία. The [Lysias] passage specifically deals with the children inheriting their father's ἀτιμία, so these must be male children. In Plato *Apol.* 34d, Socrates considers bringing in his three sons, one of whom is a μειράκιον, the other two παιδία; παιδία can therefore certainly be used of very young sons. Perhaps Philocleon's description of his voyeurism in court is meant to shock. For an exemplary modern account of a fifth century trial, see Boegehold 1995, 23–30.

27. [Xen.] *Ath. Pol.* 2.18.

28. Recorded in I.G. *Urb. Rom.* 216.8 [= Mette 1977, VI A 2,8]. Cf. the use of the term and its appeal in *Eccl.* 631, on which see p. 219 below. I do not see the basis for Kaibel's interpretation of this title (recorded in *PCG* s.v.).

29. There may be more of a problem here than either MacDowell or Sommerstein acknowledge. Strictly speaking, the *dokimasia* was not a function of the jury courts. Accusations of improper registration would indeed go to the courts on appeal, but the deme was the first venue of determination. Aristophanes may be more concerned to portray Philocleon as lascivious here (cf. the interest of Right Argument in boys' genitals at *Clouds* 973–978), or he may be subtly suggesting that Philocleon has confused the pleasures of a deme assembly with those of the courts.

30. MacDowell's view *ad loc.*

31. Plays may have been reperformed at the theater in the Peiraeus at this period. I doubt the existence of a touring circuit for plays at the Rural Dionysia as early as the 420s. See above, chapter 1, n. 2.

32. On symposium and theater cf. Mastromarco 1983, 36, citing Socrates' characterization of theater as a "great symposium."

33. Taplin 1993, 67–78, 105–110, questions the strict division between the male αὐλητής of public performance and the female αὐλητρίς of the private symposium.

Even if there are exceptions later or in Magna Graecia, at the time of *Wasps*, a flute-player performing an ἔξοδος would surely be associated in the public mind with festival performance.

34. Cf. Cratinus fr. 308 K-A.: τοὺς ἐξοδίους ὑμῖν ἵν᾽ αὐλῶ τοὺς νόμους, and the comments of Taplin 1993. 108.

35. Stockton 1990, 11, finds his figures suspiciously round but not wildly inaccurate.

36. On comedy and envy, see Carey 1994, 73–74.

37. Rau 1967, 152–155. Cf. Taplin 1972, 97 n. 123. There is real pathos as well as parody here, however: Reckford 1987, 249–250.

38. 750, ἰώ μοί μοι. = *Alc.* 862; 752–753, esp. κείνων ἔραμαι = *Alc.* 866–867. Although the plays are two years apart, it seems worth noting that Philocleon here acts out his eponymous "love" for Cleon, playing Admetus to Cleon / Paphlagon's dying Alcestis in his exit from *Knights* at 1248–1252. In a quite different vein, Bowie 1987, 114–115 and n. 16, suggests that Philocleon's disease shares a number of symptoms with the λυκάνθρωπος νόσος, including the fact that "the sufferers abandon their homes to spend the night amongst tombs."

39. Crane 1997, 218, underscores the opposition between Bdelycleon's views and those of Solon. Solon said (fr. 1 West) that the private citizen could not keep public troubles out of his *oikos*, while Bdelycleon thinks he can live best by keeping his father confined to the *oikos*, away from public space. Philocleon suffers from the opposite confusion: he thinks of the public courts as his private space. Crane 1997, 220, suggests that the old man's wish to be buried under the railings of the lawcourt, if he fails (line 386), treats the courts as his family tombs!

40. Nozick 1974, 42–45.

41. Note, though, that the protagonist of Ray Bradbury's short story, "The Happiness Machine," reaches the same conclusion as Nozick.

42. νέαισιν ἀρχαῖς, 886. The word ἀρχή means both "beginning" and "rule, government." MacDowell *ad loc.* rightly translates it here as government: Bdelycleon, like Peisetaerus a decade later in the *Birds*, is creating a new political order, here in miniature. Cf. Philocleon's "μεγάλη . . . ἀρχή" (575).

43. Noted already by Russo 1994, 128 (Italian original 1962), and Reckford 1987, 252.

44. MacDowell *ad* 240 has a full account of Laches. MacDowell 1995, 168, argues that no trial of Laches for embezzlement actually took place, because Cleon was discouraged by the parody in *Wasps*.

45. Taillardat 1962, 403–406.

46. Cf. (to Labes) ἀνάβαιν᾽, 944; *Knights* 149–150. The Theater of Dionysus also functioned as a lawcourt at times: Boegehold 1995, 24.

47. If there were only three speaking actors available in comedy (the standard view), the silence of Labes makes a joke of the fact that there is no speaking actor to play him. MacDowell 1994 argues for four actors in Aristophanes' plays. For *Wasps* his argument turns on identifying the speaking boy of 230ff. as a regular actor and on the impossibly quick change in 1412–1416 from bread-seller to accuser; contra, Marshall 1997.

48. Here the puppies are referred to as παιδία, one of the two usual terms in the orators; see n. 26, above.

49. Although the imperative κατάβα is singular, I take it to be directed to the puppies as well, since Bdelycleon has just ordered them to step up (ἀναβαίνετ᾽, 977), either with him on the speaker's platform or next to their father. We have no real resource but speculation here. Clearly all that is required for both Dog and Labes are dog masks and a furry costume. Puppies played by child performers in small masks and costumes would be a superbly funny stage effect, and so I assume its existence, although possibly the puppies were meant to be imaginary. If there was no speaker's platform on the stage, then Labes need not vacate center stage, and Bdelycleon can simply take his position beside him. The puppies can enter quickly from the *skene* when needed and crowd around the central pair.

50. On uproar in the courts, see Hall 1995, esp. 44, with ample ancient evidence.

51. Cairns 1993, 352, on the parody of the language of conscience here.

52. Hubbard 1991, 114, 132–134 (cf. now also Olson 1995), identifies Bdelycleon structurally with Aristophanes as a creator of theater, but I think it unlikely that Aristophanes wishes us to identify him closely with a *failed* dramatist such as Bdelycleon proves to be. More nuanced is the view of Reckford 1987, 252–274, of Labes' trial as "play therapy," designed to cure the old man, but he also sees the ambiguities and the painful nature of the deception Bdelycleon inflicts on his father.

53. 1010, ὦ μυριάδες ἀναρίθμητοι. The phrase is traditional, appearing in Plato *Laws* 804e, but tradition alone does not explain its use here. It helps soften the audience up for the criticism of their judgment to follow.

54. Reconstructing the exact mechanism is problematic: see Csapo and Slater 1995, 157–165. The claim of Aelian, *Varia Historia* 2. 13 that the judges went against vociferous audience acclaim for the first performance of *Clouds* is not believable.

55. Appeal to the judges: *Eccl.* 1154ff., Pherecrates fr. 102 K-A.; *Birds* 445–447 is more oblique. Plato *Laws* 659a shows that the audience tried to make its opinion known; cf. Pickard-Cambridge 1988, 95–98. Attacking the judges could well have been seen as sour grapes and possibly even antidemocratic.

56. The principal controversy is whether 1018–1029 describes a career of two or three phases. Two are clear: one in which his plays are produced by Callistratus (*Banqueters* through *Acharnians*) and another, beginning with *Knights*, which he produced in his own name. The question is whether there was an additional earlier phase, in which he contributed parts to others' comedies, as argued by Halliwell 1980 and 1989 and Sommerstein *ad loc.*; contra MacDowell 1982b. The three-phase view seems preferable.

57. Rogers *ad loc.*, citing Florent Chretien, notes the parallel to the verses sung at Spartan festivals, given in Plutarch, *Lyc.* 21. First the old men sang. Responses were then given first by a chorus of young men, then one of boys. The point of such an echo, if intended by Aristophanes, would certainly not be its Spartan associations, but the sense of calling forth a response from the next generation—which is twisted satirically by the Wasps' formidable attack on the younger generation at 1068ff.

58. Bowie 1987; Bowie 1993, 78–101.

59. Bowie 1993, 101: "At the start of the play, Philocleon was a mixture of human

and animal, mature juror and cunning ephebe, and so he remains at the end: his youthful disregard for the courts is as disordered, from the city's point of view, as his earlier obsession with them. The reversed rite of passage may have changed external features, but his basic nature appears to be unaffected." Cf. Bowie 1987, 125.

60. Bowie 1987, esp. 122–123; Bowie 1993, 48–49, 93–95.

61. Foley 1985, 223–225, with some other examples from tragedy. MacDowell *ad* 1122, 1134 notes that the τρίβων' is Philocleon's only garment; when he takes it off, he is stripped "naked," that is, down to his comic padding and phallus.

62. "Laconian shoes" were a well-known style in Athens, so the joke is very much a verbal one: as MacDowell *ad* 1159 suggests, this is as if a Cambridge man refused to wear "Oxfords." Thus, while Bowie 1987, 122, may be right on a deep structural level about the ephebic significance of this "foreign" dress (both Persian and Spartan), the audience would not necessarily perceive his new costume as "the opposite of the adult garb of the city" but simply as the equivalent of a fashionable and very expensive Italian suit today.

63. See below, p. 211, on σχῆμα at *Eccl.* 150.

64. MacDowell *ad* 1173 acutely suggests that "these antics can continue *ad lib.*, as long as the audience is laughing." A good physical comedian could build this into an extended routine. I wonder if Bdelycleon's reply at line 1172 does not in fact reflect a "generalized" text. In performance, Philocleon could do a number of exaggerated walks, with Bdelycleon identifying each as that of a particular individual. Finally, I do not share MacDowell and Sommerstein's confidence that the boil is imagined to be on Philocleon's foot.

65. And class identification: see Rothwell 1995, 244–253, for evidence that Philocleon's fondness for coarse myth and Aesopic fables strongly associates him with the lower classes.

66. See Konstan 1995, 23–28, more generally on themes of class in the play; he sees these tensions as unresolved at the play's end, but see below for a more optimistic interpretation. Davidson 1997, 233 and passim, suggests Aristophanes had democratic ideological motivations to blur or efface class distinctions.

67. The figure is low even by contemporary standards. Rosivach 1985 is a fascinating study of staffing the Athenian fleet in just this period. He argues persuasively for a smaller, year-round cohort of rowers paid a drachma a day and a larger group of rowers in the summer fleet, composed primarily of farmers who earned only three obols. Line 1189 suggests the fee was lower when Philocleon was young. More importantly, if Philocleon was a summer rower, he was likely a farmer as well: we therefore have here a country-city tension between the generations similar to that in *Clouds*. For hostility to ambassadors, see Sommerstein 1996. 328.

68. For Phanus, cf. *Knights* 1256. Theorus is one of the performing politicians exposed by Dicaeopolis in *Acharnians* 134ff.

69. Not genuinely aristocratic company in any case: Rothwell 1995, 249–250.

70. Cf. above, n. 32 and chapter 4, n. 33. Both tragic and comic poetry could be performed there. For performance of Euripides and Aeschylus, see *Clouds* 1351–1378 (cf. Lai 1997).

71. Both Antiphanes fr. 85 K-A. and Aristophanes fr. 444 K-A. refer to the Har-

modius song, which Aristophanes parodies here, and the latter to the Admetus song as well:

ὁ μὲν ᾖδεν Ἀδμήτου λόγον πρὸς μυρρίνην,
ὁ δ᾽ αὐτὸν ἠνάγκαζεν Ἁρμοδίου μέλος.

On the Admetus *skolion*, see Scodel 1979. The process of learning to sing *skolia* properly seems also to have been represented in Aristophanes' *Banqueters*: see fr. 235 K.-A. Cf. also Redondo 1993.

72. Lissarrague 1990b, 128–129 and fig. 99, discusses a cup of the Brygos painter, showing a young symposiast holding the myrtle bough and singing (Florence 3949; *CVA* 3, pl. 91).

73. This may be part of the class distinction theme as well: Philocleon has heretofore lived a simple life with no time for the indulgences of upper-class drinking parties. Vaio 1971, 339, calls attention to this distinction in the opening sequence of the play: in the guessing game "what disease does Philocleon suffer from?" Sosias hears a suggestion in the audience that the old man is a heavy drinker (φιλοπότης, 79), but he denies this, saying that drinking is a disease of the upper classes (χρηστῶν . . . ἀνδρῶν, 80).

74. The audience has just seen is a metatheatrical version of a symposium: a rehearsal in advance of the actual symposium performance offstage. Philocleon is being rehearsed in a part just as much as is the Old Relative in *Thesmophoriazusae* or all the women in *Ecclesiazusae*.

75. Hubbard 1991, 138 n. 54.

76. See MacDowell and Sommerstein *ad* 1284–91. Welsh 1990 and 1992 suggests the reference to Cleon at the end of *Knights*, while Storey 1995 (now followed by Totaro 1999, 179–195) thinks *Clouds* 575–594 was the proximate cause.

77. There may be one more fillip: Aristophanes' defiant boast comes just after he *has* put Cleon on stage in the person of Bdelycleon's performance of him at a symposium.

78. One insult has a particularly theatrical ring: he compared a fellow guest to the tragedian Sthenelus, τὰ σκευάρια διακεκαρμένῳ (1313). The scholiast identifies him here as an actor who had to sell his σκευάρια through poverty. He is later known to be a tragedian: see Aristophanes fr. 158 K.-A. and Plato Comicus fr. 136 K.-A., from the interestingly named play Σκευαί. Sommerstein *ad loc.* notes that this passage in *Wasps* is the earliest reference to Sthenelus, with most falling in the period 410–400. Perhaps this reference alludes, not to poverty (for it seems unlikely though not impossible for an actor to have accumulated sufficient costumes and props of his own to be worth selling), but to his change from performer to writer.

79. Crichton 1993, 68, sees this as a re-creation of the household. Philocleon demonstrates the truth of the joke that grandparents and grandchildren get along so well with each other because they have a common enemy.

80. Another intertextual replay of *Clouds* within *Wasps* (Hubbard 1991, 135), although note that in *Clouds* this shocking violence happens offstage: we do not actually see Pheidippides strike his father. *Wasps* gives us the actual knockabout spectacle, inverted. Kraut 1988 suggests another connection with *Clouds*: the witness summoned

by the bread-seller is Chaerephon (1408), who may well have appeared in the first version of the play. It is rare for a summons-witness to be given a personal name in Aristophanes, and Kraut suggests Aristophanes is recalling a successful comic effect from the previous play.

81. MacDowell *ad* 1450; cf. Henderson 1975, 82.

82. Sommerstein *ad* 1467.

83. Vaio 1971, MacCary 1979, Bowie 1987 and 1993, 78–101.

84. Including the suggestion that the slaves in the prologue have been drinking and therefore indulging in a "servile symposium": Vaio 1971, 338.

85. MacCary 1979, 138–142; cf. Zimmermann 1985a, 82–84.

86. MacCary 1979, 146.

87. The same five lines close *Alcestis*, *Andromache*, and *Helen*.

88. Winkler 1985 and 1990.

89. Let Winkler 1985 and Bowie 1993, 45–52, suffice; Sommerstein 1997c remains dubious about a formal institution in the fifth century, but compare now Dunbar *ad Birds* 332, suggesting an echo of the ephebic oath there.

90. Bowie 1993, 97–98. Cf. also Whitman 1964, 156–160 and the discussion by Konstan 1985, 32–33 (= Konstan 1995, 19) of the old jurors' ὀργή.

91. Philocleon is at least consistent in identifying himself as Zeus. As a juror he claimed to thunder like Zeus (619–624). Now he sees himself as the result of a gigantomachic succession motif (cf. Bowie 1993, 58–66, on *Knights*).

92. Borthwick 1968. The Aldine Σ *Wasps* 1490 mention a "Phrynichus, son of Melanthas," whereas the tragedian was Phrynichus, son of Polyphrasmon. I argue that the patronymic is simply wrong in the Aldine Σ. MacDowell *ad* 1490 suggests that the patronymic "son of Chorocles" given for Phrynichus in another scholion is an invention, as it means "famed for his choruses." Given the fame of Phrynichus as a composer of dance figures, it seems likely that he also composed pyrrhic dances. Cf. Dunbar *ad Birds* 749.

93. The allusion seems to be to Phrynichus fr. 17 *TrGF*. Borthwick 1968, 44–46, thinks the scholia wrongly attribute this to his infamous *Taking of Miletus*, arguing instead for his *Phoenissae*. In any case, the Persian associations of the dance figure are quite strong.

94. Borthwick 1968, 46. The repetition of these figures in performances of the pyrrhic dance would explain the retention in the audience's mind of the association of the figures with Phrynichus. While Herington 1985, 23–26, 48–50, argues for the survival of dance elements for long periods of time through reperformance, this seems highly improbable in the case of tragedy, for Phrynichus's tragedies were surely not reperformed in Athens in Aristophanes' time—but the pyrrhic dance was. Moreover, the pyrrhic dance forms a highly appropriate transition from the symposium to the stage for an "ephebe" such as Philocleon. Lissarrague 1990b, 102–103, 116–117, suggests that within the broad parallelism between the male collectives of the hoplite battle line and the symposium there was a more particular parallelism between pyrrhic dance and dance at the symposium. His fig. 82 (= Boardman *ARFV*, fig. 127) illustrates a vase tondo with a youth dancing the pyrrhic, whose shield further illustrates a youth dancing at the symposium.

95. Winkler 1990, 50–58.

96. Chamaileon cites as his authority a fragment of the play Σκευαί, attributing it either to Plato or Aristophanes (Plato fr. 138 K-A.).

97. Sommerstein *ad* 1501 suggests the same child actors appear here who were used to lead the chorus of old men on and probably later reused in the trial scene as kitchen utensils and Labes' "puppies." Despite MacDowell *ad* 1501, I think it unlikely Carcinus and his sons actually appeared in the *Wasps*.

98. Borthwick 1968, 49–50, with references to Lilian Lawler's discussion of this *schema* in tragedy. Lawler suggests that it is particularly appropriate to satyric drama, and indeed the one specific citation is from Aeschylus's satyr play the *Theoroi*. Someone presumably comments on the chorus performing this dance (fr. 26): καὶ μὴν παλαιῶν τῶνδέ σοι σκωπευμάτων.

99. MacCary 1979, 141.

100. Zimmermann 1985a, 83. I follow his and MacDowell's reading of ὀρχούμενος in 1537, rather than Sommerstein's ὀρχούμενον. It is also not entirely clear that Philocleon's victory in the dance competition is marked in any way on the stage. Doubtless, however, the audience understood that his coming victory and the play's were meant to be one.

101. Confirmation comes from an anonymous text called Περὶ τραγῳδίας, published in 1963 (conveniently accessible in Pickard-Cambridge 1988, 322; full text in Perusino 1993, with commentary), where we learn: τῶν δὲ ὑποκριτῶν οὐδεὶς οὐδέποτε ἐν τραγῳδίᾳ ὠρχήσατο, ἀλλ᾽ ἦν ἴδιος τοῦ χοροῦ ἡ τοιαύτη ἐνέργεια. There are some apparent exceptions: Alan Sommerstein has called my attention to Io in *Prometheus Bound*. It is far less clear to me that Cassandra's frenzied movements at *Trojan Women* 308ff. (cited by Perusino 1993 *ad loc.*) constitute dance. Comic actors dance: notably Carion in *Wealth* 290ff., and at the play's end, although there is no indication that he descends to the orchestra and joins in the choral dance.

102. I am grateful to Philip Stadter who, in response to an oral version of this chapter, drew my attention back to Philocleon's relation to the chorus at the play's beginning. Purves 1997, 18–19, intriguingly points out that, as a dancer, Philocleon cannot now be a deceptive performer (like those the play has so fiercely criticized) because he no longer relies on words.

103. [Aristotle], *Problems* 916a33: τοὺς γὰρ ἀνθρώπους φησὶν Ἀλκμαίων διὰ τοῦτο ἀπόλλυσθαι, ὅτι οὐ δύνανται τὴν ἀρχὴν τῷ τέλει προσάψαι.

104. End and beginning are the same, as Heraclitus fr. 103B points out (a reference I owe to Stephen Strange): ξυνὸν γὰρ ἀρχὴ καὶ πέρας ἐπὶ κύκλου περιφερείας. On a historical level Crichton 1993, 73, points out that men cease military service at sixty and thereupon give up their eponymous hero to that year's ephebes (Aristotle, *Ath. Pol.* 53.4–5). Philocleon returns for a new cycle.

105. That they are tragic rather than comic origins is not so grave a problem, since both shared a common origin in dithyrambic performances for Dionysus.

106. Gröbl 1889/90, 55–64, contains a full review of the arguments up to that point. Gröbl believes that Aristophanes produced *Proagon* himself, having given *Wasps* to Philonides to produce, and suggests a rather complicated textual corruption to account for the present state of the hypothesis text. Most scholars today assume the opposite, though usually without closely accounting for the present text: that is, that Philonides produced *Proagon* and Aristophanes himself *Wasps*. MacDowell's discussion

of this problem *ad loc*. rests on his belief that the name of the producer of the play alone was announced at the contest: since lines 1017–22 refer to Aristophanes, he must have been sole producer of the play. See above, chapter 3, n. 34, for the view that the audience knew very well who the author was, even when another man produced his play. MacDowell ascribes the phrase to the error of the hypothesis writer, but Gröbl makes a convincing case in general for the close reliance of the hypothesis on the Aristotelian didascalia. Gröbl's view that Aristophanes himself produced *Proagon* may deserve reconsideration. If indeed Aristophanes wrote both plays, the question becomes whether he personally backed the right or the wrong horse. Presumably he would produce personally the piece he thought more likely to win, to gain the double glory as victorious poet and producer, but the question of whether the judges concurred with his preference must remain open.

107. Halliwell 1989 argues that Aristophanes early in his career *did* contribute to the work of other playwrights. Whether he would still have been doing so at the time of *Wasps* is a difficult question. We must therefore also consider the admittedly tenuous possibility that Aristophanes contributed something (perhaps elements of the Euripides parody, apparently a central feature of *Proagon*?) to Philonides' play, although in the competitive atmosphere of the Athenian festivals it seems highly unlikely that he would assist a current rival. The *Proagon* fragments themselves (477–486 K-A. = 461–470 K), mainly drawn from Athenaeus, are remarkably unhelpful.

108. I.G. ii^2 2319 (= CIG I, No. 231 and CIA II, 2 No. 972, in Gröbl's citation), in the archonship of Diotimos. Gröbl himself does not accept this as decisive for the fifth century.

109. Gröbl 1889/90, 60.

110. Mastromarco 1978, 19–34. He bases this on a statement of Eratosthenes in P. Oxy. 2737, which has featured much more in the discussion of whether the number of comedies was reduced from five to three at the City Dionysia during the war years: see Luppe 1972, Sutton 1980, Luppe 1982, and most recently Luppe 2000a, with further citations. Rosen 1989 argues that the relegation of a poet to the less prestigious festival was a personal choice by the archon responsible, not a standing rule. If correct, Mastromarco's explanation of Aristophanes' most unusual procedure here at the Lenaea can still apply. We are less concerned with the epistemological status of the rule (was it a law, a custom, or just a good idea under the circumstances?) than with its operation. The suggestion is particularly appealing in light of the fact that a small number of poets (on the order of twelve to fifteen) seem to have dominated the comic festivals in these years. When *Acharnians* (if not *Babylonians* before it) won first prize, Aristophanes was the first new poet to do so in a number of years.

111. On the proagon itself, see Pickard-Cambridge 1988, 67–68; Csapo and Slater 1995, 109–110. A famous anecdote in the *Life of Euripides* records that Sophocles, after the death of Euripides was known in Athens, appeared in mourning at the proagon before the production of one of his own plays.

112. Arguably he did the same thing in 411, making *Lysistrata* his political play that year and *Thesmophoriazusae* the literary parody. I will argue below, however, that the *Thesmophoriazusae* too possesses a political dimension: see chapter 8.

113. MacDowell does not commit himself on whether the force of ἀνασελγαινόμενος is middle or passive; as the compound does not occur elsewhere, it is hard to

say whether it is so "opprobrious" that Aristophanes would not use it of his own play (MacDowell in asserting this has *Acharnians* and not *Proagon* in mind).

114. The order of plays in performance will have been determined by lots, probably some days before. See below for an argument that certainly lines 1158–1162 of the *Ecclesiazusae* and quite probably much of the first scene can only have been written after Aristophanes knew that his play would appear first on the day's program at the festival. One wonders also if there are direct allusions to the play of his other competitor, Leucon, in lines 54ff. Nothing beyond its title is known of his *Ambassadors*, but one wonders if Heracles might have appeared in such a play. Certainly the poets would know the general plot outlines of their rivals' pieces far enough in advance to insert such comments.

115. Dover xc–xciii. Dover took it as axiomatic that there were no "Hellenistic" productions of Aristophanes, but the Würzburg *Thesmophoriazusae* vase (H5697: Csapo and Slater 1995, 67–69 [I. 135], pl. 7A) undermines the certainty that no element of post-Aristophanic stage production could have entered the scholia. Still, it would seem a very startling innovation for a later production—and given the *Clouds'* highly Athenocentric plot, subsequent production seems highly unlikely. Sommerstein 1997b, 281–282, suggests a possible, though I think strained, explanation for the origin of the scholion in an earlier reference to fowl at 847ff. Sommerstein also objects that the Logoi could not fight while in their wicker cages, but the scholion is condensed in its expression and does not rule out the notion that they were let out of their cages after their entrance.

116. Green 1985, 95–118; Taplin 1987a and 1987b. Close dating of vases at the end of the fifth century is difficult, but pushing the date of Getty vase back far enough to represent a performance of *Clouds* in 423 (rather than *Birds* in 414) seems more so. While the representation of bird choristers as cocks has troubled more than a few, given the elaborate naming of the individual bird species in the chorus of the play, Green established that visual evidence never shows major variation in the costumes of different members of the comic chorus: Green 1991, 27–30. To this we can now add the evidence of a comic chorus depicted on an Attic vase of the second quarter of the fourth century, which, though very poorly preserved, again seems to show a chorus dressed very consistently: Pingiatoglou 1992.

117. Fowler 1989b.

118. Boegehold 1995, 24.

Chapter 6. Making Peace—Or Dionysus in '21

1. Russo 1994, 49: "*Peace* is the comedy richest in speeches addressed explicitly to the spectators."

2. Cassio 1985, 39: "L'attenzione sembra concentrata sul teatro come punto di contatto attori-coro-publico."

3. E.g., Russo 1994, 134: "*Peace* undoubtedly bears the signs of being a minor comedy." Cf. Whitman 1964, 103–104, with references.

4. See Sommerstein *ad loc.* on ἄνδρες κοπρολόγοι (9), reinforced by the address in line 13 to ὦνδρες.

5. Rosen 1984 sees a connection here to the tradition of iambic abuse.

6. See above, chapter 1, pp. 121–22.

7. On the crane see Arnott 1962, 72–78; Dearden 1976, 75–85; Robkin 1979; and Mastronarde 1990. Presumably the beetle would be fixed to the end of the crane with more than one rope to minimize sway, but considerable gyration is to be expected at first. If the reconstruction of the *mechane* as simply a long arm on a fulcrum is correct, Trygaeus presumably rose almost straight in the air over his house, was swung out over the orchestra, and then back to the other end of the *skene*, where the beetle was lowered again. The most vigorous motion would be as the crane rotated him out over the orchestra.

8. Summarized at Olson xxxiv–xxxv. Hubbard 1991, 150–151 and n. 35, suggests that the reference to this tale in *Wasps* 1448–1449 is "an intertextual hint about his next comedy."

9. Olson *ad loc.* notes the metrical joke here: after several lines of unresolved (and therefore tragic) trimeters, the resolution in the word τραγικώτερος returns us emphatically to the world of comedy.

10. There is a striking similarity here to a remarkable passage of Plautus's *Amphitruo*, where Mercury in the prologue suggests that he can change the play the audience is about to see from tragedy to comedy: eandem hanc, si voltis, faciam iam ex tragoedia / comoedia ut sit omnibus isdem vorsibus (54–55).

11. Aristophanes frr. 160 K-A. (from *Gerytades*), 192 K-A. (from *Daedalus*, perhaps Icarus speaking: see Dearden 1976, 84–85), and Strattis fr. 4 K-A. (from *Atalantos* or *Atalanta*), where a character refers to himself dangling "like a fig" (ἰσχὰς γίν[ομαι]) on the end of the crane (cf. the same image in Strattis' *Phoenissae*, fr. 46.3 K-A., probably dating after 409 B.C.). See also above, pp. 121–22.

12. I presume a stage with three doors here, following Dover 1972, 135, though most recently Olson xlvi–xlviii imagines a two-door staging with Trygaeus returning to the side of the stage from which he began. To my knowledge only Möllendorf 1995, 122–125, has recently defended the old notion that the house of Zeus was represented on the roof of the skene; for the standard view, see Mastronarde 1990.

13. Dearden 1976, 78, suggests that Hermes' entrance (182ff.) is noisy and distracting enough to cover the beetle's departure.

14. Hubbard 1991, 142 n. 9, rightly emphasizes that the plot of *Peace* is no less daring in its conception than that of *Birds*. The lack of prolonged or effective resistance to Trygaeus and his plan should not blind us to its potential to shock its original audience with its audacity.

15. *Iliad* 1.424 (χθιζός). At line 260, Polemos's helper, Kudoimos ("Hurly-burly," in Sommerstein's translation), explains to his master that they do not have a pestle because they only moved in yesterday. As Bowie 1993, 142–143, notes, there is really no mythic prototype for a mass withdrawal of the gods. This suggests considerable Aristophanic originality here. The connection of the play's action with the Anthesteria that Bowie suggests (pp. 147–150) seems somewhat more tenuous, although the fact that only Dionysus and Hermes are imagined to be present in that festival is of interest.

16. Conceivably, Aristophanes could be referring to a preceding comedy, but we know the titles of his two comic competitors, Leucon's *Phratries* and Eupolis's *Flat-*

terers, neither of which seem likely to have had gods in their casts, and in any event Aristophanes is unlikely to make any reference to a comic competitor other than a critical one. A necessary consequence of my interpretation here is that Aristophanes knew of the order of competitors far enough in advance to integrate the reference into his script, but he obviously did so in the *Ecclesiazusae* (see below, pp. 208–9, 227–28). We have no information as to what tragedies were performed at the City Dionysia of 421. The reference to divine kitchen equipment might suggest that undignified tragedian, Euripides. Note then a further bit of precision. The giant mortar Polemos will use was not part of the previous day's equipment but something he brought home "last night" (ἐσπέρας, 228).

17. There is a whiff of Middle Comedy in this line, for fourth-century mythological burlesques often reduced divine grandeur to domestic farce.

18. For σκευάρια as "props," see above, p. 16.

19. The actor playing Hermes exits and presumably returns as Kudoimos; so Olson xliii. MacDowell 1994 contends that the three-actor rule did not obtain in Old Comedy (as opposed to tragedy; contra Marshall 1997), but there is still an effort made to distribute all significant parts among the three experienced (and festival-funded) actors. Unless the two boys at the end of the play (1264ff.: see MacDowell 1994, 330) are played by the regular actors, however, there is no need for four actors in this play.

20. This may be the first representation of War on stage: MacDowell 1995, 183.

21. On the dynamics of eavesdropping scenes in ancient comedy, see Slater 1985c, 11–12, 162–165 and passim; cf. Bain 1977, 90–91. Cassio 1985, 57, sees Trygaeus as a "spettatore-guida" in the play. Particularly interesting is Trygaeus's appeal to any Samothracian initiates in the audience to pray to hobble Kudoimos (ἀποστραφῆναι τοῦ μετιόντος τὼ πόδε, 279), as images of dangerous deities were sometimes treated; see Faraone 1992, 134. Might this point ahead to the statue of Peace, which has been confined and now must be freed?

22. Hubbard 1991, esp. 151 and n. 37

23. At *Knights* 984 he is called a δοῖδυξ; the same word recurs at *Peace* 288 and 295, although here at 259 the term is ἀλετρίβανον. At 266 Cleon is said to have "disturbed" (ταράξει) all the cities of Greece, just as he once disturbed Athens (and again he is called κύκηθρον καὶ τάρακτρον at 654); on this theme see Edmunds 1987a.

24. In fact, Aristophanes seems deliberately to confuse Polemos and the dead Cleon; Olson *ad* 319–320. When Trygaeus tells the chorus to stop shouting at lines 318–329, he wants to prevent "him" (the subject of the verb must be understood) from coming out and ruining everything. Trygaeus has most recently been speaking of Cleon, and the verb he uses for ruin is literally "disturb" (συνταράξει, 319; ταραττέτω, 320), the verb he uses of Cleon in the *Knights*. Only in hindsight is it clear that the sentence must refer to Polemos, not Cleon. Aristophanes has called Cleon "Cerberus" before (*Knights* 1030), and his satisfaction that the "hound of hell" has gone home is evident.

25. Hubbard 1991, 151, though Olson *ad loc.* is skeptical.

26. For the clever slave as *architectus doli.*, see Duckworth 1952, 160–167 and passim. The image comes from Plautus, e.g., *Miles* 901–902 and *Poenulus* 1110. In Demosthenes 18.28 (*On the Crown*), the person in charge of the Theater of Dionysus and its

upkeep is called the ἀρχιτέκτων, a title also used in inscriptions, but there is no evidence for such an official in the fifth century; cf. Rhodes 1972, 125–126. It is best to take the term here simply as a general metaphor.

27. On the theme of jury service as a connection specifically back to *Wasps*, see Graves 1911 *ad* 349 and Hubbard 1991, 151.

28. The raised stage is a perennial question in studies of the fifth-century theater. Some kind of platform is certainly necessary for sound projection, at least in the Theater of Dionysus, but need not be very high: Hunningher 1956; Slater 1987, 3; and Dearden 1976, 13–18, 62–64.

29. They ask Hermes to lead them δημιουργικῶς, 429. It might be possible to argue that this implies "like a foreman," who would be outranked by "a master builder or architect (κἀρχιτεκτόνει, 305)," but we need not press the point. On Hermes' role in the *anodos* story type, see Bowie 1993, 140.

30. Eupolis *Autolycus* fr. 62 K-A., Plato Comicus, *Victories* fr. 81 K-A. Eupolis wrote two plays entitled *Autolycus*. The one dateable to 420 B.C. (Athenaeus 5. 216d) is doubtless the source for fr. 62.

31. Donohue 1988, 6, 26–27 and n. 65, shows that the term ranges widely in meaning but definitely need not connote "colossal in size." It could well mean "a column-like image." Cf. Russo 1994, 142–143, and Faraone 1992, 82–83.

32. See Faraone 1992, 136–140, on the "incarceration of dread goddesses," with a number of examples, especially statues of Artemis.

33. Compare the images of Dionysus on the so-called "Lenäenvasen" in Pickard-Cambridge 1988, 30–35 and figs. 17, 19, 21–23. Aristophanes may have had no standardized imagery of Peace as a divinity to imitate, although cults of abstractions are not unknown at this period: cf. the cult image of Nemesis carved by Agoracritus for the temple at Rhamnous about 420 B.C.

34. The contrast with Basileia in the *Birds* may be instructive. Aristophanes could have written a play in which Trygaeus danced off at the end to a wedding with Peace herself, not one of her handmaidens, but that would have been to exalt the comic hero over the needs of the hour. The world changes considerably in the seven years leading down to the wedding of Peisetaerus and Basileia. Cf. also Cassio 1985, 48.

35. Cassio 1985, 124. Olson *ad* 530 attempts to make the referent of ταύτης Peace herself rather than Showtime, apparently not seeing the wide-ranging nature of Θεωρία.

36. And after all some in the audience enjoyed those scandalous tragedies, or Euripides would never have continued to gain a chorus to perform them. See also Taaffe 1993, 159 n. 36.

37. For the debate over the Dionysiac nature of the theatrical experience in the fifth century, see Goldhill 1990, reacting to Taplin 1978, esp. 162.

38. See Bremer 1993, 151–152, for the influence of Sappho here.

39. Hermes' speech begins (603) with an allusion to fr. 109W. of Archilochus, ῏Ω λιπερνῆτες πολῖται, τἀμὰ δὴ ξυνίετε / ῥήματα. Σ *Peace* 603 notes that Cratinus quoted the same passage two years before in his *Wineflask* fr. 211 K-A. (although Kock proposed to read θεαταί in the Cratinus for πολῖται), and Eupolis fr. 392 K-A., clearly addressed to the spectators (ἀλλ᾽ ἀκούετ᾽, ὦ θεαταί, τἀμὰ . . .), echoes it. Such double intertextuality is rather unusual in Aristophanes, but we can only speculate

about its significance. Was the Archilochus poem once again popular in symposia? Then the echo of Cratinus as well is unimportant and incidental. Or is it perhaps a gracious tribute, now that the elder comic poet is dead? As such, it would be subliminal preparation for the comments on his death at 700ff.

40. Even Aristophanes does not seem to expect the audience to believe this but rather to see it as a joke as well on the gullibility of the chorus, as the line "There's a lot we don't know apparently" (πολλά γ᾽ ἡμᾶς λανθάνει, 618) suggests. See Sommerstein *ad loc.* for the real historical details behind this tangled story; MacDowell 1995, 186–189, thinks that there may have been such a rumor current.

41. See *Σ Peace* 605, conveniently translated in Pollitt 1990, 54ff. Pheidias's workshop at Olympia has been identified, establishing the chronology (p. 56).

42. Sommerstein *ad loc.*, quoting Halliwell; similarly, Olson *ad loc.*

43. Stone 1981, 60–71 and fig. 34.

44. I am indebted to a lecture by Jas Elsner in which he discussed the Pausanias and pseudo-Lucian passages as part of a larger appreciation of the function of religion in the ancient view of art. Further on moving statues in Olson *ad* 682. The effect may not have worked as well in *Peace* as Aristophanes hoped; the jokes reported above (Eupolis fr. 62 K-A., Plato Comicus fr. 81 K-A.) may suggest it miscarried. The problem may have lain in the delicate balance between maintaining an illusion (of the statue as statue) and the attempt to sacralize the theater space explicitly as a theater.

45. Even though Aristophanes may charge that the *Maricas* is simply plagiarism of his *Knights*, the very fact of Eupolis's production shows that the function of the demagogues in the city remained topical even after Cleon's death. Aristophanes seems not to have been as appalled by Hyperbolus as by Cleon, but he could not afford to be behind the times.

46. Sommerstein *ad* 729 suggests they may have been given these tools between lines 552 and 563 by the stage hands who now take them away, but what the implements are and when they are acquired is far from certain. Stone 1981, 427, suggests the reference may be to equipment or tools used in the raising of Peace.

47. It is again speculation, but one wonders if perhaps there had been a well-known theft at the theater recently (which might also lie in the background of the conceit that Hermes is guarding the σκευάρια of the gods, 201). The Choregus of Plautus's *Curculio* worries (line 464) that the title character will steal the costumes he has hired for the play! Cf. the comments of Dover 1966 [1987, 252–253]. Olson *ad loc.*, however, thinks of the theft of dramatic material by Aristophanes' dramatic rivals.

48. See Bremer 1993, 159–160, on this passage and passim for Aristophanes' self-image as part of the Greek poetic tradition.

49. Lines 752–759 repeat, largely verbatim, material Aristophanes first used at *Wasps* 1030–1037 (see Sommerstein *ad* 754 on how he has clarified the presentation here). Halliwell 1989, 522, has suggested that three other comic poets (Aristonymus, Ameipsias, and Sannyrion: see also below, n. 53) mocked Aristophanes for this boastfully Herculean self-imagery, by converting him in their references to the Heracles who was born to work for others. Presumably Aristophanes repeated himself because the lines were a success with the first audience. Did the audience of *Peace* not find them so funny here after Cleon's death, thus prompting the mockery by his fellow poets?

50. Olson *ad* 763 translates "my costume," but that meaning is not fully supported

by his parallels nor appropriate to the speech of the chorus here. At Herodotus 1.24.4–5, σκευή does mean Arion's performance robe, but that is not a costume in the sense of clothing intended to contribute to mimesis, nor is the priest's robe in Eubulus fr. 71. The old-fashioned garb in which Demos returns (*Knights* 1324) is more ambiguous, although σχῆμα (1331) seems Aristophanes' more precise word for "costume." *Frogs* 108 may be the best candidate, but even there σκευή must include not just Heracles' lionskin but also his club as part of Dionysus's "equipment." Nor does "costume" make good sense in the context of the parabasis here. The chorus is speaking in the first person for the poet: what would Aristophanes' costume be? A reference to his own costume as an actor (and Olson xxiii–xxiv n. 6 is doubtful that Aristophanes performed in his own plays) seems out of place

51. See above, chapter 1 n. 2.

52. The Muse is often invoked at the beginning of the parabasis lyrics: see Sommerstein *ad Frogs* 674. Here the scholia tell us that the invocation borrows from Stesichorus's *Oresteia*. The joyous dances she participates in are opposed to the incompetent dancing of Carcinus's sons.

53. The jabs at Carcinus (perhaps a comic, rather than a tragic, playwright: Rothwell 1994, though Olson 2000 doubts this) link back to the ending of *Wasps*. Morsimus recurs in *Frogs* 151, where writing out a speech from one of his tragedies is grounds for eternal punishment. Whether or not Morsimus's brother is to be identified as Melanthius, it is interesting that two men apparently shared the responsibility for a tragic chorus (τῶν τραγῳδῶν τὸν χορὸν εἶχον ἀδελφός τε καὶ αὐτός, 807–809), although presumably only one would have appeared as official competitor. This tends to corroborate claims of cooperation between comic poets: see Halliwell 1989 esp. 518 and 521–522, discussing the mockery of Aristophanes in Aristonymus 3 K-A., Ameipsias 27 K-A., and Sannyrion 5 K-A. as evidence for the first phase of Aristophanes' career, in which he cooperated with other poets. Melanthius was clearly topical: as Cassio 1985, 21–22, points out, all three comedies of 421 B.C. made fun of him. Olson *ad* 805 suggests the reference to Melanthius's dreadful voice suggests that he performed in his own play, rather surprising in tragedy at this date.

54. So Olson *ad* 820, based on the references to his sore legs. If so, the daughter's prediction at 147–148 has been fulfilled, and he looks like a Euripidean hero, with ample possibilities for visual parody.

55. *Peace* is the most explicit of Aristophanes' plays with regard to the transformation of the old hero (πρεσβύτης, 856) into a young man again (ζηλωτὸς ἔσει, γέρον, / αὖθις νέος ὢν πάλιν, 860–861).

56. Cf. *Knights* 1274–1289, *Wasps* 1280–1283, and fr. dub. 926 K-A. As Sommerstein notes *ad loc.*, the real point of this repeated abuse may be that Ariphrades was a rival comic poet: Aristotle *Poetics* 1458b31 refers to an Ariphrades who mocked the tragedians (τοὺς τραγῳδοὺς ἐκωμῴδει), but we have no other record of him as a poet. Olson *ad* 883 thinks he may currently have been serving on the *boule*.

57. Reading τὴν σκευήν at 886 with Meineke and Sommerstein *ad loc.*, against Olson.

58. Whitman 1964, 114, calls this a "masterpiece of montage."

59. On the *prytaneis* and the *boule*, see Stockton 1990, 67–70, 84–95. There were certainly reserved seats for the *bouletai*, as shown by *Birds* 794 and Σ *Birds* 794, but

not even all fifty *prytaneis* could have sat in the front row. That the presiding *prytanis* would have seems quite probable: see also Rhodes 1972, 13.

60. No doubt one could examine this as homosocial bonding through female exchange as well, but I forebear. The dynamic here is the inverse of that in Eupolis's *Cities* fr. 223 K-A., where an unknown speaker defends one of the personified female cities against the gaze of a lascivious viewer named Philinos: see Rosen 1997, 158–159.

61. Cassio 1985, 145, perceptively remarks on the ending: "Ma qui me pare accentuato l'elemento *spaziale*, non quello temporale;" in the farmers' return to the country "la campagna funziona . . . come spazio utopico."

62. Sommerstein *ad loc.* quotes Thucydides 5.16.1 on Cleon, suggesting that in peace the demagogues' "crimes will be more easily detected and [their] slanders less readily believed." He goes on to note that Aristophanes likes to tack the removal of Hyperbolus onto the end of a series of items (e.g., *Peace* 1319, *Knights* 1363, *Wasps* 1007), apparently as though he were so insignificant as to merit only passing reference. Even so, the mention here at 921 seems unusually brief.

63. Compare Aristophanes fr. 256 K-A. (of an altar):

μαρτύρομαι δὲ Ζηνὸς ἑρκείου χύτρας,
μεθ᾽ ὧν ὁ βωμὸς οὗτος ἱδρύθη ποτέ.

In Aristophanes fr. 591. 84–86 K-A., another image is being installed:

φέρε νῦν ἐγὼ [τ]ὴν δαίμον᾽ ἣν ἀνήγαγον,
εἶτ τὴν [ἀ]γορὰν ἄγων ἱδρύτωμαι βοΐ

Cassio 1981, commenting on this passage, suggests Hermes is present and addressed at this installation as well.

64. See Arnott 1962, 45–56, esp. 53–54, and Dearden 1976, 46–48. Rehm 1988, 306–307, thinks the altar in the center of the orchestra was used, in part arguing that the barley grains the slave throws at line 962 (see below) *would* reach the audience. He also argues that the longer distance from the stage to the central altar would allow for more comedy business.

65. Sommerstein *ad* 962, following Sharpley and Platnauer.

66. Henderson 1975, 119–120.

67. On women's attendance at the theater (probably sitting in rows behind the men, *pace* Goldhill 1994), see Henderson 1991, Olson *ad* 966–967.

68. Indeed, only the actors playing Trygaeus and his slave need be in on the joke: lines 970–972 could have been sprung as a surprise at the performance, the farcical drenching replacing a more realistic lustration in the previous rehearsals! Aristophanes clearly uses water to farcical effect in *Lysistrata* (381ff.): MacDowell 1988, 10–11. Olson's doubts *ad* 970–972 seem excessive.

69. Arnott 1962, 53–55, who also notes until recently our own stage taboos on representing certain speech acts verbatim (such as the wedding service)—an interesting reflection of belief in the "performative" power of certain utterances.

70. While Aristophanes claims in lines 741–747 to have purified comedy of such elementary slapstick, he is not above using it himself.

71. Totaro 1999 *ad* 1130 and *ad* 1154 (on the call for myrtle branches).

72. See Hubbard 1991, 141–144, on scatological themes, linking the dung beetle of the play's beginning to Trygaeus's attempt to use the breastplate the arms dealer offers him as a chamber pot (1226–1239). Cf. Bowie 1993, 136.

73. Sommerstein 1984b, 148 and n. 36. Cf. Landfester 1977, 184, who calls it "ein unerwarteter Gag."

Chapter 7. *Performing the City:* Birds

A previous version of this chapter appeared as "Performing the City in *Birds*," in *The City as Comedy*, ed. Gregory Dobrov (University of North Carolina Press, 1997). Reprinted by permission.

1. Konstan 1990.

2. Even the assignment of their lines is hotly disputed. The excellent analysis of Nesselrath 1996 makes the point that the audience at the beginning here can have no idea whether either character will play a significant role in the rest of the comedy.

3. The stage need tower like a cliff only in the imagination of performers and audience. Cf. the use of the stage front as a wall under which to hide the male overgarments of the chorus in *Ecclesiazusae* 497 (chapter 10 n. 40 below; on stage height, Csapo and Slater 1995, 258 and nos. I.131 and I.133, with plates).

4. We first heard of Tereus at line 15, but if Dunbar *ad* 16 rightly regards 16 as an interpolation, the audience will have had little notion of the journey's goal until now.

5. Dunbar *ad* 49–50 is less certain, considering line 20 possible as well.

6. Dobrov 1993, 210. In his published version, Dobrov suggests that the transformation may have been only partly illustrated, by a change in headdress or otherwise, while I would prefer to see a complete costume change.

7. A recent play by Frank Manley, *The Evidence*, offers an interesting parallel, though I should emphasize that the idea about Tereus in *Birds* occurred to me before seeing this modern production. Manley's play deals with a man who thinks he has seen a sasquatch. Although a powerful meditation on the dimensions of experience and sanity, the play was weakened by a final tableau in which the back-lit figure of the sasquatch was seen by the audience: the reality did not look otherworldly: it simply looked like a man in a gorilla suit.

8. On secondhand trade in costumes, see chapter 3 n. 49 (above) and Slater 1993a, 405 and n. 18. Bowie 1993, 154, sees Tereus's bedraggled condition as indicative of the birds' disorder. MacDowell 1995, 204, thinks Tereus in Sophocles had no feathers to begin with, but this makes for a very feeble joke.

9. Illustrated in Green 1985 (the original publication), as the frontispiece to Sommerstein's *Birds* edition, and in Taplin 1993 (pl. 24.28). Taplin 1987a suggested these birds were rather the *Logoi* from *Clouds*, although in Taplin 1993 he concedes that they should be choristers rather than actors; cf. Csapo 1993. None of these discussions addresses the apparent molting.

10. They are not jurors (ἡλιαστά), but "anti-jurors": ἀπηλιαστά, 110, an Aristophanic coinage. Konstan 1990, 190–192, defines four kinds of utopias based on their

treatment of *nomoi*: here we have the antinomian strain in *Birds*, but it slides easily into the "megalonomian" as well when Peisetaerus and Euelpides begin to describe the fantasy elements of the place they seek: that is, where the "troubles" are having too many sensual joys (128ff.).

11. For echoes of various city foundation myths in *Birds*, see Bowie 1993, 152–166.

12. The key adjective describing them is κεχηνότες, 165, in which one may hear an echo of Aristophanes' wonderful comic coinage describing the Athenians at the end of *Acharnians*: χαυνοπολίτας (635) or Open-Mouthenians, as Alan Sommerstein so aptly translates. Peisetaerus will succeed in establishing the bird city precisely because the birds are as gullible as the Athenians. This behavior is "disgraceful" (ἄτιμον, 166); Dunbar *ad* 166 says this is the only "non-political" use of ἄτιμον in Aristophanes, but there may well be a political connotation nonetheless: the birds suffer ἀτιμία because they lack a city as yet. Note also Euelpides' description of his own actions in line 264: καίτοι κέχηνά γ' εἰς τὸν οὐρανὸν βλέπων.

13. Konstan 1990, 194. Romer 1994 interprets "Melian hunger" at 186 as referring not only to Athens' blockade of Melos but also to Diagoras the Melian, denounced as a public enemy earlier on the day of the *Birds* production (see lines 1072–1075 and n. 45, below).

14. Arrowsmith 1973 already saw issues of boundedness versus unboundedness underlying this play. A neglected aspect of his article argues, based on the work of John Fine on boundary stones in Attica, that the alienability of property was a relatively new and revolutionary development in Athenian society of the fifth century. Fine's belief that commerce in (as opposed to inheritability of) property was not possible in Athens until the fifth century has not been widely accepted. Nonetheless, Arrowsmith's discussion of the issue brings out certain important elements. The process of defining boundaries made commerce in land possible. The clash of traditional concepts of landholding with new, commercial notions is still very much alive in the fifth century and energizes the jokes here in *Birds*. In W. S. Gilbert's *Patience*, the poet Bunthorne remarks: "What's the use of yearning for Elysian Fields when you know you can't get 'em and would only let 'em out on building leases if you had 'em?" Peisetaerus, of course, wants to have his Elysian fields and lease them out, too.

15. Sommerstein anticipates this reading of the space, for he chooses to translate πόλος as stage (and πόλις as state, for an equivalent pun).

16. Dobrov 1993, 190, 226; Dobrov 1997, esp. 111–115.

17. Dover 1972, 145; Mastronarde 1990, 284; and Dunbar *ad* 268–293. Given Mastronarde's reconstruction of access to the *skene* roof, these birds must appear one by one from the ladder behind and then take up positions along the "crest" (λόφον, 279, with many puns) of the *skene*. The second bird chorister is greeted with parodies of both a line in Sophocles (275, the *Tyro*, fr. 654) and of a line in Aeschylus's *Edonians* (the beginning of 276 parallels fr. 60 = 75M, quoted in the scholion); see Sutton 1971. One would very much like to know if there was a visual as well as verbal parody and whether a revival of the *Edonians* figured in the joke, but we simply cannot tell.

18. This explicit mention is a little puzzling, for it does not seem a very strong joke here. Compare the much funnier moment in *Clouds* 326, where the Cloud chorus is pointed out to Strepsiades:

{Στ.}   τί τὸ χρῆμα;
ὡς οὐ καθορῶ.
{Σω.}   παρὰ τὴν εἴσοδον.

Perhaps the birds use only one *parodos* for their entrance, as did the Clouds in their play, although see Dunbar *ad loc.* One wonders if this was standard procedure.

19. Dunbar *ad* 328–35 suggests that θεσμοὺς ἀρχαίους (331) would remind the Athenian audience of their own θεσμοί of Draco. Even more intriguingly, she suggests an echo of the ephebic oath, known from the fourth century but with language sounding older, in their reference to his violation of the ὅρκους ὀρνίθων (336). Do the choristers then conceive of themselves as ephebes, who will then be drilled and trained into a new kind of chorus by their new *chorodidaskalos*, Peisetaerus? Cf. the link between ephebes and (tragic) choristers in the ending to *Wasps* (pp. 107–9, above).

20. Is there a further dramatic, specifically tragic parody here? On the relation between tragic dancing and military drills, see Winkler 1990, 50–58. Tragic dance was rectangular, as opposed to dithyramb's "circular choruses." A key text that Winkler cites on the the connection between tragic dance and military training is Chamaileon fr. 42 Wehrli [= Athenaeus 14.268ef]. On the other hand, the taxiarch was a leader of a *tribal* unit of Athenians troops, and drama's *lack* of a tribal basis (unique among the other Athenian musical competitions) is remarkable. Winkler 1985, 45–46, took this nontribal nature of the tragic chorus to be one of its most significant features, linking it to Peisistratid reforms of the Panathenaia (cf. n. 58 below), a claim he seems to back away from in Winkler 1990. Whatever the origin of this nontribal organization, it remains a significant element. See also Bowie 1993, 157, on the birds as hoplites.

21. The pot prompts a pun about the Athenian potter's quarter, the Cerameicus, which was also where state funerals were held (395–399). The jokes here propound so many incongruities that it is hard to tell where the main focus lies. How are they going to ask the generals for a state funeral once they are dead, after all? Given that they have fled Athens, they are in reality (whatever reality means at this point!) unlikely to be welcomed back as heroes, fallen or otherwise. The joke may be a preliminary to the play's later attempts to incorporate Athens and its festivals within the new bird city, on which see below.

22. They also wonder about Peisetaerus's motivation: what will *he* get out of it?

ὁρᾷ τι κέρδος ἐνθάδ᾽ ἄξιον μονῆς,
ὅτῳ πέποιθ᾽ ἐμοὶ ξυνὼν
κρατεῖν ἂν ἢ τὸν ἐχθρὸν ἢ
φίλοισιν ὠφελεῖν ἔχειν;   (417–420)

For a thorough discussion of this conception of morality and friendship in popular thought, see Blundell 1989, esp. 26–59.

23. The formulation suggests that the vote of the judges (ten picked by lot) occasionally went against the clear demonstration of popular opinion in the theater; cf. Dunbar *ad* 445. The threat in Pherecrates fr. 102 K-A. to mock the judges in his comedies, if they judge unjustly, is surprisingly blunt. It is tempting to think that there might be a glancing parody of the voting procedure in *Eumenides* here, but we cannot

point to a specific Aeschylean revival. Gilula 1994 suggests that παραβαίην may have a second level of signification: to speak a parabasis. Thus, the chorus is promising not to speak a parabasis in praise of the poet—but if it does, it should still win, though narrowly! If this interpretation is accepted, it strengthens the notion that the parabasis as practiced by Aristophanes was not an inevitable, core element of the composition of any comedy, for here he teases the audience with the possibility of dispensing with it altogether. In fact their first parabasis (676–800) is delivered entirely in their character as birds, beginning with the famous mock theogony. The decree of Syracosius, limiting the freedom of comic attack, has been invoked to explain the unusual form of the parabasis in *Birds* (cf. Sommerstein 1986; Henderson 1990, 288–290; Hubbard 1991, 159–160; and Phrynichus fr. 27 K-A.), but this would not prevent the poet from praising himself. Sommerstein *ad Frogs* 459 suggests a self-reference there to the chorus's parabatic function.

24. It is perhaps pushing a point, but Peisetaerus specifies that new call-up notices will be posted on the πινακίοις, 450, which Sommerstein takes to be the notice boards near the Eponymous Heroes in Athens. But Nephelokokkugia both is and is not Athens: it is the theatrical city as well as the real one, and in this context πινακίοις might well be taken to mean the theatrical backdrop, the changeable scenery in the theater itself.

25. Sommerstein notes *ad* 464 that wearing a crown in order to give a speech is otherwise unattested, so Aristophanes' foreshadowing of the feast here may be quite deliberate.

26. Sommerstein *ad* 479, though Dunbar *ad* 479–480 takes it as addressed to Peisetaerus.

27. Lampon's career as an interpreter of oracles is relevant here (Dunbar *ad loc.*), but perhaps also the whole notion of euphemistic oaths (Dillon 1995, 147).

28. At 546–547 the birds say ἀναθεὶς γὰρ ἐγώ σοι τὰ νεόττια κἀμαυτὸν οἰκετεύσω. To become part of Peisetaerus's household (οἰκετεύσω) is by no means a power-neutral act: there was no equality in the Greek household. To enroll themselves in his household then *is* to become his *slaves*—and arguably they do so in the course of the play. One must note that the point here turns on an emendation by Hermann, accepted by Sommerstein and Dunbar, of οἰκετεύσω for the mss.' οἰκήσω or οἰκίσω. While it would be another century before Aristotle formulated the doctrine of "natural slavery" (*Politics* 1), the birds' eagerness here to be followers would suggest to the audience that they are not well qualified to be citizens of a democratic polis.

29. See esp. Arrowsmith 1973.

30. Silk 1980 is a wide-ranging attack on Aristophanes as a "serious" lyricist. After pillorying Aristophanes for his paucity of "pressure" and "pointedness," as though he and Pindar were writing for the same audience, Silk eventually makes some useful points about the function of the lyrics in context. He buries his disparagement of this particular lyric moment (685ff.) in a footnote *praeteritio* (p. 105 n. 24), quite ignoring Arrowsmith 1973. Perkell 1993 is a vigorous defense of Aristophanes as a lyricist, employing however the strategy of separating the birds and their songs sharply from the characters and events surrounding them.

31. Konstan 1990, 12.

32. ἐφ᾽ ἡμᾶς αὖθις αὖ κατέπτετο. This line is a key piece of evidence for the much-

discussed question of the organization of the festival during the war years and the number and order of the plays. See below, n. 45.

33. Compare *Frogs* 536–539, where Aristophanes contrasts Theramenes' success as a performer to a "painted block" (γεγραμμένην / εἰκόν). The parody of Aeschylus at line 808 also reminds us of the constructedness of the two Athenians' transformation into birds.

34. Did the onstage piper, described as a raven, actually play or only mime? See Dunbar *ad* 858 and Taplin 1993, 105–106. In any case, explicit reference to the piper's strap (861) for holding the pipes in place exposes the raven as a human performer.

35. Animal sacrifices, just like representations of human violence, do not take place on stage, though in comedy this can be turned into a joke about the saving the choregus the expense of a sheep. This is surely not squeamishness so much as some sense of religious reverence, just as, until recently, plays and films in the English language tradition did not represent God or Christ directly.

36. Smith 1989 has an excellent discussion of the corruption of political discourse Aristophanes saw in the use of oracles at this period. Cf. Slater 1996, 101–103.

37. I refer to the scene in the office of the Sylvanian ambassador in *Duck Soup*.

38. Sommerstein *ad loc.*; also considered by Dunbar. It is tempting to look for an allusion to tragedy, but the *cothornus* may have become standard acting equipment only at a later period: see Pickard-Cambridge 1988, 207–208. Also intriguing is the fact that Theramenes was nicknamed the *cothornus*, because like these boots that fit either foot, he too was very flexible in his political loyalties (Xenophon, *Hell.* 2. 3. 31).

39. Konstan 1990. 201.

40. Zimmermann 1993a, esp. 267–275, discusses the scenes with Meton and Kinesias (see below) as examples of Aristophanes' treatment of intellectuals, emphasizing that they are treated more as types than individuals, but also as representatives of those who tend to divide the city. Hubbard 1997 sees a wider anti-elite theme.

41. Dunbar *ad loc.* suggests that the Inspector also brandishes a scroll, which would reinforce his connections with both the Oraclemonger and the Decree-seller, who is just about to appear.

42. See Dunbar *ad loc.*

43. Goldhill 1990. An earlier version appeared in *JHS* 107 (1987): 58–76.

44. Cf. Pickard-Cambridge 1988, 59, 67, and Dunbar *ad* 1072, comparing the decree honoring the assassins of Phrynichus the oligarch (I.G. i^3 102 = Meiggs and Lewis 85. 12–14).

45. This passage itself is the only evidence for the reading out of such a decree about tyranny at the Dionysia. Sommerstein accepts it, perhaps too uncritically, as evidence for a practice reaching back to the beginning of the democracy (cf. Holford-Strevens 1991). Given the renewed demagoguery about tyranny in the years preceding this play, which Sommerstein notes (cf. *Wasps* 417, 463–507; *Lysistrata* 618–35), one wonders if the decree was not a more recent innovation within the festival in response to the same demagogic agitation. Another, here decidedly peripheral, but nonetheless interesting issue is raised by the emphatic τῇδε . . . θἠμέρᾳ. The obvious meaning of this is that the performance of *Birds* takes place on the same day as the proclamation. As honorary decrees were read out on day one of the festival (cf. Pickard-Cambridge 1988, 59, 67), one assumes that such decrees of punishment were read at the same time; cer-

tainly there is no other logical point in the festival program for them. Therefore *Birds* was performed on day one of the City Dionysia in 414. Romer 1994, 355 n. 14, stops just short of drawing this conclusion, although he also cites Rosenmeyer 1972, 233, for the point that "'today [i.e., τῇδε . . . θῆμέρᾳ],' in Aristophanes, always means 'on this very day.'" Cf. Totaro 1999, 153–154. This is therefore key evidence in favor of the traditional view that the City Dionysia was shortened to three days of performances (with only three comedies competing) during some of the war years and against the argument of Luppe 1972 that there was no restriction, for in its full form, the City Dionysia played all five comedies on *one* day, *after* the three days of tragedies. Luppe 1972, 72–73 discusses *Birds* 785–796, which is usually taken as proof that comedy was done in the afternoon, after tragedy. Luppe says no, that 789, ἐφ' ἡμᾶς, means simply "back to us here in the theater," not "back to the comedy." Here he relies on the scholion, which reads ἐπὶ τὸ θέατρον—but this is not the point of this phrase, which is rather a notation that the line is metatheatrical, a reference to the actual conditions of performance. I now think Luppe may well be right that in the early years of the war the number of comedies was not yet reduced (see now the arguments in Luppe 2000a with references), but the reduction is in place by 414. Sommerstein points out *ad Frogs* 376 that this line is addressed metatheatrically to the choristers *qua* performers, who, unlike the characters they play, have just had lunch before their own afternoon performance of their play. *Birds* 1072 is also incidentally further evidence that the text of plays could be altered up until very shortly before performance, since this statement could not have been made until Aristophanes had been allotted a performance time on that first day (cf. the discussion of the opening of *Ecclesiazusae*). Contra Dunbar *ad* 1072. "Sparrovian" is an inspired translation of B. B. Rogers.

46. Dunbar *ad loc.*

47. See Winkler 1990, 55–57.

48. That a tragic player *could* invade the comic stage is shown by the "Choregoi Vase" (Taplin 1993, 55–60, 66, and pl. 9.1). See chapter 8, p. 176 and n. 96, below.

49. Line 1196 is a dimeter instead of the expected trimeter. Sommerstein *ad loc.* suggests connecting it with the music effect for the sound of her wings, but φθόγγος, 1198, can equally well be a discordant sound.

50. I would dearly love for Peisetaerus's comment on her at 1211, εἰρωνεύεται, to be equally self-conscious, but there is no evidence that the fifth century thought of this as a technical term, "to play the *eiron*."

51. When Peisetaerus asks Iris to whom she thinks she is speaking, πότερα Λυδὸν ἢ Φρύγα (1244), he quotes Pheres' speech to his son in the *Alcestis*, ὦ παῖ, τίν' αὐχεῖς, πότερα Λυδὸν ἢ Φρύγα (675). Many in the audience will only have recognized the cadences of tragic parody, but for those who recognize Euripides' *Alcestis* as the source, there is an even more interesting implication: "do you think you're talking to a *barbarian*? No, you're speaking to a Greek." Peisetaerus does not now speak for birds who are fundamentally different from humanity, but for birds who, thanks to Tereus's teaching (ἐγὼ γὰρ αὐτοὺς βαρβάρους ὄντας πρὸ τοῦ / ἐδίδαξα τὴν φωνήν, 199–200), have become speakers of Greek and therefore, as antiquity measured it, Greeks. Satyrs assaulting Iris appear on a cup by the Brygos Painter (*ARV*² 370.13 [London E65]), perhaps illustrating a satyr play by Pratinas: see Simon 1982. 125–129 and Dunbar *ad* 1196–1261. There were several later satyr plays called *Iris*; one by Achaeus (*TrGF*

1 no. 20 F 19) may be a possible source, given Aristophanes' parody of Achaeus else-where (from his *Momus*: see *Σ Wasps* 1081, *Σ Peace* 356 [= Achaeus F 29]; from his satyr play *Aithon*: *Σ Frogs* 184 [= Achaeus F 11]). Achaeus seems to have specialized in satyr play, and Gauly 1991, 277–278, suggests he may even have written satyr plays for other tragedians

52. LSJ give as the second meaning for the verb ἐποικέω "to be settled with hostile views against" and cite Thucydides 6. 86. These are carpetbaggers, not philosophical enthusiasts.

53. Sommerstein *ad loc.*

54. For the ceremony and its significance, see Sommerstein *ad loc.* and Goldhill 1990. Presumably the audience had witnessed this ceremony earlier this same day (see above, n. 43). Bassi 1995, 20, even suggests that the parade of orphans, their full mas-culine identity demonstrated by their armor, functioned as "antidote" or perhaps pro-phylactic to the "compromised" figures about about to perform in the plays—which would make Aristophanes' attempt to absorb this part of the ceremony into his own play even more interesting!

55. Should it trouble us that the young man is only an orphan by intent, not in fact? Probably not. On one level the joke is surely that about the young man who killed his parents and asked the court for mercy because he was an orphan. On another level it may allude to some fears or suspicions that the benefits for orphans were being abused: Slater 1993c posits that this was the motivation behind Theozotides' proposal to exclude adopted sons from the ceremony at the Dionysia.

56. It is also consistent with his new status as ephebe. Having been armed by the bird city, he goes off to serve on the margins. Cf. Bowie 1987, 113 n. 6, who states " 'The boundaries' or 'margin' is where the ephebe belongs" and endorses the view of Gomme and others that in the fifth century ephebes were already serving as περιπόλοι, guarding the borders.

57. See Dunbar *ad* 1372–1409 and Zimmermann 1993b.

58. There is a possible relation to Konstan's theme of the unity of the birds. The dithyrambic competition, for which Kinesias's services are fought over (ὃς ταῖσι φυλαῖς περιμάχητός εἰμ' ἀεί, 1404), was tribal: it *fostered* rivalry among divisions of the citizen body, whereas comedy (before the fourth century: Aristotle, *Ath. Pol.* 56.3) and tragedy were the only nontribal *agones* at the festivals. Cf. Winkler 1985, 45: "tragedy seems never to have been organized as a competition by tribe or by naucrary or by any other subgrouping of the polis. It was from the first a celebration of the polis as a whole (here we slide over into interpretation) and not of its consituent parts." Ac-cording to the transmitted text, Peisetaerus suggests that Kinesias train the chorus of "tribe Kekrops" (Κεκροπίδα φυλήν, 1407), but Dunbar prefers Blaydes' emendation "the tribe of Crakes" (Κρεκοπίδα φυλήν); see her full discussion *ad loc.*

59. The concept of performative language was introduced by Austin and Searle (Austin 1962 and Searle 1969) in contradistinction to constative, or simply descriptive language; performative language creates reality (typical examples are a judge's sentence upon an offender, a ritual curse, ordination, or a marriage ceremony). Fish 1980, 197–245, is a now classic discussion of these topics in Shakespeare's *Coriolanus*. Philosophi-cally, the distinction collapses rather quickly, because *all* language is ultimately per-formative, informing observed reality with structures generated by the human mind

("man," "woman," and "child" are all imposed constructs, not pure descriptions, for example). The term still has some use, since the utterances Austin and Searle began by defining as performative usually call attention to their performance or are produced within strongly marked frames. Peisetaerus here foregrounds the performative power of his own language, and we need to ask why.

60. Silk 1980, 125, predictably hears only "topical satire" here. For a much more sensitive appreciation of the poety of the passage, see Moulton 1981, 28–46, especially for the wonderful image of the Cleonymus-tree, and now Perkell 1993. Rau 1967 makes no mention of possible parody.

61. Moulton 1981, 34, who also compares *Birds* 451–452.

62. The word ἄνωθεν is later repeated in contexts where it appears to mean "from up-country," as Sommerstein translates it (e.g., 1522, 1526), perhaps subtly suggesting that the established gods are at some disadvantage even before the human and avian rebellion against their authority. ἄνωθεν clearly once again means "from above (vertically)" at 1551, when Prometheus repeats his worries about Zeus seeing him. The word also occurs at 844, in regard to the birds' relation to man.

63. Cf. Ko-Ko and Pooh-Bah discussing the financing of the former's wedding in Gilbert and Sullivan's *Mikado*:

> Ko. But you said just now "Don't stint yourself, do it well."
> Pooh. As Private Secretary.
> Ko. And now you say that due economy must be observed.
> Pooh. As Chancellor of the Exchequer.
> Ko. I see. Come over here, where the Chancellor can't hear us.

Aristotle *Poetics* 1454b notes without qualification that we ascribe to the gods the power to see everything: ἄπαντα γὰρ ἀποδίδομεν τοῖς θεοῖς ὁρᾶν.

64. On his role in *Birds*, see esp. Rau 1967, 175–177.

65. For a concise and sensible summation of the argument about just what her name can mean (is she "really" a goddess or an abstraction?), see MacDowell 1995, 217–218.

66. Antiphanes fr. 204 K-A.; cf. Plato Comicus fr. 237 K-A. See Sommerstein *ad* 1549. Phrynichus was in fact competing against Aristophanes at this very festival with his play *The Hermit*, whose title character was very similar, as his fr. 19 K-A. shows: ὄνομα δὲ μοῦστι Μονότροπος / ζῶ δὲ Τίμωνος βίον . . . We cannot tell what made Timon so topical in 414. Dunbar (in my view wrongly) gives the phrase Τίμων καθαρός to Peisetaerus as the continuation of his line 1548.

67. See Dunbar *ad loc.* for the evidence of real processions, including that depicted on the Parthenon frieze.

68. I see no necessary connection, however, between Peisetaerus as a cannibal here and the past of Tereus, such as is suggested by Bowie 1993, 168. MacDowell 1995, 224–225, argues that, in the absence of any evidence that these jailbirds were not properly condemned by the democracy, the audience would not have been disturbed by this. He is doubtless right about most of the original audience; whether we should be so serene is another question.

69. See Sommerstein *ad loc.* on the halcyon.

70. In light of the use of the theme of *apate* elsewhere in Aristophanes (see esp. pp. 60–61 above, on *Acharnians*), the two competitors' terms for each other's activities are of interest here. Poseidon warns Heracles against Peisetaerus's deceptive speech (ἐξαπατώμενος, 1641), while the Peisetaerus, the consummate demagogic politician, accuses his opponent Poseidon of sophistry (περισοφίζεται, 1646). The echo of sophistic debates about the origin of the Trojan War and Helen's responsibility or innocence in line 1639 (ἡμεῖς περὶ γυναικὸς μιᾶς πολεμήσομεν;) encourages us to read this in the light of contemporary sophism.

71. Patterson 1990 is the best and most recent treatment of the νόθος in Athenian law and society. She does take Peisetaerus's citation of Solon in lines 1661–1666 as generally accurate (p. 51; cf. Sommerstein *ad* 1661–1662, Dunbar *ad* 1661–1666, and Ogden 1996, 34–37), although given what we know of Peisetaerus's methods of argument, there is ample room to wonder if it is any more accurate than some other legal "citations" in the fourth-century orators.

72. Henderson 1993, 315–316, argues strongly in favor of the *Birds* as genuinely utopian rather than satirical. The festivity of the staging reinforces this view: Bowie 1993, 165, makes a good case for Basileia and Peisetaerus appearing in a chariot for the wedding procession; cf. Dunbar *ad* 1720–1765.

73. A theme reinforced by the "unnameable fragrance" (ὀσμὴ δ' ἀνωνόμαστος) of 1715.

74. See Sommerstein *ad* 1751 on the force of νῦν. The use of the *bronteion* is not definitely proven for the fifth-century theater, although Sommerstein cites *Clouds* 292 (ἤσθου φωνῆς ἅμα καὶ βροντῆς) and Sophocles *Œdipus Coloneus* 1456ff. as parallels. Cf. Dunbar *ad* 1752.

75. For an excellent review of various interpretations of the *Birds*, especially those that have tried to find specific political allegory in the play, see MacDowell 1995, 221–228.

76. Henderson 1997, 144–145.

Chapter 8. *Cross-Dress for Success:* Thesmophoriazusae

1. Zeitlin 1981; Foley 1982.

2. Showalter 1983. I should also perhaps note that the title for this chapter occurred to me before I encountered the same phrase in Garber 1992.

3. Haldane 1965.

4. Henderson 1996, 92–93. At line 658, the women search "the whole Pnyx" (τὴν πύκνα πᾶσαν). Henderson reads this literally, as most did before the area of the Pnyx was excavated. Sommerstein *ad loc.* notes no structure for a Thesmophorion has turned up on the Pnyx and follows Broneer in placing the Thesmophorion elsewhere. Henderson rightly emphasizes, however, that Broneer's preferred site would have held only a few women, not the gathering of all citizen matrons that this play imagines. If used only during the annual festival, the Thesmophorion may have had little in the way of permanent structures.

5. Henderson's edition of *Lysistrata*, pp. xv–xxv, supports the traditional order and 411 date of two plays; more succinctly, Sommerstein's edition, pp. 1–3. Hubbard

1991, 187–189, 195–199, and esp. 243–245, notes some fragile assumptions here but supports the same date and order based on cross-citations within the two plays; cf. Storey 1998, 107–108, on paucity of personal jokes in the tense political atmosphere of 411. Rogers's edition (pp. xxviii–xxxviii) and Hall 1989 support a date of 410. Russo 1994, 193, remains apparently alone in dating *both* plays (in a parallel to *Wasps* and *Proagon*) to the City Dionysia of 411. See also n. 63 below.

6. He is addressed as ὦ γέρον by the servant at line 63, and Agathon at 164 assumes that he heard Phrynichus perform, making him at least seventy or seventy-five years old.

7. Sommerstein *ad* 1 argues that Euripides treats his relative with too little respect for the latter to be his father-in-law; cf. Rogers xvii–xviii. Arguments from verisimilitude are dangerous in Aristophanes; more important surely is Sommerstein's point that no specific historical individual is intended. The κηδεστής is simply an extension and parody of Euripides himself.

8. Compare the eavesdropping scene in *Peace* 233–288, which *is* motivated by fear of detection.

9. Made necessary by the mask and costume change, as the actor of the servant's part will also play Agathon. With superb skill Aristophanes turns this potential problem to his advantage by the careful build-up of audience interest in the question: what is Euripides worried about?

10. Mnesilochus's apparently straightforward statement is in fact controversial among ancient historians. Rhodes 1972, 185–190, suggests that it would be possible to construe the reference to the *boule* as simply intending further proof that the law courts could not be sitting, but this seems a somewhat strained interpretation, especially in light of later events in the play. See below, p. 173.

11. Apart from the question of holidays, meetings of the law courts and the assembly had to take place on separate days. If the courts are not sitting, then in principle the assembly could be. As Henderson 1996, 93, notes (citing I.G. ii² 1006. 50–51), in 122 B.C. the Athenian assembly met during the Thesmophoria—and did so in the Theater of Dionysus! Is this a subtle reminder to the audience that they are indeed a deliberative assembly?

12. On parody of tragedy, see Rau 1967, 98–114 (and on the New Music: West 1992, 356–372; Zimmermann 1993b). Taaffe 1993, 175 n. 13 discusses the scene's "self-referentiality and self-parody." Strikingly, Euripides himself had extensively employed such self-quotation very recently: his *Helen*, to be parodied by Aristophanes below, is particularly closely modeled on his earlier *Iphigeneia in Tauris*.

13. See above, chapter 3, pp. 52–57, on the *Acharnians* scene. I would only note that it is illegitimate to argue that Euripides must have been wearing one of the ragged costumes in the earlier scene because Agathon is wearing women's clothing here. Agathon's transvestism is integral to the scene here in a way that Euripides' garb in *Acharnians* is not.

14. Taaffe 1993, 83; Dover 1978, 144, on the beard. Much of this turns on the notion that Agathon is portrayed as the *eromenos*, well into adulthood, of Euripides, particularly in Aelian *Varia Historia* 13.4; cf. [Plutarch], *apophth. reg.* 177A.

15. Beautifully illustrated in color as the frontispiece in Ghiron-Bistagne 1976; also Pickard-Cambridge 1988, fig. 54a, and Winkler and Zeitlin 1990, plate 2.

16. See above, ch. 2, pp. 25–30.

17. Winkler 1990, 42–58, on the fundamental visual distinctions between actors and choristers. We know little enough about the onset of puberty in antiquity. A few eighteen-year-old choristers likely did have beards, but they would have been uncommon and not have influenced the standard representations.

18. Just as in *Acharnians* 410–411 Dicaeopolis concludes that Euripides makes lame heroes because he is lying with his feet up on his couch!

19. Most recently, Vetta 1993, 716.

20. Sommerstein *ad loc.* Mnesilochus later refers to Agathon's instrument as a *barbitos* (137), a long-armed and therefore deeper-toned lyre. West 1992, 58 n. 46, suggests it may be used as part of the parody of Aeschylus's *Edonians* here (see also passim on the cithara). Zimmermann 1988 analyzes the song and argues that it was set in the Phrygian mode.

21. Cantarella 1974 and Newiger 1961.

22. Rau 1967, 108–110, on the parody of Aeschylus's *Edonians*.

23. Sommerstein *ad* 156.

24. The sexual position "astride" was associated with prostitutes: cf. Sommerstein *ad* 153 and *Wasps* 500–501. Two vases, giving heterosexual and homosexual versions of the same scene, show the dynamics of Mnesilochus's insult: Kilmer 1993, 168 and figs. R970 and R594. Oddly, the homosexual scene is provided with an audience, but it is difficult to conclude anything more from its presence. On another level, the reference to a *Phaedra* is presumably another indirect slap at the offences of Euripides.

25. Kilmer 1993, fig. R226, illustrates such a satyr revel. Snell (*TrGF* 39 Agathon fr. 33) concluded from these lines that Agathon had in fact written satyr play, but we have no other evidence. He won his first victory in 416 at the Lenaea, where playwrights presented only two tragedies and no satyr play. Only when and if he began to compete at the City Dionysia would he have written a satyr play; no surviving fragment of his work need come from a satyr play.

26. Sommerstein's edition of *Thesmophoriazusae*, p. 6. n. 36, remarks that the *Alcestis* is second only to the *Telephus* in the number of Aristophanes' plays alluding to or parodying it and suggests that the tetralogy of 438 (containing both) might have been the first Euripides the youthful Aristophanes saw. Note also the restoration of age hierarchy: the young Agathon refuses to risk his life for the older poet.

27. Stone 1981, 408–409, thinks the shaving was mimed, but this ignores the comic possibilities of Mnesilochus's attempted escape with the mask half-shaven. A mask with a detachable beard was quite possible: cf. the women's masks with attachable beards in *Ecclesiazusae*.

28. This recalls a joke from the *Clouds* (line 355: the Cloud chorus are women because they saw Cleisthenes in the audience) and prepares the way for Cleisthenes' appearance later in the play (574).

29. Women used lamps for depilation (Kilmer 1993, 136), but a torch is very likely here. Sommerstein *ad loc.* argues that the only reason to say "bring me a torch or a lamp" is because the former is much funnier and therefore will be used. In a theater as vast as that of Dionysus and under normal light conditions, only the flame of a torch is likely to have been visible to all the spectators; cf. below, pp. 208–9, on the use of the lamp in *Ecclesiazusae*.

30. Agathon notes that he wears this headpiece at night. Is this a stock visual joke familiar to Athenian husbands (the modern equivalent being the solid helmet of roll hair curlers worn by sitcom wives), or another joke at Agathon's sexuality? He has already said at 204–205 that women accuse him of stealing men's sexual attentions away from them, and this bit of costuming may be part of that effort.

31. Taaffe 1993, 84–87.

32. Taaffe 1993, 86.

33. Mayne 1993 (with extensive bibliography) is extremely helpful in sorting out the successive views of spectatorship within film studies and also to some degree the impact of those changing views in related literary reception studies. Cf. (briefly) Bobrick 1997, 185–186, on the male gaze in this play.

34. Taaffe 1993, 87–88.

35. For charm and vividness, compare Herodas, *Mime* 4, as the women visit the shrine of Aesclepius, accompanied by a nonspeaking slave girl.

36. Both absolutely and proportionately, this is the latest entry of a chorus in Aristophanes. In the lack of a parodos song, it resembles the entrance of the chorus of *Ecclesiazusae*. One wonders if this also helps culturally to construct "feminine," since it does not march in close formation, like most male choruses.

37. My reconstruction of the movement and action of the chorus here is strongly influenced by those in *Ecclesiazusae* (see below, chapter 10, pp. 212–14), where I think Aristophanes is seeking a more startling effect.

38. See Sommerstein *ad* 295.

39. See Horn 1970, 106–115, on parabatic elements in this prayer; Haldane 1965.

40. Bowie 1993, 216–217, discusses historical parallels for women acting politically, whether at the Thesmophoria, a widespread festival in Greece, or otherwise. As Wilamowitz first noted, the parody here is the longest passage of prose in Aristophanes; more seems to be at issue than just a joke about legalistic language.

41. See Rhodes 1972, 59 n. 3, on this passage. For a brief treatment of open and specific *probouleumata*, see Stockton 1990, 77 and 89.

42. Debate rages over whether there was a νόμος εἰσαγγελτικός by the mid-fifth century, and prosecutions were limited to the categories specified therein, or whether *eisangelia* was precisely the means used to prosecute an ἄγραφον ἀδίκημα, as Pollux 8. 51–52 says. Since treason was covered whichever of these views is correct, we need not go into this in detail here, but I am inclined to agree with Sealey 1981 that no "enabling statute" was required in the fifth century.

43. Hansen 1975, 37. For other general treatments of *eisangelia* see Harrison 1971, 50–59; Rhodes 1972, 162–171; Rhodes 1979; Hansen 1980; Sealey 1981; and Stockton 1990, 101–103.

44. Rhodes and Hansen differ on a number of points, but on this they seem very close together. Cf. Rhodes 1972, 167: "the main characteristic of eisangeltic procedure in the post-Ephialtic democracy [was intended to be] that εἰσαγγελίαι were heard not by the ordinary courts but by the final authorities in Athens, the boule and demos." Rhodes 1972, 37 n. 8, notes the significant overlap between the provisions of the proclamation in *Thesmophoriazusae* 295ff. and the νόμος εἰσαγγελτικός,

45. Hansen 1975, Rhodes 1979, Hansen 1980.

46. Hansen 1975, 23. This preliminary judgment is called *katagnosis*. The decree of

the *boule* in this play is referred to neither as a *katagnosis* nor a *probouleuma* by the text itself.

47. In the fourth century the *boule* could not impose a penalty exceeding a fine of 500 drachmas on its own authority, a provision that Rhodes believes applied in the fifth century as well: Rhodes 1972, 179–207. In 403/2, however, the *boule* executed a man for violating the terms of the amnesty without further trial (ἄκριτον, *Ath. Pol.* 40.2); Rhodes 1972, 180, thinks this was "irregular."

48. Sometimes the assembly simply instructed the *boule* to prepare a case, leaving it no option. For the *boule* itself to send a case on represents in actuality a decision that the case has merit.

49. In comparison to the speakers in the *Ecclesiazusae*, note that these need no rehearsal to master the cliches of demagogic discourse!

50. There is an ironic tribute to Euripides in lines 390–391: ὅπουπερ ἔμβραχυ / εἰσὶν θεαταὶ καὶ τραγῳδοὶ καὶ χοροί. Euripides has been so successful that wherever theater is performed, people have heard his attacks on women. We ought to take more seriously the implications of these lines for the performance of Euripides outside Athens within his own lifetime. Σ *Andromache* 445 tells us that that play was first produced outside Athens; see the introduction to P. T. Stevens's edition (Oxford 1971) pp. 15–21.

51. As Bobrick 1997, 183, perceptively notes, the women's problem is not Euripides himself but the male audience's *reception* of Euripides.

52. Is there a Euripidean connection? While Aristophanes has mocked Xenocles before, this poet also unexpectedly defeated Euripides in the City Dionysia of 415 (Aelian *Varia Historia* 2. 8). Sommerstein *ad* 848 even argues that this defeat was key in turning Euripides toward a new style of composition, the romantic tragedies such as *IT* and *Helen*.

53. See Sommerstein *ad loc.*

54. Cf. πολυπλοκωτέρας at 434. Rogers *ad* 434 suggests this term ridicules Euripidean usage (cf. πολυπλόκοις in both *Medea* 481 and *IA* 197), but parody is not the only point here.

55. Heath 1987b, 274–275, suggested very briefly by Handley and Rea 1957, 34, 36.

56. Σ518 notes one line parodied from the *Telephus*, but the scholia show no consistent recognition of parody, as they do later for the *Andromeda* allusions.

57. Sommerstein *ad loc.*; Heath 1987b, 278.

58. Handley and Rea 1957, 32, suggest the chorus was of Argive elders; Heath 1987b slightly favors a chorus of soldiers for Telephus to address. Choruses of soldiers are startlingly rare in Greek drama; indeed, their rarity might be linked to the ephebic nature of the choruses and the opportunity dramatic performance offered to be something sharply "other" from what they were, i.e., young soldiers. I would therefore favor the notion of a chorus of Argive elders. In either case, the interpretation of αὐτοὶ γάρ ἐσμεν as "we are all alone" is problematic in the Argive setting of the *Telephus*. Nothing whatever would suggest that the Greeks were at war among themselves, leading them to fear people from outside the city. Moreover, Telephus himself, even when disguised as a Greek, will obviously not be an Argive, so he cannot include his hearers as "we" in that sense.

59. 534: ἀλλ' ἢ πεφάρμαχθ'. Plutarch, *Mor.* 614bc, interprets Helen's "good drug"

of *Od*. 4.220–234 as the persuasive power of the story she proceeds to tell. Perhaps an allusion to rhetoric as a drug is already present here in Aristophanes' language—or to use the language of cinema, Mica accuses the women of having been sutured into the illusion of Mnesilochus's performance.

60. Why διδαχθῇ and not some other verb for "discover, find out"? Perhaps there is a theatrical meaning here as well: the women propose to "teach" Mnesilochus different lines, to make him a disciplined player in their scenario rather than his.

61. Rogers *ad loc.* quotes the somewhat cryptic Σ536: συντιμωρεῖσθαι αὐτὸν βου-λόμενος· ἐπειδὴ ἐπὶ σκηνῆς εἰσίν.

62. While παρρησία is not "free speech" in the strictly American sense, our fifth century evidence suggests strongly that it was viewed as a very good thing, especially for the democracy. In Euripides' *Phoenissae*, Polyneices says that the worst thing about being an exile is that, like a slave, one does not have the right to speak (οὐκ ἔχει παρρησίαν, 391; cf. *Hipp*. 422, *Ion* 672). A pejorative sense ("loose, irresponsible talk") does appear in the fourth century, especially among critics of democracy, but for its defenders it was a hallmark of the city: cf. Demades fr. 115 de Falco, τοῦ τῶν Ἀθηναίων ὀνόματος ἀξίαν παρρησίαν. If *Orestes* 905, θορύβῳ τε πίσυνος κἀμαθεῖ παρρησίᾳ, is authentic (Diggle deletes in the OCT, West retains it), that would testify to a negative sense in a fifth-century political context, but otherwise it is very much a "political catchword" (Craik 1988 *ad Phoen*. 391), and the women's denial of it in their assembly ought to be disturbing to the audience.

63. So striking is this effect that I wonder if it refers to a recent event and therefore can be used to date the play. I have suggested above that Euripides is accused under the procedure of *eisangelia*. Hansen 1975, 82–83, in his collection of all known and probable *eisangeliai* lists a rather bizarre prosecution which took place between September 411 and March 410. The evidence is in Lycurgus 1. 112–115, [Plutarch] *Life of Antiphon*, and Σ *Lys*. 313. The assembly passed a decree charging the corpse of Phrynichus with treason and providing that, if convicted, the corpse be disinterred and thrown beyond the bounds of Attica. Phrynichus, one of generals who led the revolt on Samos early in 411, had been assassinated. The prosecution succeeded, and the corpse was punished. The most striking feature is that the decree provided that, if anyone defended the corpse and it was found guilty, the defenders would also be put to death. Lycurgus says two Athenians did defend and were executed. There are bizarre parallels between this incident and the *Thesmophoriazusae*. Neither the corpse nor Euripides can appear in their own defense, but surrogate defenders do volunteer—at grave peril to themselves. I am unaware of other circumstances in which the Athenians punished unsuccessful defenders for the crime of defense. If this is the precedent Aristophanes has in mind, however, the *Thesmophoriazusae* must date to 410, as Rogers originally argued (cf. Hall 1989).

64. Sommerstein *ad* 574 thinks that Cratinus fr. 208 K-A., referring to writing about Cleisthenes in a comic episode, implies such a previous appearance on stage. We do not know that he appeared in any other Aristophanic comedy. If the audience are expected to recognize this mask and costume from another production, the effect anticipates the appearance of Echo, another refugee from a past production, later in the play. It would be rather startling for Aristophanes to "quote" the appearance of a comic character in this way from a living rival, but if Cleisthenes comes from Cratinus,

that might be a gracious tribute as well to a past master. Σ215 suggests that Aristophanes borrowed elements of the scene where Euripides shaves and costumes Mnesilochus from Cratinus's otherwise unattested *Idaeans*.

65. Taaffe 1993, 93, notes the theatrical meaning of the verb and aptly compares its use in Herodotus 1. 60. 5, where Peisistratus costumes Phye as Athena for his return to power (cf. Connor 1987, 42–47).

66. Another reminder that we are spectators in the comic theater? The tips of stage phalloi were sometimes painted red, imitating the exposed glans, which less sophisticated viewers such as young boys found very funny, according to *Clouds* 539. The red color of an erect penis might also be noted (cf. *Acharnians* 787), but I do not think we are to imagine Mnesilochus's phallus as erect here. Bowie 1993, 212, suggests an allusion to women handling sexual objects as part of the Thesmophoria.

67. Taaffe 1993, 94.

68. In the 1994 RSC production of Goldoni's *The Venetian Twins* in London, a chase and sword duel were staged through the audience, at the end of which one of the actors appeared to stab an audience member accidentally. The director, thinking that even this was not enough to disconcert an audience today, had instructed the actors to stop the action, had the stage manager come out still wearing her electronic headset for supervising the production, and brought in other actors costumed as police and St. John's ambulance crew—none of which even slightly disconcerted the audience, which laughed ceaselessly throughout the episode.

69. On stage action here, see Sommerstein *ad loc.*, citing also Rehm 1988.

70. In Aeschylus, *Promethus* 1034–1035, $\alpha\dot{v}\theta\alpha\delta\dot{\iota}\alpha$ is the opposite of $\epsilon\dot{v}\beta ov\lambda\dot{\iota}\alpha$, "wise counsel": the women of the *Thesmophoriazusae* are not acting wisely or justly.

71. Illustrated in Trendall 1991, 166, fig. 68; Taplin 1993, pl. 11.4; and on the cover of Sommerstein's edition of the play.

72. The choice of precisely four major models may be significant: Angeliki Tzanetou has kindly allowed me to refer to her paper "Sex, Lies, and Women's Rituals" at the recent Performing Aristophanes conference, which suggests that these form a tragic tetralogy, followed by the comedy staged by Euripides, Fawn, and the piper (see my discussion of this as comedy below). If the audience is meant to recognize this tragic tetralogy, however, these parodies may offer further evidence in the ongoing debate about the structure of the City Dionysia: i.e., in favor of a shortened festival in the later war years in which three comedies rather than five competed, each at the end of a day after a tragic tetralogy. See further chapter 7, n. 45 above, Luppe 1972; Luppe 2000a.

73. For Zeitlin 1981, 196–197, Mnesilochus's gesture "kills" the old-fashioned Euripidean tragic plot and turns the play toward the new style of rescue drama to be parodied later. On the other hand, the very substitution of victims seems itself Euripidean, like Artemis's replacement of Iphigenaia with the deer.

74. Mnesilochus used the same expression at line 651, there taking personal responsibility for his troubles. Cf. the similarly metatheatrical use of the verb in *TrGF* II fr. 646a, line 20: $\epsilon\dot{\iota}s$ $\dot{\alpha}\pi\alpha\tau\dot{\alpha}s$ $\kappa\epsilon\kappa\dot{v}\lambda\iota\sigma\mu\alpha\iota$, with the commentary of Bierl 1990, 385–386 (which also gives the updated text of Maresch for the fragment). Mnesilochus begins his speech by looking for a $\mu\eta\chi\alpha\nu\dot{\eta}$ $\sigma\omega\tau\eta\rho\dot{\iota}\alpha s$ (765), which Sommerstein *ad loc.* describes as a "tragic catch-phrase," comparing Aeschylus *Seven Against Thebes* 209.

It points forward as well, however, to the attempt to use the stage *mechane* in the *Andromeda* parody.

75. Palamedes was sometimes identified as the inventor of writing: see Taillardat 1962, 253–254, who also compares Eupolis fr. 385 K-A. (351K), where drinking is Παλαμηδικόν . . . τοὐξεύρημα.

76. Hubbard 1991, 195–199.

77. As Sommerstein *ad* 806 points out, Aristophanes is here rubbing in the fact that the Athenians had not won a significant land battle for nearly fifty years. This sounds like he is sailing very near the wind here, but the blame is soon again turned to the leaders of the demos.

78. In fairly obvious phallic symbolism, the women have kept their "loom beam and weaver's rod" (τἀντίον, ὁ κανών, 822), while the men have lost their rod, spear, and shield. ἀντίον seems to be part for the whole, but κανών also carries connotations of "standard" as in the Polycleitan *canon*; women therefore are the maintainers of standards.

79. Sommerstein *ad* 848 suggests a deliberate change in style on Euripides' part in reaction to his unexpected defeat in 415 by Xenocles (Aelian *Varia Historia* 2. 8). We do not know how the trilogy of which *Helen* and *Andromeda* were both components placed, but it seems at least plausible that it earned one of Euripides' rare first prizes, making these plays' prominence in the parody all the more appealing.

80. Zeitlin 1981, 186–189.

81. Taaffe 1993, 96.

82. She interprets Tyndareus and Proteus as contemporary characters, insisting that the latter has been dead for ten years (876), for example.

83. Sommerstein's suggestion of sailcloth sounds plausible; as Stone 1981, 322–324, makes plain, the costume must be simple, recognizable, and easy to put on in a quick change.

84. *Pace* Sommerstein *ad* 882, it does not follow necessarily from Euripides' fear of recognition at 189 that Critylla would recognize him here. The audience must not be left in any doubt at this point that Euripides is coming to help Mnesilochus, and the mask is the key identifier. While I do believe that audiences could recognize the individual actor behind the mask by voice (and even appreciate certain ironies based on that similarity), the mask is the essential marker of identity. I accept Sommerstein's conclusion that Echo, when she appears, is to be understood as the Euripidean character and *not* Euripides *playing* that character (on which, see below): the differentiation lies precisely in the mask.

85. Since this Euripides is a comic character, whose lines are scripted by Aristophanes, this foreshadows the ultimate resolution of the play, in which a purely comic performance succeeds after the failure of at least four successive Euripidean tragedies!

86. Zeitlin 1981, 188.

87. A dedication of a thiasos of Heracles from Cydathenaeum (I.G. ii^2 2343) records an Antitheus along with a number of names from Aristophanes' plays: Dow 1969; Lind 1990, 132–141; and Sommerstein *ad loc.* Critylla does not claim to be his daughter, since the demotic is different, but the unusual name may be an in joke. A further part of the joke is surely that Critylla is positioning herself as the *opposite* of Theonoe.

88. Though the echo may be very distant, Aristophanes used this proverb, in an-

other form, at *Wasps* 175–176, where Bdelycleon, having refused his father permission to go and sell the donkey in the marketplace himself (an excuse to get out of the house and go to his jury service, of course), prematurely congratulates himself, since Philocleon is now going to try imitating Odysseus and escape by clinging to the underside of the donkey. Critylla also speaks too soon!

89. Compare 662 (τρέχειν χρῆν ὡς τάχιστ᾽ ἤδη κύκλῳ) and 954 (χώρει, κοῦφα ποσίν, ἄγ᾽ εἰς κύκλον), 665 (πανταχῇ δὲ ῥῖψον ὄμμα) and 958 (πανταχῇ κυκλοῦσαν ὄμμα).

90. Euripides fr. 125 Nauck:

> ἔα, τίν᾽ ὄχθον τόνδ᾽ ὁρῶ περίρρυτον
> ἀφρῷ θαλάσσης; παρθένου τ᾽ εἰκώ τινα
> ἐξ αὐτομόρφων λαΐνων τυκισμάτων
> σοφῆς ἄγαλμα χειρός.

91. Euripides also had an interest in statues; they are key motifs in his *Alcestis* and the lost *Laodameia*.

92. Lines 1012–1013, πάντως δέ μοι / τὰ δέσμ᾽ ὑπάρχει; cf. 851, πάντως ὑπάρχει μοι γυναικεία στολή.

93. Trendall and Webster 1971, 63–65, for the effects of Sophocles' *Andromeda*; 78–82 on Euripides' version.

94. See his superbly argued discussion *ad* 1056. Most compelling is the practical argument that an actor playing Euripides playing Echo would not have time to change for his appearance as Euripides playing Perseus on the *mechane* at 1098.

95. Trendall and Webster 1971, pl. IV, 13; Taplin 1993, pl. 10.1.

96. Trendall 1991, 165, fig. 67, and Taplin 1993, 55–60, 66, and pl. 9.1. Shapiro 1995 argues that this vase represents a (perhaps Middle Comedy) parody of the return of Aegisthus to the palace after the murder of Clytemnestra. Shapiro makes an intriguing case, but the problem of Aegisthus's realistically rendered face remains. In stage parodies of *myth*, all characters (e.g., Zeus and Hermes on a well-known vase) are represented equally comically. The only point of using a different system of representation for Aegisthus here is to point up his origin in the world of *tragedy*, in contrast to all three other figures.

97. Cf. Bunthorne to Lady Jane in Act II of Gilbert and Sullivan's *Patience*: "Do let a poet soliloquize!"

98. It is of course impossible to reconstruct what stage business might have been used, although actors in a masked drama could not use facial expressions to indicate surprise.

99. See Sommerstein *ad* 1102. While there may be a subliminal allusion to Gorgias and his views of theatrical deception (Zeitlin 1981, 194, 207–211), Sommerstein rightly insists that γραμματεύς does not mean "writer, author" in the modern sense, nor would the Archer's knowledge of individuals likely extend beyond the kind of officials he as a slave would encounter. Euripides is presumably carrying the head in a sack, as Perseus did: should we imagine a bit of stage blood dripping from it, for a comic horror effect?

100. Hall 1989, 50. Bobrick 1997, 190, therefore seems to exaggerate when she

equates the Archer's reaction with that of the male Athenian audience disturbed by Eurpides' Phaedra or Medea.

101. Lines 488ff. Presumably these lines would be proof of a 410 performance date for those who see Aristophanes as a committed opponent of the democracy, since in 411 he would scarcely wish to warn the people against Peisander and his plans to restrict the powers of the demos. Perhaps they are more likely to have been a warning in 411, however, from an Aristophanes who indeed supported democracy.

102. See above, n. 52.

103. 1163: ταῦτ' ἐπικηρυκεύομαι; cf. ἢ 'πικηρυκεύεται / Εὐριπίδῃ Μήδοις τ' (336–337) in the assembly curse.

104. E.g., Plautus, *Miles Gloriosus* 974ff., *Epidicus* 371–372.

105. There is a probably unrecoverable visual joke at 1187–1188, where the Archer apparently talks to his own phallus, at first threatening it if it does not stay "inside" (presumably his costume). He then says εἶεν· καλὴ τὸ σκῆμα περὶ τὸ πόστιον (1188). The word of course refers to posture or stance (see below, on *Ecclesiazusae* 150; cf. 482, 503), but what σκῆμα the Archer refers to is uncertain. It could either be a comic posture on his part (perhaps hunched over, like the Spartan peace delegates in the *Lysistrata* 980–1006, esp. 1003, trying to conceal their erections), or it could be a comment on a σκῆμα adopted by the dancer, perhaps coming very near to him.

106. Is the fee high, low, or reasonable? Halperin 1990, 107–112, gives literary evidence. In the next century the *Ath. Pol.* 50.2 reports prices controls capping fees for flute girls at two drachmas; the reference is brief, but the fee could cover both music and sex. Bothmer 1982, 42, discusses two cups by Makron (*ARV* [2] 469. 148, Louvre G 143; *ARV* [2] 1654. 206bis, Bochum S507) that show men offering women and boys, respectively, two coins in their extended hands, but are they obols or drachmas?

107. See Sommerstein *ad* 1208, who suggests the copyist wrote the ending -σον in anticipation of the following adjective σὸν. I rely here on Sommerstein's report of the readings.

108. Hall 1989, esp. 50–51.

Chapter 9. Glorious Mud: Frogs

1. Sommerstein 1993a.

2. No lines attributed by the scholiasts or others to one version in preference to another survive, unlike the discussion about the two versions of the *Clouds*.

3. Hooker 1980.

4. The startling suggestion that Aristophanes may have read the whole of the *Bacchae* before it was even produced in Athens *and* that Aristophanes expected some in his audience to have done the same in order to recognize the parody of an unperformed play rests on Σ *Birds* 348. The scholion claims that δοῦναι ῥύγχει φορβάν at *Birds* 348 parodies fr. 121N (ἐκθεῖναι κήτει φορβάν) of the lost *Andromeda*, a play produced two years later in 412, and that *Birds* 425–426 (καὶ τὸ κεῖσε καὶ / τὸ δεῦρο) parodies line 266 of the *Phoenissae* (κἀκεῖσε καὶ τὸ δεῦρο), produced some time after the *Andromeda*, as we learn from Σ *Frogs* 53. Hooker 1980 thus argues that if these plays could be parodied *before* they were produced, so too could *Bacchae*—presumably from

written drafts circulating in advance. Nauck on the other hand attributes the coincidence of *Birds* 348 and fr. 121N to a common source in perhaps Sophocles, whom Aristophanes then parodies and Euripides imitates. The most recent editors of the *Phoenissae* make no mention of the supposed parody of 266 in the *Birds*. The notion of a widespread market for written copies of an as yet unproduced play seems seriously anachronistic for the penultimate decade of the fifth century, even given the case Lowe 1993 makes for Aristophanes' own possession of a library of Euripidean scripts. While the overlap between the texts of *Birds* and *Phoenissae* is significant, the exact words are not so unusual that they could not be used independently by the two poets, nor is it clear how humorous the audience of *Birds* would find an echo of the nervous Polyneices, looking everywhere for potential danger as he enters Thebes. If we still do not dismiss the resemblance as simply accidental, we ought to consider as well the possibility that Euripides circulated or himself performed privately excerpts from his works in progress, without the whole of it being available in written form to the general public: Polyneices' entering monologue in *Phoenissae* might make a quite memorable party piece for the aging poet.

5. Dover 6–9, esp. 9.

6. Segal 1961.

7. I assume, more confidently than Sommerstein *ad* 1–2, that Dionysus's own iconography would have been familiar and clear enough to the audience to identify him.

8. He does very much the same thing when the Athenian ambassadors threaten the slaves with torches at the end of the *Lysistrata*. One claims that he will not perform such a "low class comic routine" (φορτικὸν τὸ χωρίον, 1218), but in response to supposed protests or requests from the audience goes ahead and does just that.

9. Known only from here and I.G. ii² 2325. 65.

10. Ghiron-Bistagne 1976. 148, strongly advocated by Heiden 1994.

11. For the number of doors, see Russo 1994, 64–65. Webster 1970², 10–11; 173 originally argued for three doors but later adopted Dale's view that only one was needed in the fifth century. Cf. Dover 104–106.

12. Described as κενταυρικῶς (38). I suspect, but cannot prove, some visual joke here. While centaurs are indeed notoriously violent (and known opponents of Heracles, as Sommerstein notes *ad loc.*: perhaps he is having a "flashback" at this point!), there are other ways to make the same point. Could Dionysus on the stage and the donkey, still on the orchestra level in front, somehow be meant to be read as a fused image by the audience at this point?

13. If Hooker 1980 is right to see any influence of the *Bacchae* on the *Frogs*, then this is also a reminisce of the famous confrontation therein of Dionysus and Pentheus, both costumed in yellow gowns. Here, however, Dionysus disguises himself as the hypermasculine Heracles, in place of Pentheus becoming the feminized Dionysus. Dover *ad* 47 suggests verbal echoes later in the scene of Lycurgus's interrogation of Dionysus in Aeschylus's *Lycourgeia*.

14. How big? "About the size of Molon" (ἡλίκος Μόλων, 55), apparently a very tall actor, who may have played the title role in *Andromeda*. The joke *may* imply that audience crushes on famous actors were already part of the culture of theatrical viewing; it may simply reflect the pleasure the (largely male) audience derived from the

damsel in distress: cf. the burst of vase paintings reflecting the production of Sophocles' version of *Andromeda* earlier in the century.

15. Dover *ad loc*. rightly notes that any notion of Dionysus taking a "return ticket" spoils the joke.

16. As Rogers *ad* 140 saw; cf. Sommerstein *ad* 140–141b and Hubbard 1991, 201. For two obols as price of theater admission, see Pickard-Cambridge 1988, 265–266. Aristophanes' *Phoenissae*, parodying Euripides' play of the same title (dating c. 409 B.C.) must be closely contemporary with the *Frogs* and refers (fr. 575 K-A.) to the θεατρο-πώλης who collected the admission money in return for keeping up the theater.

17. 151, ἢ Μορσίμου τις ῥῆσιν ἐξεγράψατο. Where the chorus of *Knights* 401 imagines the horror of rehearsing the work of Morsimus, the emphasis here on writing suggests a broader impact of literacy now twenty years later: the crime of writing out one of his speeches is presumably perpetuating the tragedian's baneful influence beyond the actual performance.

18. Hooker 1960.

19. Bowie 1993, 230–238, citing numerous elements of Eleusinian myth in the play, wishes to see a blending of Eleusinian and Dionysian elements in the play and denies that the chorus are to be associated with the lesser mysteries at Agrai (p. 228). Much of his argument rests on the notion that "the mysteries," when not further specified, *must* refer to Eleusis, but he ignores the geographical argument of Hooker 1960; in concert with the references to the Heracleion, the marsh, and indeed the theater (see below), Aristophanes' reference to the lesser mysteries should be clear enough. At times Bowie is clearly stretching to make play events fit an Eleusinian model only, as when he suggest that the whipping of Dionysus may be "symbolic" of initiation, despite the fact that no such rite is attested for Eleusis (Bowie 1993, 236).

20. Slater 1986. The Lenaion (probably in the old Agora) and the Dionysion in Limnais are distinct shrines; see also above, chapter 1, pp. 19–20. The very notion of a chorus of frogs in this play may well derive from the theater setting near or in the marshes; note their pointed praise of "Dionysus in the marshes" (Διώνυσον ἐν / Λίμναισιν, 216–217).

21. Dover *ad* 180–208; Marshall 1996, 257–259, imagines a simpler, more mobile construct. Figures of Dionysus in wheeled boats appear on vases illustrating the Anthesteria: see Pickard-Cambridge 1988, figs. 11–13. It is unclear whether these wheeled boats were included in the procession to the Dionysion in Limnais on the day of the Anthesteria (Pickard-Cambridge 1988, 12), but there may be a specific visual allusion to them in Dionysus's wheeled rowboat here.

22. Dover 39, citing fr. 268 of Eupolis, with lemmata. A contemporary vase fragment (unfortunately of very poor workmanship), illustrated in Pickard-Cambridge 1988, fig. 86, may depict this instruction scene, although Dionysus is not rowing there; cf. his fig. 87 for a comic rower. In *Taxiarchs*, Dionysus was learning to row in a trireme, but the limitations of staging and visual clarity make it unlikely that any attempt was made on stage to recreate the actual structure of a trireme, with rowers stacked above one another. Despite the considerable differences between Charon's boat and a trireme, the stage versions of these will have looked very much alike. The image of Dionysus in a boat was doubtless familiar to audiences from vase painting and other

visual media, but there he usually reclines at leisure. The joke and the precision of the visual parallel lies in his becoming a hard-working rower.

23. Dover 55–57, Sommerstein *ad* 205–206 and 404–406. On the sound of the frog chorus, see Wansbrough 1993 and Sommerstein *ad* 209. Hubbard 1991, 201 n. 123, thinks that the use of an unseen but theriomorphic chorus of the traditional type "may be meant to indicate something about the disappearance of Old Comedy;" this is quite tempting, but performance considerations tell against it. Given that this first chorus is displaced by the later one of Initiates, however, the symbolism of change Hubbard sees may still be present.

24. Marshall 1996.

25. Hegelochus was a godsend to the comedians: cf. Sannyrion fr. 8 K-A. and Strattis frr. 1 and 60 K-A. (and above, pp. 37–38). The allusion is even more pointed if Hegelochus performed this line in the Lenaean Theater, but that is unprovable and perhaps less probable. Russo 1994, 182–190, has argued from the number of surviving titles that Euripides never produced plays for the Lenaean festival, only the City Dionysia, and given that his career began before there was a tragic competition, this is not inherently improbable: the fourth-century Lenaean festival seems to have been a proving ground from which one moved up to the City festival (Camp 1971 and Rosen 1989).

26. W. W. Merry in his student commentary of 1884 (Oxford) first suggested the "weasily" pun, which has been used by subsequent translators as well.

27. Sommerstein *ad* 376 first notes that this line must refer to the choristers (and perhaps the audience too?), performing like the cast of *Birds* (786–789) on the afternoon of their day of the festival; see above, chapter 7, n. 45.

28. On tattered clothing, see Dover 62–63. Stanford *ad* 404 even suggests that the σύ of line 404 may covertly address the choregus as well as Iacchus. In this year synchoregia, the sharing of expenses between two choregoi, was introduced due to the stringencies of finance in the war's final months: see *Σ Frogs* 404 and Pickard-Cambridge 1988, 48, 86–87.

29. Sommerstein *ad loc.* takes σχῆμα as "style," implying the use of the prop club to knock on the door. See above, chapter 1, p. 14, for σχῆμα as both costume and stance.

30. Sommerstein *ad* 464.

31. Dover *ad* 503–48, on the strength of the servant's oath by Apollo (508), identifies this as a male rather than female slave, against some ancient commentators. The humor of the scene probably is increased if this is a female slave flirting with "Heracles"; cf. Sommerstein *ad* 503.

32. Heiden 1994 suggests that Aristophanes is playing Xanthias here, which encourages me to further speculation: if so, the audience will know (from the proagon at least) that this is Aristophanes and draw further amusement from this improvisatory contest in which the playwright and the god of the theater try to shift the role and the physical punishment that goes with it onto each other.

33. See below, chapter 10, pp. 214–16.

34. Dover *ad* 537a, comparing Euripides fr. 89.

35. For the κυλίνδ- root referring to the *ekkyklema*, cf. *Knights* 1249 and the use of κεκύλισμαι in *TrGF* II F646a line 20 (see Bierl 1990).

36. Euripides was showing great interest the language of painting and description at just this period: cf. the fascinating discussion in Zeitlin 1994, esp. 175–177, on the language of the *Phoenissae*. Aristophanes, however, rather than using such images to heighten his descriptions, here *opposes* Theramenes' performance to the motionless and therefore unpersuasive mimesis of painting.

37. κόθορνοι have mostly effeminate rather than tragic and performative associations in this early period: Pickard-Cambridge 1988, 207–208. Tantalizingly, Theramenes was nicknamed κόθορνος, apparently because this type of boot was so soft and flexible that it fit on either foot, just as Theramenes fitted himself to either side of the political debate, as advantage served (see Xenophon, *Hellenica* 2. 3. 30–32 and Pollux 7. 90–91). Given Aristophanes' use of μετακυλίνδειν at 536 and the brilliant theatricality of Theramenes' stampede of the assembly after Arginusae by audience-packing, one wonders if κόθορνος could not have had a theatrical association this early as well, in which case Dionysus's boots identify him as "playing a part." Cf. the comment on costume in Cratinus *Dionysalexandros* fr. 40 K-A. Sommerstein *ad* 541 even ventures to suggest that the chorus may gesture toward Dionysus's boots at the word "Theramenes."

38. Preceded by tragic parody at 580. While tragic repetition of single words is known in several sources, one wonders if οἶδ᾽ οἶδα τὸν νοῦν· παῦε παῦε τοῦ λόγου may not reflect in particular the almost comic excess of repetition in Euripides' *Phoenissae* 1284ff., recently produced.

39. Compare the discussion of "the finger" in Neil Simon's comedy, *The Sunshine Boys*. Part of the two old vaudevillians' standard comic routine involves one poking the other in the chest with his finger—until the victim puts a steel plate under his shirt and thereby sprains the finger of the aggressor!

40. Which logically should disprove his claim to godhead, but no one notices that in the rush of the moment!

41. Compare the invocation of the Muse at *Peace* 775, another play very closely tied to the performance occasion.

42. Hyp. I: οὕτω δὲ ἐθαυμάσθη τὸ δρᾶμα διὰ τὴν ἐν αὐτῷ παράβασιν ὥστε καὶ ἀνεδιδάχθη, ὥς φησι Δικαίαρχος. Goldhill 1991, 201–204, doubts that the parabasis in particular was responsible for the reperformance. He is correct that the parabasis should not be viewed as completely independent from the rest of the play, but his attempt to claim that the parabasis's appeal on behalf of "noble and sensible men" (εὐγενεῖς καὶ σώφρονας / ἄνδρας, 727–728) is undermined by Xanthias's jokes about his γεννάδας (738) master is flawed: the term γεννάδας appears nowhere in the parabasis and is by no means a synonym for the εὐγενεῖς or χρηστοῖσιν (735); see also Dover 46–47 on γεννάδας and Sommerstein *ad* 179. In his review of Dover's edition (Goldhill 1995), he is even more insistent that Dicaearchus could not have evidence for believing that the parabasis accounted for the second performance of *Frogs*. He uncharacteristically employs the logic of the great Teutonic dictum, *einmal nimmer, zweimal immer*, in an attempt to dismiss Dover's inscriptional parallels on the grounds that none of them honor a playwright for a play. Sommerstein 1993a, 461–465, however, drawing on Kaibel, convincingly argues that Dicaearchus's statement about the parabasis relies on the text of an honorific decree.

43. Compare Xanthias's discussion with Charon at 189–191. Hubbard 1991, 208–

210, sees serious social criticism in the instability of slave and free identities in this play, but that seems not to be Aristophanes' primary focus.

44. Bowie 1993, 241–242, finds reference here to ritual purification—which Cleigenes fails singularly to provide!

45. Dover 281–282 (*ad* 718–37) and Sommerstein *ad* 725; useful summary of historical background in MacDowell 1995, 287 and n. 24, with further bibliography.

46. Compare Dicaeopolis's resentment of demands of the money economy in the city (*Acharnians* 34–36) to Philocleon's delight in the independence even his three obols of jury pay bring. For the suggestion that land had only recently become an alienable commodity, see the work of John Fine cited in chapter 7, n. 14, above.

47. Sommerstein 1993a, esp. 468–469, 476, argues the second production of *Frogs* played a role in the downfall of Cleophon and considers whether Aristophanes was a witting accomplice therein. MacDowell 1995, 299–300, is more cautious.

48. The slave dialogue is reminiscent of the openings of *Knights* and *Wasps*. The feeling that the play is starting anew surely contributes to speculations about rewriting and restructuring of the play before its premiere, but it is really not surprising that, having chosen an innovative plot structure, Aristophanes here harks back to his own prologue technique to introduce the new situation.

49. We cannot prove that this uproar was audible to the audience, but in fact a strong sound cue here would help account for the abrupt transition in subject matter. Moreover, the notion that the dead are substantial enough to make an uproar may be humorous in itself; cf. also the paratragic repetition in lines 759–760.

50. Academic readers in particular must beware of thinking of this as an endowed literary chair (for which the much later chairs of rhetoric and philosophy created by the Roman emperors are perhaps a prototype). The throne here in the underworld's Prytaneum is rather a form of *proedria* (Sommerstein *ad* 765), granted for past services.

51. The Doorkeeper says he has been "performing" (ἐπεδείκνυτο, 771) for the mob (πλῆθος, 774). Most explain the verb as metaphorical, painting Euripides as one of the Sophists, who did give demonstration speeches (Dover *ad loc.*). One wonders, however, if Aristophanes is hinting that Euripides sometimes gave "performances" of his own poetry, perhaps in a symposium setting (cf. note 4, above).

52. The term ἀγῶνα is of course theatrical. Might Aristophanes be referring to a contemporary debate about Aeschylus competing with living playwrights? The evidence for the original decree (*Life of Aeschylus* 12, Σ *Ach.* 10, Σ *Frogs* 868, etc.; cf. Cantarella 1974, 412 n. 9), allowing for the production of Aeschylus's plays after his death, does not necessarily indicate that they competed with the standard festival offerings at first. Nor must we assume that these productions were only of complete tetralogies rather than of individual plays; *Persians* was certainly remounted alone in Syracuse for Hiero by Aeschylus himself. Recent productions of *Choephoroi* and *Seven Against Thebes* respectively would explain much about Euripides' *Electra* and *Phoenissae*. Cf. Newiger 1961, 427–443, on *Electra*. Later, however, revivals *did* compete with current plays (attested only in later sources, e.g., Quintilian 10. 1. 66), and this may explain different reported totals of first prizes for Aeschylus. The transition from additional presentation to regular competitor could well have happened around the end of the fifth century, and one can imagine Aristophanes would not be particularly sympathetic to the notion.

53. Dover *ad* 830–74 on staging considers but ultimately rejects the possibility that all four enter in a tableau on the *ekkyklema*. While the *ekkyklema* certainly could hold more than one person, this would probably be too crowded, *pace* Sommerstein *ad* 830. On Pluto as a speaking actor, see also MacDowell 1994, 334.

54. If the "throne of tragedy" (765) over which the poets dispute is shown on stage, it further underscores the stage picture as a mirror of the front row of the audience, where the *proedria* are centered by the throne of the priest of Dionysus. Cf. the theater critics Birdboot and Moon in Stoppard's *The Real Inspector Hound*.

55. Hubbard 1991, 218. In theory: but in fact the deceased playwright's *Bacchae* was soon to be exhibited by Euripides' son in Athens, possibly even in the same year as *Frogs* (Dover 37–38), although production at the same festival, the Lenaea, would seem to be ruled out if Σ *Frogs* 67 [= *TrGF* 1 Snell DID C 22] records the trilogy of which *Bacchae* was a part: οὕτω γὰρ καὶ αἱ Διδασκαλίαι (Aristot. fr. 627 R.) φέρουσι, τελευτήσαντος Εὐριπίδου τὸν υἱὸν αὐτοῦ δεδιδαχέναι ὁμώνυμον ἐν ἄστει Ἰφιφένειαν τὴν ἐν Αὐλίδι, Ἀλκμαίωνα, Βάκχας. Tragedians competed with only two plays each at the Lenaea: Pickard-Cambridge 1988, 41. Is Aristophanes also perhaps subtly warning against posthumous production of Euripides? Cf. note 52 (above). The ἐνθάδε of line 866 has at least a double meaning as well: the underworld and the theater itself in which the play is being performed (cf. ἐνθάδε at 783).

56. Dover *ad loc.*; Taillardat 1962, 445–446.

57. ὅ τ᾽ ἀπατήσας δικαιότερος τοῦ μὴ ἀπατήσαντος, καὶ ὁ ἀπατηθεὶς σοφώτερος τοῦ μὴ ἀπατηθέντος. See above, ch. 3, pp. 60–61. Ironically, later literary history, in the form of the poet's *Life*, claimed that Aeschylus was *not* interested in achieving *apate*: see Rosenmeyer 1955, 234–235 (though I disagree with his notion that *apate* came to mean illusion only in the fourth century).

58. Compare also the unnamed neighbor's charge in *Ecclesiazusae* 765–766 that Chremes is ἠλιθιώτατος μὲν οὖν / ἁπαξαπάντων for contributing his goods to the common store. As this passage demonstrates, however, the charge of folly is not always valid.

59. See above, chapter 4, p. 79.

60. Which is precisely *not* the "democratic" thing to do: does Aristophanes expect his audience to notice the irony? *Demokratia* assumed the equality of adult male citizens in the conduct of public affairs: placing slave and master (δοῦλος and δεσπότης, 949–950) on the same footing was the antithesis of ancient democracy. Even in the wild fantasy of making women sharers of democratic power in the *Ecclesiazusae* (see below, chapter 10), Praxagora is careful to note that slaves are left outside the new state (651). Dionysus seems to warn Euripides away from this claim, but we really cannot be sure why (see Dover and Sommerstein *ad* 953). Finally, the exchange is one argument in favor of women and slaves attending the theater: if they could not have seen Euripides' dangerous plays, Aeschylus would not be so worried about his deleterious effects on the "lower orders."

61. Dover *ad loc.* obelizes ἐρᾶν with the argument that it is "incompatible with the rational calculation" implied by the other items in the list. Euripides' point, however, is that he has taught the audience how to behave. Aristophanes puts ἐρᾶν in his mouth as a reminder that he also notoriously put the disturbing effects of Eros on stage and could thereby corrupt his audience.

62. Goldhill 1991, 213–214; Dover *ad* 970.

63. For a likely recent restriction on the freedom of comedy by the decree of Syracosius, see Sommerstein 1986, Atkinson 1992 (*contra* Storey 1998, 103–104).

64. See Stanford *ad* 1014–1015.

65. Following Dover's assignment of speakers here and note *ad loc*.

66. The phrase Ἄρεως μεστόν is Gorgianic (B24 Diels, in Plutarch, *Moralia* 715E); is it ironic to have Aeschylus characterize himself as the leading sophist of the age did?

67. On *Myrmidons* see Dover *ad* 911–12. Dover also notes *ad* 1026 that Aristophanes here reverses the correct chronology, placing *Persians* after the *Seven*, rather than five years before as we know it to have been. Did Aristophanes not know the real sequence, or did he, as Dover suggests, suit the order of the play's argument here? Or could this also reflect the order of the recent restagings?

68. See recently, however, Meier 1993. Such political commentary on contemporary issues is to be strongly differentiated from the political meaning of tragedy in a broader sense, such as Goldhill and Zeitlin have sought to elucidate. For sharp criticism of even "collective" political meaning in tragedy, see Griffin 1998.

69. 1036, τάξεις, ἀρετάς, ὁπλίσεις ἀνδρῶν. Dionysus's immediate joke that he has not taught Pantacles much suggests the claim could be made to sound a little ridiculous to the original audience as well.

70. For all that the recently deceased Euripides was at least seventy when he departed the upper world, the two poets are portrayed as arguing across a generation gap. Aeschylus seems particularly worried by poetry's effects on the young: as the schoolteacher instructs children, so should poets instruct the young. Sommerstein *ad* 1054 notes the theatrical ambiguity of διδάσκειν in this context.

71. Deceiving the demos is a serious crime and the basis for a charge of *eisangelia*.

72. Few passages in Aristophanes have been discussed in as much detail as βιβλίον τ' ἔχων ἕκαστος μανθάνει τὰ δεξιά, primarily because it seems to offer precious evidence for the degree of literacy in late fifth-century Athens. The explanation of Woodbury 1976 that possessing a book implies a certain sophistication seems best: cf. Dover pp. 34–35. Steiner 1994. 209–11 detects a pattern of associating books with a somewhat antidemocratic withdrawal from public life in this and other passages of *Frogs*.

73. Dover *ad* 1119 points out that Aristophanes need not be using the term strictly as we do, since the examples are almost all simply the first lines of plays. Cf. reference to Euripides' τῶν σῶν προλόγων . . . τῶν ἐπῶν at 1181.

74. Dover assigns this line to Euripides but notes *ad loc*. that Scaliger gave it to Dionysus (as do Rogers and Sommerstein). Given the theatrical associations of δίδαξον, it seems highly unlikely that Euripides would request "instruction" from his theatrical rival here.

75. Whitman 1969, two of whose strongest points are the opposition of the ληκύθιον to a woman's brassiere at *Thesmophoriazusae* 139 and the fact that all the prologues Aeschylus treats in this fashion have masculine subjects. Dover *ad* 1200 gives an excellent summary of the case for and against a phallic association for the ληκύθιον, including most of the relevant bibliography.

76. So Henderson 1975, 120 n. 70 (in the second edition, 1991, 247).

77. Borthwick 1993, on αὐτολήκυθος in Demosthenes 54.14, *pace* Dover; Kilmer 1993, 81–89, although the vase can appear in various shapes.

78. All of Euripides' "prologues" are in fact first lines, with the possible exception of Euripides' very first example (just as first lines of other speeches were among the most likely to be quoted: Harriot 1962, 6). The scholia tell us that "some" identified 1206–1208 as the opening of Euripides' *Archelaus*, but Aristarchus could not find them in his text or indeed any Euripidean text that had come down to him, and other lines are attested as the play's beginning in other sources. Harder 1985, 179–182, shows there are essentially three possibilities: (1) Aristophanes here records the original beginning of the play, later somehow displaced by the lines recorded elsewhere; (2) the lines are from another Euripidean prologue; or (3) Aristophanes simply made them up. Dover *ad loc.* favors the first explanation and, like Page before him, suspects the lines later recorded as the opening of the play are the result of histrionic interpolation. Harder admits that lines 3–5 of Euripides fr. 228, which she identifies as the play's opening, sound like an interpolation, but she defends the first two lines as sound and favors the second explanation, that Aristophanes is parodying the prologue of an unknown Euripidean play. Aristarchus's failure to find the lines at Alexandria tells against this (although neither could he find the source of Aeschylus fr. 238: see Σ *Frogs* 1270), and no really plausible title for a play other than *Archelaus* with this prologue has been suggested. Dover's view, however, entails more complications than he fully confronts. The evidence that the *Archelaus* was produced by Euripides at the Macedonian royal court for King Archelaus seems indisputable (see Harder 1985, 125–127). Aristophanes might conceivably have gotten a copy of the play for himself and thus been able to parody the opening, but why would he assume knowledge of it among his audience? This is the very first of the prologue parodies: Aristophanes has every reason to begin with a Euripidean prologue that is very familiar to his audience, and that implies something fresh in the audience's memory. If we were absolutely certain that ληκύθιον ἀπώλεσεν had an obscene sense, the third explanation, that Aristophanes simply created a fake Euripidean prologue, might merit more consideration: Aegyptus with his fifty sons is the most obvious candidate for sexual exhaustion in this sampling of prologues, and sufficiently riotous laughter might prevent the question forming in the audience's mind of whether this *really* by Euripides. On balance, however, the notion that Aristophanes is parodying the prologue to a play already lost by Alexandrian times seems slightly more likely than the alternatives.

79. Only Goldhill 1991, 216–217, seems to have seen that Dionysus might well take parody of a prologue narrating his own activities as having personal implications, although Whitman 1969, 111, draws the implication of the phallic image.

80. This switch to the medical meaning *lekythos* (any kind of swelling or growth) harks back to and undermines Euripides' claim to have slimmed down the "swollen" (οἰδοῦσαν, 940) art of tragedy, which he inherited from Aeschylus.

81. "Where did you get those patter songs?" (1297). Borthwick 1994, 23–26, citing Thompson 1919, explains ἱμονιοστρόφου as referring to ἱμαντελιγμός, a conjuror's game with a twisted leather, designed to make fools of unwary spectators who try it, a nice addition to the deception theme.

82. As Dover notes *ad* 1308 (with ample bibliography), it all depends on how we

interpret ἐλεσβίαζεν. Dover opts for the "old and ugly" explanation, Borthwick 1994, 26–28, for a more youthful prostitute image. Cf. Halperin 1990, 89–90, on a Phintias kylix in the Getty Museum, showing older female prostitutes.

83. Cf. the old woman dancing the *cordax* in Eupolis's *Maricas*, criticized at *Clouds* 553–556.

84. For the "New Music" and comedy see Zimmermann 1993b.

85. Borthwick 1994, 29–37. There may also be a touch of the recognition scene from Euripides *IT* 796f. as well: see Dover *ad* 1309–28. *Pace* Dover *ad* 1323, it seems highly improbable in any case that Aeschylus himself dances.

86. Borthwick 1994, 36, on the pun on the meaning "limbs" in μέλη (i.e., you criticize me for using limbs as a recognition device), as well as a discussion of "twelve" as a traditional number for a variety of sexual positions or techniques. Xenocles, son of Carcinus, the poet who shockingly defeated Euripides at the Dionysia of 415, was also called δωδεκαμήχανος by Plato Comicus, *Sophists*, fr. 143 K-A. If Plato's play preceded *Frogs*, Aeschylus may also be insulting Euripides by comparing his work to that of his clearly inferior rival, but some would date *Sophists* after 404, based on references to Apolexis (fr. 150 K-A.) and Dracontides (fr. 148 K-A.).

87. See Rogers *ad* 1370.

88. Taplin 1977, 431–433, shows there is no proof that Zeus ever appeared on stage in any fifth-century tragedy. Hermes usually holds the scales on Attic vases: see *LIMC* s.v. Memnon. Mastronarde 1990, 285, seems willing to accept his appearance and would stage the weighing scene on the theologeion, especially if this scene appeared between scenes representing mortals on the stage level.

89. A line Euripides had apparently used twice before, both in *Phrixus*, fr. 833, and *Polyidus*, fr. 638.

90. Stanford *ad* 1378 thinks the scale is brought into the orchestra, but visibility will be far better on the stage. The evidence of Pollux 4. 130 that the weighing scene in Aeschylus took place above the stage level has been doubted (most vigorously by Taplin) or seen as coming from a later production, but we must consider its possibility.

91. Sommerstein *ad* 1365.

92. Most puzzling is Dionysus's statement at 1404 that Aeschylus has "deceived" (ἐξηπάτηκεν) Euripides by throwing in two corpses and two chariots. As Dover *ad loc.* notes, Aeschylus has not tricked or deceived his opponent in the concrete sense, because he has not violated the rules of the contest. Again, I suspect a metatheatrical meaning, that Aeschylus has "deceived" Euripides by persuading him to believe in the reality of the referents of his words, but the moment passes so quickly on stage that it is hard to be certain.

93. Segal 1961, 212–217 and passim.

94. Rogers *ad* 1469 (ὤμοσας) says "it is idle to enquire" about such an oath, but Aristophanes' use of the term is not just careless exaggeration.

95. The unusual expression δυσκρίτως γ᾽ ἔχω in 1433 seems to echo Euripides' *Erectheus* fr. 365N, a play probably from the late 420s.

96. Rogers *ad* 1434 argues that Euripides' answer is clever (σοφῶς) but not really advice (the city may need and indeed want to use Alcibiades, even if it hates him), while Aeschylus's *is* advice (use him—though reluctantly); cf. Sommerstein *ad loc.* Dover *ad* 1431a and pp. 12–14 argues forcefully and with considerable evidence that σοφία in

Greek is unambiguously good and never carries the questionable associations of the English word "clever" and therefore should describe the eventual winner of the contest, Aeschylus. If σοφία is such a nonpareil, however, one wonders why Dionysus remains in any doubt. Stanford *ad* 1433–34 thinks Dionysus's judgment may be intentionally ambiguous; cf. Goldhill 1991, 218.

  97. Sommerstein 1993a, 473–475.

  98. See now Sommerstein *ad* 1442–50.

  99. On Euripides' outraged question, "how can you look me in the face?" (προσ-βλέπεις μ', 1474), see Cairns 1993, 352 n. 28 (and further references in Sommerstein *ad loc.*).

  100. See Sommerstein *ad* 1504–1507 and Dover on the the deictics.

  101. See Dover *ad loc.* on the harshness of this term.

  102. Aeschylus essentially vanished from Athenian stages in the fourth and third centuries: see Sommerstein p. 8 n. 38 for the records of Euripidean and Sophoclean revivals.

Chapter 10. Waiting in the Wings: Ecclesiazusae

A previous version of this chapter appeared as "Waiting in the Wings: Aristophanes' *Ecclesiazusae,*" *Arion* 5.1 (1997): 97–129. Reprinted by permission.

  1. Sutton 1990 probingly reappraises such notions; cf. Zeitlin 1999.

  2. See for example Muecke 1977; Foley 1988; Slater 1993a.

  3. Ussher xx–xxiii; MacDowell 1995, 303, argues for 391 B.C.

  4. The scholiast suggests Agathon or Dicaeogenes, Ussher *ad loc.* Euripides' *Phoenissae*. When *Ecclesiazusae* was produced, Euripides had been dead a number of years, and there is no evidence for Euripidean revival in Athens at this period. The scholiast's suggestions deserve a little more credence.

  5. In the fourth century, five comedies were produced, as we know from the didascalic notice attached to this play, presumably on a single day. On competitions in general, see Pickard-Cambridge 1988, 63–66. The view of Gould and Lewis that the five comedies were spread over five days seems at odds with the discussion in this play at 1154ff. *Birds* (see lines 786–789) and *Frogs* (line 376) were played in the afternoon: see above, *ad loc.* I confess I do not understand why Dover, in the introduction to his *Frogs* edition (p. 60) insists that ἠρίστηται in *Frogs* 376 can *only* refer to "breakfast" rather than "midday meal," since ἄριστον in Thucydides 4. 90 and elsewhere (see LSJ s.v.) certainly means the latter.

  6. As often noted, the signal fire in Aeschylus's *Agamemnon* that the watchman on the roof spies is the sun rising above the horizon to the east of Athens on the day of performance.

  7. Bowie 1993, 255; Zeitlin 1999, 186–187.

  8. Serious problems beset both the text of, and the scholia to, lines 21, 22, and 23 (see Ussher *ad loc.*). The most persuasive explanation suggests that we have a reference to a mispronunciation of ἑτέρας as ἑταίρας, though whether by a politician or an actor (see Σ *ad loc.*) is uncertain. Two things are worth noting. First, whether Phyromachus is politician or actor, his words are criticized as though they were a performance; Golden

1987 connects this with lines 354–357 and posits a similar pronunciation problem for an assembly speaker there (a reversal of an ἀρχ- stem to ἀχρ-). Second and perhaps more importantly, there is an emphasis on sitting down in the assembly (21, ἕδρας; also κἀγκαθιζομένας, if one accepts Rogers's reading in 23), which begins to prepare us for the arresting visual effect of having the chorus sit down in the orchestra when they arrive in this play.

9. There are obvious forerunners in Dicaeopolis's scene with Euripides in the *Acharnians*, as he begs for the costume of Telephus, and in the *Thesmophoriazusae*, where Euripides prepares Mnesilochus to play a female part. In *Ecclesiazusae* (as opposed to *Acharnians*) this process has been freed from parody of a specific source. We now have onstage plotting and rehearsal undertaken by characters using their native dramatic abilities.

10. For the importance of cross-dressing and playing outside their own natures for the choristers of tragedy, see Winkler 1985. For the Renaissance and after, Garber 1992.

11. Saïd 1979, 40.

12. Both historical sources and the conventions of the visual arts show men with much darker skin than women, since the latter spent much more time indoors.

13. Later at the assembly, the women are all believed to be shoemakers (385) because they are so pale.

14. Props are every bit as important as clothes in creating the masculine; see the discussion of such "floating signifiers" as monocles and cigars in modern male impersonation in Garber 1992, 152ff.

15. There are exceptions, of course: the male slave Chalinus in Plautus's *Casina* uses his female disguise as a cover for physical violence against his much-detested master Lysidamus.

16. Cf. *Lysistrata* 194ff., *Thesmophoriazusae* 626–633, and further examples of the topos in Henderson 1987, 119–120 and n. 104.

17. Theocritus 18. 23 uses it to describe the racing Spartan maidens. The only other instance I know of, in Dio Chrysostom *Oration* 33. 38, also deals with voice quality: ὥστε γυναικῶν λαβεῖν φωνὴν ἅπαντας καὶ μηδένα δύνασθαι μήτε πρεσβύτερον ἀνδριστὶ μηδὲν εἰπεῖν. Given that terms in Greek for language (e.g., Δοριστί) have this ending, Gordon Howie has suggested to me that ἀνδριστί may refer, not to vocal quality, but to "men's language" in an anthropological sense. Although there were gender specific oaths (line 155, and n. 21, below) and other lexical choices (Gilleland 1980 and Bain 1984), there seems to be no evidence for separate men's and women's languages in Greek (as one finds in Japanese, for example). Note that terms for the musical modes (e.g., Μυξολυδιστί) also end in -τί.

18. In lost plays Aristophanes at least alluded to varying qualities in actors' voices. Pollux (e.g., 4. 64) preserves much of this material. There were terms for light and deep voices (frr. 844 K-A., λεπτόφωνος; 793 K-A., βαρύφωνος), for a gruff, probably old voice (fr. 134 K-A., Γῆρας: ὑπόστιφρόν γε τὴν φωνήν) and comments on how to speak (fr. 790 K-A., βαλανεύειν, to speak clearly; cf. fr. 657 K-A., φθέγξαι σὺ τὴν φωνὴν ἀνατειχίσας ἄνω, to speak with a full voice). On the sound of the voice in general, see Halliwell 1990, esp. 74–75 on effeminate voice (*ad* Ar. fr. 706 K-A.). Vetta 1993, 716, suggests Agathon uses a falsetto when singing the part of the maiden chorus, but that would be a much less sustained use than here.

19. Bain 1984, 32 (following J. N. Adams on Roman comedy), notes that Menander through lexical choice does at times "accumulate markers of feminine speech (especially at the beginning of a speech)." It would not be surprising if the actor here did the same with timbre and intonation. Cf. Taaffe 1993, 115–123, on linguistic portrayal of gender here and, on the technical question of falsetto, Vetta 1993, 712.

20. Later in the play, the term σχῆμα seems virtually to mean disguise: 482, 503. Other Aristophanic uses support the notion that it refers to the whole outward appearance of a character: cf. the "King's Eye" in *Acharnians* 64 and Demos in *Knights* 1331. Sometimes it refers to a dance figure: cf. *Wasps* 1485, *Peace* 323, and fr. 696 K-A., where Aeschylus is discussing his innovations in dance. The former meaning seems more dominant, however, and reappears in Menander's *Sikyonians* fr. 2 Sandbach [=372 K-T, 439K]: . . . ὁ τοῦ στρατιώτου σχῆμα καὶ τὸ τοῦ ξένου. To Praxagora's efforts to teach the women here we may compare Albin in the original film of *La Cage aux folles*: when he receives a lesson in how to butter toast in a masculine manner, he puts his wrist into the job so vigorously that he pulverizes the toast.

21. This joke recurs when one of Praxagora's hearers praises her and swears by Aphrodite (189). Praxagora rebukes her, of course, but more importantly warns her not to make a habit of it (192, μηδ᾽ ἐθίζου νῦν λέγειν).

22. At *Lysistrata* 507–520, she speaks mostly in plural for women in general, as she recreates husband and wife dialogue. Wilamowitz assumed she had no husband, but MacDowell 1995, 241 n. 30, concluded from the κἀγώ of line 515 that she did indeed have a husband.

23. Henderson 1996, 145.

24. Saïd 1979, 39, seems to me to ignore the evidence of this scene when she insists that there is no progress in the women's efforts but finds rather that their feminine nature continually reasserts itself "malgré tous les efforts faits pour la dissimuler."

25. A result of earlier displacement, for she learned her skills while living as a refugee (ἐν ταῖς φυγαῖς, 243) near the Pnyx.

26. We are constantly in danger of taking Plato on mimesis as gospel. Though Saïd 1979, 45–46, emphasizes the view that we have here, not a real assembly of women as in *Thesmophoriazusae*, but only a rehearsal for an imitation of a masculine assembly, why should we assume that this "rehearsal" assembly is inferior to the "real" one? As Reckford 1987, 345, says, "The theatrical images . . . all serve to portray the Assembly debate as a special kind of performance." The commutative principle applies, however: the theatrical performance can be a special kind of assembly.

27. There may be some slight preparation for their extraordinary action in lines 21–23, where Praxagora in an unfortunately obscure passage refers to the women taking their seats: see Ussher *ad loc.* and Golden 1987. It is far too slight, however, to give the audience any notion of what the chorus will do here. This staging enacts the power reversal in the audience space, since women apparently sat at the back of the Theater of Dionysus (Henderson 1991; doubted by Goldhill 1994): now the men of the audience sit behind *them*. Their action is unparalleled in surviving comedy and tragedy but may have had a precedent in satyr play: a vase in Würzburg which Simon 1982, 141–142, connects with Aeschylus's satyr play *Sphinx* shows five satyrs, dressed as Theban elders, sitting in chairs before the Sphinx: these are presumably the chorus of the play. Aeschylean revivals (see above, chapter 3 n. 6) might have included satyr plays as well,

so Aristophanes could conceivably have borrowed this startling effect from Aeschylus, but he makes it all his own here.

28. Cf. also *Knights* 750 (Demos speaking). The seated posture also calls to mind that other representative body of the sovereign people, the law courts: cf. *Wasps* 90.

29. Slater 1987.

30. Rothwell 1992 cites evidence for continued flourishing of *choregeia* in the fourth century to challenge the widespread notion of choral decline. Undeniably the Athenians were spending money on choruses: there is no evidence, however, that what they got for their money was poetry from the hands of the competing dramatists, much less that those choruses sang anything to do with the play's action.

31. A chous from Anavyssos: fig. 76 in Pickard-Cambridge 1988 and Csapo and Slater 1995, pl. 4B. See also chapter 5, n. 24, above.

32. Rothwell 1990, 51–52. The verb occurs in the play only at 161.

33. Saïd 1979, 40.

34. Saïd 1979, 41.

35. Boston 98. 883, conveniently illustrated in Pickard-Cambridge 1988, fig. 34, and Winkler and Zeitlin 1990, pl. 3.

36. The technique ranges from the broad farce of Frayn's *Noises Off* to the sophisticated games of Molnar's *The Guardsman*. We might also compare Tom Stoppard's *Rosencrantz and Guildenstern Are Dead*. The title characters, minor players in *Hamlet*, become the focal point for a backstage view of Shakespeare's play. Their deaths, a minor item in Shakespeare's scheme, are for them a nightmare they struggle desperately but unsuccessfully to avoid.

This play's episode also differs significantly from a simple "dressing scene" (e.g., *Thesmophoriazusae*, where Euripides and Agathon dress the old relative). The fact that several characters are preparing to play their parts seems to suggest a different kind of rehearsal; this is not just improvisation in character but a preconcerted narrative.

37. Their actions parody female functions as well, as Blepyrus's constipation becomes a parody of childbirth (311–372). Zeitlin 1999, 187, sees in this a dark image of "the city's blocked reproductive powers" (cf. Bowie 1993, 258), but she reads back to this scene from the later confrontation between the old women and the young man, an interpretation not available to the first-time viewer.

38. He parodies the *Myrmidons*, but one might more accurately say that the *Myrmidons* parodies him. The echo directs our laughter at the man in the yellow feminizing nightgown who think Aeschylus an appropriate poet to quote under the circumstances. He attempts to theatricalize himself as a tragic hero and achieves quite the opposite effect.

39. Cf. Ussher *ad* 440.

40. Slater 1988a. Ussher *ad loc.* takes this to be the wall of Praxagora's house, but that would be set back from the orchestra by the width of the stage, nor is it part of Lenaean shrine (misidentified by Anti 1947, 242–243; see also Slater 1986). On stage height in this period, see Winter 1983 and Townsend 1986.

41. 537–538. Blepyrus equates her yellow robe with the burial shroud. At some deep level, this may reflect a Greek belief that death is somehow feminizing: see Vermeule 1979, 103, 145–177.

42. Flashar 1967, 406 n. 2, cites line 580 as proof that public taste had changed,

prompting Aristophanes to move toward Middle Comedy. This is, however, a familiar topos in Aristophanes, for as early as the *Knights* (e.g., 514–544) we find him discussing the changing tastes of the Athenian public.

43. That *Ecclesiazusae* is a parody of some early version of Plato's *Republic*, circulating perhaps in an oral version, can be firmly rejected: see David 1984. 20–29, among others. While some would still posit a lost, common source for both Plato's and Aristophanes' states (e.g., Foley 1982, 15 n. 33; Ogden 1996, 186–187), perhaps an earlier philosopher, this seems quite unnecessary.

44. Baldry 1953; Foley 1982, 18.

45. Saïd 1979; Foley 1982.

46. Foley 1982, 17, on use-values vs. exchange values.

47. For two purposes: τοῖς ἀνδράσι συγκατακεῖσθαι / καὶ παιδοποιεῖν τῷ βου-λομένῳ (614–615). Note the order. In comedy sex exists not for procreation (as in marriage) but pleasure. Saïd 1979, 55–56, makes the traditional point that marriage's social function is to provide heirs to whom property can be transmitted; once property is abolished in the new state, there is no need for marriage. We can draw the further conclusion that those wishing παιδοποιεῖν do so from private desire, not social function. Here Aristophanes clearly differentiates himself from the philosophers and social reformers, who must worry about peopling their new states. So too when Benedick in *Much Ado About Nothing* offers as a feeble excuse for his marriage that "the world must be peopled," we know he has deserted the world of comedy.

48. Note that they are not dragooned into this but do so only in order to achieve a good they think worth the price. Cf. Kerr 1967, 144–165, on the comedy of the body's sexual appetites: the young and beautiful will be the reward of those willing to work for it. Therefore Foley 1982 is not quite correct in saying all exchange values are abolished. One can still exchange the only thing one still possesses, oneself, for sexual favors.

49. Schmitt Pantel 1992, 228–229, suggests that this is a comic version of Spartan custom. In Sparta the young at the common meals listened to (and learned from) the edifying discourse of their elders; see Xenophon, *Constitution of the Lacedaemonians* 5.5 and Plutarch, *Life of Lycurgus* 12.4. While such parody is possible, we need look no further at Athens than Aristophanes, where Pheidippides recites Euripides at dinner (see *Clouds* 1371 and Dover's commentary *ad loc.*) when his father asks for Simonides. If we combine the suggestion that theatrical performance at Athens is actually an opening up of the entertainments of the aristocratic symposium to the whole city with the demonstration of Winkler 1985 that the choruses of tragedy in particular are composed of young men, then we can see that what Aristophanes proposes in an offhand manner here is actually a reversion of theater to its sympotic origins. Tragedy and comedy will not be jettisoned along with the exterior world but will be brought back within the household.

50. The belief of Ussher xxvii–xxviii and *ad* 729. Sutton 1990, 9, suggests we have simply lost these choruses; cf. Handley 1953.

51. Aristophanes may have used others' poetry for the finale of some of his earlier plays: Sommerstein *ad Acharnians* 1227 suggests perhaps a victory hymn of Archilochus at that play's end and perhaps other songs at the ends of *Knights*, *Frogs*, and *Wealth*.

52. Chremes later calls on two slaves to carry his goods, Sikon and Parmenon (867–868), but surely we must imagine more than two: if the slaves are simply lining up small items on the stage, the items will be virtually invisible beyond the middle of the theater audience.

53. We noted above the pattern of similar line endings in 221–228; cf. 799–803, here (862–864), and 1155–1557. Nowhere else does Aristophanes use this technique.

54. Douglass Parker, *The Congresswomen* (New York 1967).

55. Whitman 1964, 9, simply excludes *Ecclesiazusae* (and also *Wealth*) from his study of the Aristophanic comic hero. His lack of sympathy for this particular play is evident in his remark that it is the only one of the plays that is in danger of simply "falling apart."

56. Sommerstein 1984a. 319.

57. That universal elixir of twentieth-century criticism, irony, has indeed been called on in an attempt to demonstrate that $\tau\epsilon\rho\pi\nu\acute{o}\nu$ $\tau\iota$ $\kappa\alpha\grave{\iota}$ $\kappa\omega\mu\omega\delta\iota\kappa\acute{o}\nu$ means its exact opposite, i.e., that Aristophanes here sets out to disgust his audience. This seems unlikely, particularly in light of $\kappa\omega\mu\omega\delta\iota\kappa\acute{o}\nu$; I do not know of any instance in which Aristophanes uses this central term (or any of its cognates) ironically.

58. 890–892 (three forms of $\alpha\mathring{v}\lambda\acute{o}s$), cf. *Birds* 682–683.

59. The First Old Woman and the girl later discuss just how old a joke this is: 926–927.

60. There are considerable problems with part distribution here. Ussher gives 918–923 (with arguments *ad loc.*) to the First Old Woman, while Henderson 1996, 182, presumably anticipating his Loeb edition, makes them part of the girl's continued speech. I have preferred Ussher's assignments, wherein the old woman is already staking her claim to her lover.

61. Sommerstein 1984a, 316 and note 23.

62. MacDowell 1995, 317: "her Young Man"; Henderson 1996, 235 n. 115, on their "'romantic' relationship"; Zeitlin 1999, 174, speaks of "the young man's sweetheart."

63. As Henderson 2000, 136, notes, she is the first young woman of marriageable age with a significant role in an Attic comedy (the various daughters in *Acharnians* and *Peace* being much slighter roles and notionally in much more "private" contexts).

64. Though we as the audience might immediately recognize him by his mask and costume as Chremes' unnamed neighbor, the would-be gate-crasher of the feast (so Olson 1987, 165 n10). As we have seen, identification of the various characters in this play is one of our most difficult tasks. I have tacitly rejected above the belief of Rogers and Ussher that the unnamed neighbor who addresses Blepyrus at 327 is also the neighbor of Chremes who appears at 746 (and further the husband of the Second Woman in the opening scene with Praxagora); though it is within the realm of possibility, it seems to me unproven and unnecessary. Olson's idea is far more intriguing: the audience will retain a nagging sense of incompletion if it never knows whether the unnamed neighbor of 746ff. succeeds in his attempt at gate-crashing. If he returns as the young man, we see that he did indeed join the feast without contributing his goods, but as he attempts to take further advantage of the new state by enjoying its sexual communism, he now must "pay." I argue below that the customary bias of Old Comedy against the young (a sharp distinction from the assumptions of New Comedy) should enable us

to enjoy the triumph of the old women over the young man as a rejuvenation parallel to that enjoyed by old men in other Aristophanic plays. Any residual sympathy we might nonetheless feel for this young man would be effectively prevented, however, if we had first seen him as the thoroughly despicable scofflaw of 746ff.

65. His complaints about the tortures of love (e.g., 956–959, 976) should not be taken too metaphorically; love was a violent and physical assailant in the ancient view, not to be sentimentalized; see Henderson *ad Lysistrata* 845–846 on torture metaphors for love.

66. Most reconstructions of the staging have the girl retreat into her house and play part of the scene from an upper window (e.g., Mastronarde 1990, 257–258), though when the girl next speaks (949ff.), her words imply that she has *not* gone inside her house, as the First Old Woman believes. The girl claims to have *deceived* (ἐξηπάτησα) the old woman, who only thinks (οἰομένη) she has gone in. On the window, see Ussher *ad* 962, καταδραμοῦσα. It seems to me likely that ἄνω and κάτω on the Greek stage may mean something like our upstage and downstage (as well as onstage and offstage). All that is necessary is for both the girl and the First Old Woman to withdraw from the active playing area and be out of sight of each other. The movements of the First Old Woman are equally uncertain. She addresses the young man after he arrives, though he gives no sign of having heard. Since she concludes with a declaration that she will continue to watch him (946), she likely remains on stage unobserved. Ussher *ad loc.* assumes that she departs but offers no real evidence. If there are any projections from the stage facade behind which both women could hide from the young man's view, the scene would play far more flexibly (and the humor of the duet between young man and girl would increase).

67. 969–970, καὶ ταῦτα μέντοι μετρίως πρὸς τὴν ἐμὴν ἀνάγκην / εἰρημέν' ἐστίν. It is beyond me how Ussher *ad loc.* can take this as "and yet . . . my words have come nowhere near my feelings." The sense is much more, "enough with the love lyrics already."

68. Apparently parodying the legal language of Athenian allotment decrees: see Sens 1992 on line 999, μὰ τὴν Ἀφροδίτην, ἥ μ' ἔλαχε κληρουμένη.

69. The problems of entrances and exits in the *Ecclesiazusae* are more acute than in most Aristophanic plays. Ussher *ad* 1054–56 thinks the girl departs in terror at 1048, though the young man still appeals to her in the second person at 1054. The manner of this silent exit has great consequences for our interpretation. Does the girl leave under dire compulsion or simply give up her attempt to acquire the young man as a bad job under the new regime?

70. See Slater 1989a. Whitehorne 1989, 95–97, contributes an important discussion of the imagery the young man employs, concluding (97): "One does not need to be a Freud to guess what other sort of pit or cleft is signified by the slang term βάραθρον or how this image relates to the final image of death by drowning at the harbor's mouth." Wheat 1992 has an extremely harsh view of the death imagery, and Zeitlin 1999, 31, even imagines the tug-of-war as a *sparagmos*. Similarly, Möllendorf 1995, 211–212, sees in the Bakhtinian grotesquerie of the scene only critique of the play's utopia.

71. Konstan and Dillon 1981, 382; cf. Sommerstein 1984a, 320–321. Davidson 1997, 93, offhandedly suggests the scene may parody erotic entertainments at the sympo-

sium, an intriguing notion in light of the interiorization and domestication of space in the play. Reckford 1987, 344–353, offers the best analysis of the genuinely Aristophanic spirit of the play as a whole.

72. *Ath. Pol.* 50.2. On *auletrides*: Davidson 1997, 80–82, and passim.

73. Saïd 1979, 58, suggests that only such "sterile" unions are imagined, because this will not threaten existing definitions of legitimate citizen birth. Sommerstein 1984a, 321–322, also notes that the scene raises only a bogus spectre of incest, since children would still presumably know who their mothers are, but suppresses any notion of the real danger of father/daughter incest under such a system.

74. MacDowell 1995, 319–320, and (especially on old women) Henderson 1987, 109.

75. Elizabeth Bobrick has suggested an objection we should consider (personal communication): that the young women (such as the flute girl in *Wasps*) whom the rejuvenated heroes win in their plays are not portrayed as protesting their fate, whereas the young man here does. I do not argue that the situations are completely symmetric. We do not expect a young man to be an abstraction (such as Theoria in *Peace*). The women in situations comparable to the young man's here are all played by silent extras, and we would not expect to hear their views. One may note that Philocleon's flute girl in *Wasps* requires a bit of coaxing and so may not be entirely happy about her lot, but in the ideology of the time, she has no real choice. The young man here does: he could—temporarily—give up the young girl. That possibility is what makes his protest humorous, rather than tragic.

76. Olson 1987 has vigorously challenged those editors who identify the new arrival as Blepyrus (and therefore this servant girl as belonging to Praxagora). Since Blepyrus departs for the agora at 729, Olson asks why Blepyrus takes so long to arrive, if this is indeed he. His charge that previous commentators who have invented activities for Blepyrus to account for the time gap (e.g., Rogers) engage in the "documentary fallacy" carries some weight. This objection, however, relies on the unspoken assumption that dramatic time can run *faster* than real time but never *slower*. Amphitheos in the *Acharnians* travels to Sparta and returns in a few minutes. Why should we assume that Aristophanes cannot stretch the time scale as well? Simultaneity and sequence are problems in modern dramaturgy, not for Aristophanes. In one sense the question, "who is the man in this scene?" could only be answered by his mask. If an actor wearing Blepyrus's mask appeared, no one in the Greek audience would have demanded an accounting for his time offstage between his exit and this entrance (that notion is its own version of the documentary fallacy). If an actor in an entirely new mask appeared, the audience would doubtless have accepted that as well. I continue to find the appeal to economy (not multiplying anonymous characters unnecessarily) persuasive.

77. Rogers *ad loc.* hears sarcasm but admits the straightforward reading is quite possible. Ussher *ad loc.* for some reason takes the maid seriously but suspects the chorus of sarcasm.

78. As Ussher *ad* 1138, 1151 points out, the women referred to cannot be the chorus, because the chorus also refers to them; they must be a παραχορήγημα, perhaps of dancers.

79. The order may be significant. Though the vote of the judges determined the

outcome, the acclaim of the audience doubtless influenced the vote. Moreover, it seems to have been better to win by a clear demonstration of public approval than simply by the judges' vote in a close contest. Compare *Birds* 445–447 (and chapter 7, n. 23, above).

80. See Ussher *ad loc.* and Sommerstein 1984a, 322 n. 53, who points to the parallels of *Lysistrata* 1043–1071, 1189–1215, and also Plautus's *Rudens* 1418–1422, *Pseudolus* 1331–1334, and *Stichus* 775.

81. Aristophanes elsewhere sings the praises of feasts in his plays, but the theme is most emphatic here. In my more cynical moments, I wonder if this might not be an attempt at subliminal sabotage of his rivals. If we combine the mouthwatering word here with Blepyrus's invitation to the audience to join the feast *by going home*, we might suspect that Aristophanes is trying to make his audience hungry enough to skip the next couple of plays in order to go home for a meal. Audiences did bring food with them to the theater, but it was more on the order of Dicaeopolis's bread and onions, which he takes to the assembly in the *Acharnians*. If Blepyrus can turn the audience's thoughts to more substantial fare, Aristophanes' next rival might be greeted by the sight of large numbers leaving the theater before his play.

82. Sommerstein 1984a, 315–316, has an excellent review of interpretations; further, Flashar 1967, 405–411. Rothwell 1990, 6–7, offers some salutary criticisms of the "irony hunt" (a term borrowed from Wayne Booth) conducted by many scholars through this play.

83. Sommerstein 1984a, 319–320.

84. See Sommerstein 1984a, 321 n. 48, on the emphatic μόνην of line 947. Cf. MacDowell 1995, 319–320.

85. Sommerstein 1984a, 322.

86. Saïd 1979, 55.

87. Schmitt-Pantel 1992 concludes from the material on food she has gathered from Aristophanes that he draws a sharp, moral distinction between public and private feasting, the latter being an unqualified good, the former usually a symptom of public corruption. I cannot review all the material she so admirably analyzes but will only say that, while Aristophanes clearly condemns the entertainment of corrupt political figures at public expense, the case of the people at large is quite different. Public feasts would seem to an Athenian audience a natural democratic good.

88. Zeitlin 1999, esp. 172–190.

89. Saïd 1979, 45–46; Zeitlin 1999 has a more nuanced but not dissimilar view of gender in the play.

90. Her final vision of this play is apocalyptic: "un retour à l'indifférenciation générale et au chaos" (Saïd 1979, 55). Zeitlin 1999, 185–186, also sees a failure of masculine identity in the play.

91. Saïd 1979, 34.

92. As Aristophanes' deprecation of attacks on Hyperbolus (*Clouds* 551ff.) suggests. Certainly experience would suggest that the removal of any individual politician had not yet cured the problems of the democracy.

93. Henderson 1990.

94. There is a curious prefigurement here of the notion of Svenbro 1993, 192, that reading is a feminizing activity, involving submission to the author. Svenbro ultimately

redeems his reader by making him an active participant in the process, and we should remember that spectators in the theater are also key participants in the creation of the dramatic experience.

95. Taaffe 1993, 182–183 n. 1, with references to Strauss 1987.

96. Adeleye 1977/78 tries to defend Theramenes' actions here by impugning Xenophon's account and denies he had any role in recruiting people to attend the assembly, but Buck 1995 seems a more just view.

97. See OCD s.v. Apaturia. Bowie 1993, 49, notes that "ancient etymology derived the name Apaturia from . . . *apate*."

98. See Strauss 1987, 28–31, and his discussion of "action-sets" and "quasi-groups" in assembly politics.

99. Xenophon, *Hellenica* 1. 7. 15. I confine one further speculation to the notes. Xenophon reports that a key element in moving the assembly to condemn the generals was a report from a man who said he survived by clinging to a barley barrel (τεύχος ἀλφίτων, 1.7.11) and further said that the dying told him to report back to the demos that they had died because the generals did not save them. The barley barrel is a very nice touch, and to my knowledge no one has ever doubted the authenticity of this survivor's report. Given the careful preparation of the audience by and including Theramenes' followers, I do wonder if he was such a transparently true witness. Where was he, for example, during the assembly's first debate? His name remained unrecorded, while those who sponsored various motions and countermotions in that debate but were well-known political leaders are all duly noted by name.

Chapter 11. Reprise—And Coming Attractions

1. The choices are not just comedy and tragedy, of course, but comedy and almost all other kinds of poetry that dealt with characters either mythic or historic. See the excellent discussion of this division in Lowe 2000.

2. Aristotle, *Poetics* 1449ab, Sommerstein 1997a, 69.

3. Another response is to postulate a substantial difference between theater audience and assembly audience, as Sommerstein 1997a does.

4. See above, chapter 2, pp. 22–23 and Plutarch, *Life of Solon* 30, where Peisistratus wounds himself, then demands a public bodyguard to protect him from his enemies.

5. Kerr 1967.

Bibliography

EDITIONS

The following editions of individual plays are referred to in the notes by editor's name alone, without date. Unless otherwise noted, the text quoted is regularly that of Sommerstein (1980–), where available, or that of Coulon.

Coulon, Victor. 1948–54. *Aristophane*. 5 vols. Paris.
Dover, K. J. 1968. *Aristophanes: Clouds*. 2nd ed. Oxford.
———. 1993. *Aristophanes: Frogs*. Oxford.
Dunbar, Nan. 1995. *Aristophanes: The Birds*. Oxford.
Henderson, Jeffrey. 1987. *Aristophanes: Lysistrata*. Oxford.
Henderson, Jeffrey. 1998–. *Aristophanes*. Loeb Classical Library. Cambridge, Mass. and London.
———. forthcoming. *Aristophanes: Knights*. Oxford.
MacDowell, D. M. 1971. *Aristophanes: Wasps*. Oxford.
Neil, R. A. 1909. *The Knights of Aristophanes*. Cambridge.
Olson, S. Douglas. 1998. *Aristophanes: Peace*. Oxford.
Platnauer, M. 1964. *Aristophanes: Peace*. Oxford.
Rogers, Benjamin Bickley. 1910–1916. *The Comedies of Aristophanes*. London
Sommerstein, Alan. 1980–. *The Comedies of Aristophanes*. Warminster, England.
Stanford, W. B. 1958. *The Frogs*. London.
Starkie, W. J. M. 1909. *The Acharnians of Aristophanes*. London.
Ussher, R. G. 1973. *Aristophanes: Ecclesiazusae*. Oxford.

SECONDARY LITERATURE

Abel, Lionel. 1963. *Metatheatre: A New View of Dramatic Form*. New York.
Adeleye, Gabriel. 1977/78. "The Arginusae Affair and Theramenes' Rejection at the *Dokimasia* of 405/04 B.C." *Museum Africum* 6: 94–99.
Allison, Richard H. 1983. "Amphibian Ambiguities: Aristophanes and His Frogs." *G&R* 30: 8–20.
Anti, Carlo. 1947. *Teatri Greci Arcaici da Minosse a Pericle*. Padua.
Arnott, Peter. 1962. *Greek Scenic Conventions in the Fifth Century B.C.* Oxford.
Arrowsmith, William. 1973. "Aristophanes' *Birds*: The Fantasy Politics of Eros." *Arion* n.s. 1/1: 119–167.

Atkinson, J. E. 1992. "Curbing the Comedians: Cleon Versus Aristophanes and Syracosius' Decree." *Classical Quarterly* 42: 56–64.

Auger, Danièle. 1979. "Le Théâtre d'Aristophane: Le mythe, l'utopie et les femmes,"
Aristophane: "Les Femmes et la Cité." Cahiers de Fontenay 17. Fontenay aux Roses.

Austin, Colin. 1974. "Catalogus Comicorum Graecorum," *ZPE* 14: 201–225.

Austin, J. L. 1962. *How to Do Things with Words*. Oxford.

Bailey, Cyril. 1936. "Who Played Dicaeopolis?" in *Greek Poetry and Life*, ed. Bailey et al.
Oxford.

Bain, David. 1977. *Actors and Audience*. Oxford.

——. 1984. "Female Speech in Menander." *Antichthon* 18: 24–42.

——. 1987. "Some Reflections on Illusion in Greek Tragedy." *Bulletin of the Institute
of Classical Studies* 34: 1–14.

Baldry, H. C. 1953. "The Idler's Paradise in Attic Comedy," *G&R* 22: 49–60.

Bassi, Karen. 1995. "Male Nudity and Disguise in the Discourse of Greek Histrionics."
Helios 22: 3–22.

Bennett, L. J. and W. B. Tyrrell. 1990. "Making Sense of Aristophanes' *Knights*." *Arethusa* 23: 235–254.

Bierl, Anton. 1990. "Dionysus, Wine, and Tragic Poetry: A Metatheatrical Reading of
P. Köln VI 242A = *TrGF* II F646a." *GRBS* 31: 353–391.

Blundell, Mary Whitlock. 1989. *Helping Friends and Harming Enemies*. Cambridge.

Boardman, John. 1974. *Athenian Black Figure Vases*. London.

——. 1975. *Athenian Red Figure Vases: The Archaic Period*. London.

Bobrick, Elizabeth. 1997. "The Tyranny of Roles: Playacting and Privilege in Aristophanes' *Thesmophoriazusae*." Pp. 177–197 in *The City as Comedy: Society and Representation in Athenian Drama*, ed. Gregory W. Dobrov. Chapel Hill, N.C.

Boegehold, Alan. 1991. "Three Court Days." Pp. 165–182 in *Symposion 1990: Vorträge
zur griechischen und hellenistischen Rechtsgeschichte*, ed. Michael Gagarin. Köln.

Boegehold, Alan et al. 1995. *The Lawcourts at Athens: Sites, Buildings, Equipment, Procedures, and Testimonia*. Athenian Agora 28. Princeton, N.J.

Borthwick, E. K. 1968. "The Dances of Philocleon and the Sons of Carcinus in Aristophanes' *Wasps*." *CQ* n.s. 18: 44–51.

——. 1992. "Observations on the Opening Scene of Aristophanes' *Wasps*." *CQ* n.s.
42: 274–278.

——. 1993. "Autolekythos and Lekythion in Demosthenes and Aristophanes." *LCM*
18.3: 34–37.

——. 1994. "New Interpretations of Aristophanes *Frogs* 1249–1328." *CQ* n.s. 18: 44–
51.

Bothmer, Dietrich von. 1982. "Notes on Makron." Pp. 29–52 in *The Eye of Greece:
Studies in the Art of Athens*, ed. Donna Kurtz and Brian Sparkes. Cambridge.

Bowie, A. M. 1982. "The Parabasis in Aristophanes: Prolegomena, *Acharnians*." *Phoenix* 48: 21–41.

——. 1987. "Ritual Stereotype and Comic Reversal: Aristophanes' *Wasps*." *BICS* 34:
112–125.

——. 1993. *Aristophanes: Myth, Ritual and Comedy*. Cambridge.

Bowie, Ewen L. 1988. "Who Is Dicaeopolis?" *JHS* 108: 183–185.

Braund, David. 2000. "Strattis' *Kallipides*: The Pompous Actor from Scythia?" Pp. 151–158 in *The Rivals of Aristophanes: Studies in Athenian Old Comedy*, ed. David Harvey and John Wilkins. London.

Bremer, J. M. 1993. "Aristophanes on His Own Poetry." Pp. 125–165 in *Aristophane*, ed. Bremer and E. W. Handley. Entretiens Hardt 38. Vandœvres-Genève.

Brillante, Carlo. 1987. "La figura di Filocleone nel prologo delle Vespe di Aristofane." *QUCC* 55: 23–35.

Brock, R. W. 1986. "The Double Plot in Aristophanes' *Knights*." *GRBS* 27: 15–27.

———. 1991. "The Emergence of Democratic Ideology." *Historia* 40: 160–169.

Brown, E. L. 1974. "Cleon Caricatured on a Corinthian Cup." *JHS* 94: 166–170.

Buck, R. J. 1995. "The Character of Theramenes." *Ancient History Bulletin* 9: 14–24.

Buttrey, T. V. 1977. "Ὑπο- in Aristophanes and ὑποκριτής." *GRBS* 18: 5–23.

Cairns, Douglas L. 1993. *Aidos: The Psychology and Ethics of Honour and Shame in Ancient Greek Literature*. Oxford.

Calderwood, James. 1971. *Shakespearean Metadrama*. Minneapolis.

Camp, John McK. 1971. "Greek Inscriptions, Tragedies Presented at the Lenaia of 364/3 B.C." *Hesperia* 40: 302–307.

Cantarella, R. 1974. "Aristophanes' *Plutos* 422–425 und die Wiederaufführungen aischyleischer Werke." Pp. 405–435 in *Wege zu Aischylos* Vol. I, ed. H. Hommel. Darmstadt. [*RAL* 20 (1965) 363–381].

Carawan, E. M. 1990. "The Five Talents Cleon Coughed Up (Scho. Ar. *Ach.* 6)." *CQ* n.s. 40: 137–147.

Carey, Christopher. 1993. "The Purpose of Aristophanes' *Acharnians*." *RhMus* 136: 245–263.

———. 1994. "Comic Ridicule and Democracy." Pp. 69–83 in *Ritual, Finance, Politics: Athenian Democratic Accounts Presented to David Lewis*, ed. Robin Osborne and Simon Hornblower. Oxford.

Cartledge, Paul. 1990. *Aristophanes and His Theatre of the Absurd*. London.

Cassio, A. C. 1981. "A 'Typical' Servant in Aristophanes (Pap. For. 112, Austin 63, 90FF.)." *ZPE* 41: 17–18.

———. 1985. *Commedia e partecipazione: La Pace de Aristofane*. Naples.

Chapman, G. A. H. 1983. "Some Notes on Dramatic Illusion in Aristophanes." *AJP* 104: 1–23.

Cole, Susan G. 1993. "Procession and Celebration at the Dionysia." Pp. 25–38 in *Theater and Society in the Classical World*, ed. Ruth Scodel. Ann Arbor, Mich.

Compton-Engle, Gwendolyn. 1999. "From Country to City: The Persona of Dicaeopolis in Aristophanes' *Acharnians*." *CJ* 94: 359–373.

Connor, W. R. 1987. "Tribes, Festivals, and Processions: Civic Ceremonial and Political Manipulation in Archaic Greece." *JHS* 107: 40–50.

———. 1989. "City Dionysia and Athenian Democracy." *Classica et Medievalia* 40: 7–32.

Crahay, R. and M. Delcourt. 1952. "Les ruptures d'illusion dans les comédies antiques." *Annuaire de l'Inst. Phil. et Hist. Orientale de Bruxelles* 12: 83–92.

Craik, Elizabeth. 1988. *Euripides: Phoenissae*, ed. with trans. and comm. Warminster, England.

Crane, Gregory. 1997. "Oikos and Agora: Mapping the Polis in Aristophanes' *Wasps*." Pp. 198–229 in *The City as Comedy: Society and Representation in Athenian Drama*, ed. Gregory W. Dobrov. Chapel Hill, N.C.

Crichton, Angus. 1993. " 'The Old Are in a Second Childhood': Age Reversal and Jury Service in Aristophanes' *Wasps*." *BICS* 38: 59–80.

Csapo, Eric. 1993. "Deep Ambivalence: Notes on a Greek Cockfight." *Phoenix* 47: 1–28, pls. 1–4; 115–124.

Csapo, Eric and William J. Slater. 1995. *The Context of Ancient Drama*. Ann Arbor, Michigan.

Dale, A. M. 1961. "A Heroic End." *BICS* 8: 47–48 [= *Collected Papers of A. M. Dale*, 170–172].

———. 1969a. "Interior Scenes and Illusion in Greek Drama." Pp. 259–271 in *Collected Papers*. Cambridge.

———. 1969b. "The *Acharnians* of Aristophanes." Pp. 281–294 in *Collected Papers of A. M. Dale*. Cambridge.

David, E. 1984. *Aristophanes and Athenian Society of the Early Fourth Century B.C.* Leiden.

Davidson, James. 1997. *Courtesans and Fishcakes: The Consuming Passions of Classical Athens*. London and New York.

de Ste. Croix, G. E. M. 1972. *The Origins of the Peloponnesian War*. Ithaca, N.Y.

Dearden, C. W. 1976. *The Stage of Aristophanes*. London.

Dedoussi, Christina. 1995. "Greek Drama and Its Spectators: Conventions and Relationships," Pp. 123–132 in *Stage Directions: Essays in Ancient Drama in Honour of E. W. Handley*, ed. Alan Griffiths [= *BICS Supplement* 66].

Dickerson, G. W. 1974. "Aristophanes' *Ranae* 862." *HSCP* 78: 177–188.

Dillon, Matthew. 1995. "By Gods, Tongues, and Dogs: The Use of Oaths in Aristophanic Comedy." *G&R* 42: 135–151.

Dinsmoor, William. 1951. "The Athenian Theater of the Fifth Century." Pp. 309–330 in *Studies Presented to David Moore Robinson*, ed. G. E. Mylonas. Saint Louis.

Dobrov, Gregory. 1993. "The Tragic and the Comic Tereus." *AJP* 114: 189–234.

———. 1997. "Language, Fiction, and Utopia." Pp. 95–132 in *The City As Comedy: Society and Representation in Greek Drama*, ed. G. Dobrov. Chapel Hill, NC.

Donohue, A. A. 1988. *Xoana and the Origins of Greek Sculpture*. Atlanta.

Dover, K. J. 1963. "Notes on Aristophanes' *Acharnians*." *Maia* 15: 6–25.

Dover, K. J. 1966 [1987]. "The Skene of Aristophanes," *Proceedings of the Cambridge Philological Society*. No. 192 (n.s. 12): 2–17 [= pp. 249–266 in Dover, *Greek and the Greeks*, Blackwell, 1987]

Dover, K. J. 1967. "Portrait Masks in Aristophanes." Pp. 16–28 in *ΚΩΜΩΙΔΟΤΡΑΓΗΜΑΤΑ: Studies in Honor of W. J. W. Koster*. Amsterdam. [= Newiger 1975: 155–169]

———. 1972. *Aristophanic Comedy*. Berkeley and London.

———. 1978. *Greek Homosexuality*. London.

Dow, Sterling. 1969. "Some Athenians in Aristophanes." *AJA* 73: 234–35.

Duckworth, George E. 1952. *The Nature of Roman Comedy*. Princeton, N.J.

Edmonds, J. M. 1957. *The Fragments of Attic Comedy*. Vol. 1. Leiden.

Edmunds, Lowell. 1980. "Aristophanes' *Acharnians*." *YCS* 26: 1–41.

———. 1987a. "The Aristophanic Cleon's 'Disturbance' of Athens." *AJP* 108: 233–263.

———. 1987b. *Cleon, Knights, and Aristophanes' Politics*. Lanham, Md.

Ehrenberg, Victor. 1962. *The People of Aristophanes: A Sociology of Old Comedy*. 3rd ed. New York.

Faraone, Christopher A. 1992. *Talismans and Trojan Horses: Guardian Statues in Ancient Greek Myth and Ritual*. Oxford.

Fish, Stanley. 1980. *Is There a Text in This Class?: The Authority of Interpretive Communities*. Cambridge, Mass.

Fisher, N. R. E. 1993. "Multiple Personalities and Dionysiac Festivals: Dicaeopolis in Aristophanes' *Acharnians*." *G&R* 40: 31–47.

Flashar, H. 1967. "Zur Eigenart des Aristophanischen Spätwerks." *Poetica* 1: 154–175 [= Newiger 1975: 405–434—pages cited from this reprint].

Flickinger, Roy C. 1918. *The Greek Theater and Its Drama*. Chicago.

Foley, Helene P. 1982. "The 'Female Intruder' Reconsidered: Women in Aristophanes' *Lysistrata* and *Ecclesiazusae*." *CP* 77: 1–21.

———. 1985. *Ritual Irony: Poetry and Sacrifice in Euripides*. Ithaca, N.Y.

———. 1988. "Tragedy and Politics in Aristophanes' *Acharnians*." *JHS* 108: 33–47. [shorter version pp. 119–138 in R. Scodel, ed., *Theater and Society in the Classical World* (Ann Arbor, Mich., 1993)]

Fowler, Don P. 1989a. "Correspondence." *LCM* 14: 3.

———. 1989b. "Taplin on Cocks." *CQ* 39: 257–259.

Garber, Marjorie. 1992. *Vested Interests: Cross-Dressing and Cultural Anxiety*. New York and London.

Garzya, A. 1987. "Gorgias et l'*apate* de la tragedie." Pp. 149–165 in *Anthropologie et théâtre antique*, ed. Paulette Ghiron-Bistagne Cahiers du GITA 3. Montpellier.

Gauly, Bardo et al. 1991. *Musa Tragica: Die griechische Tragödie von Thespis bis Ezechiel*. Göttingen.

Gebhard, Elizabeth. 1974. "The Form of the Orchestra in the Early Greek Theatre." *Hesperia* 43: 428–440.

Gelzer, Thomas. 1960. *Der Epirrhematische Agon be Aristophanes*. Zetemata 23. Munich.

———. 1971. *Aristophanes der Komiker*. Stuttgart [= cols. 1392–1570, Supplement-Band XII der Paulyschen Realencyclopädie].

———. 1976. "Some Aspects of Aristophanes' Dramatic Art in the *Birds*." *BICS* 23: 1–14.

Ghiron-Bistagne, Paulette. 1976. *Recherches sur les acteurs dans la Grèce antique*. Paris.

Gilleland, M. E. 1980. "Female Speech in Greek and Latin." *AJP* 101: 180–183.

Gilula, Dwora. 1994. "An Unnoticed Second Meaning: Ar. *Birds* 445–7." *LCM* 19: 19.

Golden, Mark. 1987. "Aristophanes, *Ecclesiazusae* 354–357." *Hermes* 115: 500–502.

Goldhill, Simon. 1989. "Reading Performance Criticism." *G&R* 36: 172–182.

———. 1990. "The Great Dionysia and Civic Ideology." Pp. 97–129 in *Nothing to Do with Dionysos? Athenian Drama in its Social Context*. ed. John J. Winkler and Froma I. Zeitlin. Princeton, N.J.

———. 1991. *The Poet's Voice*. Cambridge.

———. 1994. "Representing Democracy: Women at the Great Dionysia." Pp. 347–369 in *Ritual, Finance, Politics: Athenian Democratic Accounts Presented to David Lewis*, ed. Robin Osborne and Simon Hornblower. Oxford.

Goldhill, Simon. 1995. review of K. J. Dover, *Aristophanes: Frogs* (Oxford, 1993). *CP* 90: 86–91.

Graves, C. E. 1911. *Aristophanes: The Peace*. Cambridge.

Green, J. Richard. 1985. "A Representation of the *Birds* of Aristophanes." Pp. 95–118 in *Greek Vases in the J. Paul Getty Museum* 2. Malibu.

———. 1991. "On Seeing and Depicting the Theatre in Classical Athens," *GRBS* 32: 15–50.

———. 1994. *Theatre in Ancient Greek Society*. London.

Green, J. R. and Eric Handley. 1995. *Images of the Greek Theatre*. London.

Greenblatt, Stephen. 1980. *Renaissance Self-Fashioning: From More to Shakespeare*. Chicago.

———. 1988. *Shakespearean Negotiations: The Circulation of Social Energy in Renaissance England*. Oxford.

Griffin, Jasper. 1998. "The Social Function of Attic Tragedy." *CQ* 48: 39–61.

Gröbl, J. 1889/90. *Die ältesten Hypotheseis zu Aristophanes*. Dillingen.

Haldane, J. A. 1965. "A Scene in the *Thesmophoriazusae* (295–371)." *Philologus* 109: 39–46.

Hall, Edith M. 1989. "The Archer Scene in Aristophanes' *Thesmophoriazusae*." *Philologus* 133: 38–54.

———. 1995. "Lawcourt Dramas: The Power of Performance in Greek Forensic Oratory." *BICS* 40: 39–58.

———. 1996. *Aeschylus: Persians*. Warminster, England.

Halleran, Michael R. 1985. *Stagecraft in Euripides*. Totowa, N.J.

Halliwell, F. Stephen. 1980. "Aristophanes' Apprenticeship." *CQ* 30: 33–45.

———. 1989. "Authorial Collaboration in the Athenian Comic Theatre." *GRBS* 30: 515–528.

———. 1990. "The Sounds of the Voice in Old Comedy." in *"Owls to Athens": Essays on Classical Subjects Presented to Sir Kenneth Dover*, ed. E. M. Craik. Oxford.

———. 1991. "Comic Satire and the Freedom of Speech in Classical Athens." *JHS* 111: 48–70.

———. 1993. "Comedy and Publicity in the Society of the Polis." Pp. 321–340 in *Tragedy, Comedy, and the Polis*, ed. Alan Sommerstein et al. Bari.

Halperin, David. 1990. *One Hundred Years of Homosexuality*. New York.

Hammond, N. G. L. 1988. "More on Conditions of Production to the Death of Aeschylus." *GRBS* 29: 5–33.

Handley, E. W. 1953. "*XOPOY* in the *Plutus*." *CQ* n.s. 3: 55–61.

———. 1965. *The Dyskolos of Menander*. London.

———. 1993a. "Aristophanes and His Theatre." Pp. 97–123 in *Aristophane*, ed. J. M. Bremer and Handley. Entretiens Hardt 38. Vandœvres-Genève.

———. 1993b. "Aristophanes and the Generation Gap." Pp. 417–430 in *Tragedy, Comedy and the Polis*. ed. Alan Sommerstein et al. Bari.

Handley, E. W. and J. Rea. 1957. *The Telephus of Euripides*. *BICS* Supplement 5. London.

Hansen, M. H. 1975. *Eisangelia*. Odense.

———. 1980. "Eisangelia in Athens: A Reply." *JHS* 100: 89–95.

Harder, Annette. 1985. *Euripides' Kresphontes and Archelaos*. Leiden.

Harriott, Rosemary. 1962. "Aristophanes' Audience and the Plays of Euripides." *BICS* 9: 1–8.

Harrison, A. R. W. 1971. *The Law of Athens*. Vol. 2, *Procedure*. Oxford.

Heath, Malcolm. 1987a. *Political Comedy in Aristophanes. Hypomnemata* 87. Göttingen.

———. 1987b. "Euripides' *Telephus*." *CQ* 37: 272–280.

———. 1990. "Aristophanes and His Rivals." *G&R* 37: 143–158.

Heiden, Bruce. 1994. "Two Notes on the *Frogs*." *LCM* 19: 8–12.

Helmbold, H. 1890. *Aristophanis Pax superstes utrum prior sit an retractata*. Jena.

Henderson, Jeffrey. 1975. *The Maculate Muse: Obscene Language in Attic Comedy*. New Haven, Conn. [2nd ed. New York, 1991].

———. 1980. *Aristophanes: Essays in Interpretation. YCS* 26. New Haven.

———. 1987. "Older Women in Attic Old Comedy." *TAPA* 117: 105–129.

———. 1990. "The Dêmos and the Comic Competition." Pp. 271–313 in *Nothing to Do with Dionysos? Athenian Drama in Its Social Context*, ed. John J. Winkler and Froma I. Zeitlin. Princeton, N.J.

———. 1991. "Women and the Athenian Dramatic Festivals." *TAPA* 121: 133–147.

———. 1993. "Comic Hero Versus Political Élite." Pp. 307–319 in *Tragedy, Comedy, and the Polis*, ed. Alan Sommerstein et al. Bari.

———. 1996. *Three Plays by Aristophanes: Staging Women*. New York and London.

———. 1997. "The Comic Heroism of Peisetairos." Pp. 135–148 in *The City as Comedy: Society and Representation in Athenian Drama*, ed. Gregory W. Dobrov. Chapel Hill, N.C.

———. 2000. "Pherecrates and the Women of Old Comedy." Pp. 135–150 in *The Rivals of Aristophanes: Studies in Athenian Old Comedy*, ed. David Harvey and John Wilkins. London.

Herington, C. J. 1985. *Poetry into Drama: Early Tragedy and the Greek Poetic Tradition*. Berkeley, Calif.

Higgins, W. E. 1977. "A Passage to Hades: The Frogs of Aristophanes." *Ramus* 6: 60–81.

Holford-Strevens, L. A. 1991. "Killing Dead Tyrants (Ari., *Birds* 1072–7)." *LCM* 16: 68.

Horn, W. 1970. *Gebet und Gebetsparodie in den Komödien des Aristophanes*. Nürnberg.

Hooker, G. T. W. 1960. "The Topography of the *Frogs*." *JHS* 80: 112–117.

Hooker, J. T. 1980. "The Composition of the *Frogs*." *Hermes* 108: 169–182.

Hornby, Richard. 1986. *Drama, Metadrama, and Perception*. Lewisburg, Pa.

Hubbard, Thomas K. 1991. *The Mask of Comedy: Aristophanes and the Intertextual Parabasis*. Ithaca, N.Y.

———. 1997. "Utopianism and the Sophistic City in Aristophanes." Pp. 23–50 in *The City as Comedy: Society and Representation in Athenian Drama*, ed. Gregory W. Dobrov. Chapel Hill, N.C.

Hubert, Judd. 1991. *Metatheater: The Example of Shakespeare*. Lincoln, Nebr., and London.

Hunningher, Benjamin. 1956. *Acoustics and Acting in the Theatre of Dionysos Eleuthereus*. Amsterdam.

Hunter, Richard L. 1976. "The Comic Chorus in the Fourth Century." *ZPE* 36: 23–38.

Jouan, François. 1983. "Réflexions sur le rôle du protagoniste tragique." Pp. 63–80 in *Théâtres et spectacles dans l'antiquité*. Leiden.

Kaimio, Maarit. 1971. *The Chorus of Greek Drama within the Light of the Person and Number Used*. Helsinki.

Kannicht, R. 1971. "Aristophanes Redivivus: über die Aktualität der 'Akarner.'" *Dioniso* 45: 573–591.

Kerr, Walter. 1967. *Tragedy and Comedy*. New York.

Ketterer, R. G. 1980. "Stripping in the Parabasis of *Acharnians*." *GRBS* 21: 217–221.

Kilmer, Martin F. 1993. *Greek Erotica*. London.

Koepke, E. 1856. *De Chamaeleontis Heracleotae vita librorumque reliquiis*. Berlin.

Kolb, F. 1981. *Agora und Theater, Volks- und Festversammlung*. Berlin.

Konstan, David. 1985. "The Politics of Aristophanes' *Wasps*." *TAPA* 115: 27–46.

———. 1990. "A City in the Air: Aristophanes' *Birds*." *Arethusa* 23: 183–207.

———. 1995. *Greek Comedy and Ideology*. New York.

Konstan, David and Matthew Dillon. 1981. "The Ideology of Aristophanes' *Wealth*." *AJP* 102: 371–394.

Körte, A. 1897. "Zu attischen Dionysos-Festen." *RhMus* 52: 168–176, esp. 172–174.

Kourouniotes, K. and H. A. Thompson. 1932. "The Pnyx in Athens." *Hesperia* 1: 90–217.

Kraus, Walther. 1985. *Aristophanes' politische Komödien*. Vienna.

Kraut, Bruce. 1988. "The Reappearance of Chaerephon in Aristophanes' *Wasps*." Pp. 129–136 in *Text and Presentation*. ed. Karelisa Hartigan. Comparative Drama Conference Papers 8. Lanham, Md.

Lada, Ismene. 1993. "'Empathic Understanding': Emotion and Cognition in Classical Dramatic Audience-Response." *PCPS* 39: 94–140.

Lai, Alberta. 1997. "La circolazione delle tragedie eschillee in ambito simposiale." *Lexis* 15: 143–148.

Landfester, Manfred. 1967. *Die Ritter des Aristophanes*. Amsterdam.

———. 1977. *Handlungsverlauf und Komik in den frühen Komödien des Aristophanes*. Berlin and New York.

Larson, Catherine. 1994. "Metatheater and the *Comedia*: Past, Present, and Future." Pp. 204- 221 in *The Golden Age Comedia: Text, Theory, and Performance*, ed. Charles Ganelin and Howard Mancing. West Lafayette, Ind.

Lefkowitz, M. R. 1981. *The Lives of the Greek Poets*. Baltimore and London.

Lenz, Lutz. 1980. "Komik und Kritik in Aristophanes' 'Wespen'." *Hermes* 108: 15–44.

Ley, Graham, and Michael Ewans. 1985. "The Orchestra as Acting Area in Greek Tragedy." *Ramus* 14: 75–84.

Lind, Hermann. 1990. *Der Gerber Kleon in den "Rittern" des Aristophanes*. Frankfurt am Main.

Lissarrague, François. 1990a. "Why Satyrs Are Good to Represent." Pp. 228–236 in *Nothing to Do with Dionysos? Athenian Drama in its Social Context*, ed. John J. Winkler and Froma I. Zeitlin. Princeton, N.J.

———. 1990b. *The Aesthetics of the Greek Banquet*. Princeton. N.d.

———. 1999. "Publicity and Performance: *Kalos* Inscriptions in Attic Vase-Painting." Pp. 359–373 in *Performance Culture and Athenian Democracy*. ed. Simon Goldhill and Robin Osborne. Cambridge.

Littlefield, David J. 1968. "Metaphor and Myth: The Unity of Aristophanes' *Knights*." *Studies in Philology* 65: 1–22.

Long, Timothy. 1976. "The Parados of Aristophanes' *Wasps*." *Illinois Classical Studies* 1: 15–21.

Lowe, Nicholas J. 1993. "Aristophanes' Books." *Annals of Scholarship* 10: 63–83.

———. 2000. "Comic Plots and the Invention of Fiction." Pp. 259–272 in *The Rivals of Aristophanes: Studies in Athenian Old Comedy*, ed. David Harvey and John Wilkins. London.

Luppe, W. 1972. "Die Zahl der Konkurrenten an den komischen Agonen zur Zeit des peloponnesischen Krieges." *Philologus* 116: 53–75.

———. 1982. "ἀπεώσθη πάλιν εἰς τούς Ληναικούς." *ZPE* 46: 147–159.

———. 2000a. "Ein weiteres Zeugnis für fünf Konkurrenten an den Komödien-Agonen während des peloponnesischen Krieges." *ZPE* 129: 19–20.

———. 2000b. "The Rivalry between Aristophanes and Kratinos." Pp. 15–21 in *The Rivals of Aristophanes: Studies in Athenian Old Comedy*, ed. David Harvey and John Wilkins. London.

MacCary, W. Thomas. 1979. "Philokleon *Ithyphallos*: Dance, Costume, and Character in the *Wasps*." *TAPA* 109: 137–147.

MacDowell, Douglas M. 1972. "The Frogs' Chorus." *CR* 22: 3–5.

———. ed. and trans. 1982a. *Gorgias: Encomium of Helen*. Bristol.

———. 1982b. "Aristophanes and Kallistratos." *CQ* 32: 21–26.

———. 1983. "The Nature of Aristophanes' *Acharnians*." *G&R* 30: 143–162.

———. 1988. "Clowning and Slapstick in Aristophanes." *Themes in Drama* 10 (*Farce*): 1–13.

———. 1994. "The Number of Speaking Actors in Old Comedy." *CQ* 44: 325–335.

———. 1995. *Aristophanes and Athens*. Oxford.

Macleod, Colin. 1974. "Euripides' Rags." *ZPE* 15: 221–222 [reprinted in *Collected Essays of Colin Macleod*. (Oxford 1983)].

———. 1980. "Euripides' Rags Again." *ZPE* 39: 6 [reprinted in *Collected Essays of Colin Macleod*. (Oxford 1983)].

Maidment, K. J. 1935. "The Later Comic Chorus." *CQ* 29: 1–24.

Marshall, C. W. 1996. "Amphibian Ambiguities Answered." *Echoes du Monde Classique/Classical Views* 15: 251–265.

———. 1997. "Comic Technique and the Fourth Actor." *CQ* 47: 77–84.

Mastromarco, G. 1978. "Una norma agonistica del Teatro di Atene." *Rh.Mus.* 121: 19–34

———. 1979. "L'esordio 'segreto' di Aristofane." *Quaderni di Storia* 10: 153–196.

———. 1983. *Commedie di Aristofane*, Vol. I. Turin.

Mastronarde, D. J. 1990. "Actors on High: The Skene Roof, the Crane, and the Gods in Attic Drama." *CA* 9: 247–294.

Mayne, Judith. 1993. *Cinema and Spectatorship*. New York.

Meier, Christian. 1993. *The Political Art of Greek Tragedy*. Trans. A. Webber. Oxford.

Mette, H. J. 1977. *Urkunden dramatischer Aufführungen in Griechenland*. Berlin and New York.

Möllendorf, Peter von. 1995. *Grundlagen einer Ästhetik der Alten Komödie: Untersuchungen zu Aristophanes und Michail Bachtin*. Classica Monacensia 9. Tübingen.

Moulton, Carroll. 1981. *Aristophanic Poetry*. Hypomnemata 68. Göttingen.

Muecke, Frances. 1977. "Playing with the Play: Theatrical Self-Consciousness in Aristophanes." *Antichthon* 9: 52–67.

———. 1982a. "'I know you—by your rags'—Costume and Disguise in Fifth Century Drama." *Antichthon* 16: 17–34.

———. 1982b. "A Portrait of the Artist as a Young Woman." *CQ* 32: 41–55.

Neil, R. A. 1909. *The Knights of Aristophanes*. Cambridge.

Neri, Camillo. 1997. "Il figlio di padre Caprese (Ar. 'Ach.' 848–53)." *Lexis* 15: 149–158.

Nesselrath, H-G. 1996. "Die Tücken der Sprecherverteilung: Euelpides, Peisetairos und ihre Rolle in der Eingangspartie der aristophanischen *Vögel*." *MusHelv* 53: 91–99.

Newiger, H-J. 1957. *Metapher und Allegorie*. Zetemata 16. Munich.

———. 1961. "Elektra in Aristophanes' Wolken." *Hermes* 89: 422–430.

———. 1975. *Aristophanes und die Alte Komödie*. Darmstadt.

———. 1976. "Zwei Bemerkungen zur Spielstätte des attischen Dramas im 5. Jahrhundert v. Chr." *WS* 10 n.f.: 80–92.

———. 1980. "War and Peace in the Comedies of Aristophanes." *YCS* 26: 219–237.

Nozick, Robert. 1974. *Anarchy, State, and Utopia*. Oxford.

Ober, Josiah. 1989. *Mass and Elite in Democratic Athens*. Princeton.

O'Connor, John B. 1908. *Chapters in the History of Actors and Acting in Ancient Greece*. Chicago.

Ogden, Daniel. 1996. *Greek Bastardy*. Oxford.

Olson, S. Douglas. 1987. "The Identity of the Δεσπότης at *Ecclesiazusae* 1128f." *GRBS* 28: 161–166.

———. 1990. "The New Demos of Aristophanes' *Knights*." *Eranos* 88: 60–63.

———. 1991. "Dicaeopolis' motivations in Aristophanes' *Acharnians*." *JHS* 111: 200–203.

———. 1992. "Names and Naming in Aristophanic Comedy." *CQ* 42: 304–319.

———. 1995. "Politics and Poetry in Aristophanes' *Wasps*." *TAPA* 126: 129–150.

———. 2000. "We Didn't Know Whether to Laugh or Cry: The Case of Karkinos." Pp. 65–74 in *The Rivals of Aristophanes: Studies in Athenian Old Comedy*, ed. David Harvey and John Wilkins. London.

Owen, A. S. 1936. "The Date of the Electra of Sophocles." Pp. 145–157 in *Greek Poetry and Life: Essays Presented to Gilbert Murray*, ed. Cyril Bailey et al. Oxford.

Parker, L. P. E. 1991. "Eupolis or Dicaeopolis?" *JHS* 111: 203–208.

Patterson, Cynthia B. 1990. "Those Athenian Bastards." *CA* 9: 40–73.

Pavlovskis, Zoja. 1977. "The Voice of the Actor in Greek Tragedy." *CW* 71: 113–123.

Perkell, Christine. 1993. "On the Two Voices of the Birds in *Birds*." *Ramus* 22: 1–18.

Perusino, Franca. 1986. *Dalla Commedia antica alla commedia di messo. Tre studie su Aristofane*. Università di Urbino, serie di linguistica letteratura arte 8. Urbino.

———, ed. 1993. *Anonimo (Michele Psello?): La Tragedia Greca*. Urbino.

Pfeiffer, Rudolf. 1968. *History of Classical Scholarship: From the Beginnings to the End of the Hellenistic Age*. Oxford.

Pickard-Cambridge, A. W. 1946. *The Theatre of Dionysos at Athens*. Oxford.

———. 1962. *Dithyramb, Tragedy and Comedy*. 2nd ed. rev. by T. B. L. Webster. Oxford.

———. 1988. *The Dramatic Festivals of Athens*. 2nd ed. rev. by J. Gould and D. M. Lewis, reissued with supplement and corrections. Oxford.

Pingiatoglou, Semeli. 1992. "Eine Komödiendarstellung auf einer Choenkanne des Benaki-Museums." Pp. 291–300, pls. 63–65 in *Kotinos: Festschrift für Erika Simon*. Mainz.

Pöhlmann, E. 1989. "Suchszenen auf der attischen Bühne des 5. und 4. Jh.s. Zur Bühnentechnik der Eumeniden, des Aias, der Acharner und des Rhesos." *Xenia* 22 (*Festschrift Robert Werner*) 41–58.

Poland, F. 1934. s.v. "Technitai." *RE* 5B, Nachträge 2473ff.

Pollitt, J. J. 1990. *The Art of Ancient Greece: Sources and Documents*. Cambridge.

Purves, Alex. 1997. "Empowerment for the Athenian Citizen: Philocleon as Actor and Spectator in Aristophanes' *Wasps*." Pp. 5–22 in *Griechisch-römische Komödie und Tragödie II*. Drama 5. Stuttgart.

Radermacher, L. 1922/23. "Zum Prolog der Eirene." *Wiener Studien* 43: 105–115.

Rau, Peter. 1967. *Paratragodia: Untersuchung einer komischen Form des Aristophanes*. Munich.

Reckford, Kenneth J. 1987. *Aristophanes' Old-and-New Comedy*. Chapel Hill, N.C..

Redfield, James. 1990. "Drama and Community: Aristophanes and Some of His Rivals." Pp. 314–335 in *Nothing to Do with Dionysos? Athenian Drama in its Social Context*, ed. John J. Winkler and Froma I. Zeitlin. Princeton, N.J.

Redondo, J. 1993. "La poésie populaire grecque et les *Guêpes* d'Aristophane." Pp. 102–121 in *Intertextualität in der griechisch-römischen Komödie*. Drama 2. Stuttgart.

Rehm, R. 1988. "The Staging of Suppliant Plays." *GRBS* 29: 263–307.

———. 1992. *Greek Tragic Theatre*. London and New York.

Reinders, Peter. 1995. "Der Demos in den *Rittern* des Aristophanes am Beispiel des Amoibaions in den Vv. 1111–1150." Pp. 1- 20 in *Griechisch-römische Komödie und Tragödie*. Drama 3. Stuttgart.

Rhodes, P. J. 1972. *The Athenian Boule*. Oxford.

———. 1979. "*ΕΙΣΑΓΓΕΛΙΑ* in Athens." *JHS* 99: 103–114.

Ringer, Mark. 1998. *Electra and the Empty Urn: Metatheater and Role Playing in Sophocles*. Chapel Hill, N.C.

Robertson, Noel. 1992. *Festivals and Legends: The Formation of Greek Cities in the Light of Public Ritual*. *Phoenix* Supplement 31. Toronto.

Robkin, A. L. H. 1979. "That Magnificent Flying Machine: On the Nature of the *Mechane* of the Theatre of Dionysos at Athens." *ArchNews* 8: 1–6.

Roccos, L. J. 1995. "The Kanephoros and Her Festival Mantle in Greek Art." *AJA* 99: 641–666.

Rogers, B. B. 1910. *The Knights of Aristophanes*. London.

Rohde, E. 1883. "Scenica." *RhMus* 38: 251–292, esp. 285–286.

Romer, F. E. 1983. "When Is a Bird Not a Bird?" *TAPA* 113: 135–142.

———. 1994. "Atheism, Impiety and the *Limos Melios* in Aristophanes' *Birds*." *AJP* 115: 351–365.

Rosellini, Michèle. 1979. "*Lysistrata*: une mise en scène de la féminité." in *Aristophane: "Les Femmes et la Citè*." Cahiers de Fontenay 17. Fontenay aux Roses.

Rosen, Ralph M. 1984. "The Ionian at Aristophanes *Peace* 46." *GRBS* 25: 389–396.

———. 1989. "Trouble in the Early Career of Plato Comicus: Another Look at P. Oxy. 2737.44–51 (*PCG* III 2, 590)." *ZPE* 76: 223–228.

———. 1997. "The Gendered Polis in Eupolis' *Cities*." Pp. 149–176 in *The City as*

Comedy: Society and Representation in Athenian Drama, ed. Gregory W. Dobrov. Chapel Hill, N.C.

———. 2000. "Cratinus' *Pytine* and the Construction of the Comic Self." Pp. 23–39 in *The Rivals of Aristophanes: Studies in Athenian Old Comedy*, ed. David Harvey and John Wilkins. London.

Rosenmeyer, T. G. 1955. "Gorgias, Aeschylus, and *Apate*." *AJP* 76: 225–260.

———. 1972. "Notes on Aristophanes' *Birds*." *AJP* 93: 223–238.

———. 1982. *The Art of Aeschylus*. Berkeley, Calif.

Rosivach, V. J. 1985. "Manning the Athenian Fleet, 433–426 BC." *AJAH* 10 (1985 [1992]) 41–66.

Rothwell, Kenneth S. 1990. *Politics and Persuasion in Aristophanes' Ecclesiazusae*. Mnemosyne Supplement 111. Leiden.

———. 1992. "The Continuity of the Chorus in Fourth-Century Attic Comedy." *GRBS* 33: 209–225 [= Pp. 99–118 in *Beyond Aristophanes: Transition and Diversity in Greek Comedy*, ed. G. W. Dobrov (Atlanta, 1995)].

———. 1994. "Was Carcinus I a Tragic Playwright?" *CP* 89: 241–245.

———. 1995. "Aristophanes' *Wasps* and the Sociopolitics of Aesop's Fables." *CJ* 93: 233–254.

Russo, C. F. 1994. *Aristophanes: An Author for the Stage*. London.

Saïd, Suzanne. 1979. "L'Assemblée des Femmes: les femmes, l'économie et la politique," Pp. 33–69 in *Aristophane: "Les Femmes et la Citè."* Les Cahiers de Fontenay 17. Fontenay aux Roses.

Schmitt Pantel, Pauline. 1992. *La Cité au banquet*. Collection de l'École Française de Rome 157. Rome.

Schnurr, Ch. 1995a. "Die alte Agora Athens." *ZPE* 105: 131–138, pls.

———. 1995b. "Zur Topographie der Theaterstätten und der Tripodenstrasse in Athen." *ZPE* 105: 139–151, pls.

Scodel, Ruth. 1979. "Ἀδμήτου Λόγος and the Alcestis." *HSCP* 83: 51–62.

Seale, David. 1982. *Vision and Stagecraft in Sophocles*. Chicago.

Sealey, R. 1981. "Ephialtes, *Eisangelia*, and the Council." Pp. 125–131 in *Classical Contributions: Studies in Honor of Malcolm F. McGregor*, ed. G. S. Shrimpton and D. J. McCargar. Locust Valley, N.Y.

Searle, John. 1969. *Speech Acts*. Cambridge.

Seeberg, Axel. 1995. "From Padded Dancers to Comedy," Pp. 1–12 in *Stage Directions: Essays in Ancient Drama in Honour of E. W. Handley*, ed. Alan Griffiths [= *BICS* Supplement 66].

Segal, Charles P. 1961. "The Character and Cults of Dionysus and the Unity of the *Frogs*." *HSCP* 65: 207–242.

———. 1962. "Gorgias and the Psychology of the Logos." *HSCP* 66: 99–155.

———. 1982. *Dionysiac Poetics and Euripides' Bacchae*. Princeton, N.J.

Segal, Erich. 1972. "The φύσις of Comedy." *HSCP* 77: 49–56.

Sens, Alexander. 1992. "The Luck of the Draw: Ar. *Ecc.* 999." *CQ* 42: 529.

Shapiro, Alan. 1987. "Kalos-Inscriptions with Patronymic." *ZPE* 68: 107–118.

———. 1995. "Attic Comedy and the 'Comic Angels' Krater in New York." *JHS* 115: 173–175 and plate IV.

Shear, T. Leslie. 1995. "Bouleuterion, Metroon, and the Archives at Athens." Pp. 157–

190 in *Studies in the Ancient Greek Polis*, ed. M. H. Hansen and K. Raaflaub. *Historia* Einzelschrift 95. Stuttgart.

Showalter, Elaine. 1983. "Critical Cross-Dressing: Male Feminists and the Woman of the Year." *Raritan* 3: 130–149.

Sidwell, Keith. 1994. "Aristophanes' *Acharnians* and Eupolis." *C&M* 45: 71–115.

Sifakis, Gregory M. 1967. *Studies in the History of Hellenistic Drama*. London.

———. 1971. *Parabasis and Animal Choruses*. London.

———. 1979. "Boy Actors in New Comedy." Pp. 199–208 in *Arktouros*, ed. G. W. Bowersock, W. Burkert, and M. C. J. Putnam. New York and Berlin.

———. 1992. "The Structure of Aristophanic Comedy." *JHS* 112: 123–142.

———. 1995. "The One-Actor Rule in Greek Tragedy." Pp. 13–24 in *Stage Directions: Essays in Ancient Drama in Honour of E. W. Handley*, ed. Alan Griffths [= *BICS* Supplement 66].

Silk, Michael. 1980. "Aristophanes as a Lyric Poet." Pp. 99–151 in *Aristophanes: Essays in Interpretation*, ed. Jeffrey Henderson. *YCS* 26. Cambridge.

———. 1990. "The People of Aristophanes." Pp. 150–173 in *Characterization and Individuality in Greek Literature*, ed. C. B. R. Pelling. Oxford 1990.

Simon, Erika. 1982. "Satyr-Plays on Vases in the Time of Aeschylus." Pp. 123–148 in *The Eye of Greece: Studies in the Art of Athens*, ed. Donna Kurtz and Brian Sparkes. Cambridge.

Slater, Niall W. 1985a. "Play and Playwright References in Middle and New Comedy." *Liverpool Classical Monthly* 10: 103–105.

———. 1985b. "Vanished Players: Two Classical Reliefs and Theatre History." *GRBS* 26: 333–344.

———. 1985c. *Plautus in Performance: The Theatre of the Mind*. Princeton, N.J.

———. 1986. "The Lenaean Theatre." *ZPE* 66: 255–264.

———. 1987. "Transformations of Space in New Comedy." *Themes in Drama* 9 (*Space*): 1–13.

———. 1988a. "The τειχίον of *Ecclesiazusae* 497." *LCM* 13:105.

———. 1988b. "The Date of Euripides' *Oineus*." *LCM* 13:147–148.

———. 1988c. "Problems in the Hypotheses to Aristophanes' *Peace*." *ZPE* 74: 43–57.

———. 1989a. "*Lekythoi* in Aristophanes' *Ecclesiazusae*." *Lexis* 3: 43–51.

———. 1989b. "Aristophanes' Apprenticeship Again," *GRBS* 30: 67–82.

———. 1990. "The Idea of the Actor." Pp. 385–395 in *Nothing to Do with Dionysos? Athenian Drama in Its Social Context*, ed. John J. Winkler and Froma I. Zeitlin. Princeton, N.J.

———. 1993a. "Space, Character, and *AΠATH*: Transformation and Transvaluation in the *Acharnians*." Pp. 397–415 in *Tragedy, Comedy, and the Polis*, ed. Alan Sommerstein et al. Bari.

———. 1993b. "From Ancient Performance to New Historicism," Pp. 1–13 in *Intertextualität in der griechisch-römischen Komödie*, ed. Slater and Bernhard Zimmermann. Drama 2. Stuttgart.

———. 1993c. "Theozotides on Adopted Sons (Lysias fr. 6)." *Scholia* 2: 82–86.

———. 1995. "The Fabrication of Comic Illusion." Pp. 29–45 in *Beyond Aristophanes: Transition and Diversity in Greek Comedy*, ed. Gregory Dobrov. Atlanta.

————. 1996. "Literacy and Old Comedy." Pp. 99–112 in *Voice into Text: Orality and Literacy in Ancient Greece*, ed. Ian Worthington. Leiden.

————. 1997. "Waiting in the Wings: Aristophanes' *Ecclesiazusae*," *Arion* 5.1: 97–129.

————. 1999. "The Vase as Ventriloquist: *Kalos*-inscriptions and the Culture of Fame." Pp. 143–161, pl. 16, in *Signs of Orality: The Oral Tradition and its Influence in the Greek and Roman World*, ed. E. Anne Mackay. Leiden.

————. 2000. *Plautus in Performance: The Theatre of the Mind*. 2nd ed. Greek and Roman Theatre Archive Vol. 2. Amsterdam.

Smith, Nicholas D. 1989. "Diviners and Divination in Aristophanic Comedy." *CA* 8: 140–158.

Sommerstein, Alan H. 1984a. "Aristophanes and the Demon Poverty." *CQ* 34: 314–333.

————. 1984b. "Act Division in Old Comedy." *BICS* 31: 139–152.

————. 1986. "The Decree of Syrakosios." *CQ* 36: 101–108.

————. 1993a. "Kleophon and the Restaging of *Frogs*." Pp. 461–476 in *Tragedy, Comedy, and the Polis*, ed. Sommerstein et al. Bari.

————. 1993b. "Aristoph. *Ach*. 1103–17." *Museum Criticum* 25–28: 139–144.

————. 1996. "How to Avoid Being a *Komodoumenos*." *CQ* 46: 327–356.

————. 1997a. "The Theatre Audience, the *Demos*, and the *Suppliants* of Aeschylus." Pp. 63–79 in *Greek Tragedy and the Historian*, ed. Christopher Pelling. Oxford.

————. 1997b. "The Silence of Strepsiades and the *agon* of the first *Clouds*." Pp. 269–282 in *Aristophane: la langue, la scène, la cité*. ed. Pascal Thiercy and Michel Menu. Bari.

————. 1997c. "Response." Pp. 53–64 in *Education in Greek Fiction*. Nottingham Classical Literature Studies 4, 1996 [1997], ed. Sommerstein and Catherine Atherton. Bari.

Spence, I. G. 1990. "Perikles and the Defence of Attika During the Peloponnesian War." *JHS* 110: 91–109.

————. 1993. *The Cavalry of Classical Greece*. Oxford.

Spitzbarth, Anna. 1946. *Untersuchungen zur Spieltechnik der Griechischen Tragödie*. Zurich.

Spyropoulos, E. S. 1975. "Μάγνες ὁ κωμικὸς καὶ ἡ θέση του στὴν ἱστορία τῆς ἀρχαίας ἀττικῆς κωμῳδίας." *Hellenika* 28: 247–274.

Steiner, Deborah Tarn. 1994. *The Tyrant's Writ*. Princeton, N.J.

Stockton, David. 1990. *The Classical Athenian Democracy*. Oxford.

Stone, Laura M. 1981. *Costume in Aristophanic Poetry*. New York.

Storey, Ian C. 1987. "Old Comedy 1975–1984." *Echoes du Monde Classique/Classical Views* 6: 1–46.

————. 1993. "Notus est omnibus Eupolis?" Pp. 373–396 in *Tragedy, Comedy, and the Polis*, ed. Alan Sommerstein et al. Bari.

————. 1995. "*Wasps* 1284–91 and the Portrait of Kleon in *Wasps*." *Scholia* 4: 3–23.

————. 1998. "Poets, Politicians, and Perverts: Personal Humour in Aristophanes." *Classics Ireland* 5: 85–134.

Strauss, Barry S. 1987. *Athens after the Peloponnesian War*. Ithaca, N.Y.

Styan, J. L. 1975. *Drama, Stage and Audience*. Cambridge.

————. 1977. *The Shakespeare Revolution: Criticism and Performance in the Twentieth Century*. Cambridge.

Sutton, Dana F. 1971. "Aeschylus' *Edonians*," Pp. 387–411 in *Fons Perennis*. Turin.

———. 1980. "Plato Comicus Demoted: A Reconsideration." *ZPE* 38: 59–63.

———. 1987. "The Theatrical Families of Athens." *AJP* 108: 9–26.

———. 1988. "Dicaeopolis as Aristophanes, Aristophanes as Dicaeopolis." *LCM* 13.7 (July): 105–108.

———. 1990. "Aristophanes and the Transition to Middle Comedy." *LCM* 15.6 (June): 81–95.

Svenbro, Jesper. 1993. *Phrasikleia: An Anthropology of Reading in Ancient Greece*. Trans. J. Lloyd. Ithaca, N.Y.

Taaffe, Lauren K. 1993. *Aristophanes and Women*. London.

Taillardat, Jean. 1962. *Les Images d'Aristophane*. Paris.

Talcott, Lucy. 1939. "Kourimos Parthenos." *Hesperia* 8: 267–273.

Taplin, Oliver. 1972. "Aeschylean Silences and Silences in Aeschylus." *HSCP* 76: 57–97.

———. 1977. *The Stagecraft of Aeschylus*. Oxford.

———. 1978. *Greek Tragedy in Action*. London.

———. 1983. "Tragedy and Trugedy." *CQ* 33: 331–333.

———. 1986. "Fifth-Century Tragedy and Comedy: A *Synkrisis*." *JHS* 106: 163–174.

———. 1987a. "Phallology, *Phlyakes*, Iconography and Aristophanes." *PCPS* 213 (n.s. 33) 92–104.

———. 1987b. "Classical Phallology, Iconographic Parody, and Potted Aristophanes." *Dioniso* 57: 95–109.

———. 1991. "*Auletai* and *Auletrides* in Greek Comedy and Comic Vase-Paintings." *Quaderni Ticinesi di Numismatica e antichità classiche* [= *NumAntCl*] 20: 31–48.

———. 1993. *Comic Angels*. Oxford.

Thompson, D'Arcy. 1919. "*ΙΜΑΝΤΕΛΙΓΜΟΣ*." *CR* 33: 24–25.

Totaro, Piero. 1999. *Le Seconde parabasi di Aristofane*. Drama Beiheft 9. Stuttgart.

Townsend, Rhys F. 1986. "The Fourth Century Theatre of Dionysos." *Hesperia* 55: 421–438.

Trendell, A. D. 1991. "Farce and Tragedy in South Italian Vase-Painting." Pp. 151–182 in *Looking at Greek Vases*, ed. Tom Rasmussen and Nigel Spivey. Cambridge.

Trendell, A. D. and T. B. L. Webster. 1971. *Illustration of Greek Drama*. London.

Ussher, R. G. 1969. "The Staging of the *Ecclesiazusae*." *Hermes* 97: 22–37 [= Newiger 1975: 383–404].

Vaio, John. 1971. "Aristophanes' *Wasps*: The Relevance of the Final Scenes." *GRBS* 12: 335–351.

Verdenius, W. J. 1981. "Gorgias' Doctrine of Deception." Pp. 116–128 in *The Sophists and their Legacy*. Hermes Einzelschrift 44. Wiesbaden.

Vermeule, Emily. 1979. *Aspects of Death in Early Greek Art and Poetry*. Berkeley, Calif.

Vetta, M. 1993. "La voce degli attori nel teatro attico." Pp. 703–718 in *Traduzione e Innovazione nella cultura Greca da Omero all' Età Ellenistica*, vol. 2, ed. Roberto Pretagostini. Rome.

Wansbrough, Henry. 1993. "Two Choruses of Frogs?" *JHS* 113: 162.

Webster, T. B. L. 1952. "Chronological Notes on Middle Comedy." *CQ* 2: 13–26.

———. 1960. "Greek Dramatic Monuments from the Athenian Agora and Pnyx." *Hesperia* 29: 254–284, pl. 65–68.

———. 1967. *The Tragedies of Euripides*. London.

———. 1970. *The Greek Chorus*. London.

———. 1970². *Greek Theatre Production*. 2nd ed. London.

Welsh, D. 1983. "The Chorus of Aristophanes' *Babylonians*." *GRBS* 24: 137–150.

———. 1990. "The Ending of Aristophanes' *Knights*." *Hermes* 118: 421–429.

———. 1992. "Further Observations on the Ending of the *Knights*." *Hermes* 120: 377–380.

Wendling, Emil. 1899. s.v. "Chamaileon." *RE* 3: 2103–2104.

West, M. L. 1982. *Greek Metre*. Oxford.

———. 1992. *Ancient Greek Music*. Oxford.

Wheat, Jennifer. 1992. "Terminal Sex: Feasts into Funerals in the *Ecclesiazusae*." *Pacific Coast Philology* 27: 166–173.

Whitehead, David. 1986. *The Demes of Attica 508/7–ca. 250 B.C.* Princeton, N.J.

Whitehorne, John. 1989. "Punishment Under the Decree of Cannonus." Pp. 89–97 in *Symposion 1985: Vorträge zur griechischen und hellenistischen Rechtsgeschichte*, ed. G. Thür. Cologne.

Whitman, Cedric H. 1964. *Aristophanes and the Comic Hero*. Cambridge, Mass.

———. 1969. "*ΛΗΚΥΘΙΟΝ ΑΠΩΛΕΣΕΝ*." *HSCP* 73: 109–112.

Wiles, David. 1987. "Reading Greek Performance." *G&R* 34: 136–151.

———. 1997. *Tragedy in Athens*. Cambridge.

Wilkins, John. 1997. "Comic Cuisine: Food and Eating in the Comic Polis." Pp. 250–268 in *The City as Comedy: Society and Representation in Athenian Drama*, ed. Gregory W. Dobrov. Chapel Hill, N.C.

Wills, G. 1969. "Aeschylus' Victory in the *Frogs*." *AJP* 90: 48–57.

Wilson, A. M. 1973. "Not Callias, but Ecphantides?" *CR* n.s. 23: 126–127.

———. 1977. "The Individualized Chorus in Old Comedy." *CQ* n.s. 27: 278–283.

———. 1978. "Breach of Dramatic Illusion in the Old Comic Fragments." *Euphrosyne* 9: 145–150.

Wilson, Peter. 1997. "Leading the Tragic *Khoros*: Tragic Prestige in the Democratic City." Pp. 81–108 in *Greek Tragedy and the Historian*, ed. Christopher Pelling. Oxford.

———. 2000. *The Athenian Institution of the Khoregia: The Chorus, the City and the Stage*. Cambridge.

Winkler, John J. 1985. "The Ephebes' Song: *Tragôidia* and *Polis*." *Representations* 11: 26–62.

———. 1990. "The Ephebes' Song: *Tragôidia* and *Polis*." Pp. 20–62 in *Nothing to Do with Dionysos? Athenian Drama in its Social Context*. ed. John J. Winkler and Froma I. Zeitlin. Princeton, N.J.

Winkler, John J. and Froma I. Zeitlin. 1990. *Nothing to Do with Dionysos? Athenian Drama in Its Social Context*. Princeton, N.J.

Winter, F. E. 1983. "The Stage of New Comedy." *Phoenix* 37: 38–47.

Woodbury, L. 1976. "Aristophanes' *Frogs* and Athenian Literacy: *Ran.* 52–53, 1114." *TAPA* 106: 349–57.

Worthen, William B. 1984. *The Idea of the Actor: Drama and the Ethics of Performance*. Princeton, N.J.

Worthington, Ian. 1990. "Aristophanic Caricature and the Sam Wide Group Cups." *Eranos* 88: 1–8, pls. 1–2.

Wurster, W. W. 1979. "Die neuen Untersuchungen im Dionysostheater in Athen." *Architectura* 9: 58–76.

Zeitlin, Froma I. 1980. "The Closet of Masks: Role-Playing and Myth-Making in the *Orestes* of Euripides." *Ramus* 9: 51–77.

———. 1981. "Travesties of Gender and Genre in Aristophanes' *Thesmophoriazusae*." Pp. 169–217 in *Reflections of Women in Antiquity*, ed. Helene Foley. London and New York.

———. 1985. "Playing the Other: Theater, Theatricality, and the Feminine in Greek Drama." *Representations* 11: 63–94.

———. 1994. "The Artful Eye: Vision, Ekphrasis, and Spectacle in Euripidean Theatre." Pp. 138–196 in *Art and Text in Ancient Greek Culture*, ed. Simon Goldhill and Robin Osborne. Cambridge.

———. 1999. "Aristophanes: The Performance of Utopia in the *Ecclesiazusae*." Pp. 167–197 in *Performance Culture and Athenian Democracy*, ed. Simon Goldhill and Robin Osborne. Cambridge.

Zimmermann, Bernhard. 1983. "Utopisches und Utopie in den Komödien des Aristophanes." *WJA* 9: 57–77.

———. 1984. "The Parodoi of the Aristophanic Comedies." *SIFC* 3rd ser. 2: 13–24.

———. 1985². *Untersuchungen zur Form und dramatischen Technik der Aristophanischen Komödien*, Vol 1, *Parodos und Amoibaion*. 2nd ed. Beiträge zur Klassischen Philologie 154. Meisenheim.

———. 1985a. *Untersuchungen zur Form an dramatischen Technik der Aristophanischen Komödien*, Vol 2: *Die anderen lyrischen Partien*. Beiträge zur Klassischen Philologie 166. Meisenheim.

———. 1985b. "Aristophanes, Lysistrate V. 1295." *Hermes* 113: 374–376.

———. 1987a. *Untersuchungen zur Form an dramatischen Technik der Aristophanischen Komödien*, Vol 3: *Metrische Analysen*. Beiträge zur Klassischen Philologie 178. Meisenheim.

———. 1987b. "Ioniker in den Komödien des Aristophanes." *Prometheus* 13: 124–132.

———. 1987c. "L'Organizazione interna delle commedie di Aristofane." *Dioniso* 57: 49–64.

———. 1988. "Critica ed imitazione. La nuova musica nelle commedie di Aristophane." Pp. 199–204 in *La Musica in Grecia*, ed. Andrew Barker, Bruno Gentili, and Roberto Pretagostini. Rome and Bari.

———. 1992a. *Dithyrambos: Geschichte einer Gattung*. Hypomnemata 98. Göttingen.

———. 1992b. "Der Forschungsbericht: Griechische Komödie." *Anzeiger für di Altertumswissenschaft* 45: 161–184.

———. 1993a. "Aristophanes und die Intellectuellen." Pp. 256–286 in *Aristophane*, ed. J. M. Bremer and E. W. Handley. Entretiens Hardt 38. Vandœvres-Genève.

———. 1993b. "Comedy's Criticism of Music." Pp. 1–13 in *Intertextualität in der griechisch-römischen Komödie. Drama 2*. Stuttgart.

———. 1995. "Der Tanz in der Aristophanischen Komödie." Pp. 121–132 in *Primeras Jornadas Internacionales de Teatro Griego*. ed. A. Melero Bellido and J. V. Bañuls Oller. Valencia.

Index Locorum

Fragments are listed in numerical order after surviving whole works. Scholia to an author follow whole works and fragments.

Index Nominum et Rerum